China-Pakistan Military Nexus

Implications for India

China-Pakistan Military Nexus

Implications for India

Editors

Lt Gen PC Katoch, PVSM, UYSM, AVSM, SC (Retd)

Gp Capt Sharad Tewari, VM (Retd)

UNITED SERVICE INSTITUTION OF INDIA
NEW DELHI

PENTAGON PRESS LLP

China-Pakistan Military Nexus: Implications for India

Editors: Lieutenant General PC Katoch, PVSM, UYSM, AVSM, SC (Retd)
Group Captain Sharad Tewari, VM (Retd)

First Published in 2019

ISBN 978-93-86618-93-1

Published by
PENTAGON PRESS LLP
206, Peacock Lane, Shahpur Jat
New Delhi-110049
Phones: 011-64706243, 26491568
Telefax: 011-26490600
email: rajan@pentagonpress.in
website: www.pentagonpress.in

Printed at Aegean Offset Printers, Greater Noida, U.P.

Dedicated since 1870

to

'The furtherance of Interest and Knowledge in the art, science and literature of National Security in general and of the Defence Services in particular'

China-Pakistan Military Nexus

Implications for India

<u>OVERSIGHT</u>

Lieutenant General P K Singh, PVSM, AVSM (Retd) – Director, USI

Major General BK Sharma, AVSM, SM** (Retd) – Deputy Director (Research)

<u>RESEARCH TEAM</u>

Lieutenant General P C Katoch, PVSM, UYSM, AVSM, SC (Retd) – Chairperson and Editor

Major General RPS Bhadauria, VSM (Retd)

Major General Rajiv Narayan, AVSM, VSM (Retd)

Commodore Lalit Kapur (Retd)

Group Captain Sharad Tewari, VM (Retd) – Co-editor

Dr (Mrs) Roshan Khanijo

CONTENTS

FOREWORD

India, by virtue of its size, location; economic and political potential, should assume a natural leadership role in South Asia. However, the existence of three nuclear powers, having territorial disputes among them, makes South Asia a vulnerable region in the world. Relations between India and Pakistan have always been complex and uneasy due to a number of historical and political events. Even though the two South Asian nations share linguistic, cultural, geographic and economic links, their relationship has throughout been plagued by hostility and suspicion. At the same time, China's contemporary geopolitics is shaped by its Middle Kingdom mind set with the idea of creating a China-centric Asia and polycentric world. Much of China's strategic orientation is driven by competition with the US for domination of resources, locations and influence. China's main geopolitical focus in South Asia is to restrain India as a competitor by using Pakistan as a proxy. China's growing economic and security relation with Pakistan remains a major worry for India as the growing Chinese involvement is bound to erode India's influence in the region.

However, the major concern for India is neither China nor Pakistan in isolation but the 'unholy nexus' that the two have. Pakistan and China enjoy exemplary friendly ties, which have not only sustained changes of governments and the ups and downs in the regional and global situation, but, in fact, have been expanding and becoming even deeper. The lack of credible Indian deterrence to prevent such nexus further aggravates the concern. The need of the hour, thus, was to have an in-depth analysis and a detailed study on the subject, which has not been undertaken earlier.

This book is the culmination of a series of discussions held under the aegis of the United Service Institution of India on the subject of Sino-Pak Collusivity and Hybrid Warfare. The book contains details on Concepts and Determinants of Hybrid Warfare, an objective assessment of the China–Pakistan Collusive Threats and their Implications for India, and makes Policy recommendations for India in the Time-Frame up to 2030.

My compliments to Lt Gen PC Katoch, PVSM, UYSM, AVSM, SC (Retd), and the entire team of researchers on their tremendous efforts in the research on the subject that culminated in the publication of this book.

New Delhi
May 2019

Lt Gen PK Singh, PVSM, AVSM (Retd)
Director, USI of India

EDITOR'S NOTE

Hybrid warfare is raging globally, including India where China and Pakistan are jointly waging against us. Yet, no study or book on hybrid warfare has been authored by an Indian. The China-Pakistan hybrid warfare nexus, developing over the past five decades, has seen a spurt with Chinese President Xi Jinping in great hurry to realise his pet project, the 'China Dream' that would put him at par with Mao Zedong and make China a 'Great Power'. China having voted to permit Xi to serve indefinitely (read for life), China's all-round aggression is likely to aggravate. Geopolitics in South Asia is changing fast with the China-Pakistan Economic Corridor (CPEC), People's Liberation Army (PLA) base in Skardu, China developing Gwadar (Pakistan) and Hambantota (Sri Lanka) Ports, future People's Liberation Army (Navy) (PLAN) deployment in Gwadar and additional PLA bases likely in Jiwani (Pakistan), Gadhoo (Maldives) and Badakshan (Afghanistan). CPEC is not only China's flagship project for its 'One Belt, One Road' (OBOR) initiative, but is also its strategic highway to the Indian Ocean. However, the economic gains of CPEC to China are somewhat suspect without India joining it, which India has refused for valid reasons. China needs the OBOR and the proposed Maritime Silk Route (MSR) for its future economic sustenance and employment for the Chinese population, but since their success will have strategic ramifications for global power play, these are not likely to go uncontested. Chinese forays into the Indian Ocean Region (IOR) and the Gwadar's proximity to the Straits of Hormuz pose threat to the Persian Gulf.

China is intent on extending her illegal territorial gains astride the Himalayas, her recent forays into and establishing herself in the North Doklam Plateau of Bhutan, in complete disregard to previous agreements, being just one example. With her economic and military might, China is endeavouring to draw India's close neighbours (like Nepal, Sri Lanka, and Maldives) into her gravitational pull, aimed at weaning them away from India. The Rohingya crisis and the Western onslaught against the Myanmar Government have provided China the opportunity to get a deeper grip on the internal affairs of Myanmar. Both China and Pakistan have developed proactive sub-conventional capabilities that they are employing in South Asia, including in J&K and other parts of India. China's entry in PoK-Pakistan has made India's western front vulnerable, and raised possibilities of a two-front collusive hybrid conflict, also employing state as well as non-state actors opening a third front within India, in addition to possible skirmishes/conflict at sea. China has advanced cyber-warfare capabilities, which along with China's 'Assassin's Mace' weaponry can be passed on to Pakistan on 'selective' basis. India's lack of effective deterrence to proxy wars magnifies the China–Pakistan anti-India hybrid threat. Hybrid warfare in the nuclear backdrop too needed to be taken into account.

In consideration of the above, the USI decided on in-house research to be undertaken to carry out an objective assessment of the China-Pakistan Collusive Hybrid Threats, their Implication for India, and for making policy recommendations in the time-frame up to 2030. In conjunction with Major General BK Sharma, AVSM, SM** (Retd), Deputy Director (Research), chapterisation of the study was arrived at as follows: Ch 1, Concepts and Determinants of Hybrid Warfare; Ch 2, Hybrid Warfare in Nuclear Backdrop as Grand Strategy; Ch 3, Pakistan's Hybrid Warfare Strategy and Capabilities 2030; Ch 4, China's Hybrid Warfare Strategy and Capabilities 2030; Ch 5, Pakistan–China Hybrid Warfare Collusivity; Ch 6, Challenges and Implications for India; Ch 7, India's Strategy and Capability Scan; Ch 8, Grand Strategy to Mitigate Collusive Threats and Ch 9, Policy Recommendations.

Detailed inputs for this book, based on extensive research, have been provided by Dr (Mrs) Roshan Khanijo on all aspects related to the nuclear, including the nuclear strategy of China and Pakistan, by Major General RPS Bhadauria, VSM (Retd) on Pakistan-China hybrid warfare collusivity, by Commodore Lalit Kapur (Retd) on all aspects related to the naval capabilities of China and Pakistan and the threat that India faces at sea, and by Group Captain Sharad Tewari, VM (Retd) in SWOT analysis and scenario building toward the China-Pakistan collusive threat. Major General Rajiv Narayanan AVSM, VSM (Retd) has provided valuable inputs with respect to China's strategic behaviour. The research that has gone into this study is based on the data and inputs available in the public domain and open sources. It is also pertinent to highlight that not much material is available on the hybrid warfare potential and stratagem of these countries, scarce in case of China in particular. It is hoped that the book will be enjoyed by readers and prove useful for the policy makers.

—Lt Gen P C Katoch, PVSM, UYSM, AVSM, SC (Retd)

1

CONCEPT AND DETERMINANTS OF HYBRID WARFARE

Conventional War and Hybrid War

There is a general perception in some cross sections, especially in India, that war implies conventional war. This belief is mostly because the differences between conventional war and hybrid war are often not understood. A conventional war is part of the hybrid war. It is a war that is declared and is fought astride defined borders. In contrast, hybrid war encompasses 'all forms' of warfare. This is a war that is ongoing—in perpetuity. It is not only undeclared, it is ambiguous and borderless. Hybrid wars are vicious and dirty and adhere to no rules or regulations.

Historical Perspective

From the 'trench warfare' (of World War I) to the era of conventional wars, modern-day asymmetric wars and irregular wars in today's information age that include increasing use of irregular forces, warfare has remained in transition and will continue to be so, with ambiguous battlefields sans borders and nations being threatened from multiple directions including some threats being faceless. The transition in generations of warfare is depicted in Figure 1.1. Over the years, the description of warfare has taken many forms like asymmetric warfare, terrorism, guerrilla warfare, irregular warfare, unconventional warfare, special operations, long war, fourth/fifth–generation warfare, hybrid warfare, etc. But hybrid warfare always was an integral part of warfare right since ancient civilisations took to fighting. Not much is written about hybrid warfare in ancient Indian history but Chanakya had **advocated a six-fold policy to interact with the neighbours that included co-existence, neutrality, alliance, double policy, march and war, and that** '*If the end could be achieved by non-military method, even by methods of intrigue, duplicity and fraud, he would not advocate an armed conflict*'.[1] *Much of this was practiced in Ramayana and Mahabharata, as well as in ancient Indian wars by Maurya and Gupta dynasties and others.* Sun Tzu had similarly said, **'To win one hundred victories in**

one hundred battles is not the acme of skill. To subdue the enemy without fighting is the acme of skill' and that *'those skilled in war subdue the enemy's army without battle'.*[2]

Figure 1.1: Transition: Generational Wars

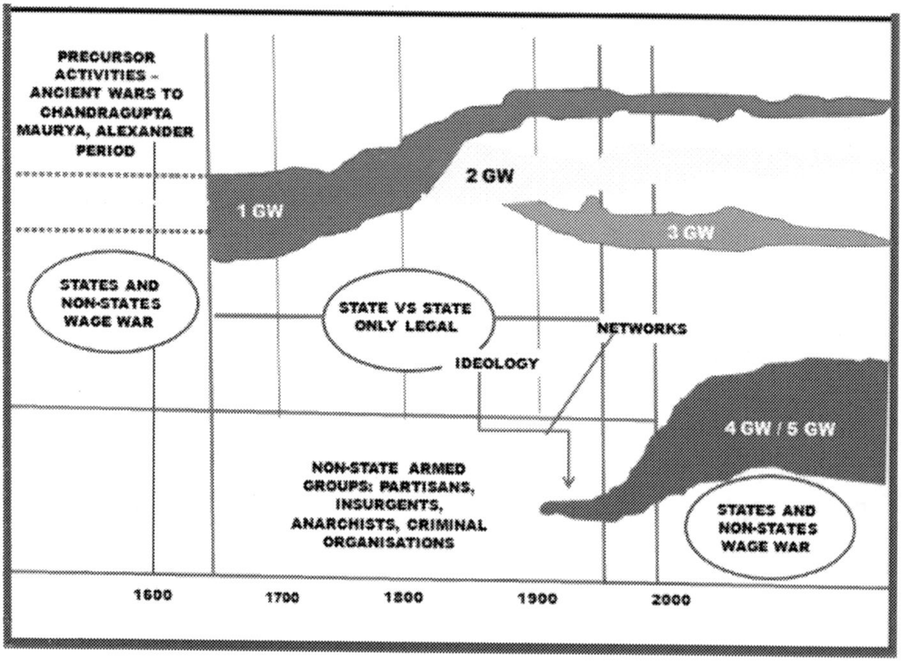

Hybrid warfare has been waged globally, including in the two world wars, many revolutions, American Civil War, Franco-Prussian War, Boer Wars, Sino-Japanese Wars, Vietnam War, and modern day conflicts in Middle East, West Asia, Ukraine and Afghanistan. Another description of hybrid warfare can be gleaned from Clausewitz's work wherein he said,

War is more than a true chameleon that slightly adapts its characteristics to the given case. As a total phenomenon its dominant tendencies always make war a paradoxical trinity—composed of primordial violence, hatred, and enmity, which are to be regarded as a blind natural force; of the play of chance and probability within which the creative spirit is free to roam; and of its element of subordination, as an instrument of policy, which makes it subject to reason alone.[3]

These factors have been part of war since the dawn of recorded history, even though some say that the term *hybrid warfare* is not warranted since any warfare includes multiple manifestations. However, as 21st-century wars morph into multiple forms of warfare, combining regular and irregular forces both using kinetic and non-kinetic means, the term hybrid warfare appears most appropriate. The combination of conventional and irregular methods is not new and has been used throughout history. The American Revolution saw a combination of Washington's Continental Army with militia forces, and similarly, in the Napoleonic Wars British regulars cooperated with Spanish guerrillas.[4] What is new is the sophistication and lethality of non-state and state-supported non-state actors that are well armed with technologically advanced weapons and wherewithal like mobile phones and digital networks adapted to the battlefield—all of which challenge and exploit weaknesses in conventional military structures.[5]

Definitions

There is no universally accepted definition of hybrid warfare. Generally, it is considered to be a military strategy that combines conventional warfare, irregular warfare and cyber warfare. Within the US, one finds different descriptions referring to this type of threat. In 2011, US Army defined a hybrid threat as, 'the diverse and dynamic combination of regular forces, irregular forces, criminal elements, or a combination of these forces and elements all unified to achieve mutually benefiting effects'.[6] The US Joint Forces Command defines a hybrid threat as, 'any adversary that simultaneously and adaptively employs a tailored mix of conventional, irregular, terrorism and criminal means or activities in the operational battle space. Rather than a single entity, a hybrid threat or challenger may be a combination of state and non-state actors'.[7] General George W Casey, former US Army Chief, described a new type of war that would become increasingly common in the future, 'A hybrid of irregular warfare and conventional warfare'.[8] Yet another view expressed by the National Defence University, Washington, DC, is that hybrid warfare is only a part of 'compound warfare' as depicted in Figure 1.2.[9] However, according to James G Hoffman, as difficult as compound wars have been, the operational fusion of conventional and irregular capabilities in hybrid conflicts may be even more complicated. Compound wars offered synergy and combinations at the strategic level, but not the complexity, fusion and simultaneity we anticipate at the operational and even tactical levels in wars where one or both sides are blending and fusing the full range of methods and modes of conflict into the battle space.[10]

With reference to hybrid warfare, NATO uses the term to describe 'adversaries with the ability to simultaneously employ conventional and non-conventional means adaptively in pursuit of their objectives'.[11] According to Agus Harimurti Yudhoyono, 'In the future, we should anticipate seeing more hybrid wars where conventional warfare, irregular warfare, asymmetric warfare, and information warfare all blend

Figure 1.2: Compound Warfare

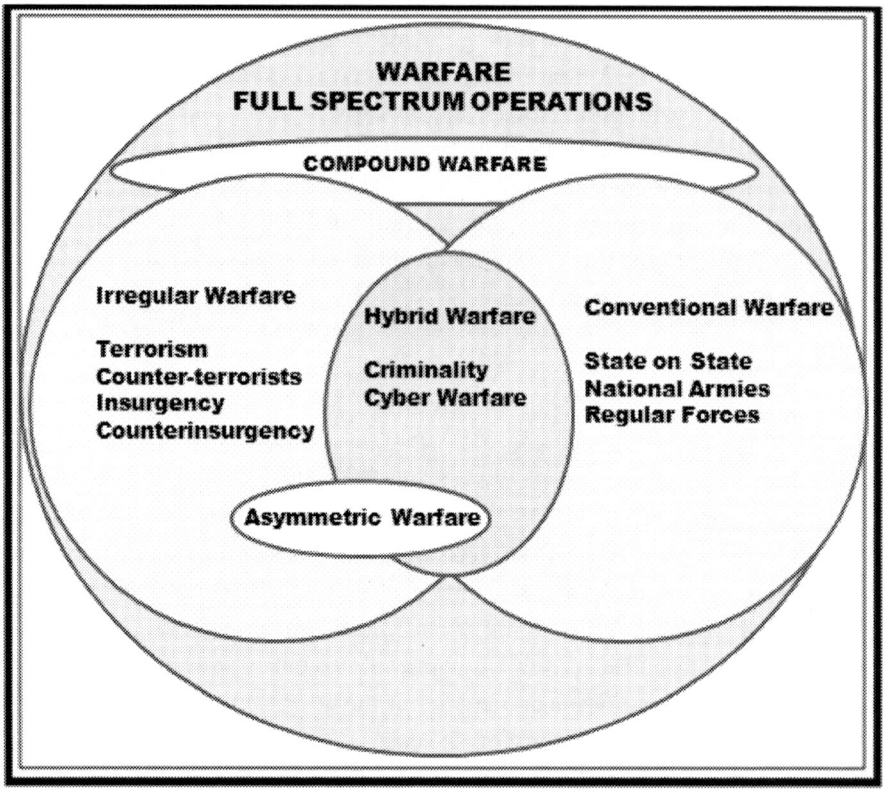

together, creating a very complex and challenging situation to the combatants; therefore it will require military forces to possess hybrid capabilities, which might help deal with hybrid threats'.[12]

Examination of the aforementioned definitions leads to the following *characteristics of hybrid warfare*:

- ✓ **Ambiguous and Complex Adversary**. The hybrid adversary can be state, non-state, state-sponsored non-state, or a mix of all. For example, in Afghanistan, the government is battling the Afghan Taliban as well as proxies of Pakistan, as perhaps also some non-state forces like Islamic State Khorasan and Al Qaeda, even if they have underhand links with Pakistan's ISI. Similarly, in the Israel–Hezbollah Conflict and the Syrian Civil War, the main adversaries are non-state entities within the state system. These non-state actors can act as proxies for countries but have independent agendas as well. For example, Iran is a sponsor of Hezbollah but it was Hezbollah's, not Iran's, agenda that resulted in the kidnapping of Israeli troops that led to the Israel–Hezbollah war. However, US-NATO describe the Russian involvement in Ukraine as a traditional state actor waging a hybrid war, in addition to using a local hybrid proxy, even as Russia denies any such involvement in the Ukraine conflict.

- ✓ **Multiple Simultaneous Methods**. Methods and tactics include employment of conventional capabilities, irregular forces and tactics, irregular formations, mass violence and terrorist acts, criminal activity and the like. The hybrid adversary also uses clandestine actions to avoid attribution or retribution. These methods are used simultaneously across the spectrum of conflict with a unified strategy. A significant example is the Islamic State that plans a Global Caliphate and the 40-nation coalition battling it. ISIS has structured formations, sizeable strength with steady stream of volunteers across the globe, blended tactics and an array of weaponry including access to chemical and radiological warfare material, in addition to sufficient financial back-up through sale of oil.[13]
- ✓ **Adaptability**. The hybrid adversary enjoys the big advantage of mingling and merging in the population, which is the biggest asset. The adversary has the advantage of foreseeing actions of conventional forces and the inhibitions that conventional forces have in terms of collateral damage involving human rights issues. This enables adapting to the changing tactics of conventional forces. The ISIS response to the US aerial bombing campaign was to quickly reduce the use of cell phones, move in smaller convoys and avoid use of checkpoints. ISIS cadres dispersed among the civilian population and civilians were used as shields against ground attacks. Collateral damage and civilian casualties became the tool for recruiting more youth in the name of jihad.[14]
- ✓ **Advance Weaponry and Disruptive Technologies**. Advanced weaponry is now available on the world market that can be bought at bargain prices, with global players also arming irregular forces and non-state actors in furtherance of their own national interests. Modern technologies like cellular networks are being adapted to the battlefield. In 2006, Hezbollah was found armed with high-tech weaponry like precision-guided missiles. Hezbollah shot down Israeli helicopters, severely damaged a patrol boat with a cruise missile and destroyed Israeli tanks by firing guided missiles. They are also reportedly using unarmed aerial vehicles (supplied by Iran) to gather intelligence, communicate with encrypted cell phones and monitoring Israeli troop movements with thermal night-vision equipment.[15]
- ✓ **Propaganda through Mass Communication**. The growth of mass

communication networks offers powerful propaganda and recruiting tools. Not only is video-streaming being used effectively, fake new websites to spread false stories are being exploited as a tool of hybrid warfare.[16] Pakistan has been exploiting mass communication for radicalising the youth of Kashmir Valley and causing social unrest in India. This was very evident during the recent turmoil in J&K post the killing of Burhan Wani and the sustained campaign to denounce the use of pellet guns, even showing photos of children injured in the Middle East and West Asia.

- ✓ **Multiple Battlefields**. Hybrid war takes place on three battlefields: *one* the conventional battlefield, *two*, the indigenous population of the conflict zone and *three*, the international community.[17]

On balance, *hybrid warfare can be defined as a cocktail of conventional military capabilities, insurgencies, terrorism, guerrilla warfare, organized crime, cyber warfare and advanced military technology*. This kind of warfare may also include violations of international laws of war, and will often also include non-state actors and organizations, supported by states with dubious agendas. All these ingredients may be blended together with an equivocal number of ingredients affecting the outcome at the same time. The magnitude of each ingredient may vary significantly during the war depending on the phase of the war or its immediate effectiveness.[18] Technology assisting hybrid warfare would include drones and robotics, cyber weapons, virtual terrorism, exploitation of electronic and social media, directed energy weapons, smart and stealth technologies, directed energy plasma and laser weapons, nano-technologies, hypersonic and space platforms, etc.

Concepts and Determinants

There are a variety of terms used to refer to the hybrid war concept: hybrid war, hybrid warfare, hybrid threat, or hybrid adversary. Since hybrid war merges different methods and theories of war and warfare at different levels of war, in different realms and domains, especially the cognitive and moral domains, by a blend of actors, arranged in time and space to achieve objectives at all levels of war, it poses a novel threat to conventional armies even when they give attention to irregular warfare. One of the biggest challenges hybrid war present is exploitation of the cognitive and moral domains vis-à-vis the physical domain that all conventional armies traditionally concentrate on.[19] The two Gulf Wars witnessed the use of large numbers of regular forces, heavy armour, air supremacy, cruise missiles and technological advantage over the adversary. The effective use of technology was keenly studied by the Chinese who went in for *Informatisation* of the PLA. But post 9/11, when Al Qaeda hit the Twin Towers and Pentagon using hijacked passenger planes, and US-NATO attacked and occupied Afghanistan and Iraq, they found themselves embroiled in a different type of war-fighting hybrid war with non-state actors.[20]

> **Every age has its own kind of war, its own limiting conditions, and its own peculiar preoccupations.**
>
> ***—Carl von Clausewitz***

In the late 1980s, Fourth-Generation Warfare (4 GW) theorists began to recognise a shift in warfare that they assumed was both in the character and nature of war. Their ideas and publications triggered a captivating dialogue on how warfare was changing. This debate helped prompt militaries to recognize the change and look at transformation. Over the ensuing years, a number of military thinkers and strategists demonstrated that the 4GW theorists were not the ultimate. They set the stage for a generation of subsequent theorists to follow with their own predictions of future warfare. Frank Hoffman compellingly argued that warfare is converging, blending into a hybrid form, wherein adversaries will use all capabilities at their disposal. The key to success in such a period of change and persistent conflict is an agile strategic approach that relies on a wide array of capabilities. Fourth-Generation Warfare proponents also noted that historically most wars have usually turned into irregular warfare after the invader had defeated an adversary's regular force. In the case of the US-NATO invasions of Afghanistan and Iraq, they either did not have a regular force to start with, or the one they had was defeated quickly and decisively. The mismatch of resources practically forced these adversaries to employ insurgent and terrorist strategies from the start. It is within this complex and dynamic setting that a new form of warfare has materialized. Many see a prospect of enduring conflict ahead in which state, non-state and individual actors increasingly resort to violence to pursue their political and ideological goals. Over the ensuing decades, particular global trends will merge with existing local and regional tensions to fuel the frequency, intensity and extent of conflict around the world.[21]

A prominent global trend of the new strategic environment is the advancement of 'globalization' and 'technology'. While this has led to better global connectivity and scientific advances that are driving world-wide prosperity, at the same time, they also underscore disparities in wealth and power among populations. These phenomena, working in tandem, have inadvertently provided the means to export terror and extremism around the world.[22] In addition, several cultures have seen an increase in radicalism. In today's post-modern world, those who feel victimized or threatened by the cultural and economic impacts of globalization have become increasingly attracted to radical and religious extremist groups. Aided by the power of many followers, the motivations and activities of radical groups, particularly religious radicals, are difficult to moderate and often intensify and lengthen a conflict. Another important reason why hybrid warfare has emerged as the preferred mode of warfare in the 21st century is the huge cost of waging conventional wars, both in terms of lives and finances, which even a superpower like the US finds difficult to live with. As per a report in the *Times* magazine, of January 1, 2015, the true cost to the US wars in Afghanistan and Iraq is pegged at between $4 trillion and $6 trillion.[23] The number of US troops that were killed in fighting the wars in Iraq and Afghanistan had passed 6,800 in the beginning of 2015.[24] However, the total US casualties in Afghanistan had increased to 7,905 by January 2017, while the combined US-NATO 'killed' alone in Afghanistan and Iraq by January 2017 totalled to 8,362.[25] What also emerged over the years is that while proxy forces were being used by nations to bridge conventional asymmetry vis-à-vis superior adversary, now even major powers are using proxy forces to further their own national interests; 'boots on ground' have 'largely' been replaced by 'proxy boots on ground'. This phenomenon is observed more and more in great power games.

Hybrid war uses all forms of kinetic and non-kinetic means. Therefore, special operations are of great significance in this type of warfare. Amid an increasingly fluid and challenging contemporary security environment, there is increased demand worldwide for military forces skilled in operating below the threshold of large-scale armed conflict. As United States (US) Army General Joseph Votel said in August 2014, US Special Operations Command (SOCOM) has entered the 'golden age for special operations'. Also, a major part of non-kinetic means is psychological operations. Psychological warfare includes an action that forces the enemy to divert men and equipment from the active front, to tie down men and arms in preparation for defence against an attack that never comes. Political warfare adds the important idea that all instruments of policy need to be correlated in the conduct of war. The British programme for political warfare during World War II was carried out through three agencies: the Political Warfare Executive, a secret organisation for propaganda against enemy and for enemy-occupied countries; the Ministry of Information, which dealt with British public and Allied and neutral countries and the Overseas Services of the BBC, which broadcast to all countries receiving guidelines from the Political Warfare Executive and Ministry of Information. Psychological warfare was recognized as a military instrument, sharing honours, powers and responsibilities with the military, economic and diplomatic agencies of modern war.

With hybrid warfare here to stay as the most likely form of warfare to be faced, the importance of air power is equally true as it is for conventional warfare. At the same time, while airpower has great utility, there are limitations to its effectiveness and therefore can't be termed the 'silver bullet'. The importance of air power is more in conventional conflict, than in hybrid warfare. For hybrid warfare, there needs to be a greater investment in mobility and Intelligence, Surveillance and Reconnaissance (ISR) and there remains an over investment in control of the air platforms. But notwithstanding this, airpower can never be the sole solution to hybrid threats as may be seen in the case of US-NATO operations in Afghanistan and Iraq battling irregular forces, where an adversary without air power could not be wholly taken out despite overwhelming technological superiority. While the hybrid actor rarely contests control of the air directly, however, the presence of Surface to Air Missiles (SAMs) and proliferation and sophistication of Man-Portable Air Defence Systems (MANPADS) put caution on the attacker's air campaign. The hybrid actor may seek to neutralize the space advantage through cyber-attack or by physically attacking the ground stations. No doubt, time-sensitive targeting, persistence, all-weather precision and low-yield weapons have increased the utility of air power; however, its greatest utility remains against conventional targets and it is believed that it will remain having little utility against terrorist and criminal activities. Attacks will remain sensitive to GPS jamming as well as the exploitation of the media. However, mobility has more of an all-weather capability now and the ability to carry out Combat Search and Rescue (CSAR) operations that reinforces the moral component.

From the foregoing, the concept of hybrid warfare can be described as, 'involvement, employment, pursuit and blending, at operational level of kinetic and non-kinetic tactics, regular and irregular combatants, state and non-state actors, physical, psychological, low-tech and high-tech means aimed at generating advantage relative to the adversary with a view to achieve surprise, seize and maintain the initiative, generate deception and ambiguity, maximizing deniability, subduing the adversary and advancing own national interests'. The hybrid conundrum is depicted in Figure 1.3.

The success or failure of the US invasion of Afghanistan and Iraq, more conventional than hybrid, has been questioned within the US itself, particularly with respect to Afghanistan, even though the true aim of US and NATO remains ambiguous. In the case of US operations in the Middle East, these did exponentially increase arms sales of the US, besides control of oil and territory in the region directly or indirectly, which helped sustain America's image of a global superpower. The application of hybrid warfare, though a global phenomenon, must have certain degree of success. At the same time, *application of hybrid warfare involves certain determinants*, which can be summarized as follows:

✓ **Geostrategic Interests of the Aggressor**. These may range from capture of

Figure 1.3: Hybrid Conundrum

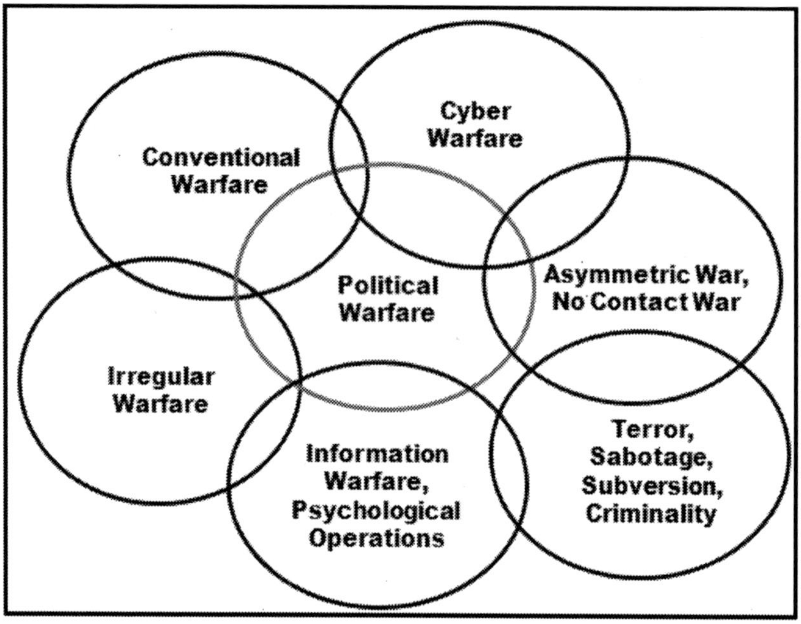

territory; control of oil and energy resources; access to sea; facilitating own economy and trade; gaining access to regions of own interest; denying outside influence to own fault-lines (demographic, societal, economy, and defence); negating geopolitical and economic competition; force adversary to subordinate role; compel adversary to fall in line with own policies and ambition and time table to become regional and global superpower.

✓ **Proficiency of Aggressor**. In terms of the formulation of strategy of hybrid war at the strategic level, the aggressor should have proficiency in terms of strategic judgment, strategic decision making and strategic planning. In addition would be the need for adequate preparation, control, strategic defence and principles for waging hybrid war, latter varying from nation to nation as well as who is the adversary. The performance of the aggressor during the hybrid war will be dependent upon the strategic guidance, establishment and employment of kinetic and non-kinetic forces using low-tech and high-tech. It will be contingent upon strategic command, strategic offence activating multiple battle fronts in multiple domains through the spectrum of conflict as warranted; strategic manoeuvre; information warfare; psychological operations; strategic defence; strategic support; escalation control and periodic course corrections as required.

- ✓ **Profile, Fault-lines and Weaknesses of Adversary**. Success of hybrid war, over and above the proficiency of the aggressor (as mentioned above) would depend on the adversary's profile, fault-lines and weaknesses such as geography; socio-political fabric; economy and development; demography, human development index and unemployment; national interests and strategic culture; cultural traditions and role of religion; strategic culture, degree of ethical views on warfare; strategic orientation and lack of institutionalized capacity to evolve national and defence policies in the long term; type of leadership; prominence of military in decision making; corruption and susceptibility to being bribed; military capabilities on land, sea, air, space and cyberspace; indigenous defence-industrial complex and degree to which they can support defence forces; Information Warfare (IW) and Electronic Warfare (EW) capabilities deterrence created against hybrid war and irregular warfare; indigenous insurgencies and terrorist organizations; foreign alliances and the degree to which outside assistance expected during conflict, other fault-lines including paucity of energy resources, susceptibility to encirclement and the like.

Russian Hybrid Warfare

Western scholars and media started talking of hybrid warfare in recent years during Russia's involvement in Crimea and the conflict in Ukraine. Russia's successful use of non-military instruments and of information, in particular, in the annexation of Crimea was the reason why the 'hybrid warfare' label gained so much traction in its aftermath. Western depiction of the Russian concept of hybrid war is shown in Figure 1.4. General Valery Gerasimov, Chief of the General Staff of Russian Federation, went on record to say, 'Methods of conflict have changed, and now involve the broad use of political, economic, informational, humanitarian, and other non-military measures. All of this could be supplemented by firing up the local populace as a fifth column and by concealed armed forces'. The *Financial Times*, in 2014, referred to Russia's unorthodox methodology, and drew a simile to Russia's hybrid war in Ukraine with Leo Tolstoy in his *War and Peace*, wherein described Field Marshal Mikhail Kutuzov's partisan campaign against Napoleon as 'dropping the sword and picking up the club', expressing that Moscow's intervention and covert war in Crimea and the Lugansk and Donetsk regions had set a high watermark in the art, laying bare the weakness of NATO's ossified military deterrent—the centrepiece of international security order that was supposed to be hardening, not weakening.[26]

Figure 1.4: Russian Hybrid Warfare

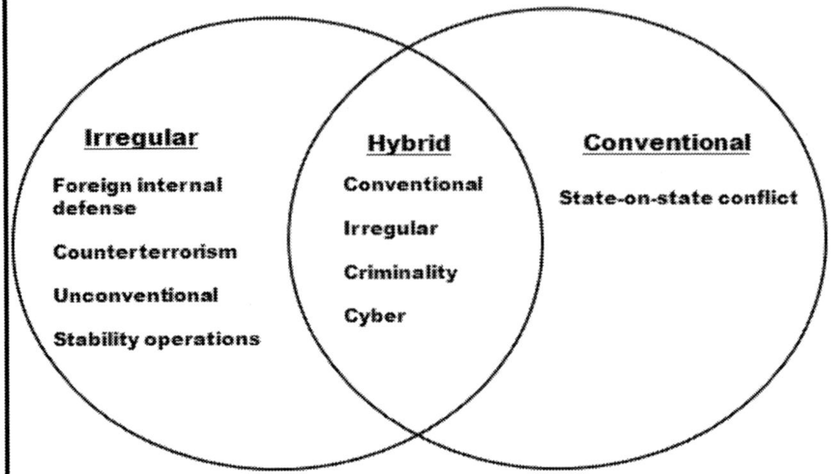

Kennan Cable, Wilson Centre, April 2015.

Russia's hybrid warfare has its roots in Soviet forces practicing and mastering the 'Reflexive Control' theory, defined as a 'means of conveying to a partner or an opponent specially prepared information to incline him to voluntarily make the predetermined decision desired by the initiator of the action'. It is a sort of coercion through means of information warfare, which will incline a great power's opponents to act in a pre-simulated way.[27] As per current Russian military operational doctrine, Information Operation (IO) implies everything that would involve information. Therefore, propaganda, disinformation, psychological operations and even cyber warfare, which stay below the bar to invite retaliation, all fall within this arc. Recent Russian claims that Russian Electronic Warfare (REW) troops can detect and neutralise any target from a ship's system and radar, to a satellite; can immobilise entire US Navy through an *electronic bomb* and are capable of creating electronic jamming domes over their bases that make them invisible on radar screens.

General Gerasimov advocates the use of a modern version of partisan warfare that targets an adversary's weaknesses and avoids direct, overt confrontations.[28] Additionally, Gerasimov proposes a correlation of non-military to military measures of 4 to 1. His non-military measures include efforts to shape the political, economic and social landscapes of the adversary state through subversion, espionage and propaganda, potentially in combination with cyber-attacks. Grounded in *maskirovka*, the Soviet doctrine of denial and deception, this new employment of ambiguous warfare keeps opponents wondering and hesitating by resolutely denying Russian involvement while working through as many agents as possible. In Ukraine, for example, third-party deniable agents included pro-Russian loyalists and local paramilitary commanders, as well as gangsters who spotted an opportunity for profit and power. In the second phase, Russia uses economic warfare and diplomatic/political pressure to intimidate, coerce, punish and undermine governments in target states as means of further weakening them. In the third phase, Russia infiltrates ambiguous military and security personnel into the target country, and activates criminal and other networks to further foment unrest and ignite open conflict. In the fourth phase, Russia's military engages in a campaign to isolate government positions, seize key terrain and destroy the defence and security apparatus of the target country. In the fifth phase, Russia conducts information operations to deny involvement and seed doubt and discord in the minds of other foreign governments as to what is occurring and how they might respond. In the sixth and final phase, Russia consolidates its gains in the target country, takes actions to de-escalate the conflict and reduce tensions and installs a government amenable to Russian influence (see Figure 1.5).

Figure 1.5: Russia's Non-Linear Warfare

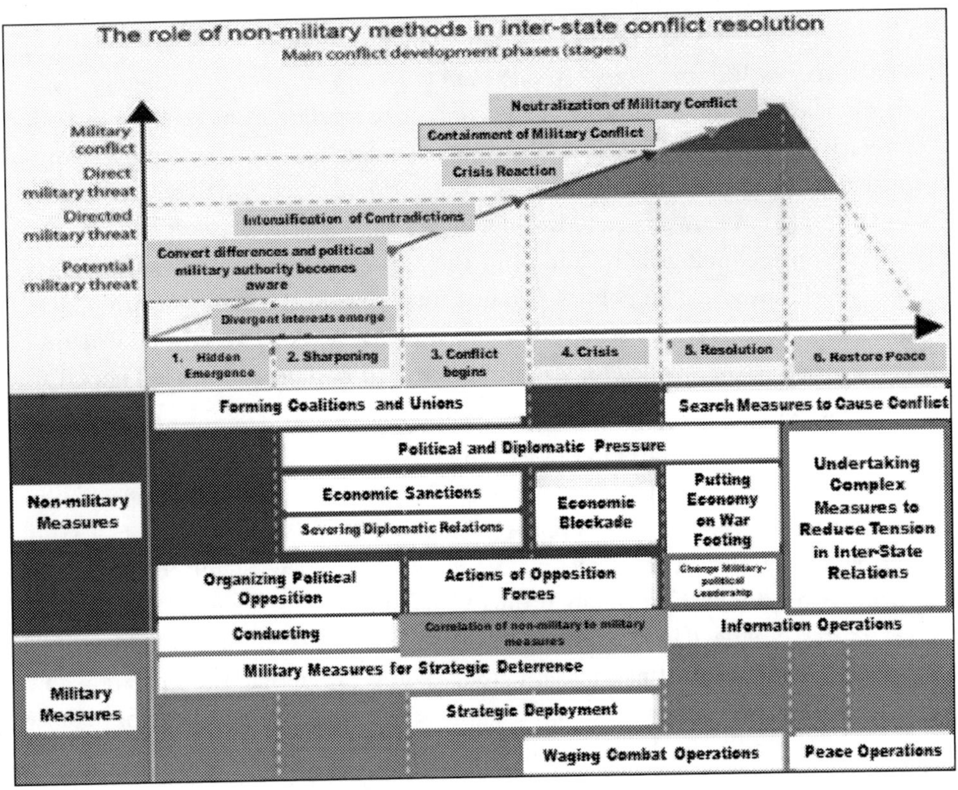

Russia's conquest of Crimea highlighted the following: *one*, effective operational demonstration of Russia's newly created Special Operations Forces (SOF), which were deployed with high speed and to great effect albeit Ukraine was without such matching capability; *two*, Russian leadership's ability to co-ordinate all relevant instruments of state power, including SOF, information operations including state media, elements of cyber warfare, deterrence and coercion through staged military exercises and the use of proxy fighters, for the successful achievement of objectives and three, military exercises staged by Russia during the Ukraine crisis were unprecedented in size and served as an impressive show of force, exhibiting latest advances in Russia's conventional military forces.[29] The debate over hybrid warfare, however, continues in the West, with some scholars questioning whether hybrid warfare even exists, on the grounds that any threat can be hybrid as long as it is not limited to a single form and dimension of warfare. When any threat or use of force is defined as hybrid, the term loses its value and causes confusion instead of clarifying the "reality" of modern warfare.[30]

Chinese Hybrid Warfare

In 1999, China came up with the concept of 'Unrestricted Warfare' worked out by two PLA Colonels, Qiao Liang and Wang Xiangsui, and which was later published as *Unrestricted Warfare: China's Master Plan to Destroy America.*[31] The book's main thesis called for the expansion of the concept of warfare from military to both military and non-military means, the argument being that such conceptual change increases the capacity in violence in other dimensions, such as politics, economics and information networks, and this rise in violence-capacity is precipitated by the increase in technologies. In addition, the authors advocate for warfare what Machiavelli advocated for politics, that is, warfare constitutes an independent sphere of action in which ethical standards are not applicable. A thematic representation of the means recommended for waging unrestricted warfare is shown in Figure 1.6.

This concept literally shocked the Western world, as described by Brigadier (later Lieutenant General) HS Lidder, who was then posted as the Indian Defence Advisor at Washington, DC. It took the US scholars two years to come up with the counter-term 'hybrid warfare', even as it remains shuttling between acceptance and denial, as indicated in the above-mentioned NATO review. Significantly, veteran Major General John K Singlaub, former Chief of Staff, US Forces, Korea went on record to say, 'The 9/11 attacks may have been just the beginning of Unrestricted Warfare. Many terrorist nations and groups will try to imitate this operation and China's war book Unrestricted Warfare will be their text'. China's hedging actions in Western Pacific are also part of hybrid warfare even as actual clash in terms of

Figure 1.6: China's Unrestricted Warfare

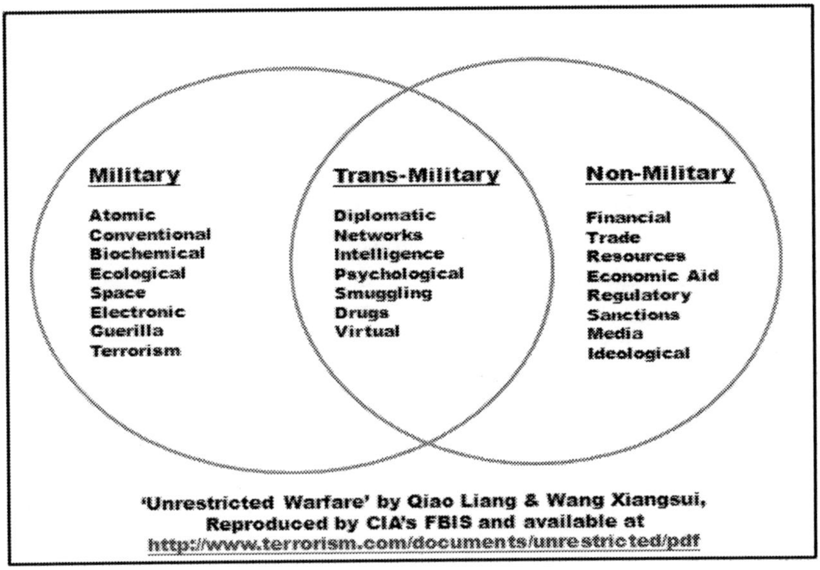

conventional clash has not taken place. This includes reclaiming and militarisation of islands and reefs in disputed areas in a bid to 'legalise' illegal claims. Another example is the use of China's fishermen-turned-militia.[32]

China's 'Unrestricted Warfare' has eight pillars as under:

✓ The *first pillar* is that this form of warfare takes place globally or on a 360° observation and design, and utilises all forms of kinetic and non-kinetic defence capabilities and factors. The financing and support of crime, addiction, corruption, arms transfers, illegal smuggling and the corruption of public and governmental institutions across the globe certainly matches with this requirement. This 'omni-directionality', to use the authors' term, eliminates distinctions between what is and is not the battlefield in pursuit of strategic advantages. Using IT and the other tools of the trade, purveyors of this warfare, essentially, have taken the Leninist solution of using Socialist movements and ramified Communist party political and military organisations as surrogates for the lack of an organised or capable army to a new level. Every conceivable avenue of approach is, therefore, sanctioned, as this war knows no restrictions. And thus, wars of these kinds encompass the entire network of a society's relationships.

✓ The *second pillar* is synchrony, actions taking place at the same time across the depth of the entire 'theatre'. All the activities described here are ongoing and occurring globally. But they can ideally be orchestrated or turned on and off like a rheostat as circumstances in any particular theatre warrant. For instance, principals could decide at any given time to elevate the crisis in Latin America while downgrading support for insurgencies in Africa or vice versa.

- ✓ The *third pillar* is limited objectives. The aim is not to destroy the nation and its military or government or necessarily those of any other state but rather to weaken them and prevent their ability to restrict the aggressor's activity. The goal is to keep the level of provocation below that threshold (unless necessary) where the targeted state might lash out and destroy the network in his country or Russian, Chinese or Democratic People's Republic of Korea (DPRK) capabilities altogether. Nevertheless, in targeted Third-World areas the cumulative impact of these operations over time is to destabilize or even take over the targeted states if not entire regions around them, e.g., Colombia.
- ✓ The *fourth pillar* logically follows that in pursuit of the limited objectives, which are within the reach of the active network waging this kind of war and within that framework of limited goals, the attacking force should pursue 'unlimited measures'. This entails the unrestricted employment of measures that are restricted only to the pursuit of those objectives. For Chinese writers, Sherman's march to the sea represents a burn-and-plunders operation that shunned actual combat in order to achieve a limited objective of attacking the South's will and capacity to fight without giving battle. That exemplifies an unlimited measure in support of a limited objective.
- ✓ The *fifth pillar* is asymmetry, operations conducted in ways contrary to enemy expectations or understanding of the balance of symmetry. The breadth and scope of the operations described in these papers certainly lend themselves to that kind of asymmetric operations since their initiators now command not only a global reach but also a diverse global portfolio of capabilities with which to conduct their operations anywhere in the world.
- ✓ The *sixth pillar* is minimal consumption. What this means is waging this war with the least necessary expenditure of resources. And as we know, from US experience, this translates to a cost-imposing strategy, e.g., the minimal cost of the Al Qaeda 9/11 operation versus the huge costs of operation in Afghanistan, not to mention Iraq. The orchestrators of these kinds of operations, whether they be in Moscow, Tehran, Caracas, Pyongyang or elsewhere have within their capability the means to (or they may so believe) to launch similar cost-imposing crises against a nation or the US in 'peripheral

areas' that Washington and its allies must nonetheless spend time, money and men to defend while they can initiate them at minimal cost.

- ✓ The *seventh pillar*, which flows from the foregoing pillars, is that of multi-dimensionality, namely, the coordination and allocation of all forces, military and otherwise, that can be mobilized, for accomplishment of the task at hand and realization of the objective in question. This entails coordination and cooperation among all kinds of forces in different spheres, e.g., the coordination of partisan with regular army warfare on the Eastern Front in World War II.
- ✓ Lastly, the *eighth pillar* is the continuous adjustment and control of the entire process in dynamic fashion, using all the instruments of warfare, as conceived here, and of national power toward accomplishment of the objective.

IW is a key aspect of unrestricted warfare. IW in this context does not refer primarily to the disabling of physical infrastructure, e.g., electricity grids, power plants, etc., like the well-known Stuxnet virus used against Iran's nuclear programme, but rather, as defined by Russian and Chinese authorities alike to a much broader concept. For example, in 2009, First Deputy Chief of the Russian General Staff, Alexander Burutin stated that IW is not only essential in disabling Command Control (C2) structures of military establishments, but more importantly, the essence of contemporary information attacks lies in altering the outside principles of societal structure and the life of society with the help of information expansion. This can be done by imposing onto the citizens' moral norms and cultural traditions that are foreign to them. China's hybrid threats as related to India are discussed in subsequent chapters.

Pakistan's Hybrid Warfare

Pakistan's hybrid warfare is being discussed in detail in subsequent chapters. However, at this stage, it is highlighted that Pakistan has used a mix of regular and irregular forces, right since its birth, in all wars against India. In addition, Pakistan is continuously using proxy forces for mounting terrorist attacks on India. Religion is being used as a tool to wage Islamic jihad in India—under the 'Quranic Concept of War'. Pakistan has been exploiting information operations, optimising mass media communications. Its hybrid warfare modes include cyber warfare, narcotics, flooding India with fake Indian currency and the like. There is Pakistan–China collusivity in waging hybrid war on India. Pakistan frequently resorts to nuclear sabre rattling for facilitating irregular war on India, largely so because India has not called Pakistan's nuclear bluff.

America's Hybrid Warfare

It is but natural that not much would be written about the hybrid war waged by the US-NATO forces save by the Russians. But then the US raised the Al Qaeda to oust the Soviets from Afghanistan, fought them as part of Global War on Terrorism (GWoT), later used them in Libya and Iraq and appears fighting the outfit again. With reference to Russian hybrid warfare in Ukraine, Chris Donnelly, former British military officer and Special Adviser to the NATO Secretary General, said, 'We are there already', implying US-NATO employ similar strategy and tactics.[33] According to William Blum, US historian who has also served in the State Department, 'Since 1945, US has tried to overthrow more than 50 governments, many of them democratically elected; grossly interfered in 30 countries; bombed the civilian population of 30 countries; interfered in elections in 30 countries; used chemical and biological weapons; and attempted to assassinate foreign leaders. In many cases Britain has been a collaborator'.[34] That these actions of the US were part of America's hybrid warfare needs no emphasis. General Wesley Clark, former NATO Supreme Commander had disclosed in 2014 that the US had already decided to take out seven countries in five years while the bombing of Afghanistan was still underway prelude to the US invasion.[35]

A Russian view is that currently the US is the only country that is practicing hybrid warfare; Russia has tangentially recognised this new development in May 2014 at the Moscow Conference on International Security, and is still struggling to make sense of it all; the Chinese and Iranians have not responded to the findings of the conference, but as with Russia, they too are existentially affected by its findings; it may take half a decade for any other country to adequately understand hybrid war to the point of being able to defend against it, let alone practice it on its own.[36] This Russian view is quite understandable because while US, Russia and China have all been waging hybrid war, the element of deniability being uppermost, none will admit to it. Significantly, General Michael Flynn, former head of US Defense Intelligence Agency, had gone public to say in 2015 that the rise of Islamic State and Jabhat al Nusra was 'Willful Decision' of the US.[37] Former British army officials training ISIS militants in Iraq also was reported during August 2014.[38]

A *typical US-sponsored insurgency* is orchestrated on the following lines[39]:

- ✓ **Phase I: Preparation**. Preparation phase for unconventional warfare begins with the approval of the President or Secretary of Defense to execute an unconventional warfare campaign. Intelligence and psychological preparation continues throughout.
- ✓ **Phase II: Initial Contact**. Ideally, a pilot team makes initial contact with an established or potential irregular element. A pilot team is typically an ad

hoc element composed of individuals possessing the specialized skills appropriate to the particular mission.

- ✓ **Phase III: Infiltration**. During this phase, special operations forces infiltrate the unconventional warfare operating area. Infiltration may be as overt as using a chartered civilian flight or as discreet as a clandestine insertion.
- ✓ **Phase IV: Organization**. Once US advisors link up with resistance leadership, the objective is to determine and agree upon a plan to organize the resistance for expanded operations. In addition to physical preparations, this entails a confirmation of mutual objectives and prior agreements. This requires a period of rapport-building to develop trust and confidence, as well as a period of discussion of expectations from both sides.
- ✓ **Phase V: Build-up**. Plans agreed to in Phase IV are implemented in Phase V. The amount of effort required to conduct organization building will be based on the insurgent or resistance organization that may already exist. Organization could be time consuming and painstaking or friendly forces could fall in on well-established and robust organizations.
- ✓ **Phase VI: Employment**. This will be a series of many events, both lethal and nonlethal, throughout Phases IV through VII. In other words, Phase V does not come to a complete stop when Phase VI begins. Nevertheless, this may represent a planned surge or maximum growth of organization effectiveness synchronized with planned future operations.
- ✓ **Phase VII: Transition**. When unconventional warfare ends in overthrow of a state or liberation of occupied territory and leads to a new government, Phase VII will include those activities contributing to the promotion of the new government's legitimacy. In such cases, the unconventional warfare effort will transition to foreign internal defense at some point.

The overall US purpose in the field of political warfare is to maintain an advantageous position on the world stage without resorting to defensive or offensive war by countering aggressors' attempts to gain advantage over subject states or by subverting the government of a subject state whose actions are inimical to US interests.[40] *America's political warfare objective is to isolate, erode, manipulate, exhaust, wear down, attrite, overthrow, reduce, replace, or create the conditions to coerce a belligerent government or regime to acquiesce to US national objectives, without going to war.*

As part of political warfare, the US enters into a competition with an opposing power over contested territory—the subject. The subject may be an entire state or, more commonly, a border adjustment involving only a part of a state.[41] The US may play the role of either status quo power or revisionist power. Other interested external powers may enter into the competition. When the US is in the role of status quo power, it opposes the aggressor in the competition over the subject territory. Direct military intervention, counterinsurgency and foreign internal defence are methods used to assist the subject state in defending against an insurgent force whether it is an indigenous effort or a proxy force assisted by an outside aggressor. In this situation, the aggressor is waging unconventional warfare while the US wages counter-unconventional warfare. When the US is the revisionist power, it intervenes against the established government of the subject state possibly using foreign proxies. In this situation, the US wages unconventional warfare and may be opposed by other external powers waging counter-unconventional warfare. In both cases, the US is engaged in a strategic competition with other external powers and a more tactical competition involving proxy forces including the forces of the subject state's established government. All instruments of national power are employed in a coordinated mix of overt, clandestine and covert actions. The resources in the subject state and those of interested external actors are marshalled to reduce costs to the US and to raise costs to the opposing power.

Key Issues

- ✓ *Hybrid warfare, combining conventional, irregular and cyber war, is not new but advancements in technology, weaponry and communications have enhanced lethality of this type of warfare.*
- ✓ *In hybrid warfare, the adversary is ambiguous and complex employing multiple kinetic and non-kinetic means simultaneously, adapting to changing situations, using advance weaponry and disruptive technologies, optimizing propaganda through mass communications.*
- ✓ *Special operations, information warfare and psychological operations are of vital importance in hybrid warfare.*
- ✓ *Air power has utility in hybrid warfare but it has limitations and is certainly not the 'silver bullet'. Its utility is more in conventional warfare.*
- ✓ *Concept of hybrid warfare can be described as involvement, employment, pursuit and blending, at operational level of kinetic and non-kinetic tactics, regular and irregular combatants, state and non-state actors, physical, psychological, low-tech and high-tech means aimed at generating advantage relative to the adversary with a view to achieve surprise, seize and maintain initiative, generate deception and ambiguity, maximizing deniability, subduing the adversary and advancing own national interests.*
- ✓ *Successful application of hybrid warfare involves geostrategic Interests and requisite proficiencies on the part of the aggressor, and exploiting the traits, fault-lines and weaknesses of the adversary.*

✓ *Global players like US, Russia and China are all practicing hybrid warfare in furthering their national interests, employing all instruments of national power in a mix of coordinated mix of overt, clandestine and covert actions.*

NOTES

1 Reza, Akash, 'China and India in the Perspective of Sun Tzu and Kautilya's Thought', July 29, 2008, https://ishakhan.wordpress.com/2008/07/29/china-and-india-in-the-perspective-of-sun-tzu-and-kautilya%E2%80%99s-thought/

2 Six Principles of Sun Tzu & the Art of Business, http://www.suntzustrategies.com/resources/six-principles-of-sun-tzu-the-art-of-business.

3 Michael, Howard, Michael and Parte, Peter, Carl von Clausewitz, '*On War*', Princeton: Princeton University Press, 1976/1984, p. 89 (p. 101 in Knopf's 'Everyman's Library' edition).

4 Hoffman, Frank, 'Conflict in the 21st Century: The Rise of Hybrid War', Potomac Institute for Policy Studies, Arlington, 207, pp. 20–22.

5 Jasper, Scott; Moreland, Scott (2014-12-02), 'The Islamic State is a Hybrid Threat: Why Does That Matter?"', Small Wars Journal, Small Wars Foundation, retrieved 2015-08-05.

6 Fleming, Brian P, 'Hybrid Threat Concept: Contemporary War, Military Planning and the Advent of Unrestricted Operational Art' (pdf), United States Army Command and General Staff College, 2011, retrieved 2015-08-05.

7 Ibid.

8 Grant, Greg, 'Hybrid Wars', Government Executive, National Journal Group, 2008, retrieved 2015-08-05.

9 Petri Huovinen, Petri, 'Hybrid Warfare – Just a Twist of Compound Warfare?' National Defence University, Washington DC, April 2011.

10 Frank, Hoffman G, 'Hybrid Warfare and Challenges', NDU Press, JFQ/issue 52, 1st quarter, 2009.

11 Jasper, Scott; Moreland, Scott, 'The Islamic State is a Hybrid Threat: Why Does That matter?', 2014, Small Wars Journal, Small Wars Foundation, retrieved 2015-08-05.

12 Agus Harimurti Yudhoyono Quotes, https://www.goodreads.com/author/quotes/7224099.Agus_Harimurti_Yudhoyono.

13 Pindják, Peter, 'Deterring Hybrid Warfare: A Chance for NATO ad EU to Work Together?', 2014, NATO Review, archived from the original on 2015-08-05, retrieved 2015-08-05.

14 El Mawy, Reda 'Islamic State Adapting to US-led Air strikes', BBC News, BBC, 2014, archived from the original on 2015-08-05, retrieved 2015-08-05.

15 Deep, Alex, 'Hybrid War: Old Concept, New Techniques', *Small Wars Journal*, Small War Foundation, 2015, retrieved 2015-08-05.

16 Lucian Kim, 'Russia Having Success in Hybrid War Against Germany' at http://blogs.reuters.com/great debate/2016/02/07russia-having-success-in-hybrid-war-against-germany/

17 McCuen, John J, 'Hybrid Wars', Military Review, 88 (2), p. 107.

18 Petri Huovinen, op. cit.

19 Lasica, T Daniel, 'Strategic Implications of Hybrid War: A Theory of Victory', United States Army Command and Staff College, AY 2009.

20 Ibid.

21 'The Army Strategy', US Department of Army, Washington DC, August 22, 2008, p. 1.

22 US Joint Forces Command, 'The Joint Operating Environment: Challenges and Implications for the Future Joint Force', Norfolk, VA: U.S. Joint Forces Command, November 2008, p. 13.

23 Thompson, Mark, 'The True Cost of the Afghanistan War May Surprise You', Times, 1 January 2015, http://time.com/3651697/afghanistan-war-cost/.
24 'US and Allied Killed', Costs of War, Watson Institute, Brown University, http://watson.brown.edu/costsofwar/costs/human/military/killed
25 'iCasualties: Operation Iraqi Freedom and Operation Enduing Freedom/Afghanistan', icasualties.org, http://icasualties.org/.
26 Jones, Sam, 'Ukraine: Russia's New Art of War', Financial Times, 28 August 2014, http://www.mediapool.bg/files/224/Ukraine_%20Russia%E2%80%99s%20new%20art %20 of% 20 war%20-%20FT.pdf.
27 Russian military has a dedicated information warfare force (VOI: Войска информационных операций, Voiska informatsionnykh operatsii). Per current Russian military operational doctrine, information operations (IO) means everything that would involve information. Therefore, propaganda, disinformation, psy-ops, and even cyber warfare which stays below the bar to invite a retaliation all falls within this arc.
28 Connell, Mary Ellen and Ryan Evans, 'Russia's "Ambiguous Warfare" and Implications for the U.S.', Marine Corps, CAN Occasional Paper, May 2015. https://www.cna.org/cna_files/pdf/dop-2015-u-010447-final.pdf.
29 Renz, Bettina and Smith Hanna, 'Russia and Hybrid Warfare – Going Beyond the Label', Aleksanteri Papers 1/2016, http://www.helsinki.fi/aleksanteri/english/publications/presentations/papers/ap_1_2016.pdf.
30 NATO Review Magazine, 'Hybrid War – Does It Even Exist?' http://www.nato.int/docu/review/2015/also-in-2015/hybrid-modern-future-warfare-russia-ukraine/EN/index.htm.
31 Liang, Qiao and Xiangsui, Wang, 'Unrestricted Warfare: China's Master Plan to Destroy America', Pan American Publishing Company, Panama, 2002.
32 Burgers, Tobias J and Romaniuk, Scott N, 'Hybrid Warfare in the South China Sea: The United States' "Little Grey (Un)Men"', The Diplomat, 31 December 2016, http://thediplomat.com/2016/12/hybrid-warfare-in-the-south-china-sea-the-united-states-little-grey-unmen/.
33 Jones, Sam, 'Ukraine: Russia's New Art of War', Financial Times, 28 August 2014, http://www.mediapool.bg/files/224/Ukraine_%20Russia%E2%80%99s%20new%20art%20of%20 war%20-%20FT.pdf.
34 Pilger, John, 'In Ukraine the US is Dragging Us Towards War with Russia', The News, 14 May 2014, http://www.theguardian.com/commentisfree/2014/may/13/ukraine-us-war-russia-john-pilge.r
35 Clark, Wesley, 'We're Going to Take Out 7 Countries in 5 Years: Iraq, Syria, Lebanon, Libya, Sudan and Iran', Global Research, 12 July 2014, http://www.globalresearch.ca/we-re-going-to-take-out-7-countries-in-5-years-iraq-syria-lebanon-libya-somalia-sudan-iran/5166.
36 Horybho, Andrew, 'Hybrid Wars: The Indirect Approach to Regime Change', Project of the Institute of Strategic Studies, Peoples' Friendship University of Russia, 2015, p. 74.
37 Clark, op. cit.
38 Former British army officials now training ISIS militants in Iraq: MI6, CIA, News, webindi123, 31 August 2014, http://news.webindia123.com/news/articles/India/20140831/2450603.html.
39 United States Political Warfare Policy, January 2015, http://orchestratingpower.org/lib/LIC/PW/2015%20draft%20PWP.pdf.
40 Ibid.
41 Ibid.

2

HYBRID WARFARE IN NUCLEAR BACKDROP AS GRAND STRATEGY

General

Nuclear weapons have an important role in geopolitics and big power relations. In December 2011, Vladimir Putin, then Prime Minister of Russia, had stated while presiding over a banquet that the only reason the US had any interest in relations with Moscow was that Russia was the only country that could 'destroy America in half an hour or less'.[1] Though nuclear weapons are the ultimate in warfare, they are considered as deterrent because of their massive destructive power. However, the role of nuclear weapons is important and is increasingly visible as a bedrock on which a more aggressive grand strategy of hybrid warfare is based; the credibility and effectiveness of hybrid warfare campaigns by nations is being backed by the potential to use of full spectrum of military capabilities, including conventional and nuclear forces, even as the nuclear remains ambiguous and controversial.

The deterrence value of nuclear power also facilitates nations going rogue and the international community restricting their actions to financial sanction, desisting from physical action against them, North Korea being one example. Nuclear posturing and messaging is important since these frame requirements add to or detract from stability, and can affect outcomes when deterrence fails, which can well happen. Therefore, depending on the dynamics of geopolitics, nuclear posturing and messages are changed by nation states. In the case of the non-declared nuclear states, like Israel, South Korea and perhaps Japan that is one screw away, their nuclear posturing and messaging of necessity remains opaque.

> **Not just North Korea, but Russia, Pakistan, and others have made counterproductive moves that only increase the risk that nuclear weapons could be used in a regional conflict in Europe, South Asia, or East Asia.**
>
> ***—Joe Biden***

Role of Nuclear Weapons in Hybrid War

Hybrid warfare is essentially a combination of conventional warfare, irregular warfare and cyber warfare in the nuclear backdrop, spanning the domains of air, land, sea, space, and cyberspace. While nuclear weapons remain a deterrent, the irregular warfare ushers in the aspect of nuclear terrorism. Ban Ki-moon, former UN Secretary General, went on record to say, 'Nuclear terrorism is one of the most serious threats of our time. Even one such attack could inflict mass casualties and create immense suffering and unwanted change in the world forever. The prospect should compel all of us to act to prevent such catastrophe'. A study undertaken by Brookings Institution during 2008 noted, 'Unless the world community acts decisively and with great urgency, it is more than likely than not that a weapon of mass destruction will be used in a terrorist attack somewhere by the end of 2013'.[2]

> **The threat of nuclear terrorism is growing faster than our ability to prevent an attack.**
>
> ***—Joe Liberman***

The Center for Non-proliferation Studies (CNS) Global Incidents and Trafficking Database published in 2016 identified 188 publicly reported incidents from 26 countries of nuclear or other radioactive material outside of regulatory control in 2015. Only eight of these incidents involved nuclear materials (uranium, thorium and plutonium-beryllium), and in all eight cases the material was recovered.[3] There have been reports of Al Qaeda and ISIS pursuing the acquisition of weapons of mass destruction (WMDs) past several years though the exact status in this regard is difficult to establish. More significant is the possibility of rogue and terror exporting nations providing nuclear material or WMDs to their proxies or through their proxies to another terrorist organisation in order to obfuscate the trail. Barak Obama, former US President, had said, 'When we think of our national security, the first to come to mind are nuclear proliferation, rogue states and global terrorism'. In the above-mentioned Brookings Institution study, Daniel Byman, Senior Fellow at Brookings Institution, referring to 'WMD Threats in Pakistan' had said,

> In my judgement Pakistan today is the most dangerous country in the world with regard to the proliferation of nuclear terrorism. Pakistan hosts most of the al-Qaida core, has an established nuclear programme and is prone to political instability. Some parts of its military and intelligence services have also evinced sympathy for the jihadists. This problem may grow as the civilian government control over the country is weak and its relationship with the military troubled.[4]

The aspect of big powers providing WMDs to proxy forces has also come to light in recent years. One example is the use of sarin gas in Syria by anti-government forces. In 2013, the Federal Security Service of the Russian Federation (FSB) circulated on the web evidence hacked that 'Britain Defence', one of the largest private mercenary forces in the world, was instructed by Washington to deliver a chemical weapon to Homs (Syria), a Soviet-origin g-shell from Libya similar to the one that Assad should have. Britain Defence was asked to deploy Ukrainian personnel who should speak Russian and make a video recording.[5] So, if chemical weapons can be provided to proxy forces in big power play, the possibility of nuclear material being provided can hardly be ruled out altogether. In 2009, Thomas Reed, former US Air Force Secretary (himself having designed two nuclear devices), in his book *The Nuclear Express: A Political History of the Bomb and Its Proliferation*, pointedly states that China has intentionally proliferated nuclear technology to risky regimes, particularly Pakistan. More significantly, in his interview with *US News*, Reed explained that China under Deng Xiaoping decided to proliferate nuclear technology to communists and Muslims in the third world based on the strategy that if the West started getting nuked by Muslim terrorists or another communist country without Chinese fingerprints, it would be good for China.[6] What reinforces Chinese denials of nuclear proliferation is that while China raised a host of objections to exposures in Reed's book, all were withdrawn subsequent to discussion with Chinese scientists as claimed by Reed. China, now having subsumed Pakistan and vetoing Pakistani terrorist like JeM chief Masood Azhar being branded 'terrorist', can well support, even instigate Pakistan into nuclear terrorism in pursuit of its 'Great Power' ambitions.

Of late, there has been increasing discussion about the possible use of tactical nuclear weapons (TNWs). While Pakistan has deployed these extensively, American scholars at the closed-door Defence Forum on Regional Security held at Taiwan in 2012 were of the view that China may well use TNWs in a bid to force India to give up territory. These views perhaps would undergo change with an increased reach of India's nuclear weapons and deployment of BrahMos weapon systems.

> **The use of TNW [tactical nuclear weapons] in Southeast Asia would be highly damaging to the U.S. whether or not the use remains unilateral.**
>
> ***—Nautilus Institute***

Nuclear Posturing and Messaging

Nuclear posturing and messaging varies among nations. It is a dynamic phenomenon that undergoes change with the prevailing geostrategic environment and what the host country perceives best in its national defence, and best suited as deterrence. One view is that there are three basic models to choose from: (1) assured retaliation, (2) catalytic posture (designed to prompt the intervention of a patron) and

(3) asymmetrical escalation. At present, India and China have adopted assured retaliation. South Africa, Israel, and Pakistan initially chose catalytic postures. France, and now Pakistan, adheres to asymmetrical escalation. Also, an assured retaliation posture doesn't fare well when paired up against asymmetrical escalation.[7] All nuclear postures may project mixed messages of catalytic, assured retaliation, and asymmetric escalation capabilities; however, the primary envisioned employment of these three postures is mutually exclusive.

According to the book *Nuclear Strategy in the Modern Era: Regional Powers and International Conflict* (which won the 2015 Best Book, International Security Studies Section of the International Studies Association), states optimize force structure and posture for their external security and their internal threats and constraints. If the state has a reliable patron, catalytic posture could fit. If the nation has assertive civil–military relations and confidence in its conventional capabilities, assured destruction is a good fit. But if the state is disadvantaged conventionally and its military hold sways, then it looks for TNWs and asymmetric escalation.[8] The posture optimization theory is described as a flowchart in Figure 2.1.

Figure 2.1: Posture Optimisation Theory

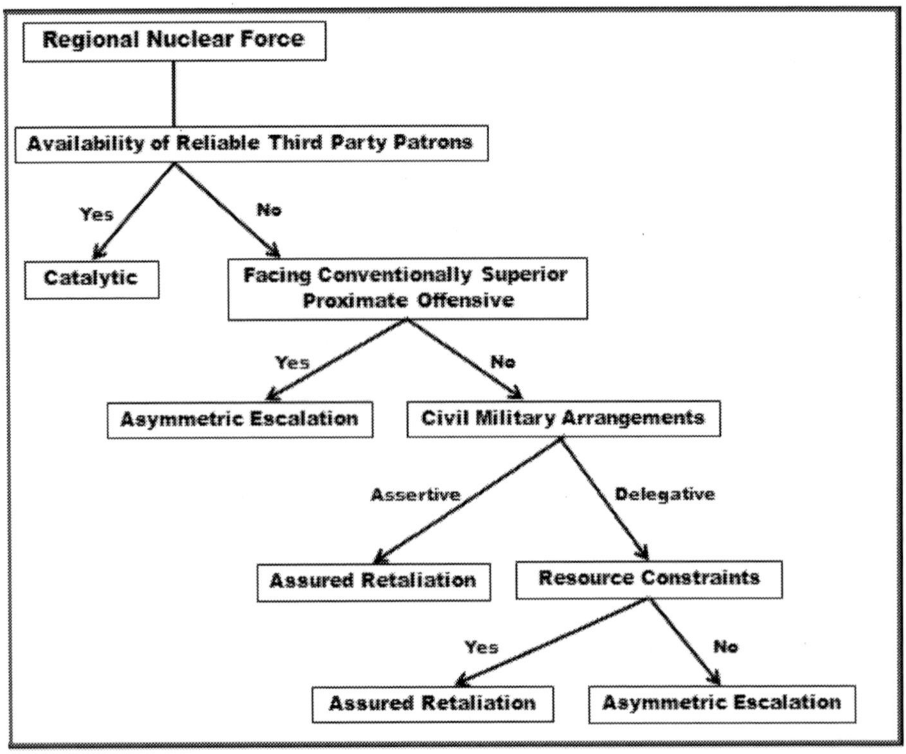

Pakistan's Nuclear Genesis

Pakistan nuclear programme commenced in late 1950s, and by 1956, Pakistan Atomic Energy Commission (PAEC) was established.[9] By mid-1970s, Pakistan started uranium enrichment to realize aspirations for developing nuclear weapons. In 1975, during AQ Khan's tenure in URENCO Enrichment Corporation, Netherlands, he clandestinely acquired centrifuge designs to start his work on the uranium enrichment facility in Pakistan. Simultaneously, Pakistan under Munir Ahmad Khan was also developing the plutonium route despite initial hurdles of sanctions and technological challenges. Pakistan's nuclear programme got a boost when China got actively involved in this programme. In late 1970s, Beijing provided Islamabad, with various levels of nuclear and missile-related assistance, including centrifuge equipment, warhead designs, highly enriched uranium (HEU), components of various missile systems, and technical expertise.[10] Finally (amidst rumours of China conducting the 'Cold Test' for Pakistan), Pakistan conducted its first nuclear test in 1998 (five explosions on May 28 and a sixth on May 30, 1998). Since then, Pakistan has enhanced its uranium and plutonium enrichment capabilities through the construction of plutonium production reactors at Khushab and uranium enrichment plant at Kahuta.[11]

Pakistan does not have a written doctrine, and hence its nuclear policies are periodically indicated by its military and diplomatic leaders. Pakistan has often threatened the 'First Use' of nuclear weapons in the early phase of the war, if its 'Red Lines' are violated. Lt Gen Lodhi (Retd), in the *Pakistan Defence Journal*, states, 'In a deteriorating military situation when an Indian conventional attack is likely to break through our defence or has already breached the main defence line causing a major setback to the defences which cannot be restored by conventional means at our disposal, the government would be left with no option except to use nuclear weapons to stabilize the situation', adding, 'India's superiority in conventional arms and manpower would have to be offset by nuclear weapons. Pakistan's nuclear doctrine would, therefore, essentially revolve around the first-strike option. In other words, we will use nuclear weapons if attacked by India even if the attack is with conventional weapons'.[12]

The civilian rulers also agreed with this view, as Abdul Sattar (former Pakistani foreign minister), Agha Shahi and Zulfiqar Ali Khan jointly authored an article in 1999 stating, 'The exigency under which Pakistan may use nuclear weapons is spelt out as: although the precise contingencies in which Pakistan may use nuclear weapons have not been articulated or even defined by the government, the assumption has been that if the enemy launches a war and undertakes a piercing attack to occupy large territories or communication junctions, the weapon of last resort would have to be invoked'.[13] Lt. Gen. Khalid Kidwai, the head of the Strategic Planning Division, in Pakistan commented in an interview, 'nuclear weapons would be used only if the very existence of Pakistan as a state is at stake'.[14] Thus, for the first time a few red lines or thresholds under which nuclear weapons could be used were elaborated by him. These red lines are Space, Military, Economic thresholds and also if India pushes Pakistan into political destabilization or creates a large-scale internal subversion in Pakistan.[15]

Pakistan's nuclear strategy is India-centric, but it has tried to rationalise the escalatory nuclear strategy by bringing in the defensive concept of 'Minimum Credible Deterrence'. PM Nawaz Sharif, in 1999, stated that, 'Nuclear restraint, stabilisation and minimum credible deterrence constitute the basic elements of Pakistan's nuclear policy'.[16] In an op-ed by Agha Shahi, Zulfiqar Ali Khan and Abdul Sattar remarked about quantum of nuclear weapon to be developed, saying, 'Of course, minimum [credible deterrence] cannot be defined in static numbers. In the absence of mutual restraints, the size of Pakistan's arsenal and its deployment pattern have to be adjusted to ward off dangers of pre-emption and interception',[17] adding, 'Obviously our deterrence force will have to be upgraded in proportion to the heightened threat of pre-emption and interception'.[18] The Minimum Credible Deterrence that has evolved as a result of these strategies has four main objectives[19]:

- ✓ Deterrence from all forms of external aggression;
- ✓ Building an effective combination of conventional and strategic forces;
- ✓ Avoiding a pre-emptive strike through protection and the threat of nuclear retaliation;
- ✓ Stabilising strategic deterrence in South Asia.

Apart from that, Pakistan has frequently adjusted its nuclear doctrine. By improving and diversifying nuclear force structures, Pakistani interlocutors are highlighting other aspects of nuclear strategy like 'full spectrum deterrence' or building deterrence 'at all levels of the threat spectrum',/'flexible deterrence options'.[20] Thus, Pakistan's nuclear posture has developed according to its perceived strategic environment, which is often considered as a reaction to the hostile Indian behaviour.

Pakistan–China Strategic Nuclear Nexus

> **If you subtract Chinese help there wouldn't be a Pakistani Programme.**
>
> ***—Gary Mihollin, Nuclear Analyst***

Pakistan–China nuclear cooperation began in 1971 when Bhutto persuaded the Chinese to help them in their nuclear programme. In 1976, AQ Khan met three

Chinese nuclear officials including Jiang Shengjie, China's Nuclear Bureau Chief. Cooperation increased between 1986 and 1996 with China transferring nuclear technology and blueprints of bombs and missiles to Pakistan. In 1982, China gave Pakistan weapon-grade uranium for two atomic bombs. Chinese assistance range included special industrial machine tools, ring magnets, Tritium gas, etc. In 1989, China offered its test facilities at Lop Nor to Pakistan. Same year, Prime Minister Benazir Bhutto admitted that a Cold Test had been conducted. Thereafter, Chinese assistance to Pakistan has been continuing: assistance in Kahuta Nuclear Reactor; supply of Heavy Water (D2O) to the Kannupp Reactor; agreement to build the Chashma 300 MW Nuclear Power Reactor in 1991; construction of 40-MW nuclear reactor at Khushab.

Pakistan's Posturing and Nuclear Communication Strategy

Pakistan has communicated unambiguously that Pakistan's nuclear weapons are guarantors of Pakistan's territorial integrity and sovereignty, and, also, that Pakistani threat perceptions are only India-centric where the sole aim of having these weapons is to deter India from aggression such as to counter India's conventional superiority.[21] India's lead in conventional weapons has compelled Pakistan to go in for a strategy of 'First use', as they believe that this 'First use' posture can deter India from fighting conventional war with impunity. However, Pakistan has developed a strategy of 'offensive-defence', believing these weapons give her leverage, to counter countries that are conventionally superior. They also believe they have successfully pushed in defensive mode, simultaneous to their successful strategy of using non-state actors. They believe that through nuclear sabre rattling/nuclear blackmail, India has been dissuaded from conventional attack. This lowering of threshold by deliberate threat of use of nuclear weapons intensified after the development of TNWs. Politicians, diplomats and strategic thinkers excessively communicate verbally in national/international dailies, the use of TNWs on violation of their red lines. These tactics also allow Islamabad to 'internationalise the crisis and invite outside intervention in unfavourable circumstance'.[22] Pakistan's aim is to have an external balancing factor, particularly through propaganda, in the 'Kashmir Dispute'.

China's Concept of Nuclear War and Nuclear Doctrine

The 21st century, as 'Asian Century' implies global activities would be dominated by two major countries in Asia, namely, China and India. David Lai has noted, 'The Chinese way of war places a strong emphasis on the use of strategy, stratagems, and deception. However, the Chinese also understand that their approach will not be effective without the backing of hard military power. Hence, China's grand strategy is to take the next 30 years to complete China's modernization mission, which is ultimately expected to turn China into a true 'great power'.[23] To achieve this, China on one hand has systematically worked to build its economy, and on the other hand, China is utilizing economic gains in modernising its army. This smart amalgamation of economics and military has given China enormous dividends. As a result, externally China has become more assertive, and internally the Chinese leaders are trying to strike a chord with the locals, by raising the nationalistic fervor of the Chinese people through the propaganda of 'The China Dream'. In China's power projection plan, coupled with soft power, the Chinese military, especially the PLA Rocket Force (PLARF) or the guardian of China's missile forces would play a key role.

China conducted its first nuclear fission test on 16 October 1964, and its first thermonuclear test on 17 June 1967. In July 1966, China established a special force, named the Second Artillery Force (SAF), directly under the control of the CMC, which was responsible for the development of China's nuclear force and the nuclear strategy. This force was rechristened as the PLARF in December 2015. While PLARF retains its old characteristics and the functions of SAF, significantly it is now considered the fourth service in China's armed forces, on an equal footing with the PLA Army, Navy and Air Force.[24] Geostrategic challenges of past years had compelled China to rethink its nuclear policies. Deng Xiaoping had once commented that 'we must have what anyone else has, and anyone who wants to destroy us will be subject to retaliation'.[25] This statement set the tenor of China's nuclear doctrine. China's nuclear thought process was influenced by the book *Guidelines for the Development of Nuclear Weapons*.[26]

In July 2000, at the CMC's Conference, President Jiang Zemin gave out 'Five Musts on Nuclear Weapons' expounding China's need to have five key basics, namely, (1) definitive quality and quantity of nuclear weapons to ensure national security, (2) ensure safety of strategic nuclear bases, (3) keep nuclear weapons in high degree of war preparedness, (4) be able to launch nuclear counter-attacks and (5) adjust strategic nuclear weapon development strategy in a timely manner.[27]

Nuclear Doctrine

Initially, China's nuclear force was developed as a 'basic retaliatory' force. Since then, it has undergone substantial role evolution leading to structural and technological modifications. The *basic tenants of China's nuclear doctrine* are (1) *conditional 'No First Use'* (NFU), (2) *credible minimum deterrence* (CMD), (3) counter-strike through developing '*second-strike retaliatory capability*' and (4) *survivability* of China's nuclear force.

Implications of China's Nuclear Doctrine

First, China professes that it will not use or threaten to use nuclear weapon against any 'non-nuclear' weapon states or those within any Nuclear Weapon–Free Zones. At the same time, its nuclear posture is ambiguous as far as newly declared 'nuclear weapon states' are concerned, implying China can use or threaten to use nuclear weapons against a country like India if it finds that the country's core interest is threatened.

Second, China has developed limited but reliable, precise and effective nuclear force, capable of surviving the first strike, ability to effectively counter-strike through its nuclear triad. In recent publications, the PLA has also been using the term 'Effective Nuclear Deterrence' *(you xiao he weishe)* and this has been interpreted as being a 'reliable, survivable delivery system, capable of penetrating the adversary's missile defences'.[28]

Third, counter-strike *(zhongdian Fanji)* is one of the pillars of China's policy of 'Active Defence'. It is the offensive after strike that would damage massive military and civilian targets, especially the command and control systems, thereby reducing the enemy's war-making potential and forcing him to end the nuclear exchange. Counter-attack campaign is planned jointly by PLARF and PLAN/PLAAF. Hence, its retaliatory counter-value posture is in stark contrast to America's counterforce targeting policy. China focuses on the quality rather than the quantity of its nuclear force, and it is the accuracy and the penetrating ability of its nuclear arsenal that has become important.

China has significantly increased the size of its conventional weapons, especially its Land Attack Cruise Missiles (LACM). This policy of counter strike is possible through developing a strong 'Survivable Second Strike Capabilities'. In the same vein, China test fired a multiple independently targetable vehicle (MIRV) missile with ten warheads in January 2017, attaining the advanced US level of warhead miniaturization. While the Chinese have had trouble with their MIRV technology, especially the guidance aspects, it wasn't expected that they would overcome the technical problems so fast and so well. Essentially, this means the Second Artillery Strategic Forces (SASF) have nuclear/thermonuclear warheads clocking in at around 100-kg weight, which is an astounding achievement. According to a study undertaken by Prof. Phillip Karber, China has a vast network of underground tunnels, often referred to as China's underground Great Wall that is 3000 miles and could host about 3000 nuclear weapons, while Chinese are also converting their land-based missile system into tunnel-based system.[29]

China perceives warfare having become more localised and limited to China's periphery. Hence, information in terms of advanced computer usage, information technology and communication networks to gain operational advantage over the adversary have become important milestones.[30] In other words 'high-intensity, information-centric regional military operations of short durations' is the key.[31] The nature of China's nuclear force has therefore undergone change from a simple retaliatory force to a force that has the capabilities for power projection.

In the eighties, China added the concept of 'Dual Deterrence and Dual Operations' for SAC, and the 'conventional guided missile campaign army group' were made an integral part of the erstwhile SAC. This was in continuation of the principles mentioned in the Science of Second Artillery Campaigns, emphasizing that 'nuclear missile force deterrence actions and conventional missile strike operations must be fused together and mutually interwoven'. The focus of research thereafter shifted from using nuclear tactics to accomplish the mission of nuclear counter attacks, to using dual operation tactics. The strategy now is to use both nuclear and conventional missile forces in warfare, with greater importance being given to the sophistication of conventional missile force (*hechangjianbei, yichangweizhu*).

Finally, China has also changed the content of research from focusing on strategizing in the past, to focusing on a combined use of strategy and technical means.[31] In other words, it means aggressively explore and boldly innovate (*jijitansuo, dadanchuangxin*). All this required a different kind of force, which China aims to achieve through modernizing and diversifying its forces. The new PLARF is carrying out more joint manoeuvres with other services and branches across multiple military regions, in addition to practicing operating under harsh conditions, which may include contingencies like loss of communication with the command chain, constrained mobility, and electronic attacks.[32]

Is China's NFU Policy Changing?

Though the NFU in China's nuclear policy remains conditional, this has been reinforced in recent years. In a speech during 2012, President Xi Jinping, C-in-C of PLA including PLARF, told his troops to 'maintain a high alert level assuring that if something happens we're ready to go'.[33] In 2013, an updated edition of a standard text on Chinese military strategy, partially translated by the Union of Concerned Scientists, said China's nuclear forces will move towards a 'launch-on-warning' posture, where 'under conditions confirming the enemy has launched nuclear missiles against us, before the enemy nuclear warheads have reached us [we can] quickly launch a nuclear missile retaliatory strike'.[34] These and some other statements suggest that a domestic conversation about raising the alert level of China's nuclear forces is taking place.

The Grand Strategy

The concept of deterrence can be defined as the use of threats by one party to convince another party to refrain from initiating some course of action. The threat can be credible only if the country convinces its adversary that the damage will be disastrous both in terms of cost and human life if the warning is disregarded. With advent nuclear weapons, the deterrence theory has been expediently used by nations to justify possession of nuclear weapons. Nuclear weapons are considered ultimate weapons, especially by those nations whose conventional capability is insufficient to deter the adversary. Mostly nations with not a strong conventional arsenal resort to nuclear blackmail, to mitigate superior conventional arsenal of their adversaries. Since hybrid war combines conventional warfare and irregular warfare besides cyber warfare, nuclear weapons are applicable as deterrent both in case of conventional warfare and hybrid warfare.

America's Nuclear Posture Review states, 'The fundamental role of US nuclear weapons, which will continue as long as nuclear weapons exist, is to deter nuclear attack on the United States, [its] allies, and partners'.[35] Because of the vast and indiscriminate destructive power of nuclear weapons, there is a general consensus that their sole legitimate purpose is to deter the use of WMDs by potential enemies, and that their use in war should be initiated only as a last resort to prevent the military defeat of the nation or an ally. There is also a belief that these weapons clearly are irrelevant to current international security challenges such as non-state terrorist expansion in Iraq and Syria, the Ebola virus in Africa or even Russian aggression in Ukraine.[36]

The western view is that Russia has been suspected of lowering its nuclear threshold and developing new low-yield nuclear warheads for more than a decade.[37] Russia has regularly issued nuclear threats related to missile defence in Europe, carrying out exercises on battlefield use of nuclear warheads and simulating nuclear strikes against NATO and EU member states, albeit the evolution of Russia's nuclear strategy was only fully revealed in the Ukraine crisis. Without the nuclear posturing that accompanied Russia's aggressive actions against Ukraine, Kremlin's re-emphasis on nuclear power would have continued to go largely ignored.[38] At best, it would have been rationalized as a legitimate attempt to counter NATO's overall superiority in conventional capabilities or as part of a desire to preserve Russia's waning superpower status. As part of its nuclear messaging, in December 2015, Putin personally emphasised that air- and sea-launched cruise missiles, which were showcased in Syria, can deliver both conventional and nuclear warheads.[39]

Examination of open-source documents on China's grand strategy reveals an intriguing thread that weaves its way through the corpus of thought on its grand strategy and the role of nuclear weapons within it. The result is, not surprisingly, ambiguity.[40] The Chinese would like adversaries to believe that even their leadership has not fully decided which path to pursue. The Science of Military Strategy, written by two PLA Major Generals states, 'At the most important position of the strategic structure is China's national strategy. While no national strategy has been formally issued so far, its contents are embodied in a series of general and specific policies worked out by the Chinese Communist Party and Chinese government'.[41] This passage is deliberately vague and leaves outsiders to ponder whence China has gone with its strategy, thereby making it difficult to develop possible counter measures.[42]

Pakistan has adopted the nuclear posture of asymmetric escalation, using the concept of lowering the nuclear threshold, threatening use of TNWs in the case of violation of its red lines for counter-Indian conventional threat. This has led Pakistan to believe that it can continue proxy war on India with immunity, which the Pakistani military has sold to the Pakistani public, as successful grand strategy, through propaganda. It is because of this that Pakistani radical mullahs like Hafiz Saeed and Masood Azhar openly threaten nuclear war on India, as do the political and military hierarchies of Pakistan. But this is largely because India has not developed effective deterrent to Pakistan's proxy war, taking control of Pakistan's numerous fault lines, even though Pakistani red lines include the use of nuclear weapons in the event of Pakistan nearing balkanising due to Indian sub-conventional operations, should India employ such option.

Key Issues

- ✓ *Though nuclear weapons are the ultimate in warfare, they are considered as deterrent because of their massive destructive power despite miniaturization.*
- ✓ *Credibility and effectiveness of hybrid warfare campaigns by nations is being backed by potential to use full-spectrum military capabilities including nuclear forces, even as the nuclear remains ambiguous and controversial.*
- ✓ *Possession of nuclear power facilitates nations going rogue, international community imposing financial sanction but desisting physical action.*
- ✓ *Nuclear posturing and messaging are important since these add to or detract from stability, and can affect outcomes when deterrence fails.*
- ✓ *Depending on dynamics of geopolitics, nuclear posturing and messages are changed by nation states.*
- ✓ *China's grand strategy is to induce deliberate ambiguity including the role of its nuclear weapons; NFU policy too is conditional.*
- ✓ *Pakistan has adopted nuclear posture of asymmetric escalation, and keeps lowering the nuclear threshold to message use of TNWs in case of violation of its red lines.*

✓ *Pakistan believes, with messaging nuclear response, it can continue proxy war on India with immunity because it can deter Indian conventional response. But this is largely because India has not developed effective deterrent to Pakistan's proxy war, taking control of Pakistan's numerous fault lines.*

NOTES

1 Macias, Amanda, 'Putin Once Casually Said Over Dinner That He Could Destroy America in A Half-Hour (or Less)', Business Insider, 04 January 2016, http://www.businessinsider.in/Putin-once-casually-said-over-dinner-that-he-could-destroy-America-in-a-half-hour-or-less/articleshow/50443170.cms.

2 Byman, Daniel, 'Recommendations for the Commission on the Prevention of Weapons of Mass Destruction Proliferation and Terrorism', 13 June 2008, https://www.brookings.edu/wp-content/uploads/2016/06/0613_terrorism_byman-1.pdf.

3 CNS Global Incidents and Trafficking Database - 2015 Annual Report, March 2016, http://www.nti.org/media/documents/global_incidents_trafficking_report.pdf.

4 Ibid.

5 Katoch, PC, 'The Currency of Terror', USI of India, 2013, http://usiofindia.org/Article/?pub=Strategic%20Perspective&pubno=37&ano=1883.

6 Kingsbury, Alex, 'Why China Helped Countries Like Pakistan, North Korea Build Nuclear Bombs, US News, 2 January 2009, http://www.usnews.com/news/world/articles/2009/01/02/why-china-helped-countries-like-pakistan-north-korea-build-nuclear-bombs.

7 Krepon, Michael, 'Nuclear Postures', Arms Control Wonk, 25 February 2015, http://www.armscontrolwonk.com/archive/404492/nuclear-postures/.

8 Narang, Vipin, 'Nuclear Strategy in the Modern Era: Regional Powers and International Conflict', Princeton University Press, 2014.

9 Pakistan's Nuclear Doctrine, ***Patron Lt Gen (Retd) Sardar FS Lodi, Defence Notes***, http://www.defencejournal.com/apr99/pak-nuclear-doctrine.htm.

10 Lodi, FS (Lt Gen, Retd, Pakistan Army), 'Pakistan Nuclear Doctrine', ***Defence Notes,*** Pakistan Defence Journal, 1999, http://www.defencejournal.com/apr99/pak-nuclear-doctrine.htm.

11 Paul, TV, 'Chinese-Pakistani Nuclear/Missile Ties and the Balance of Power', *The Non-Proliferation Review,* Summer 2003.

12 Lodi, op. cit. at nm 10.

13 Ibid.

14 *Dawn* (Karachi), 5 Octobe 1999.

15 Dr Shalini Chawala, Nuclear Pakistan, KW Publishers, New Delhi.

16 As cited in the Landau Report on 'Nuclear Safety, Nuclear Stability and Nuclear Strategy in Pakistan', Prepared by Prof Paolo Cotta-Ramuniso and Prof Maurizio Matellini.

17 'Remarks of the Prime Minister of Pakistan, Nawaz Sharif, on Nuclear Policies and the CTBT', National Defence College, Islamabad, 20 May 1999.

18 Shahi, Agha, Zulfiqar Ali Khan and Abdul Sattar, 'Securing Nuclear Peace', The News, 5 October 1990.

19 Ibid.

20 Durrani, MA, 'Pakistan's Strategic Thinking and the Role of Nuclear Weapons', Cooperative Monitoring Center Occasional Paper 37, Sandia National Laboratories, July 2004, http://www.cmc.sandia.gov/cmc-papers/sand2004-3375p.pdf.

21 Inter Services Public Relations, Press Release No. PR130/2012-ISPR, 29 May 2012, http://

www.ispr.gov.pk/front/main.asp?o=t-press_release&id=2074. Also see Adil Sultan, 'Pakistan's Emerging Nuclear Posture', p. 163.

22 Latif, Amir, 'A Comparative Study of Nuclear Doctrines of India and Pakistan', Journal of Global Peace and Conflict, June 2014, Vol. 2, No. 1.

23 Lai, David, 'The Agony of Learning: The PLA's Transformation in Military Affairs', in *Learning by Doing: The PLA Trains at Home and Abroad*, Roy Kamphausen, David Lai, and Travis Tanner (eds), Carlisle, PA: Strategic Studies Institute, US Army War College, November 2012, p. 369.

24 Tiezzi, Shannon, 'The New Military Force in Charge of China's Nuclear Weapons, Goodbye Second Artillery Force; Hello PLA Rocket Force', 5 January 2016, http://thediplomat.com/2016/01/the-new-military-force-in-charge-of-chinas-nuclear-weapons/.

25 Nair, Vijai K, 'China's Evolving strategic capabilities :Doctrine, Concept, Force- Structure', South Asia Strategic Forum, 25 May 2013.

26 Lin, Chong-Pin, *China's Nuclear Weapon Strategy: Tradition within Evolution*, Lexington: Lexington Books, 1988, p. 144.

27 Nair, op. cit.

28 Medeiros, Evan S, 'Minding the Gap: Assessing the Trajectory of the PLA's Second Artillery', Chapter 4, p. 153, in *Rightsizing the People's Liberation Army: Exploring the Contours of China's Military*, Carlisle: Strategic Studies Institute, US Army War College, September 2007.

29 'China's Nuclear Weapons Modernization: Intentions, Drivers, and Trends' by Hui Zhang, p. 5.

30 DOD, Military and Security Development Involving the People's Republic of China, 2013.

31 Ibid.

32 Science of Second Artillery Campaigns [English Translation]; Beijing, PRC: PLA Press, 2004, p. 13.

33 'Pentagon Report and Chinese Nuclear Forces', Federation of American Scientists, 18 May 2016, https://fas.org/blogs/security/2016/05/chinareport2016/.

34 Ibid.

35 Gard, Robert andGreg Terryn, 'American Nuclear Strategy: The Case for a Minimal-Deterrence Policy', 1 December 2014, http://nationalinterest.org/feature/american-nuclear-strategy-the-case-minimal-deterrence-policy-11755.

36 Ibid.

37 Ibid.

38 For a background reading on Russia's approach to nuclear weapons over past two decades, see, for example, Yost, David S, 'Russia's Non-strategic Nuclear Forces', International Affairs, 2001, 77 (3); McDermott, Roger N, 'Russia's Conventional Military Weakness and Substrategic Nuclear Policy', The Foreign Military Studies Office, Fort Leavenworth, 2011, http://fmso.leavenworth.army.mil.

39 'Putin says he "hopes" nuclear warheads will never be needed against Isis ... or anyone else', The Independent, 9 December 2015, www.independent.co.uk.

40 Rickard, James, 'Sun Tzu, Nuclear Weapons and China's Grand Strategy', Centre for Contemporary Conflict, http://www.au.af.mil/au/awc/awcgate/nps/rickard_chin_grand_strat_jul08.pdf.

41 Guangqian, Peng and Yao Youzhi (eds), The Science of Military Strategy, Beijing: Military Science Publishing House, 2005, p. 22.

42 Brad, Roberts, 'Alternative Futures', in *China's Nuclear Future*, Paul Bolt and Albert Willner (eds), pp. 188-89. 'China provides almost no official information on the disposition and modernization policies for its nuclear forces'.

3

PAKISTAN'S HYBRID WARFARE STRATEGY AND CAPABILITIES 2030

General

Pakistan had earlier placed Jamaat-ud-Dawa (JuD) chief Hafiz Saeed's name on the exit control list along with four of his aides.[1] This action was under US pressure but meant little because Saeed was not travelling outside Pakistan. He was also reportedly placed under house arrest for 90 days but despite the US designating him as 'global terrorist', he has been released from house arrest, absolved of all charges and is conducting open rallies calling for jihad against India. This time his organisation's name has been changed from JuD to Tehreek-e-Azadi J&K (TAJK) to escape any action. Despite the image-building efforts of the Pakistan Army Chief, the army and purported success of Operation 'Zarb-e-Azb' by the Inter-Services Public Relations (ISPR), secessionist movements in the Khyber–Pakhtunkhwa and Baluchistan and rising spectre of Jihadi violence, including the Sunni and Shia sectarian conflict, are threatening the existence of Pakistan as a viable nation state. The success of Zarb-e-Azb against Tehrik-e-Taliban of Pakistan (TPP) is very questionable with regional reporters talking of advance warning of aerial bombardment and artillery barrages enabling the terrorist leadership to escape to safe havens in south-eastern Afghanistan. Relocation of some of these terrorist groups to Baluchistan too is by design of Pakistan's ISI as counter to the Baluch freedom movement.

Pakistan continues to perceive India as an existential threat and ipso facto adheres to its policy of using Jihad to destabilize India or gain strategic depth in Afghanistan. Pakistan, therefore, will continue to be a major source of instability in the region. Dire internal security scenario in Pakistan is closely linked with militancy in Afghanistan and proxy war in Kashmir. What is more worrisome is that the security scenario in Afghanistan remains bleak although US President Trump has signalled that US forces will remain in Afghanistan in support of the Afghan National Security Forces (ANSF). However, continued political uncertainty in Afghanistan and incapacity of the ANSF to tide over expanding violence in the wake of possible withdrawal of the US/NATO forces will lend the country susceptible to scenarios that could range from virtual Taliban rule in Pashtun belt or a simmering civil war degenerating into balkanization of the country along ethnic lines.

While the volatile internal security scenario in Pakistan coupled with failing economy is a recipe for collapse, it has reportedly leased out Gilgit-Baltistan (GB) for 50 years to China, made territory available for the China Pakistan Economic Corridor (CPEC) and allowed China to develop Gwadar port. Jiwani is likely to come up as a larger PLA base, closer to the Straits of Hormuz than Gwadar. The CPEC facilitates PLA's covert lodgement in Gilgit-Baltistan, Gwadar and Jiwani, also making Pakistani ports of Omari and Karachi open to Chinese naval vessels. Pakistan expects 700,000 jobs for Pakistanis, and more importantly, in-built deterrence against perceived Indian attacks because of the presence of the Chinese. The calls by both China and Pakistan for India to join the CPEC are aimed at augmenting this deterrence, and legitimizing Chinese presence and projects in Pakistan-Occupied Kashmir (POK) undertaken without reference to India.[2] The US-led effort to place Pakistan on the 'Grey List', during the plenary session of the Financial Action Task Force (FATF), in February 2018 will put greater financial squeeze on Pakistan, when formalised in June 2018. But by propping up the Hafiz Saeed led LeT-JuD political party, Milli Muslim League, Pakistan will perhaps attempt to deflect terror financing to political financing.

In one of its quarterly report on the state of the economy last year, the State Bank of Pakistan says that the latest macroeconomic data signal a stable growth momentum in Q1 FY 2017.[3] Agriculture employs 40 per cent of the people with an output of 20 per cent of GDP. GDP in 2015 was $271 billion. GDP growth was expected to pick up to 5.1 per cent in FY 2017, supported by expansionary fiscal and monetary policies, as well as by rising investment, driven by the USD 46 billion CPEC programme. In FY 2018, GDP growth is set to decelerate to 4.8 per cent. Pakistan's external debt in terms of percentage of GDP stands at $22.7 billion. Pakistan's unemployment rate stood at 5.9 per cent in January 206 and is expected to be around 5.7 per cent by 2020.[4] China has emerged as Pakistan's largest trading partner replacing the US in 2012. The China–Pakistan Free Trade Agreement is a major trade agreement that exists between the two countries. Trade volume due to this agreement was $13 billion in 2013, while it reached $20 billion by 2015. As per China, the trade volume between China and Pakistan grew from $5.7 billion to $100.11 billion during a 15-year period from 2000 to 2015 while total value of contracts signed between the two in this period went from $1.8 billion to $150.8 billion.[5]

Capabilities of Pakistan's nuclear and conventional forces have traditionally been oriented and structured against a prospective threat from India. Since 2008, however, counter-insurgency and counter-terrorism have been of increasing importance and are now the forces' main effort, despite an increase in cross-border incidents with Indian forces since summer of 2015. The air force is modernising its inventory while improving its precision-strike and Intelligence, Surveillance, and Reconnaissance (ISR) capabilities. Pakistan produces the Chinese JF-17 combat aircraft and a third squadron transitioned to this newer aircraft in 2016. Pakistan has declared that its 'short-range low-yield' battlefield nuclear capability based on the Nasr missile has become operational. Major investment in this programme continues. As part of the CPEC initiative, the army is raising a 15,000-strong dedicated security force to protect the project. Major defence-industry partners include China and Turkey, with a number of programmes in their early stages. However, according to Pakistan's minister for defence production, Pakistan has significantly reduced its reliance on external sources for defence procurement. The navy is currently too small to sustain a long campaign against a significant competitor, but recent and likely future investment in Chinese-supplied frigates, missile craft, and submarines could improve sea-denial capabilities. Year 2016 saw the start of a number of upgrades to maritime capabilities, including the development with Turkey of the navy's new fleet tanker, which should form the backbone of Pakistan's naval-auxiliary support. The army continues to contribute to UN peacekeeping operations. The Pakistan Navy took over the rotational command of the Combined Maritime Forces' Task Force 150 maritime-security operation in August 2016.

Pakistan's Geostrategic Importance and Strategic Objectives vis-à-vis India

Since its inception in 1947, India and Pakistan have had a troubled relationship. At the core of these animosities lies the question of Kashmir. It has 1,046 km of coastline along the Arabian Sea, the Gulf of Oman as also land boundaries with Afghanistan (2410 km), Iran (999 km), India (3323 km) and China (523 km). Pakistan is the epicentre of international Jihadi terrorism. Geopolitics of Pakistan devolves around its strategic location as a frontline state, chronic animosity towards India, Jihadi ideology and ethno-regional and sectarian conflicts. The main aspects of Pakistan's geostrategic importance are as follows:

- ✓ Pakistan's pivotal location at the crossroads of South Asia, Arabian Sea, the Middle East and Central Asia endows it with critical significance. Pakistan connects South Asia to Central Asia and China to West Asia. *It also has the potential to influence shipping lanes in the Arabian Sea.*

- ✓ Bolan Pass and Khyber Pass connect Afghanistan and Pakistan. The supply routes passing through these passes are vital for sustenance of US and NATO forces in Afghanistan. It is one of the major leverages used by Pakistan against US-NATO forces in Afghanistan. Around 80 per cent of food supplies and military armaments to US-NATO forces go through this pass. Pakistan from time to time has closed these passes and denied flow of US logistics supplies into Afghanistan. These passes are also crucial for the smooth de-induction of US/NATO troops from Afghanistan.
- ✓ In regard to providing access to China and Central Asia to Arabian Sea, the CPEC assumes immense strategic importance. Energy supplies from Iran or Africa across Strait of Malacca take 16 to 25 days to reach China through Indian Ocean and Western Pacific. The domination of SLOCs by the US Navy poses maximum concern, what is commonly known as Malacca Dilemma for China. Once Gwadar and Karakoram rail and pipeline route is operationalised, it will take only 48 hours for energy resources to reach Kashgar in Xinjiang province across the Kunjerab pass.
- ✓ *Ethno-regional fault lines have the potential to undermine Pakistan's strategic advantage in many ways.* The dispute over Durand line can spark off a strong movement for independent Pakhtunistan with Pashtun's in Afghanistan and Khyber Pakhtunkhwa joining ranks. Sectarian violence in Karachi, secessionist movement in Baluchistan and ethnic strife in northern areas can destabilize Pakistan and threaten the CPEC. These developments can potentially pose multiple criticalities and multi-front dilemmas for Pakistan and undermine China–Pakistan strategic nexus.

The Indian Independence Act of 1947 averred that the sovereigns of princely states could choose which state to join. As is well-known, Maharaja of Kashmir Hari Singh only acceded to India after Pakistan dispatched irregular forces to seize the terrain by force. In fact, Pakistan makes this claim based upon the Two-Nation Theory, its communally bigoted founding ideology.[6] Pakistan has tried ever since to wrest Kashmir from India who it considers as enemy number one, even though Pakistan controls approximately 37 per cent of Kashmir, namely Pakistan-Occupied Kashmir and the northern areas of Gilgit-Baltistan. Though Pakistan keeps demanding plebiscite in Kashmir based on the 1948 UN Resolution on Kashmir, the resolution itself is not binding because it required Pakistani security forces to vacate POK first, which Pakistan did not. In fact, Pakistan did the reverse: increased deployment of its security forces in POK and changed its demography by bringing in settlers from outside. The Shia population of Gilgit-Baltistan has already been reduced from 70 per cent to 50 per cent.

The genocide unleashed by General Tikka Khan in East Pakistan flooded India with millions of refugees that led to the liberation of Bangladesh. The loss of Bangladesh was a severe blow to Pakistan and it wants to take revenge and keeps looking for an opportunity to balkanize India. The Pakistani army is using proxies for exporting terror as institutionalized state policy both in India and Afghanistan. This helps the Pakistani army retain a stranglehold on the country and continue to enjoy power and money, having infiltrated every branch of the government, administrative and civilian set-up. It is well known that Pakistan's defence and foreign policies are scripted and executed by the Pakistani army. In this backdrop, Pakistan's strategic objectives vis-à-vis India can be summarised as under:

- ✓ Wrest J&K fully from India.
- ✓ Continue to pursue jihad in a bid to further destabilise/balkanise through proxy war and exploiting Indian fault lines.
- ✓ Deny land access to India through Pakistan-POK to Afghanistan and Central Asia.
- ✓ Restrict India's strategic space in South Asia and IOR, in conjunction China.
- ✓ Stymie India's economic growth and development, as possible, in conjunction China.

HYBRID WARFARE STRATEGY

Jihad and Pakistan's Quranic Concept of War

Pakistan considers itself as the leader of the Sunni-Muslim world in the region and in a way ahead of even Saudi Arabia because of its nuclear weapons. Radicalization, is therefore, institutionalized in educational institutions, not the 32,000 madrassa and seminaries alone in the country. Pakistani scholars have termed it a hugely successful 'monstrous experiment' successful in brainwashing children on a par with, if not worse than, Nazi Germany's eugenics, producing millions of neo-drones, indoctrinated about the fanciful world that awaits him in the heaven, and that in order to attain that he has to destroy everything that stands in his way, including his own body.[7] As far back as 2009, a noted nuclear physic of Pakistan had noted that the promotion of militarism in Pakistan's schools, colleges and universities had a profound effect on young people, with militant jihad having become a part of the culture in college and university campuses, and armed groups inviting students for jihad in Kashmir and Afghanistan.[8]

Meet a Pakistani army officer today and he will tell you the Pakistani army is the "Army of Allah" first and then the Pakistani Army. The roots of this lie in the book 'The Quranic Concept of War', published in 1979, written by Brigadier SK Malik, a Pakistani army officer. The preface of the book is written by Allah Bukhsh K. Brohi, the former Pakistani ambassador to India, and Zia-ul-Haq, former President of Pakistan and Pakistani Army Chief of Staff, opens the book by focusing on the concept of jihad within Islam and explaining it is not simply the domain of the military. Most significantly, it justifies terrorism,[9] *which amounts to distorting the teachings of Quran. The teachings of Quran have been debated in multiple international forums discussing countering transnational forums including in Iraq and Afghanistan between Muslim scholars and clerics, with the latter stating that it is the distorted interpretation of the Quran that is causing the violence. Using its own interpretation of the Quran, Zia-ul-Haq institutionalized radicalization of Pakistan, assiduously preparing the whole population, particularly youth, for holy jihad.* Quran is presumed to be the revealed word of God as spoken through his chosen prophet, Mohammed. As per SK Malik, 'As a complete Code of Life, the Holy Quran gives us a philosophy of war as well.... This divine philosophy is an integral part of the total Quranic ideology'. *The Quranic Concept of War* is a treatise with historical, political, legalistic and moralistic ramifications on Islamic warfare. It seemingly is without parallel in the western sense of warfare since the 'Quran is a source of eternal guidance for mankind'.[10]

Jihad is not the exclusive domain of the professional soldier, nor is it restricted to the application of military force alone. The professional soldier in a Muslim army, pursuing the goals of a Muslim state, cannot become 'professional' if in all his activities he does not take the 'colour of Allah'.[11] The non-military citizen of a Muslim state must, likewise, be aware of the kind of soldier that his country must produce and the only pattern of war that his country's armed forces may wage.[12] All Muslims play a role in jihad, a mainstream concept of the Quran, that jihad in terms of warfare is a collective responsibility of the Muslim *ummah*, and is not restricted to soldiers. This is the 'only pattern of war', or approach to war that an Islamic state may wage.

In the abovementioned book, the author categorises humans in three archetypes: (1) those who fear Allah and profess the Faith, (2) those who reject the Faith and (3) those who profess, but are treacherous in their hearts. Examples of the Prophet and the instructions to him by God in his early campaigns should be studied to fully understand these three examples in practice. According to him, the 'divine philosophy on war' was revealed gradually over a 12-year period, its earliest guidance dealing with the causes and objects of war, while later guidance focused on Quranic strategy, the conduct of war, and the ethical dimensions of warfare.

Crux of Pakistan's Quranic Concept of Warfare

The nature and dimension of war is considered the greatest single characteristic of Quranic warfare that distinguishes it from all other doctrines. The crux of the concept is summarised as under:

- ✓ *Muslims are required to wage war with the spirit of religious duty and obligation. In return for fighting in the way of Allah, divine, angelic assistance will be rendered to jihad warriors and armies*; divine assistance requires divine standards on the part of the warrior mujahedeen for the promise of Allah's aid to be met.
- ✓ For *the Muslim warrior*, for whom fighting is prescribed, to be unmatched, *to be the bravest and the most fearless; he can only do so through the correct spiritual preparation, beginning with total submission to God's will*; moral forces are the real issues involved in the planning and conduct of war.
- ✓ The *Quran instructs the jihad warrior to fight with total devotion and never contemplate a flight from the battlefield for fear of death*. The jihad warrior, who dies in the way of Allah, does not really die but lives on in heaven.
- ✓ The *Quranic dimensions of war are revolutionary, conferring on the jihad warrior a personality so strong and overbearing as to prove himself equal to, indeed dominate, every contingency in war*; becoming a purer and more disciplined Muslim serves the cause of Islam better in peace and war.
- ✓ *Restraint in warfare is a two-sided affair.* Where the enemy (not defined) fails to exercise restraints and commits 'excesses' (not defined), then the very injunction of preserving and promoting peace and justice demands the use of limited force. *Islam permits the use of the sword for such purpose.*[13]
- ✓ *While moral and spiritual forces are predominant in war, focus is on a broader application of power; jihad is a continuous and never-ending struggle waged on all fronts including political, economic, social, psychological, domestic, moral and spiritua*l to attain the objectives of policy, bringing with it the power of God—the strategy is therefore divine theory.[14]
- ✓ *When God wishes to impose His will on his enemies, He chooses to do so by casting terror into their hearts; the Quranic military strategy enjoins Muslims to prepare for war to the utmost in order to strike terror into the hearts of the enemies*, known or hidden, while guarding ourselves from being terror-stricken by the enemy—terror is an effect, the end-state.[15]
- ✓ The *centre of gravity in war is the human heart, [man's] soul, spirit, and faith*, latter meaning more than simple moral courage or fortitude. Faith in this sense is in the domain of religious and spiritual faith; this is the centre of gravity in war.
- ✓ *Need for creating a wholesome respect for the cause of Islam, seeded in advance of war and conflict in the minds of the enemies.*
- ✓ *If properly prepared (informational, psychological and perception management*

included), the 'war of muscle', the physical war, will already be won by the 'war of will'—through beautiful and handsome ways or by the strategic application of terror.

✓ The point where the means and the end meet; *terror is an objective principle of war; once terror is achieved, the enemy reaches his culminating point.*

Why *The Quranic Concept of Warfare* has become the Bible of the Pakistani army is because it helps (1) the army retain a stranglehold on the country enjoying total power and access to money; (2) breed and nurture host of powerful proxies (currency for geopolitical power play through hybrid war) because of which Pakistan has managed to balance its relations with the US, China and Russia; (3) divert attention from instability within Pakistan; (4) enlarge strategic depth in Afghanistan—bringing more areas under Pakistani influence and (5) keep India embroiled internally with proxy war coupled with nuclear sabre rattling, which deters India from actions to retake POK. The Zia-ul-Haq–Malik duo's deliberately distorted teachings of Quran, and cobbled together their version of the 'Quranic Concept of Warfare' aimed at above fallouts, which has served them well even though Islamic terrorism perpetuated by Pakistan has brought Islam to disrepute. The ground truth is that the elimination of terrorism protects human lives and the Quran allows the liquidation of a 'fasadi' (troublemaker) and this can save a whole community.[16] At a time when radicalisation among some sections of Muslims threatens to distort reality and the message of Islam, India is contemplating hosting an international conference on counter-radicalisation.

Conventional Component

The Pakistani Military is the sixth largest in the world in terms of active military personnel and the largest among Muslim countries. Since the 1963 Sino-Pak Agreement, the military has had close military relations with China, working jointly to develop the JF-17, the K-8 and other weapons systems. Both nations also cooperate on the development of nuclear and space technology programmes. Both armies hold institutionalized periodic joint military exercises. The Pakistani military also maintains close relations with the US, which gave Pakistan a major non-NATO ally status in 2004. Pakistan gets the bulk of its military equipment from local domestic suppliers, China and the US.

The need for border management led to the creation of paramilitary forces to deal with civil unrest in the North-West and security of border areas in Punjab and Sindh by paramilitary troops. In 2016, the military had approximately 617,000 personnel on active duty, with 513,000 in the reserves, 402,000 in the paramilitary forces and approximately 20,000 serving in the Strategic Plans Division Forces, giving a total of almost 1,500,000 soldiers. The armed forces have a large pool of volunteers so conscription has never been needed, though the Pakistani constitution and supplementary legislation allow for conscription in a state of war. Existing and future capabilities of the Pakistani Military are discussed later in this chapter.

Since the founding of Pakistan, the military has played a key role in holding the state together, promoting a feeling of nationhood. However, since the rule of Zia-ul-Haq, radicalization and the abovementioned *Quranic Concept of War* has become the Bible of the Pakistani military. Pakistan is a large contributor to UN missions. Other foreign deployments have consisted of Pakistani military personnel serving as military advisers in African and Arab countries. The Pakistani military had maintained combat divisions and brigade-strength presences in some of the Arab countries during the Arab-Israeli Wars, aided the Coalition forces in the first Gulf War, and participated in conflicts in Somalia and Bosnia.

Irregular Component

The time since it was born, Pakistan has sought to seize Kashmir through the use of state proxies; during the first Indo-Pak War of 1947–1948, Pakistan invaded Kashmir with irregulars (Razakars) mixed with regulars. The same format was used by Pakistan during the 1965 Indo-Pak War and the 1999 Kargil Conflict, both lost by Pakistan. Since 1989, it has cultivated a proxy war, of varying intensity over time, in Kashmir. But it is not Kashmir alone where Pakistan is using proxy forces to wage war on India. Pakistan has raised terrorist organizations specific to India, supports insurgencies and terrorist movement in India, and is infiltrating terrorists into India. As early as 1992–93, the process of 'transplanting armed modules' in the heartland of India had started taking cognizable shape. Some of these cells were identified in Assam, West Bengal, Bihar, Uttar Pradesh, Delhi, Kota/Ajmer region of Rajasthan, Gujarat, Maharashtra, Andhra Pradesh and Kerala. Students' Islamic Movement of India (SIMI) had already started deputing 'volunteers' to Pakistan for training along with the Mujahedeen, Taliban, and Al Qaeda cadres. They established firm linkages with Islamic Chhatra Shibir, Al Qaeda–affiliated HUJI, Al Badr and Al Jihad, and other organisations in Bangladesh were trained in facilities located inside Bangladesh and under the very noses of DGFI and BDR.[17]

Pakistan's ISI is linked with some 15 regional and international terrorist organizations including ISIS, Al Qaeda, Taliban, LeT, JeM, LeJ, HuM, Sipah-e-Sahiba, IM, SIMI, Muslim militant groups in our northeast, Popular Front of India (PFI), etc. Stratfor had warned in 2008 that ISI was forging alliance with Indian Maoists. It was the ISI that arranged training in IEDs/explosive for Maoists with LTTE. As early as 2005, ammunition with Maoists was found to bear Pakistan

Ordnance Factory markings. In 2008, reports also emerged of 500 Maoists having been trained by SIMI. Al Qaeda and ISI in Kerala were behind the establishment of PFI, who though armed and trained are presently dormant. ISI-sponsored terrorist attacks have repeatedly targeted India, including attack on Parliament, 26/11 Mumbai terrorist attacks and during 2016 Pathankot IAF airbase and Uri attacks besides many others. The so-called non-state actors in Pakistan enjoy the protective umbrella of the ISI. Radical terrorist-mullahs like Hafiz Saeed and Masood Azhar are de facto foreign policy spokespersons of Pakistan and act as advisors to the Pakistani military. The AQIS chief, South Asia, is Pakistani national Asim Umar, who recently gave a call urging Muslims in India to undertake 'lone wolf' attacks to target senior IPS and IAS officers.

Collusivity

The China–Pakistan nexus dates back to 1960s when Chou En-Lai suggested to Ayub Khan that Pakistan should prepare for prolonged conflict with India instead of short-term wars. He advised Pakistan to raise a Militia Force to act behind enemy (Indian) lines. In 1963, when Pakistan illegally ceded Shaksgam Valley to China, began the massive military, nuclear, missile knowhow assistance from China to Pakistan. In 1966, when a Pakistani military delegation visited Beijing, Chou En-Lai while discussing India raised his clenched fist and said, 'This is capable of delivering a forceful blow, but if you cut off one finger, the fist loses its power, not by one-fifth, but by fifty per cent. If you wipe out a couple of hundred thousand of the enemy spread over a long front, its impact is not as great as wiping out an entire battalion or a brigade—the enemy's morale is dealt a devastating blow. We know this from practical experience'.

Collusive threat to India emanates from the China–Pakistan nexus with their strategic aims coalescing. Pakistan wants to capture J&K and balkanize India as revenge for the loss of East Pakistan. China is in illegal possession of 5,180 km^2 of Shaksgam and 38,000 km^2 of Aksai Chin, and eyes more including 90,000 km^2 of Arunachal Pradesh. China wants a 'Multi-Polar World but China-centric Uni-Polar Asia'. Hence, China wants to restrict India to within South Asia. India feels there is adequate space for both India and China to grow economically but China goes strictly by what Zbigniew Brzezinski wrote in his book *The Grand Chess Board* in 1997, 'China and India are destined by geography to be rivals. With venerable culture and vast population, are likely to compete with each other for resources and influence'.

China provides tacit support to Pakistan's anti-India *jihad* policy. China has blatantly and repeated protected Masood Azhar, Jaish-e-Mohammed (JeM) chief from being branded terrorist by the UN. The potency of the China–Pakistan collusivity is more because India has an adverse strategic asymmetry vis-à-vis the China-Pakistan; while China and Pakistan have advanced sub-conventional capabilities, India is lagging behind having not developed the proactive component for employment at a strategic level. Besides, China has invested heavily in force development (cyber, information and electromagnetic warfare included) plus what it terms as 'Assassin's Mace Weapons', and Pakistan's collusivity with China can make many of these technologies accessible to Pakistan.

Nuclear Dimension

While the China–Pakistan collusivity includes the nuclear domain, Pakistan is estimated to possess about 100–120 nuclear weapons for delivery by aircraft and land-based missiles. It is widely believed that, in peacetime, Pakistan stores its nuclear warheads separate from their delivery vehicles. However, the Strategic Plans Division (SPD), which operates Pakistan's nuclear forces, has never confirmed such arrangements. Pakistan's current warhead designs are believed to use HEU. Pakistan continues to produce HEU for military purposes and its total stockpile was estimated at 2.7–3.5 tonnes in 2014. The enrichment takes place at the gas centrifuge facilities located at Kahuta and Gadwal in Punjab.[18]

The nuclear weapons of Pakistan have two dimensions in terms of warfare: *first*, possibility of Chemical, Biological, Radiological, Nuclear (CBRN) terrorism through proxy terrorist organisations, and *second*, deterrence against Indian conventional attack in retaliation to Pakistan's proxy war and terrorist attacks. Latter is because India has never called Pakistan's nuclear bluff. Despite the blowbacks like the terrorist attack on the army school in Peshawar, Pakistan remains undeterred, and even evermore resolute, in its addiction to 'jihad' to achieve its foreign policy objectives in India, as well as Afghanistan.[19] The bottom line is that Pakistan's army uses terrorism, under the safety of its ever-expanding nuclear umbrella, because it works, is cost-effective, and offers putatively plausible deniability because Pakistan's own security forces are not engaged in the butchery.[20]

Hybrid Warfare Strategy

The hybrid warfare strategy of Pakistan, therefore, combines *jihad in backdrop of the Quranic Concept of War; conventional forces; collusivity with China throughout the spectrum of conflict and effective nuclear deterrent cover to continue waging proxy war on India*—largely because India has not called Pakistan's nuclear bluff. Jihad and the Quranic Concept of Warfare enable Pakistan to produce millions of terrorists consistently and wage a low-cost war against India, with its military largely untouched.

CAPABILITIES 2030

Conventional

Defence Spending. In June 2016, Pakistan announced a defence budget of Rs 860 billion for fiscal 2016–2017, an 11 per cent hike from the previous year. This did not include military pensions (averaging at Rs 127 billion since 2010), the nuclear programme and the army's operations in the Federally Administered Tribal Areas (FTA). Of the Rs 860 billion allocation, about Rs 2 billion was to be spent on defence ministry establishment where the remaining Rs 858 billion would be distributed among the three services: Army, Air Force and Navy. The three services were to spend Rs 211 billion on local purchases and import of arms and ammunition; Rs 216 billion on operational expenses; Rs 327 billion on salaries of soldiers and officers and Rs 104 billion on maintenance of its buildings and construction of new ones. Comparing these with the previous year, the increase is the highest in acquisition of weapons, followed by operational expenses, which cover transport costs, ration, treatment and training. In May 2017, Pakistan announced Defence Budget for FY 2017–2018 at Rs 920.2 billion (see Figure 3.1). The total budget was Rs 4.75 trillion of which 19.36 per cent was allotted to Defence Affairs and Services head. The operating expense for armed forces was Rs 225.5 billion. The government was to separately pay Rs 180 billion for military pensions. This did not count in the budget allocated to defence services. Pakistan also announced 10 per cent increase in the pay of all military personnel as a 'special allowance' in recognition for their sacrifices in the ongoing conflicts across the country. Pakistan is also launching a new scheme through the Central Directorate of National Savings (CDNS) for the welfare of families of martyrs, guaranteed and enhanced profit to support martyrs' families.

In June 2016, the US Senate passed draft of the National Defence Authorisation Bill, including a provision to set up a new fund to reimburse Pakistan for its efforts in the war against terrorism, authorizing $800 million under a provision called the 'Pakistan Security Enhancement Authorisation'. It also fenced $300 million behind a similar Haqqani network provision that has existed in the annual defence authorisation acts since the fiscal year 2015. The proposed reimbursement mechanism for Pakistan replaced the Coalition Support Fund (CSF), latter ending in October 2016. Pakistan had received a total of $3.1 billion since 2013 under the CSF. Pakistan considers that the US through this new provision delinks Pakistan from Afghanistan, recognising it as a country with its own strategic value for US interests.[21] However, besides action against Haqqani network, the bill requires Pakistan to keep open ground communication lines to Afghanistan for receiving

Figure 3.1: Defence Spending (Rs in billions)

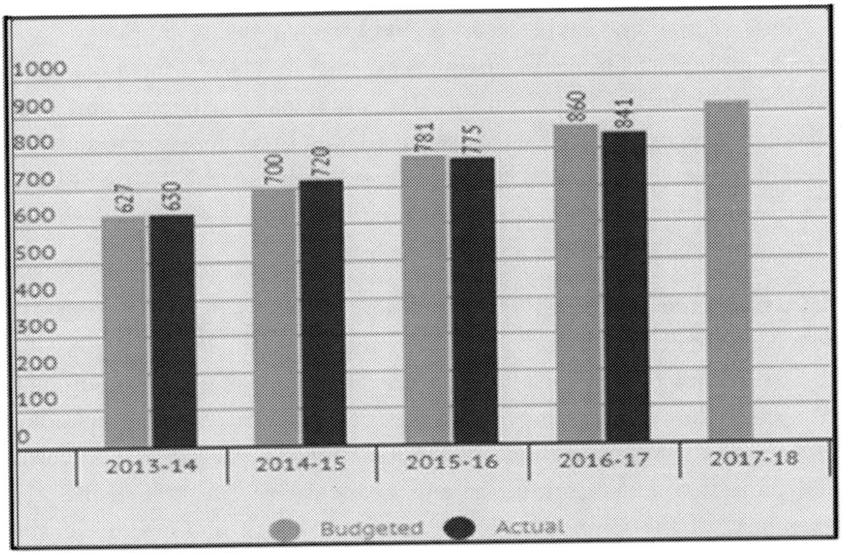

reimbursements from this fund. The Trump Administration has recently introduced a bill to cease non-military financial aid to Pakistan.

Higher Defence Organisation. While determining the causes of Pakistan's defeat in 1971, The Hamood-ur-Rehman Commission had pointed out lack of inter-services coordination as a major weakness. To address this inadequacy, the structure of its Higher Defensive Organisation (HDO) was revamped in 1976.

Defence Industry. Pakistan is becoming an increasingly important player in the world with distinct focus towards export. Pakistan's major defence manufacturing companies are owned and operated by 'Pak military'. It has over 20 major Public Sector Units (PSUs) and over 100 private sector firms. PSUs undertake production and assembly of weapons and equipment where as private sector firms supply components. Major PSUs include Pakistan Ordnance Factory (POF), Heavy Industries Taxila (HIT), Pakistan Aeronautical Complex, Karachi Shipyard and Engineering Works (KSEW). Joint development/production with China of Al-Khalid Tank, Al-Zarrar Tank, Agosta Submarine, Mushshak Aircraft, JF-17 Aircraft, Transport aircraft, different variants of APCs, Frigates and UAV variants, with Chinese collaboration are examples towards self-reliance in the field of defence production. JF-17 fighter aircraft a Joint venture with China has potential buyers like Bangladesh, Venezuela, Morocco, and Turkey and is being projected to be sold in developing countries. Pakistan has been able to boost its capabilities for high technology aerial warfare, to enable response to the new emerging challenges to combat insurgents especially when the Americans are reluctant to give 'Drones' or the Drone technology. Pakistan's UAV industry is growing exponentially with demand explosion for Drones by foreign companies. Pak UAV companies specialise in air frames, launch and propulsion systems, signal intelligence and training simulators. Pakistan military firms have signed joint development, production and marketing agreements with defence firms from South Korea, France and Ukraine. These agreements include new reactive armour bricks, 155-mm artillery shells, and other developments in armour and land weaponry.

Defence Cooperation. China is the largest supplier of armament to Pakistan, while Turkey has supplied Pakistan 52 MKEK Panter 155-mm Artillery guns during 2008-2012. Since 1962, China has been a steady source of military equipment to the Pakistani Army, helping establish ammunition factories, providing technological assistance and modernizing existing facilities. China and Pakistan are involved in several projects to enhance military and weaponry systems, which include the development of the Chinese tailor made for Pakistan JF-17 Thunder fighter aircraft, K-8 Karakorum advance training aircraft, a training aircraft for the Pakistan Air Force (PAF) based on the Chinese domestic Hongdu L-15, space technology, AWACS systems, Al-Khalid tanks, which China granted license production and made modifications based on the initial Chinese Type 90 and/or MBT-2000. China has helped Pakistan in launching communication satellite PAKSAT 1R, 57 optical satellite and high-resolution remote sensing satellite system to be launched in 2016. China is also providing GPS coverage to Pakistan and training Pakistani astronauts for space flights on board Chinese space crafts. The Chinese has designed advanced weapons for Pakistan, making it a strong military power in the Asian region. The armies have a schedule for organising joint military exercises.

US Assistance. Pakistan has received economic and military aid from US since 1947. During the period 1951-2011, Pakistan received nearly $67 billion from US. In 2010, military assistance to Pakistan totalled $2.5 billion—including $1.2 billion in CSF. CSF has accounted for nearly half of US financial transfers to Pakistan since 2001; as of June 2013, nearly $10.7 billion had been disbursed. The amount equals roughly one-fifth to one-quarter of Pakistan's total military expenditures during this period. Nearly all reimbursements are for Pakistan army expenses; navy and air force expenses account for only about 2 per cent of all Pakistani military claims under CSF.[22] The US has also made total Foreign Military Sales (FMS) agreements with Pakistan worth $5.2 billion for FY 2002–2011 (sales of F-16 combat aircraft and related equipment account for more than half of this). Congress also has appropriated more than $3 billion in Foreign Military Financing (FMF) grants to Pakistan since 2001; more than two-thirds has been disbursed to date. These funds are used to purchase US military equipment for longer term modernisation efforts. Pakistan also has been granted US defence supplies as Excess Defence Articles (EDA). Major post-2001 defence supplies provided or soon to be provided under FMF include:

- Eight P-3C Orion maritime patrol aircraft and their refurbishment (valued at $474 million; four delivered, but three of these were destroyed in a 2011 Islamist militant attack on Pakistan Naval Station Mehran)
- 2,007 TOW anti-armour missiles ($186 million)
- 5,600 military radio sets ($163 million)
- Six AN/TPS-77 surveillance radars ($100 million)
- Six C-130E transport aircraft and their refurbishment ($76 million)
- USS McInerney, an ex-Perry class missile frigate (via EDA, $65 million for refurbishment, delivered and now the PNS Alamgir)
- 20 AH-1F Cobra attack helicopters (via EDA, $48 million for refurbishment, 12 delivered).

Supplies paid for with a mix of Pakistani national funds and FMF include

- Up to 60 Mid-Life Update kits for F-16A/B combat aircraft (valued at $891 million, with $477 million of this in FMF; Pakistan's plans are to purchase 45 such kits, 8 have been delivered)
- 115 M-109 self-propelled howitzers ($87 million, with $53 million in FMF).

Notable items paid for entirely with Pakistani national funds include:

- 18 new F-16C/D Block 52 combat aircraft (valued at $1.43 billion)
- F-16 armaments including 500 AMRAAM air-to-air missiles; 1,450 2,000-pound bombs; 500 JDAM bomb tail kits for gravity bombs and 1,600 Enhanced Paveway laser-guided bomb kits, also for gravity bombs ($629 million)
- 100 Harpoon anti-ship missiles ($298 million)
- 500 Sidewinder air-to-air missiles ($95 million)
- Six Phalanx Close-In Weapons System naval guns ($80 million).

PAKISTAN ARMY (PA)

The Pakistan Army is organised into ten corps. The Army Strategic Forces Command corps has been the latest addition to the already existing nine corps and was established in February 2000; it is responsible for the training, deployment and activation of nuclear missile assets. In 2006, the government set up separate commands in its three services equipped with nuclear weapons and missiles capable of retaliating for any first nuclear strike. Detailed force levels as per International Institute for Strategic Studies (IISS) Military Balance 2017 are described in Appendix 'A'.

Most of Pakistan's ground units are deployed along the Indian border. The deployment of forces is based on the need for creation of reserves due to lack of geographical depth. One holding Corps (X Corps) is responsible for the Line of Control including Siachen with XI Corps as the dedicated reserve for Kashmir. Three Corps (IV, XXX and XXXI) are deployed for defence of the border with India from the Chenab River to Sir Creek with V and XII Corps as strategic reserves. I and II Corps (Strike Corps) are deployed for offensive employment north and south of the Ravi River. XI and XII Corps have the principal responsibility for counter-insurgency in Khyber Pakhtunkhwa (KP) and Baluchistan and 323 Infantry Brigade, part of Forces Command Northern Areas (FCNA), on the Siachen Glacier.

Modernisation and Expansion of Army. As part of the Armed Forces Development Programme (AFDP) 2019, Pakistan has invested in the build-up of the Army, managed to expand the land equipment and has also initiated an infantry modernisation programme for its special, regular and paramilitary forces. The Army is raising a 15,000 strong special division for the protection of the CPEC. There are no other known expansion plans.

Capability of Army – 2030. The Pakistani Army is well equipped even as it has never won any war. With China's strategic engagement with Pakistan, China can be expected to continue arming it well. Its proactive sub-conventional stance gives it a distinct advantage in addition to its close defence relationship with China. However, *in case Pakistan undergoes an implosion because of terrorist blowback, with or without external assistance, the Army may well be stretched beyond limits.*

PAKISTAN NAVY (PN)

Major combatant components of Pakistan Navy are as follows: Commander of Pakistan Naval Fleet (COMPAK). The command heads the surface, sub surface and aviation commands: Commander COAST (COMCOAST). The special command of SSG (N), Marines and Coastal stations, Commander North (COMNOR), looks after the naval installations in the north of Pakistan. The COMNOR commands the naval facilities in North-west Pakistan, Azad Kashmir, and Northern Areas of Pakistan. The COMNOR is also a major part of Pakistan's Northern Naval Command, Commander WEST (COMWEST), and looks after the naval installations in the west of Pakistan. The naval bases are Omari, Pasni, Gwadar and Jiwani. The COMWEST is a major component of the Western Naval

Command of Pakistan Navy; Commander Naval Air Arm (COMNAV) looks after the naval air stations, and is the commander of the Naval Aviation, and Flag Officer Sea Training (FOST). It conducts all types of operational training at Sea. The Pakistan Navy comprises 11 Frigates, 12 fast attack crafts, 3 mine hunters, 12 hovercrafts, 17 Coastal patrol boats and 8 auxiliary vessels. Detailed force levels incorporating IISS Military Balance 2017 are given in Appendix 'B'.

Naval Acquisition Plans

- **Submarines**. Media reports indicate that the PN will acquire 8 new submarines from China by 2028.[23] The first four are expected to be built by China and delivered by 2023; the next four will be built by KSEW and be delivered by 2028.[24] The type of submarine to be supplied has not been specified. Analysts, however, believe that it will be a lighter, AIP equipped S 20 export version, something between the Type 039 that entered service in 1989 and Type 041, first seen in 2006.[25] The number of submarines may go up to 12.[26] The projected weapon fit will include 6 torpedo tubes, capable of launching either the Yu-4 torpedo with a range of 15 Km or the YJ-82 anti-ship cruise missile, 40 Km range. The package includes a training centre at Karachi and reported access to China's Beidou-II satellite navigation network,[27] supporting target positioning at the tactical level, use by precision strike weapons and providing a common operating picture of friendly force locations.[28] There is some speculation that the supersonic YJ-18B SLCM[29] with a range of 290 km and similar to the Klub Submarine-Launched Cruise Missile (SLCM) used by the Indian Navy, may be provided to Pakistan along with these submarines. It is also possible that these submarines may be modified to launch the naval version of Babur SLCM.
- **Naval Platforms**. The traditional sources of supply have been USA and UK. These sources appear to have dried up for political and economic reasons. Both USA and UK are no longer likely to transfer warships at friendship prices, although UK may be willing to sell at market price. The PN, however, doesn't have the ability to buy at market prices. Essentially, the only reliable sources of supply appear to be China [PN vessels of Chinese origin in service include Zulfiqar class frigates, Azmat Class Fast Attack Craft (FAC) (M) and the fleet tanker PNS Nasr. Two 1,500-ton OPVs for Pakistan's Coast Guard are under construction at KSEW] and Turkey (Turkish origin ships are the Zarrar Class FAC (M) and a 17,000 ton fleet tanker launched by KSEW in August 2016,[30] due for delivery in April 2017). Russia could emerge as a future source of supply. Unconfirmed reports indicate that Pakistan is looking for four improved Zulfiqar class frigates,[31]

or the bigger Type 054A Jiangkai class. Some reports claim that these have been ordered.

- **Brown Water Platforms.**
  - ✓ **Houbei Class Catamarans**. Reports indicate that Pakistan has contracted to build six Houbei class Stealth catamaran; 83 of these are reported to have entered PLA Navy service since 2004. The PN version is likely to be fitted with C-802 Surface-to-Surface Missile (SSM) of 180 km range, man portable SAMs and a Chinese close-in weapon system (CIWS).
  - ✓ **Corvettes**. Reports indicate that Pakistan is looking to build four corvettes indigenously, with designs chosen from among the French DCN Gowind Class, German Meko A-100D and the Turkish Milgem Class. Other reports talk of acquiring four Ada class corvettes from Turkey, three of which will be constructed by KSEW. Weapons carried include 8 Harpoon SSMs, an effective CIWS using RIM-116 Rolling Airframe Missiles and 12.7 mm machine guns, a 76-mm gun, 2 triple torpedo launchers for Mk 46 torpedoes and a hangar and platform for the S-70B Seahawk helicopter or UAVs. Since USA may be unwilling to release the RIM-116 system to Pakistan, the reports indicate that Pakistan may be looking to fit the South African Denel Dynamics Umkhonto SAM in lieu.

Maritime Capabilities 2030

- **Submarines**
  - ✓ **Nuclear Deterrence**. Pakistan inaugurated its Naval Strategic Forces Command in 2012 and declared its intent to develop its own sea-based deterrent.[32] By dispersing low-yield nuclear weapons across a variety of naval platforms, Pakistan aims to acquire escalation dominance and greater strategic depth, reducing incentives for a pre-emptive Indian strike on its nuclear assets.[33] Guarding its nuclear assets against seizure by US or Indian Special Forces is a greater concern for Pakistan than their seizure by terrorists.[34] The sea-based deterrent will probably be a navalised version of Pakistan's Babur cruise missile, modified for launch from its French Agosta or the new Chinese origin submarines. As observed by Admiral Arun Prakash, 'navalisation of the Babur will mean modifying it for launch from the 533 mm torpedo tube of the submarine and interfacing its Chinese guidance control with the submarine's fire control system'.[35] Given that Chinese help is likely to be available; this is not beyond the bounds of possibility.[36]
  - ✓ **Nuclear Strike.** The same submarine could also be used to launch a nuclear

first strike, particularly on counter force and counter value targets within SLCM range (presently thought to be about 800 km). The immediate impact of development of a nuclear tipped SLCM would be to force the IN to shift from tactical Anti-submarine Warfare (ASW) (directed towards preventing submarine attack on surface vessels and thus relatively localized) to strategic ASW, focused on seeking and destroying PN submarines before they can reach anywhere within the SLCM range of targets on the Indian coast. This would, in effect, cover the entire Arabian Sea.

- ✓ **Land Attack.** The induction of the YJ-18B SLCM would give the PN the capability to carry out precision attack on high-value economic infrastructure on India's Western seaboard while remaining at a safe, standoff distance from the coast. This includes refineries at Jamnagar, Koyali, Mumbai, Mangalore and Kochi; all major ports, international airports at Mumbai, Goa and Kochi and all heavy industry on the coast and much more. The damage done by such attacks could, in the opinion of some Pakistan analysts, do sufficient damage to India's economic infrastructure to substitute the tactical use of nuclear weapons[37] early in a conflict. As such, they could give Pakistan the ability to inflict heavy costs for Indian actions such as the cross-border strikes following the Uri attack, while remaining below the nuclear threshold given India's 'no first use' policy.
- ✓ **SLOC Interdiction**. Submarines are best suited for Sea Lanes of Communication (SLOCs) interdiction tasks. India's trade already constitutes 42 per cent of its GDP[38] and dependence on trade is bound to grow as India continues to integrate with the global economy. A key vulnerability is energy imports: the gap between demand and supply of crude oil was 4.1 million barrels per day in 2015 and this gap is bound to grow given continued robust economic development and the government's focus on development of highway and road infrastructure, as well as the 'Make in India' policy. Nearly 60 per cent of India's crude imports come from the Middle East, with the concerned SLOCs falling well within range of PN submarines. India is also the world's fourth largest importer of natural gas (after Japan, South Korea and China), with imports, which accounted for 37 per cent of the demand in 2014, increasing. Supplies come primarily from Qatar and are vulnerable to interdiction by PN submarines. India also became the world's largest importer of coal in 2015, buying over 226 million tons from overseas, primarily for its Iron and Steel industry. Coal imports come primarily from Australia, Indonesia

and South Africa and the SLOCs are thus less vulnerable to PN submarines, but the threat exists.[39]

- ✓ **Sea Denial**. Denying the IN the ability to bring its superior surface force to bear in the North Arabian Sea, for operations such as a blockade. PN submarines could be tasked to interdict any Indian surface units approaching the Pakistan coast, as well as to seek out high-value units operating in the Arabian Sea. An example of this deployment is Pakistan's use of PNS Ghazi to search for INS Vikrant in the 1971 war.
- ✓ **Anti-Submarine (Hunter/Killer)**. Given the hydrographic conditions prevalent in the North Arabian Sea, PN submarines could be deployed for hunter/killer operations against IN submarines attempting to interdict Pakistan's SLOCs.
- ✓ **Clandestine Raids on Coastal and Offshore Infrastructure**. PN submarines could be used to land saboteurs for clandestine missions including raids on India's coastal and offshore economic infrastructure. They could also be deployed during peacetime to infiltrate personnel anywhere on the West Coast of India. The midgets are particularly suited for such operations.
- ✓ **Mining of West Coast Harbours**. All PN submarines including the midgets have the ability to carry mines. They could thus be deployed for mine laying in the approaches to Indian harbours, where any mine explosion would strike fear into the hearts of merchant traffic.

➢ **Blue-Water Capability**

- ✓ Six of Pakistan's 10 blue-water ships are more than 35 years old, in need of replacement. They are well suited for the diplomatic, constabulary and benign roles, as well as military roles against other regional nations.
- ✓ PN ships do carry anti-ship missiles and do have a helicopter to help with Over the Horizon Targeting (OTHT). They can also receive target information from LRMP aircraft. They would, however, suffer from a range disadvantage of more than 150 km against Indian ships equipped with Brahmos (Rajput, Kolkatta, Visakhapatnam and Shivalik classes, as well as INS Teg onwards from the Talwar class) and 60 km against ships equipped with the Klub missile (Talwar and Kamorta classes). PN missiles are of comparable range to the Uran fitted on Delhi, Brahmaputra, Khukri and Kora classes. PN ships have a good CIWS and ECM to defend themselves against enemy anti-ship missiles, except the supersonic Brahmos, against which their capability must be considered suspect. SAM

capability is restricted to short range systems (15–18 km). They can engage low-flying cruise missiles and UAVs, but their range is not sufficient to take on IN aircraft or helicopters firing anti-ship missiles from standoff range. Area AD capability is conspicuous by its absence.

- ✓ None of the PN surface fleet has any land attack missiles and given the likely opposition by shore-based anti-ship missile batteries, they are not likely to be able to carry out shore bombardment as was done in 1965. This position could change if the Babur cruise missile is successfully miniaturised and fitted on to surface platforms.
- ✓ PN anti-submarine capability must be considered limited, particularly in the difficult waters of the Arabian Sea. Details of sonars fitted on the Zulfiqar class are not available, while those on the Type 21s and Alamgir would be aged. The integral helicopter with dunking sonar seems to be their best ASW solution. Numbers available are not really sufficient for an effective search.
- ✓ Surface warships are inherently not suited for clandestine missions.
- ✓ All in all, PN blue-water ships, both current and future, appear suited for diplomatic, constabulary and benign functions, including in distant waters. They could be used for escort operations particularly while operating in the vicinity of the Makran coast, under shore-based air cover. Their survivability in open ocean operations against the IN would appear to be doubtful. Until such time as they are retro-fitted with land attack missiles such as the Babur (seaborne version under development), they pose little threat to India and the IN.

➢ **Brown-Water Capability**

- ✓ Harbour defence tasks, particularly defence of the Karachi citadel, for which they are best suited. They could, in a pinch, be used for strikes on Indian ports as was done by India in 1971, but given their short legs and the availability of better units, are not likely to be used for these tasks.
- ✓ Swarm attacks against IN ships approaching Pakistan's coast, where sheer numbers of platforms and missiles launched could overwhelm the approaching force.
- ✓ Constabulary tasks close to Pakistan's coast, or as sentinels to provide warning of incoming Indian strikes.

➢ **Naval Aviation**

- ✓ Keeping the North Arabian Sea, defined as north of the line connecting the Gulf of Aden to Mumbai, under reasonable surveillance against surface vessels. The efficacy of this surveillance would reduce if the Indian Carrier Battle Group were to operate in this area since PN MR Aircraft would be forced to adopt tactics guarding against the threat posed by carrier borne interceptors.

- ✓ Maritime strikes against vessels in the North Arabian Sea, both using integral weapons on the MR aircraft as well as by vectoring in strikes by fixed wing aircraft or submarines.
- ✓ Limited surveillance and ASW operations against Indian submarines off Pakistan's coastal belt.
- ✓ In sum, Pakistan's naval aviation, both current and projected future, based on available information, poses limited threat to IN units.

➢ **Special Services Group Navy (SSGN)**

- ✓ Coastal and covert beach reconnaissance, preliminary to amphibious landings. This could also include landing by irregular forces, including terrorist elements.
- ✓ Covert landings on India's coast, particularly North of Mumbai.
- ✓ Seizure of vessels and installations, either from pirates, or from the regular crew.
- ✓ Operations against offshore and coastal installations, including of the deniable variety.
- ✓ Raids targeting vessels in harbour, including possible attempts to block harbour entrances.
- ✓ In sum, the SSGN provides Pakistan with a number of options for deniable sub-conventional operations.

Summary of PN Capability. The PN is, in sum, structured as a coastal sea denial navy, capable of denying IN units the ability to operate in the vicinity of Pakistan's coastline, but not of controlling the waters. This broad categorisation is unlikely to change, unless the PN can find a way to change Pakistan's continental mindset and enhance its budget share considerably. Perhaps it's most potent and underestimated capability remains the SSGN, which could find substantial utility in hybrid, sub-conventional wars. At the conventional level, perhaps the biggest concern for India would be shift of the nuclear deterrent to sea (with China's assistance if need be). This would force the IN to invest heavily in ocean surveillance and ASW, both areas where its capability is limited.

PAKISTAN AIR FORCE (PAF)

The PAF is divided into five commands: Northern Air Command (NAC) Peshawar; Central Air Command (CAC) Lahore; Southern Air Command (SAC) Faisal, Karachi; Air Defence Command (ADC) Chaklala, Rawalpindi, and Air Force Strategic Command (AFSC), Islamabad. Pakistan has 11 active airbases and currently operates approximately 450 combat aircraft of four different types. There are around 20 frontline squadrons. Details of equipment holding as per IISS Military Balance 2017 are given in Appendix C.

Modernisation of PAF

- The 'Air Force Development Plan 2025' was launched in 2003/04 by then President Pervez Musharraf. Under the plan, the PAF received money by the federal government only till 2007. Thereafter, PAF suspended its upgradation and development plan. The expenditure on the entire package would be met from PAF share in Armed Forces Development Programme (AFFDP 2019). The Cabinet (Interim Government), according to the document, allowed PAF to set up Joint Working Group (JWG) with CATIC for procurement of 36 FC-20 aircraft. The government was also seeking for PAF in securing long-term credit financing for the J-10 aircraft from Chinese government, besides allowing PAF to initiate a Letter of Request (LoR) for the F-16 package and equipment through the Defence Ministry.
- In June 2006, PAF had signed a deal for the supply of six Saab 2000s. However, because of shortage of funds, the number of aircraft was revised to five. Another report suggests that the Erieye airborne surveillance system deal involves up to eight Saab 2000 aircraft. The first Saab 2000 AEWC aircraft ordered for the PAF was rolled out on 3 April 2008 at the SAAB factory in Sweden. The ERIEYE, developed by the Ericsson Microwave Systems, comprises fixed, dual-sided and electronically scanned phased-array pulse-Doppler radar mounted on top of the fuselage.
- PAF received the delivery of a second Gulfstream 450 aircraft in November 2007. The first aircraft was delivered in December 2005.
- On 25 January 2009, Pakistan's defence minister informed the parliament that Pakistan has placed a $278 million order for the Chinese AWACS system ZDK-03 based on the Chinese Y-8 aircraft.
- In January 2009, PAF received delivery of two IL-78 tanker aircraft from Ukraine, out of the four ordered. Once the IL-78 tanker aircraft has been commissioned into service, it will enhance the long-range capability of PAF.

- By 2014, Pakistan was concentrating on modernising its air power, still in line with the Armed Forces Development Plan 2025, by seeking defence deals with China and Russia.
- In July 2004, PAF finalised a deal with Libya to buy its fleet of 50 Mirage IIIs and Vs, 150 sealed pack engines and a huge quantity of Mirage spares. Libya had purchased the Mirage jets in the 1970s, and they had been grounded for the previous decade following sanctions imposed after the Boeing 747 was blown up over Lockerbie. With these airframes, Pakistan operated more Mirages than the French Air Force. It is believed that jets would be cannibalized for spare parts to provide spares for the PAF fleet of Mirages for the next seven to ten years. As of 2009, the Mirage Rebuild Factory, which is a part of PAC, had been rebuilding the 35-year-old version of the Mirage aircraft that were bought as scrap from various countries.
- The PAF was offered the J-10 by the Chinese government as the future part of PAF, and the purchase of 36 J-10 aircraft, modified according to the requirements of PAF, was approved on 12 April 2006. The export version to the Pakistan would be called FC-20 (J-10B). PAF planned to purchase 36 to 100 FC-20 aircraft. It was initially planned that China would start exporting FC-20s to Pakistan in the 2014 to 2015 period.
- In August 2011, it was reported that the Chinese government had offered to provide its advance fourth-generation J-10B fighter jets to the PAF to meet its requirements of high-tech fourth-generation frontline fighter aircraft. The J-10B is an improved version of the basic J-10A powered by the Chinese WS-10 engine. Pakistan has a total requirement of 150 frontline fourth-generation aircraft that will be met with the induction of Chinese J-10B/FC-20, F-16AM/BM and F-16 C/D Block 52+ fighter aircraft. In September 2013, it was reported that PAF would receive its first FC-20/J-10B fighter jet in 2014.

Acquisition Plan PAF. Pakistan has been on a steady acquisition spree to modernise its Air Force over the past decade, accelerating the process during the last few years. Significantly, Pakistan's weapon acquisitions have been exclusively cantered on modernization and build-up of the PAF. The future (2020) acquisitions of the PAF as compared to 1990s would enhance both the quality and quantity of equipment (Figure 3.2).

Figure 3.2: PAF Capability 2020

	1990s	2020
Combat Aircraft	380	420
AEW&C	Nil	8
Air-to-Air Refueling	Nil	4
Maritime Patrol and Strike Aircraft	3	18

PAF Capabilities

- The PAF currently operates a fighter force comprising F-16s, Dassault Mirage IIIs and 5s, Chengdu F-7s, and JF-17s. F-16s, with their tactical nuclear delivery capabilities, play a particularly important role for Pakistan in bolstering its conventional abilities against India. The acquisition of F-16s ex US may not come through. Should Pakistan seek to purchase Sukhoi Su-35 fighter jets, that are far more advanced than the F-16s, the Russian-made jets could be a great asset for PAF.
- PAF aircraft are either of Western stock or Chinese and are far more maintenance friendly. Pakistan has also been upgrading its aircraft massively and has incorporated a complex combination of technology from across the globe—from China to Brazil, from South Africa to the US.
- PAF aircraft are also 'pimped' in that they have been extensively modified. Thus, while on paper PAF is flying ancient Mirages that were bought second-hand from the Australians, when one actually examines any such model, one is surprised at how extensively they have been rebuilt—almost from scratch and the hardware is extremely lethal.

Sub-Conventional Capability

The irregular component of Pakistan has been discussed earlier in this chapter. With its penchant for jihad, this capability will expand especially with China's support and American intransigence. The latter, so far, is only concerned with Pakistan's proxy war in Afghanistan and US-NATO casualties in that country. Pakistan's ISI is linked with and targets India through the Indian Mujahedeen (IM), Student Islamic Movement of India (SIMI), Popular Front of India (PFI), Maoists and Muslim groups in the northeast. This is in addition to the Pakistan-POK based Lashkar-e-Taiba (LeT), Jamat-ud-Dawa (JuD), Tehreek-e-Azadi J&K (TAJK), Hijbul Mujahedeen (HuM) and many of the numerous other terrorist organizations of Pakistan. LeT and Al Qaeda footprints were detected in 2000 that led to the rise of the PFI. In 2005, five cadres of PFI were caught in Kupwara trying to cross over to POK. Stratfor had warned as early as 2008 that the ISI was forging alliance with Indian Maoists and SIMI had trained 500 Maoists on the behest of ISI, even as ammunition with Pakistan Ordnance Factory (POF) markings were found with Maoists since 2005. The ISI had also arranged IED, mines and explosives training for a core group of Maoists by the LTTE.

Pakistan has been successful in radicalizing some five districts of J&K, replacing the Sufi culture with hardcore Wahabism and nurturing the anti-India sentiment. The anti-India sentiment and violence was seen spread to even rural areas in the spate of violence post the killing of Burhan Wani, albeit this was more so due to lack of any anti-radicalization policy or programme on India's behalf. Also, the Hurriyat separatists had virtually free-hand with our intelligence agencies terming them as irrelevant, even as they continued to spread anti-India venom. Ironically, India continues to rely on diplomacy to isolate Pakistan which in no way has succeeded in raising the cost of Pakistan's proxy war, surgical strikes notwithstanding. Asim Umar, Al Qaeda in the Indian Subcontinent (AQIS) South Asia head who is a Pakistani national, has been giving calls for Indian Muslims to undertake 'lone wolf' attacks against senior IAS and IPS officers. Fake currency continues to surface in India and ISI is looking at new ways of targeting India, one example being NIA reports indicating that the brain for the recent train derailments in India is located across the border, and physical contacts for coordinating the sabotage was done by travelling to India via Nepal.

Given the trend of not raising the costs of Pakistan's proxy war, future sub-conventional capability can manifest as under:

- ➢ Radicalising more Indian Muslims in the name of jihad, particularly J&K. In doing so, Pakistan will also incorporate illegal Bangladeshi and Myanmar immigrants, including the large number of Rohangiya Muslims who have managed to settle in the Jammu region despite Article 370.
- ➢ Enlarge pockets of Muslim population within India in order to force non-Muslims to flee. Ethnic cleansing of Hindus from Kashmir Valley is one example, recent one being Kairana in Uttar Pradesh.
- ➢ Raise the level of terror attacks: car/truck bombs, drones, shoulder-fired AD weapons, hand-held EW weapons, CBRN attacks and the like.
- ➢ Target critical infrastructure, security forces, their training establishments and personnel, financial institutions.
- ➢ Rally insurgents and terrorists in India under common/regional umbrella.
- ➢ Increased suicide attacks and hostage taking to subjugate the higher leadership.
- ➢ Optimise radicalism in India's neighbourhood to destabilise India; Bangladesh, Myanmar, Maldives, Nepal and Muslims in northern Sri Lanka.
- ➢ Ecological terrorism.

Cyber and Info Warfare (IW)

Limited cyber skirmishes between India and Pakistan had already begun in 2008. Pakistani hackers defaced many Indian websites in what Pakistan described as counter cyber strikes in retaliation to Indian hackers when a group of Indian hackers purportedly defaced the website of Ministry of Oil and Gas, Government of Pakistan. Given the influential nature of cyberspace, Pakistan is going in for a dedicated professional force to fight against all cyber warfare tactics. A special wing inside armed forces is also being raised to counter advanced cyber threats. In early 2013, Pakistan launched Operation 'Arachnophobia', advanced persistent threat/cyber espionage activity featuring a custom malware family dubbed Bitterbug that serves as the backdoor for siphoning stolen information.[40] The Bitterbug malware is geared for cyber espionage purposes and was hidden behind pilfered US infrastructure as a way to hide its origins. Specifically, the attacks employ infrastructure from a US virtual private server. The Pakistani hosting provider appears to have leased its command and control infrastructure from a US VPS provider. The goal was to make the attacks appear to come from the US. Operation Arachnophobia was named after the Pakistani security firm Tranchulas, whose name appeared in some of the malware samples studied by Fire Eye researchers. 'The "Tranchulas" name was in a string' of the malware, says Mike Oppenheim, principal threat intelligence analyst at Fire Eye. Tranchulas was supposedly a security company that does penetration testing. The researchers say it supports 'national level cyber security programmes' and the development of 'offensive and defensive cyber capabilities'.

The cyber war between India and Pakistan is an ongoing affair. While programmes of both nations are at a nascent stage, Pakistan being the protégé of China has the advantage of being helped by China in undertaking cyber-attacks on India. At the same time, reports indicate that India is adopting a joint approach against Pakistan with the help of Israel.[41] Israel established a cyber-task force for cyber warfare in 2008 with a budget of $1,50,000,00 that also covers Pakistan.

Cyberspace, electronic and social media can be exploited by Pakistan, manifesting in following threats:

- Espionage and attacking critical infrastructure, government websites, command and control nets of security forces.
- Nuclear installations, dams, communication networks including of important services like airports, railways, harbours, etc., especially where Supervisory Control and Data Acquisition (SCADA) software is in use.
- Planning and coordinating terror attacks.
- Radicalisation and spreading social unrest/riots.

Electronic Warfare

Number 24 Squadron of PAF (Blinders) is responsible for electronic warfare. It was originally raised in 1962 and operated RB-57 aircraft for electronic surveillance till 1977 when it was disbanded. The same squadron was re-raised in 1987, equipped with Dassault Falcon 20F aircraft and tasked for electronic warfare. The aircraft are fitted with an electronic warfare suite, tasked with providing ESM and ECM support to other PAF squadrons. Electronics and Air Defence officers are also trained in electronic warfare concepts, equipment and operational tactics by the squadron. In various exercises, the squadron's aircraft have provided Airborne Early Warning of intruding aircraft to participating squadrons, as well as communications jamming, radar jamming and radar spoofing. They have been used to expose PAF aircrews in operating under degraded environments and train pilots and controllers in ECM.

During the international exercises Inspired Alert 94, Inspired Alert 95 and Sea Spark 95, the squadron's ESN equipment has been employed to gain intelligence on radar capabilities and tactics used by aircraft of participating countries. As well as international exercises, the squadron flies extensively during Indian military exercises to ensure complete coverage. Aircraft of the Blinders squadron form an integral part of trans-frontier photo-reconnaissance missions flown by the PAF's reconnaissance aircraft, providing protection and early warning.

In 2012, Pakistan signed a $54 million contract with ITT Exelis for 18 AIDEWS and four pod shells. PAF already possessed AIDEWS, the internally carried version, for their then recently purchased Block F-16 aircraft. The new AIDEWS pods purchased were to be used on the upgraded but older F-16s of the PAF fleet. The systems are interchangeable but not interoperable. Part of the ALQ-211 electronic warfare self-defence system family, AIDEWS detects, denies, disrupts and degrades lethal threats and provides multi-spectral situation awareness.

Space

Pakistan's space agency, the Space and Upper Atmosphere Research Commission (SUPARCO), was established in 1961. The first successful spaceflight launched its first weather rocket, Rehbar-I. SUPARCO mainly focuses on areas related to understanding the solar system, space weather, astrophysics, astronomical observation climatic studies, space and telemetric, remote sensing and the earth observation. In 2011, Paksat-1R satellite was launched from China and was deployed successfully at 38° E in the geo-stationary orbit. This satellite, however, was not indigenously built and China was behind Paksat-1R's design, built, launch and even funding; only a few components were built by Pakistani engineers. In the 1980s there was reorganisation of space department and new research areas like rocketry programmes were included in the space programme. This aided in the development of Pakistan's missile programme and Haft and Shaheen series were developed subsequently. In the 1990s, the Space programme slowed down due to slot crisis and failures; however, due to Chinese assistance and cooperation, Pakistan is now gradually moving ahead. All Pakistani satellites in space have been launched primarily by China; in fact Pakistan's only communication satellite was built and launched by China. For purposes of surveillance and monitoring the borders, China provides satellite cover to Pakistan.

Space Vision 2040 programme was approved by then Prime Minister Yousaf Raza Gilani in January 2012 and the main motto, according to SUPARCO Chairman Maj. Gen. (Retd) Ahmed Bilal, was 'to be able to make, produce and launch our own satellite [in the future]—we should have at least three remote sensing satellites that should be launched every three years'.[42] Pakistan planned to launch five GEO satellites and six low earth orbit (LEO) satellites between 2011 and 2040. However, in reality, Pakistan, has limited space capabilities and has not been able to build or launch its own satellite to date. SUPARCO, though raised in 1961, has not been able to maintain momentum due to economic challenges, poor governance and sanctions.

Nuclear Dimension

Pakistan's nuclear arsenal probably consists of approximately 100–120 nuclear weapons for delivery by aircraft and land-based missiles. Islamabad is producing fissile material, adding to related production facilities, and deploying additional delivery vehicles. These steps could enable Pakistan to undertake both quantitative and qualitative improvements to its nuclear arsenal. Pakistan does not have a public, declared nuclear doctrine, but its 'minimum credible deterrent' is widely regarded as designed to dissuade India from taking military action against it. With long-standing disputes, limited resources to match Indian conventional military capability and lack of support from its principal ally, the US, Pakistan during various crises reinforced its India-specific threat perception, and made the nuclear weapons pursuit a national imperative that no successive leadership could reverse. Several factors contribute to a state's nuclear choices, but in Pakistan's case, the concern about national security has been the chief catalyst. The stated policy is that of 'minimum deterrence', yet it is not clear as to what 'minimum deterrence' implies. It follows a principle of nuclear retaliation in the case of a preventive or pre-emptive strike, and does not subscribe to the 'no-first use doctrine'. The Pakistani concept of nuclear deterrence is India specific and aims, first and foremost, to deter Indian conventional as well as nuclear aggression.

In an interview Lt Gen Khalid Kidwai, the head of Strategic Plans Division responsible for nuclear planning and implementing decisions taken by Pakistan's National Command Authority (NCA), reportedly stated that nuclear weapons would be used only 'if the very existence of Pakistan as a state is at stake'. While describing the range of contingencies, he said that nuclear weapons are aimed solely to deter India. In case that deterrence fails, these will be used if, India attacks Pakistan and conquers large part of territory (space threshold), India destroys a large part either of its land or air forces (military threshold), India proceeds towards economic strangulation of Pakistan (economic threshold), and, if India pushes Pakistan into political destabilisation or creates large-scale internal subversion in Pakistan (domestic destabilisation). The NCA has decided to further develop the country's nuclear weapons programme for preserving 'full spectrum deterrence' against any possible external aggression. Further development implies that the perceived gaps in the programme would be plugged. The country has already been pursuing this track and has developed short-range and low-yield TNWs in response to India's cold start doctrine.

The NCA (see Figure 3.3) is responsible for the operational control of all strategic forces. The army and air force strategic forces are responsible for technical aspects, training and administrative control of the services' nuclear assets.

Figure 3.3: National Command Authority

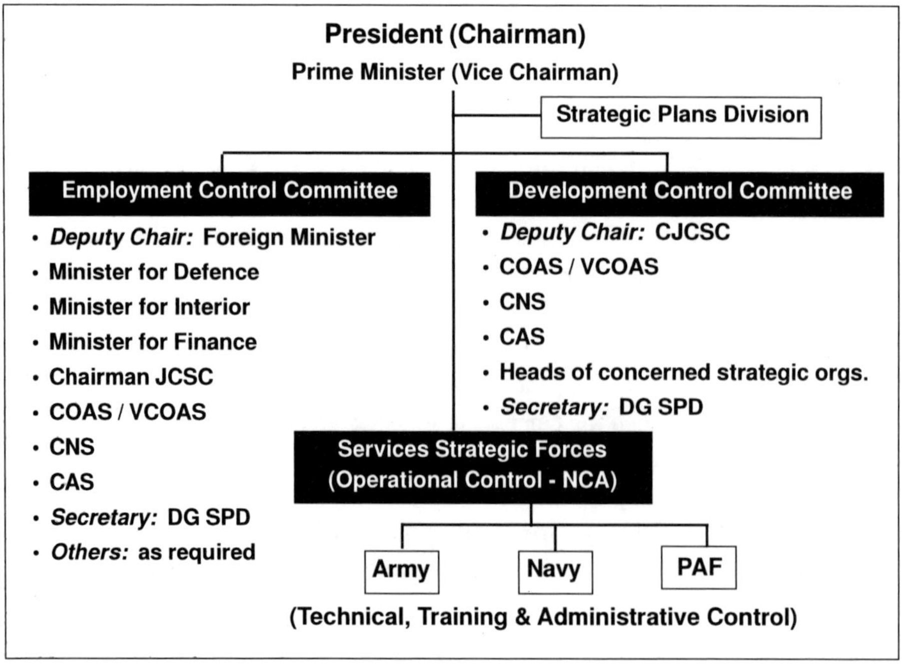

Force Structure. Pakistan has seen a shift in its 'Nuclear Doctrine' as the posture has changed from 'Minimum Credible Deterrence' to 'Full Spectrum Deterrence', and hence its force structure has also undergone a transformation accordingly. This strategy was basically developed to counter India's 'Cold Start Doctrine'. The new strategy of 'Full Spectrum Deterrence' included the use of TNWs; hence, the force structure has become more diverse to cater for battlefield targets (Counter force). The detail of the force structure is given in the following table.

Pakistan Nuclear Force 2015

Type	Number of Launchers	Range (km)	Warheads Per Launcher	Number of Warheads
Aircraft				
F-16A/B	~24	1,600	1	-32
Mirage III/V	~12	2,100	1	-16
Subtotal	~36			
Land-Based Ballistic Missiles				
Abdali (Hatf-2)	Few	180	1	Few
Ghaznavi (Hatf-3)	16	290	1	16
Shaheen-1 (Hatf-4)	16	750	1	16
Shaheen-1A (Hatf-4)	-	900	1	N/A
Shaheen-2 (Hatf-6)	-8	1500	1	-8
Shaheen-3 (Hatf-?)	-	2750	1	N/A
Ghauri (Hatf-5)	-40	1250	1	-40
Nasr (Hatf-9)	-6	60	4	-6
Subtotal	-86	-86		
Cruise Missiles				
Babur (Hatf-7)	-8	350	3	-8
Ra'ad (Hatf-8)	-	350	1	N/A
Subtotal	-8 130			
Total	130			

Source: Hans M. Kristensen and Robert R. Norris, 'FAS Nuclear Notebook: Pakistani Nuclear Forces, 2015', *Bulletin of the Atomic Scientists.*

Land-Based Missiles including TNWs. Pakistan possesses a wide variety of nuclear capable medium-range ballistic missiles with ranges up to 2,500 km. Pakistan also possesses nuclear tipped Babur Cruise missile with ranges up to 700 km. In April 2012, Pakistan launched a Hatf-4 Shaheen-1A, said to be capable of carrying a nuclear warhead designed to evade missile-defence systems. The Babur cruise missile range can also be extended to 1,000 km or more. These land-based missiles are controlled by Army Strategic Forces Command of Pakistan Army. Pakistan has developed TNWs for use on the battlefield with ranges up to 60 km such as the

Nasr missile. On 19 April 2011, Pakistan successfully tested the Hatf IX, named Nasr, a solid fuelled battlefield range ballistic missile. The missile has been developed by Pakistani National Development Complex and carries a sub-kiloton nuclear war head. The engine comprises a single-stage rocket motor and has an operational range of 60 km. The launch platform is a Transport Erect Launcher (TEL) and is a multi-tube ballistic system. Two Hatf IX Nasr Ballistic Missiles can be carried by a single TEL. Nasr is a quick response system that has shoot and scoot nuclear delivery capability. A quick response system with regard to nuclear weapons is definitely destabilising as supposedly nuclear weapons ought to be used in the gravest circumstances.

Aerial Systems. The PAF has two dedicated units operating 18 aircraft in each squadron of the JF-17 Thunder, believed to be the preferred vehicle for delivery of nuclear weapons. These units are major part of the Air Force Strategic Command, a command responsible for nuclear response. The PAF also operates a fleet of F-16 fighters, of which 18 were delivered in 2012 and are capable of carrying nuclear weapons. With a third squadron being raised, this would bring the total number of dedicated nuclear capable aircraft to a total of 54. The PAF also possesses the Ra'ad Air-Launched Cruise Missile (ALCM), which has a range of 350 km and can carry a nuclear warhead with a yield of between 10 to 35 kt. It has also been reported that an air-launched cruise missile (ALCM) with a range of 350 km has been developed by Pakistan, designated Hatf 8 and named R'aad ALCM, which may theoretically be armed with a nuclear warhead. It was reported to have been test-fired by Mirage III fighter and is believed to be capable of penetrating some air defence/missile defence systems.

Sea-Based Ballistic Missiles. In 2004, Pakistan Navy established the Naval Strategic Forces Command and made it responsible for countering and battling naval-based WMDs. Pakistan is developing a sea-based variant of the Hatf VII Babur, which is a nuclear-capable ground-launched cruise missile, and claimed to have successfully tested it in early 2017. With a stockpile of plutonium, Pakistan would be able to produce a variety of miniature nuclear warheads that would allow it to nuclear-tip the C-802 and C-803 anti-ship missiles as well as being able to develop nuclear torpedoes, nuclear depth bombs and nuclear naval mines.

Nuclear Trajectory – 2030. If Pakistan's internal dynamics remain stable and the China–Pakistan nuclear alliance continues unabated, then Pakistan would have most likely developed its third leg of triad—its naval vector by 2030. Pakistan would generally have 250–300 nuclear weapons (if the nuclear fissile material, especially Plutonium production continues unhindered). This would lead to more diversification of its nuclear assets, especially if its Shaheen-3 and Ra'ad (Hatf-8) get operationalized. Pakistan, thus, has the basic edifice for full-spectrum deterrence and by 2030, both the short- and medium-range missile systems would be available to Pakistan catering for full-spectrum use. But availability of sufficient numbers of warheads, to set full-spectrum deterrence into practice, will depend on many intangible variables. Since the functional parameters are not transparent and uniform, hence accurate prediction of nuclear arsenal becomes difficult. However, Pakistan's delivery systems will likely be a mix of solid-fuelled surface-to-surface ballistic missiles with short and medium ranges, ground and air-launched cruise missiles (some of which may be deployed on surface naval vessels and submarines), gravity bombs delivered by appropriate aerial platforms and maybe Pakistan may acquire nuclear powered submarines.

Doctrinal Thought

Pakistan Army's doctrine of 'offensive defence' seeks to respond to an Indian attack with aggressive counterattacks on Indian Territory. While the Indian doctrine envisages limited objectives, but it in no way can predict the Pakistani response to an offensive into its heartland. In the case of Pakistan, critical value objectives and essential lines of communication lie within tactical depth. Any offensive that threatens these will draw violent reaction and has the potential of escalating beyond India's control and trigger a nuclear response. This doctrine entails Pakistan in the event of hostilities with India will not wait for the enemy's offensive, but rather launch an offensive of its own. The offensive will be a limited advance along narrow fronts with the aim of occupying territory near the border to a depth of 40–50 km. Since Indian forces will not reach their maximum strength near the border for another 48–72 hours, Pakistan might have parity or numerical superiority against the Indians. The Pakistani Army hopes to accomplish three things by this strategy:

- The enemy is kept off-balance as it will be tied up containing the Pakistani offensive into its territory rather than launching an offensive into Pakistani territory.
- The Pakistani Army hopes to contain the fighting on the Indian side of the border so that any collateral or other damage will be suffered by India.
- Indian Territory of strategic importance once seized, will give the Pakistani Army a bargaining chip to be used in the aftermath of a ceasefire brought about by international pressure after 3–4 weeks of fighting.
- The use of tactical battlefield nuclear missiles that provide maximum damage against troop concentrations.

Pakistan has now adopted a revised doctrine that calls for immediate mobilisation of one-fourth of its reserves to defensive positions along the Indian border in case there is a major terrorist attack in India. In the 1990s, Pakistan had added a fourth element, seeking 'strategic depth' against India by establishing a sphere of influence in Afghanistan and Central Asia. Pakistan remains vitally concerned with developments in Iran and Central Asia in general and Afghanistan in particular, as instability on its western border can have dangerous repercussions inside Pakistan.

Key Issues

- ✓ *Pakistan continues to perceive India as an existential threat and ipso facto adheres to its policy of using Jihad to destabilize India or gain strategic depth in Afghanistan.*
- ✓ *Ethno-regional fault lines and secessionist movements in Pakistan have the potential to undermine Pakistan's strategic advantage and can potentially pose multiple criticalities and multi-front dilemmas for Pakistan including undermining China– Pakistan strategic nexus.*
- ✓ *Pakistan's strategic objectives vis-à-vis India include wresting J&K; continue destabilizing India; deny India land access to Afghanistan and Central Asia; and, in conjunction China, restrict India's strategic space in South Asia-IOR and stymie India's economic growth.*
- ✓ *The Pakistani army is following the 'Quranic Concept of War', defined in-house as a distorted version of Islam, which approves use of terror, and assiduously prepare its population, particularly youth, for holy jihad.*
- ✓ *China–Pakistan collusivity is total and spans complete spectrum of hybrid warfare.*
- ✓ *Hybrid warfare strategy of Pakistan combines jihad in the backdrop of the Quranic Concept of War; conventional forces; collusivity with China throughout the hybrid warfare spectrum and effective nuclear deterrent cover for continuing proxy war on India—largely because India has not called Pakistan's nuclear bluff.*
- ✓ *Application of jihad and the Quranic Concept of Warfare enable Pakistan to produce millions of terrorists consistently and wage a low cost war against India, with its military largely untouched.*
- ✓ *Pakistan in conjunction China has an asymmetric edge over India at the sub-conventional level.*
- ✓ *India needs to establish effective deterrent against Pakistan's proxy war and call Pakistan's nuclear bluff in order to raise the cost of Pakistan's proxy war to a level that forces Pakistan to abandon it; exploit Pakistan' fault-lines; present two-*

front dilemma to Pakistan in conjunction Afghanistan and weaken China–Pakistan nexus.

- ✓ *India will continue to face hybrid threats on dual front and must look at its military structures including the Higher Defence Organisation and the war fighting doctrines.*
- ✓ *Western experts have been talking of Balkanisation of Pakistan for quite some time. President Trump has indicated he wants to eradicate Islamic terrorism. Pakistan being the hub of Islamic terrorism in South Asia, India needs to explore the possibility of Balkanizing Pakistan with various stakeholders as this would be strategically advantageous to India.*
- ✓ *Pakistan's deployment of nuclear weapons at sea and change in nuclear strategy from 'Minimum Deterrence' to 'Full Spectrum Deterrence' including use of TNWs for battlefield targets need to be taken note of.*
- ✓ *India must enhance non-contact and asymmetric capabilities speedily in conjunction strategic partners.*

NOTES

1 Jamaat-ud-Dawa Chief Hafiz Saeed Placed on Pak's Exit Control List', The Indian Express, 1 February 2017, http://indianexpress.com/article/world/jamaat-ud-dawa-chief-hafiz-saeed-placed-on-paks-exit-control-list-4502943/.

2 Katoch, PC, 'Why India Should Never Join CPEC', SP's MAI, 10 January 2017, http://www.spsmai.com/experts-speak/?id=311&q=Why-India-should-never-join-CPEC.

3 Pakistan Economic Outlook, Focus Economics, 24 January 2017, http://www.focus-economics.com/countries/pakistan.

4 Pakistan Unemployment Rate Forecast 2016-2020, Trading Economics, http://www.tradingeconomics.com/pakistan/unemployment-rate/forecast.

5 'Trade Between Pakistan and China Continues to Grow at Steady Pace', Balochistan Times, 27 April 2016.

6 Fair, Christene, 'Denying Pakistan the Dividends of Terror', Open Magazine, 23 September 2016, http://www.openthemagazine.com/article/cover-story/denying-pakistan-the-dividends-of-terror.

7 Mirza, Nazir Abbas, 'A Monstrous Experiment', Daily Times, 11 May 2009, https://therearenosunglasses.wordpress.com/2009/05/12/a-monstrous-experiment/.

8 Hoodbhoy, Pervez, 'Pakistan's Westward Drift', Islamic Research Foundation International Inc., 8 September 2008, http://www.irfi.org/articles2/articles_3251_3300/pakistan's%20westward%20 drifthtml.htm.

9 Myres, Joseph C, 'The Quranic Concept of War', http://insct.syr.edu/wp-content/uploads/2013/03/MyersJoseph.Quranic-Concept-of-War.pdf.

10 Ibid.

11 Ibid.

12 Ibid.

13 Ibid.

14 Ibid.

15 Ibid.
16 'Quran Allows Elimination of Troublemakers: M J Akbar', The Times of India, 10 February 2017, http://timesofindia.indiatimes.com/india/quran-allows-elimination-of-troublemakers-m-j-akbar/articleshow/57071594.cms.
17 Dhar, Maloy Krishna, *Open Secrets – India's Intelligence Unveiled*, New Delhi: Manas Publications, 2005.
18 Pakistan, SIPRI, https://www.sipri.org/research/armaments-and-disarmament/nuclear-weapons/world-nuclear-forces/pakistan.
19 Fair, op. cit.
20 Ibid.
21 'US Senate Passes $800m Pakistan Fund', *Dawn*, 16 June 2016, http://www.dawn.com/news/1265197.
22 Congressional Research Service, Pakistan: US Foreign Assistance, 01 July 2013, www.crs.org.
23 Usman Ansari, "Pakistan, China Finalise 8-Sub Construction Plan".
24 Report published by *Hindustan Times*, 21 October 2016, see http://www.hindustantimes.com/world-news/china-confirms-sale-of-8-attack-submarines-to-pakistan-first-delivery-by-2023/story-kqSiZxhkB6r60QvhF2G7CK.html.
25 Alex Calvo, 'Pakistan's Navy: A Quick Look', published by CIMSEC 23 March 2016, sourced from http://cimsec.org/pakistans-navy-quick-look/23227.
26 Ibid.
27 Listner, Michael J, 'Pakistan to Have a Functioning Global Navigation Satellite System by June 2013', published by Space Safety Magazine, 07 November 2012.
28 Ian A Rinehart, 'The Chinese Military: Overview and Issues for the Congress', CRS Report R44196, 24 March 2016, sourced from https://www.fas.org/sgp/crs/row/R44196.pdf.
29 For a discussion on YJ-18 performance, see Goldstein, Lyle J, 'China's YJ-18 Supersonic Antiship Cruise Missile: America's Nightmare', published by National Interest, 1 June 2015, http://nationalinterest.org/feature/chinas-yj-18-supersonic-anti-ship-cruise-missile-americas-13010.
30 'PN Fleet Tanker, Pakistan', published by Naval Technology, see http://www.naval-technology.com/projects/pn-fleet-tanker/. See also, report in *Daily Sabah* on 19 August 2016, http://www.dailysabah.com/defense/2016/08/20/turkish-made-military-tanker-ship-joins-pakistan-navy.
31 Ansari, Usman, "Pakistan Seeks to Energize Naval Modernisation", published by Defense News, 17 June 2015, see http://www.defensenews.com/story/defense/naval/ships/2015/06/17/pakistan-revive-naval-modernization-shipbuilding-china-frigates-dockyard-ksew/71074464/.
32 See Rehman, Iskander, 'Murky Waters: Naval Nuclear Dynamics in the Indian Ocean', published Carnegie Endowment, 9 March 2015, see http://carnegieendowment.org/2015/03/09/murky-waters-naval-nuclear-dynamics-in-indian-ocean-pub-59279.
33 Javeed, Nusrat, 'Indians Aiming at Strikes on Pakistan's Nukes', see http://www.rense.com/general18/indiansaimingatstrikes.htm.
34 See Dalton, Toby and George Perkovitch, 'Alliance is Unstable, not Pakistan's Nukes', published Carnegie Endowment, 16 May 2011, http://carnegieendowment.org/2011/05/16/alliance-is-unstable-not-pakistan-s-nukes/2oi.
35 Quoted by Rehman in 'Murky Waters', op. cit.
36 Bloomberg News, 'Pakistan Could Put Nukes on New Submarines Sold by China', published by Trib Live, 17 April 2015, http://triblive.com/usworld/world/8194853-74/pakistan-nuclear-india.
37 See, for example, Cdr Muhammad Azam Khan (Retd), 'India's Cold Start is Too Hot', published in USNI Proceedings, March 2011, 137 (3), p. 1297.

38 As per World Bank Data, see http://data.worldbank.org/indicator/NE.TRD.GNFS.ZS.

39 Data for imports of hydrocarbons and coal obtained from Energy Information Administration Country Brief for India, updated 14 June 2016. See https://www.eia.gov/beta/international/analysis.cfm?iso=IND.

40 http://paper.seebug.org/papers/APT/APT_CyberCriminal_Campagin/2014/ThreatConnect_Operation_Arachnophobia_Report.pdf.

41 Ibid.

42 https://tribune.com.pk/story/415738/lagging-behind-2040-pakistans-space-oddyssey/.

4

CHINA'S HYBRID WARFARE STRATEGY AND CAPABILITIES 2030

Victorious warriors win first and then go to war, while defeated warriors go to war first and then seek to win.

—Sun Tzu

Background

Comprehensive National Power (CNP) is a sum total of a State's Hard and Soft power. It has many constituents, of which the military power is a major component and also called the ultimate yard stick of national power. With the objective of becoming a 'Great Power', lead Asia as China-Centric and emerge as a strong pole in a Multi-Polar World (Global Power by 2050), China has toiled relentlessly on building its CNP. China's observance of the Gulf Wars led to the *informatisation* of the PLA. But China also witnessed conflicts where crafty diplomacy, wily espionage, terrorism (including cyber terrorism), low-intensity conflict, proxy war, employment of WMDs like dirty/chemical/radiological bombs through non-state actors and a host of other asymmetric approaches were being used to advance own national interests including control of energy sources; principles of asymmetric war were not to use armed forces to compel the enemy to submit to one's will but use all means including armed forces, military and non-military, lethal and non-lethal measures to compel the enemy to accept one's interests. Asymmetric wars exploited the fault-lines of the adversary, instigating weaker/under privileged sections of the society, propagating to its advantage the issue of not so good political health of a nation, exploitation of the diversity based on caste, creed, and community and expressing ethnic affinity towards a particular segment of masses to arouse anti-government sentiments. Such methods adopted to target different sections of the society led to waging asymmetric war on different planes. Therefore, China devised its own way of war fighting.

As per China's White Papers, China seeks to be the 'Sole Asian Power' by 2020 and become a 'Great Power (Global Power)' by 2049 (see Figure 4.1) and this assertion is reinforced by Xi Jinping in his 'China Dream slogan'. In shaping of its strategic space, China aspires to gain a balance of power with a China-led unipolar Asia and a bipolar World with China and USA as its prominent poles. By all indications, China considers India as a rival and is working assiduously to shrink India's strategic space in South Asia (SA) and the IOR despite successive Indian Prime Ministers stating that there is enough space for both India and China to grow. Gandhi ji had once said, 'There is enough in the world for everyone's need, but there isn't enough in the world for everyone's greed'. In China's greed to dominate the world, it shows scant regard to her neighbours, methods, international norms and laws. Therefore, China will pursue a policy of strategic ambivalence against India and at the same time build up its military muscle to asymmetric proportions with a view to coerce India into making policy choices, which are favourable to China's long-term strategic interests.

Figure 4.1: China's Strategic Objectives

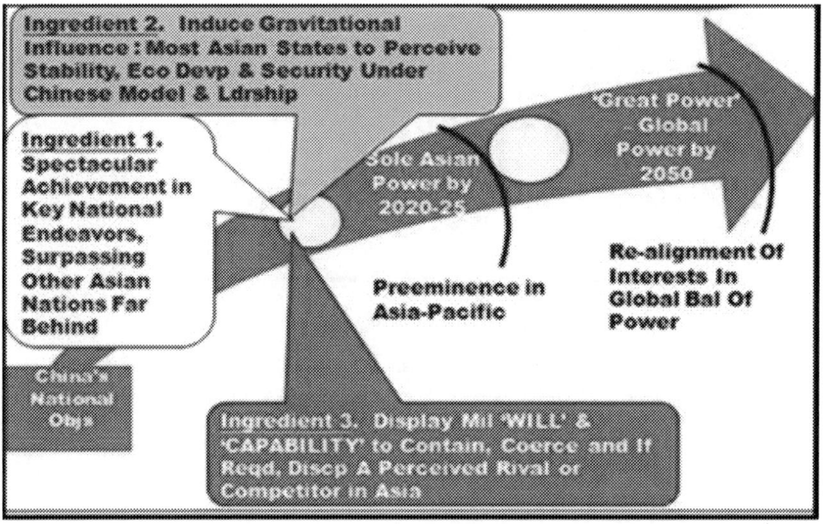

Economy is the main determinant of China's CNP and is a critical driver for its military modernisation. China's economic growth had witnessed an unparalleled rise in the last three decades to a 9-10 per cent growth rate and despite the global slump continued to have a growth rate around 7.4 per cent till 2014, after which there have been more downward fluctuations. As per Trading Economics, GDP Annual Growth Rate in China is expected to be 6.70 per cent by the end of first quarter of 2017, and is expected to fall to 6.5 per cent in 12 months' time. In the long-term, the China GDP Annual Growth Rate is projected to trend around 5.80

per cent in 2020.[1] To boost its economy, China has invested $1.25 trillion abroad through China Development Bank and China Exim Bank, and launched the One Belt-One Road (OBOR) initiative. With Chinese participation in the Regional Comprehensive Economic Partnership (RCEP) that involves 10 ASEAN states, and its FTA partners, involving three billion plus people and combined GDP of about $17 trillion, China contributes to 35 per cent of world trade. China also seeks greater voting rights in World Bank and the Asian Development Bank. See Figure 4.2 also.

Figure 4.2: China GDP Annual Growth Rate

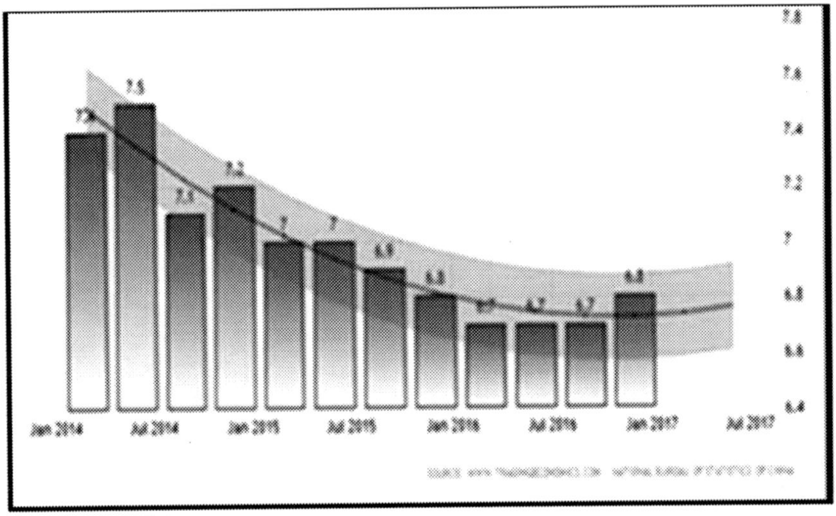

In March 2018, China said its defence spending would increase at the quickest pace in three years, as President Xi Jinping pursues a 'world-class' military capable of projecting force further from the country's coasts. The central government's military outlays are expected to rise 8.1 per cent, to 1.11 trillion yuan ($175 billion) this year; the Chinese Ministry of Finance has said,[2] 'Last year's budget had called for an increase of 7.1 per cent, the slowest pace since at least 1991'. However, no one really knows what is the actual defence spending of China because of multiple factors including the PLA's commercial and private enterprises. Given that China has massive in-house arms manufacturing capabilities as well as resources for indigenous operations and maintenance requirements, the correct means of comparison of defence spending is on Purchasing Power Parity (PPP) basis.[3] Therefore, comparing military spending among major powers using a common US dollar metric may not bring out the correct matrix. On the PPP datum, and using military spending data from SIPRI and economic data from the IMF, the results are quite different from dollar terms; in 2015, the US spent $596 billion in international dollars (the PPP currency) on defence, while China spent \$374 billion and Russia spent a further \$187 billion. Combined Russia and China spent \$561 billion almost at par with the US—just \$35 billion short. Add \$34 billion spent by Iran and China, Russia, Iran combined defence spending equals the US. This is significant considering the dynamics of changing geopolitical equations. As for the defence spending of \$175 billion announced in March 2018, while the figure equals about one-quarter of US outlays, the Stockholm International Peace Research Institute (SIPRI) estimates that China's actual spending is about 55 per cent more than officially stated. See Figure 4.3.

Figure 4.3: China's Defence Budget 2011-2018

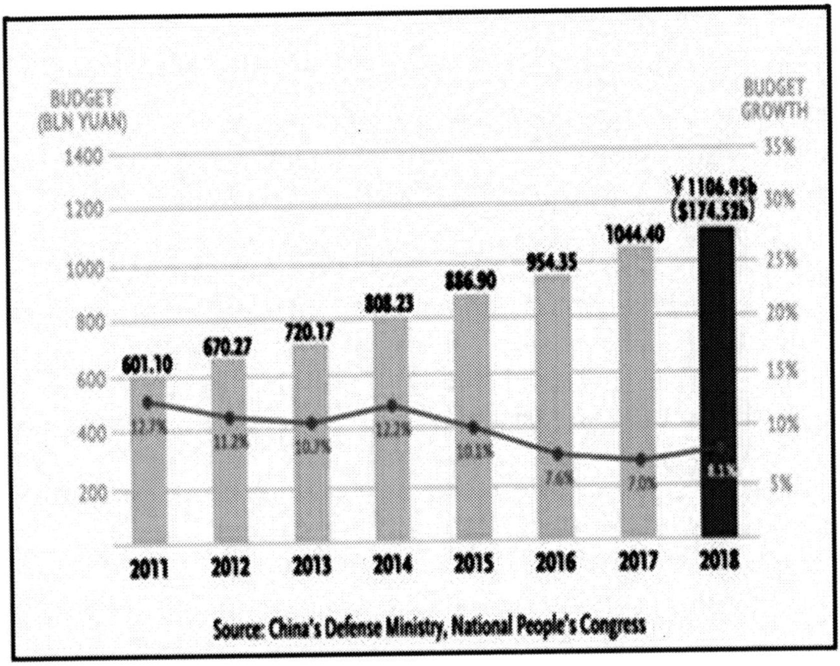

Geostrategic Location of China

China is geographically restrained in the East and the South China Sea and is surrounded by a web of countries that contest China's maritime claims and enjoy defence alliances with the US. The US together with these countries is well postured to exploit China's critical vulnerability, i.e. domination of SLOCs and compounding China's Malacca Dilemma. Equally imperative is the control of China's peripheral 'Non-Han' strategic buffers for the security of the Heartland and for fructifying China's Eurasia and South Asia strategy. In this calculus, the growing salience of Xinjiang and China's maritime outreach stands out. Shaping of strategic space is extremely crucial for China before it can up the ante to alter the balance of power. In this, China needs to be cognisant of its vulnerabilities opened up by the US re-balancing to Asia and the covert actions it is taking to limit China's inroads into Africa and West Asia, and this covert rivalry has the potential to spread to the South American continent in the future.

The geographic configuration of Indian Peninsula and strategic location of Andaman and Nicobar afford India a competitive advantage to dominate China's SLOCs in the Indian Ocean, the Bay of Bengal and the Arabian Sea and petrochemical hubs along the transportation corridors leading to Kunming and Xinjiang respectively. It is for this reason that China has established the CPEC and the Gwadar Port, with CPEC also connected to the Pakistani ports of Omari and Karachi.

China's 19th Congress and Rise of Xi Jinping

China's 19th Congress, held from 18 to 25 October 2017, was used by Xi Jinping to retire his anti-corruption Tsar, Wang Qishan, due to his age [though in the 13th National People's Congress (NPC) held in March 2018, Wang Qishan was made the Vice President with both, President and Vice President not restricted by any tenure and thus, Wang Qishan and Xi Jingping can rule China till their demise], yet in all else he has followed no convention having filled up the Politburo Standing Committee (PBSC), the Central Military Commission (CMC) and the Politburo with his chosen allies, and not brought in anyone from the 6th Generation as nominee(s) for succession in 2022 to circumvent the inner party tussles, thereby enabling his firm grip on the Party. Xi has hidden his true intentions, how he intends to lead China, though he has given some new timelines on the route to his China Dream (little different from the previous): become a 'moderately prosperous society' by 2020, a 'basically modernised nation' by 2035 and a 'rich and powerful socialist nation' by 2050. However, now that the Chinese Constitution has allowed Xi Jinping to serve as President indefinitely (read 'for life'), there is no gainsaying that he may not become more aggressive in making China a 'Great Power'.

Significantly, during the 90th Anniversary of the PLA in Aug 2017, while addressing the troops in Zhurihe Combined Arms Training Base, Xi focused on the party's goal of building a strong military under 'the new situation', which he briefly summarised as having three core elements: building a people's army which obeys the party's command and can fight and win battles and has excellent work style; creating a new military strategic command and developing new military strategies and guidelines. The tasks given to the PLA by Xi Jinping while making major structural changes to the CMC and the PLA since Dec 2015 demanded increased levels of joint/integrated training for its operational and tactical units, higher quality of joint Tactical Command, service headquarters, and unit staffs that would be crucial for the planning, command, and control of campaigns. But the changes to the 19th CMC, which indicate very close oversight, run contrary to these requirements. The problems envisaged then—that some commanders cannot judge the situation; understand intention of higher authorities; make operational decisions; deploy troops and deal with unexpected situations—would continue for some time more as apparently the leadership may feel inhibited from such independent decision making, a key requirement necessary to win future network centric hybrid wars.

China's Strategic Objectives vis-à-vis India

There is no doubt that India and China are simultaneously moving upward on relative power trajectories; both are expanding economies supporting rising defence budgets and capabilities including nuclear weapons, combined with the availability of massive manpower reserves. Both China and India are ancient civilisations that merit future 'great power' status. However, China's intent for the international relations of the Indo-Pacific region to be reordered to reflect its historical position as the 'Middle Kingdom' is fuelling concerns that it wants India to play the subordinate role. The Sino-Indian relationship is complex, as a result of not only history and unresolved borders but also because underlying tensions are being exacerbated by current-day expectations of greatness and a trend of mistrust of their respective geopolitical intent. China's 'Great Game' is the containment of India and that, while the initial focus of Sino-Indian competition was centred on South Asia, China is concerned that an emerging India poses a strong competitor for China from South, West, Southeast and Central Asia to the Indian and Pacific Oceans, where their interests and influences will clash. China, because of its rapid rise and past history, views itself as the natural leader in Asia, with a resultant propensity to contain the rise of rivals, and India as its major medium- to long-term competitor. China's ultimate objective would seem to be to curb the influence of India, the other rising Asian power and a perceived rival in South Asia, India's traditional backyard.

In South Asia, China's manoeuvrings for influence and power can best be seen in the Sino-Pakistan alliance. This relationship, established in 1962, is the strongest in the region encompassing formal military, nuclear and economic alliance between the two nations. It has provided China with geopolitical and geostrategic advantages over India in both South and Central Asia. It has provided China to use Pakistan to counterbalance India, preventing India from only focusing on China, and China gaining the strategic land route to the Indian Ocean through Pakistan. The centrality of China in Pakistan's strategic calculus, at the expense of its relationship with India, has further soured the mistrust between India and Pakistan. The Sino-Pakistan alliance has provided China with a key ally in its strategy to constrain India, which will be discussed later in the paper. The alliance has also provided critical strategic benefits to Pakistan, to the detriment of India's balance of power. These benefits include diplomatic support, military-to-military cooperation, and nuclear capability. Diplomatically, China has consistently defended Pakistan in international forums and provided Pakistan with moral support in times of need.[4] The Sino-Pakistan military-to-military cooperation has been the most enduring pillar of their alliance and is aimed at their shared anxiety of India. The alliance has emphasized the need to counterbalance the relative strength of India's military capability in comparison to Pakistan's. A key component is based on China's assessment that it must ensure that Pakistan has the appropriate military capabilities to defend its interests from the perceived threats of its rival India.[5] As a result, after the US failed to support Pakistan after the 1965 Indo-Pakistan war, China has continued to provide Pakistan with modern military equipment and arms.

Chinese assistance to counter India is not just confined to military equipment sales; it also involves the modernisation of Pakistan's military industrial complex. The modernisation is focused on Pakistan's naval capability and developing its military aircraft manufacturing capability. Such support is aimed at countering India's military strength in South Asia and meets Beijing's long-standing policy to arm Islamabad with every weapon system that India has (and will have) in order to maintain a favourable balance of power in South Asia. The final component of Sino-Pakistan military cooperation, aimed at countering India, is the development of Pakistan's nuclear capability. This cooperation commenced in 1974 includes Chinese assistance in building Pakistan's three nuclear power plants/laboratories and nuclear weapons. China has also supported Pakistan's development of its short- and medium-range ballistic missile capability and the transfer of technology. This nuclear cooperation is seen as a critical pillar of the alliance and is aimed at balancing India's conventional and nuclear capability, if not ensuring that Pakistan enjoys an edge over India in the nuclear sector.

Beijing views the Sino-Pakistan alliance as a lasting partnership that has helped contain India despite the pressures of time and shifting geopolitical and geostrategic landscapes. The alliance meets China's strategic goals in South Asia as Beijing prefers a powerful and well-armed Pakistani military that helps mount pressure by proxy on India.[6] From India's perspective, Beijing's overt conventional and secretive nuclear support to Pakistan only adds further to India's mistrust of China's intent in South

Asia. China would continue to attempt to isolate India and the region and beyond. It would aim to undercut India's economic growth from within, using its 'deep connections' and create socio-political and socio-economic turmoil to subvert India's steady rise. It would aim to curtail India's outreach within the region and within ASEAN to enable it to secure its 'edge and sides', as part of its strategy based on the principles of *Wei Qi*. At an opportune moment, in the near to medium term, it would attempt to cause a politico-military embarrassment for India.

In the above backdrop, China's strategic objectives vis-à-vis India would likely be as follows:

- Strengthen Pakistan to countervail India and confine India to South Asia.
- Expand power asymmetry exponentially to keep India subdued.
- Nudge India to accept subordinate role in Asia.
- Hedge India's economic rise asymmetrically.
- Calibrate economic engagement to ensure availability of Indian markets.
- Shrink India's Strategic Space in South Asia/IOR through gravitational pull to smaller states to wean them away from India; cultivate Bhutan and Nepal as strategic buffers; indirect posturing in POK; leverage border and water Issues; perpetuate two-front collusive hybrid threat dilemma; maximize Chinese influence and freedom of manoeuvre in IOR; undermine Indian influence in Afghanistan and neutralise Tibet Card.
- Realise own territorial claims in western, central and eastern sectors including Arunachal Pradesh.
- Prevent India capture POK.
- Consolidate Sino-Russia-Iranian Alliance.
- Scuttle India's entry into Nuclear Suppliers Group (NSG), United Nations Security Council (UNSC) and UN resolution against Pakistan.

HYBRID WARFARE STRATEGY

Abetting Insurgencies in India

During Mao's time, Chinese intelligence infiltration operations into Nepal and Burma (now Myanmar) led to the rise of Maoist insurgencies in Nepal, aim being to install a regime that was not friendly to India and US, as revealed by Debka files. Similar Chinese intelligence operations led to the rise of the Japanese Red Army, the New People's Army of Philippines, Khmer Rouge of Cambodia and Shining Path in Peru. For decades, Naga rebels and other northeast insurgents had been travelling to China through northern Myanmar for training, arms and financial support. When the Royal Bhutan Army routed ULFA and Bodo camps in Bhutan, China provided refuge to their cadres on Chinese soil and continued to support and provide arms to them. In 2014, four Chinese nationals were apprehended with fake Indian documents, on a mission to meet Naga rebels in the northeast.

China has been supporting and arming the Indian Maoists, PLA of Manipur and Kachen rebels in Myanmar. When ULFA militant leader Paresh Barua was kicked out from Bangladesh, China provided sanctuary to him at Ruli in China. The NSCN (K) abrogated its 13-year ceasefire with India on behest of China. In April 2015, Chinese intelligence established the United Liberation Front of West, South, East Asia (ULFWSEA) in Myanmar, bringing under common umbrella nine insurgent groups in the northeast including the NSCN (K) and ULFA.[7] China has also established a deadly proxy in Myanmar in the United Wa State Army (UWSA) in the Shan province of Myanmar that straddles the Golden Triangle. China has armed the UWSA with machine guns, armoured vehicles, shoulder-fired air defence weapons and even missile-fitted helicopter flown in via Thailand.[8]

China had developed links with the Taliban even before the US invasion of Afghanistan, and was providing training to them in China. China had reportedly been providing advisors and IR SAMs to the Taliban to fight US and NATO forces in Afghanistan. By abetting insurgencies, China keeps its adversaries destabilised, suppressed and forced to look inwards, keep Chinese assets safe (like economic ventures in Afghanistan), and further own national interests.

Playing Pakistani Jihadi Card

China provides tacit approval to Pakistan's anti-India jihad because it meets China's strategic objectives vis-à-vis India as discussed above. This helps keep India internally embroiled, keeping the Indian security establishment taxed besides being a drain on the economy. Same is the case in Afghanistan where China wants to, in conjunction with Pakistan, boot out US and NATO forces even it means complete takeover by Taliban and the end of democracy with Sharia imposed. China has emerged as the central actor behind the problems in J&K. China has entrench itself fully in projects in POK-Pakistan, CPEC, and Gwadar. Pakistani proxies and radical mullah-terrorists are benefited from Chinese veto at the UN; China has repeatedly barred the UN from branding Masood Azhar, JeM chief as terrorist. Earlier, China was doing so under the pretext of putting the motion on 'technical hold'; however, China has now said that she is doing so on 'professional' grounds. This is abetment of terrorism, but China has no compunctions of doing this openly. In return, Pakistan puts a lid on Chinese genocide in Xinjiang and keeps the East Turkestan Islamic Movement (ETIM) cadres in Pakistan under check. China also needed to divert

Uighur youth from Xinjinag, and who better than Pakistan to provide terrorist training and send them off for *jihad*. For some time now, intelligence inputs were indicating LeT (covert arm of ISI) providing terrorist training to Uighurs. Concurrently, reports and photographs have appeared of Uighurs fighting China's proxy war in faraway Syria.

Afghan terrorists have been operating in J&K in the past; it is perhaps a matter of time when Uighur terrorists will be infiltrated into J&K for jihad. After all, it is a method of providing employment and what better than to divert radicalized youth to J&K for jihad rather than undertaking terrorist acts in Xinjiang. Significantly, the BSF has already found a diary written in Chinese on the body of a terrorist killed along the LoC last December. Intelligence agencies have reported that Chinese funds are coming into J&K for terrorism. This is a significant development, much more than the recovery of Chinese flags in Baramula during search operations last year and sighting of PLA soldiers on Pakistani posts along the LoC. China has dug some 22 tunnels in Gilgit-Baltistan under the garb of hydel projects where locals are not permitted to approach anywhere in the vicinity. These tunnels are reportedly being used to deploy strategic weapons and house missiles. Pakistan's export of terrorism both in India and Afghanistan has gone up with China's entry into POK and Pakistan. That is why ceasefire violations, terror attacks, infiltration, and violence in J&K have shot up exponentially. The China factor in Kashmir must always remain in focus of Indian policy makers.

Cyber Warfare

Cyber plays vital role in hybrid warfare. China is one of the most active nations in cyberspace and has made no secret that President Xi Jinping's 'new model of great power relations' policy means that it will not be afraid to challenge the US and the rest of the world in areas it considers a core interest, such as cyberspace. Substantial money, manpower and resources are devoted to develop China's cyber capabilities: mix of dedicated personnel, advanced equipment, and cyber-attack methodologies. PLA's 'Unit 61398' is dedicated for cyber warfare. It has a staff of 'hundreds if not thousands' of people, trained in advanced network security, digital signal processing, and covert communications who have access to extensive infrastructure of computer systems around the world.[9] Taiwan recently identified another unit of the General Staff Department's (GSD's) Third Department that is involved in cyber-activities, engaged in technical aspects of surveillance and intelligence gathering on the Taiwanese agencies, intercepting telecommunications signals, hacking computers and mobile phone service networks and satellite imagery reconnaissance.

China has 'reached out' to people with the necessary cyber skills in the IT sector and academic community to help fill any gaps in state expertise and personnel when needed. There is also ample evidence that China uses hackers and other cybercriminals to accomplish operations that it is officially unwilling or unable to commit. To be sure, cybercrime is often intimately tied to state-sponsored threats to cyber security. The use of affiliated hackers is based on the idea that cybercriminals can be used to escape the attribution that may otherwise provide the necessary legal, military or diplomatic links that other countries can use to prove China's official participation in cyber attacks. In October 2014, the FBI issued a warning that a Chinese hacking collective known as Axiom has been engaged in a well-resourced, sophisticated campaign to steal valuable data from US government agencies. According to the warning, Axiom, and other state-sponsored Chinese hacking groups like them, are 'exceedingly stealthy and agile by comparison' to Unit 61398.

China's cyber capabilities are organized based on a strategy that calls for early application of its cyber warfare units against an adversary to establish information dominance, taking and maintaining control of an adversary's access to its own information, and disrupting the flow of information necessary for 'decision-making or combat operations'. Information dominance requires that Chinese cyber capabilities are deployed pre-emptively or as early as necessary to support more traditional combat actions; however, in the event of asymmetric operations not including conventional operations, these cyber warfare capabilities will be employed continuously. China also has a fundamentally different understanding of aggression. For the Chinese, there is little difference between peacetime and wartime cyber espionage, and they have engaged in cyber warfare whenever they so want.

Space

China spends $2 to $3 billion annually on its space programme compared to some $19 billion by NASA. Although China remains decades behind the US in terms of space technology and know-how, it has managed to fast-forward innovation by leveraging existing technologies,[10] its inexpensive labour and material markets. After successfully launching 19 missions in 2015, China planned more than 20 space missions in during 2016, range of civilian and military missions to test new rockets, launch a space laboratory, hone China's manned spaceflight capability and loft new satellites into orbit—all while furthering plans to bring a habitable space station online by 2022 and put Chinese astronauts on the moon in the mid-2020s. At the same time, China is investing in anti-satellite (ASAT) technologies that would destroy or disable space-based assets in the event of conflict.

Considering the fact that even a superpower like the US relies heavily on satellites for intelligence collection and communication, in 2007, China publicly demonstrated a ASAT weapon strike by launching a ground-based interceptor missile at one of its own defunct satellites in orbit, destroying it (and creating a cloud of dangerous space debris). With respect to ASATs, the CSIS states, 'There are a lot of avenues to go after satellites, and what worries people, is that the Chinese are pursuing all of them. The question becomes, 'if they're so into peace, why are they building so many weapons'? China's space activities certainly need monitoring considering the manner in which these can contribute in hybrid warfare with militarization of space.

Conventional

China's conventional forces and their capabilities are discussed later in this chapter (also see Appendix 'D' attached). These are under reorganisation presently. Before 2016, besides the Central Military Commission CMC, there were four General Departments, seven Military Regions (MR), the Air Force, the Navy, and the Second Artillery. The reorganised PLA is the CMC, Army, Air Force, Navy, Rocket Force, Strategic Support Force, and five Theatre Commands. The Second Artillery has been renamed Rocket Force. The Strategic Support Force combines the functions of intelligence, technical reconnaissance, electronic warfare, cyber warfare and space warfare. The Western Theatre Command (WTC) is the largest of the five commands, responsible for China's borders with Myanmar, India, Bhutan, Nepal and Afghanistan. It also looks after the turbulent region of Xinjiang, and TAR (see Figure 4.4).

Figure 4.4: Organisational Structure—PLA

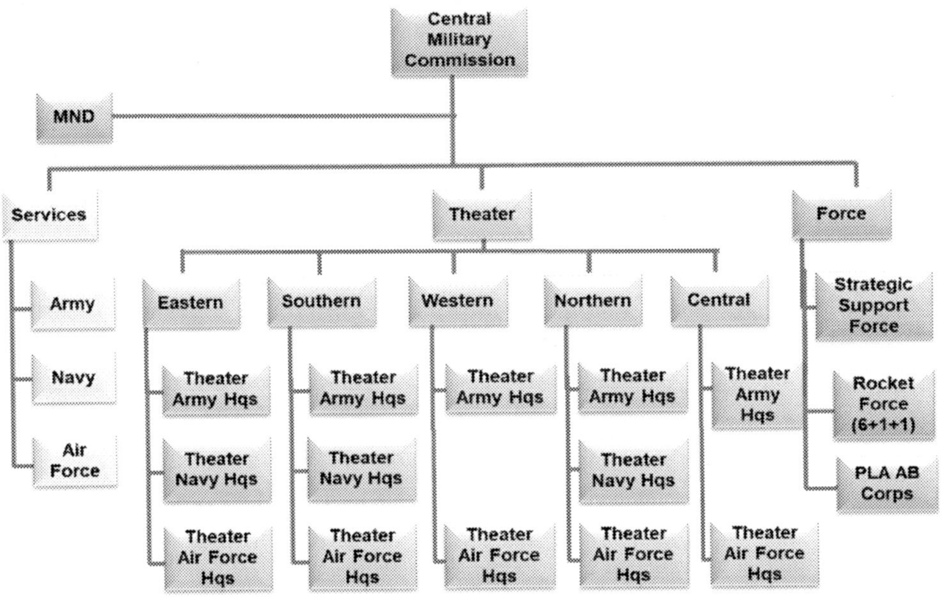

Conscription is enshrined in Article 55 of China's Constitution, 'It is a sacred duty of every citizen of the People's Republic of China to defend his or her motherland and resist invasion. It is an honored obligation of the citizens of the People's Republic of China to perform military service and to join the militia forces'. The legal basis of conscription was stated to be the 1984 Military Service Law, which describes military service as a duty for all citizens without distinction of race and religious creed. But due to large population, conscription only exists in theory. However, every Chinese citizen, both male and female, who attend further education are reportedly required to attend a military training period of around 20 days as a part of a military education. While conventional forces are part of hybrid warfare, the advantage that China has is that development projects undertaken globally by China are executed either by PLA-owned companies or companies contracted by them, and in both cases have a mix of regular and former PLA personnel in form of managers, technicians or workers in civilian garb. There is adequate sprinkling of intelligence and special operations operatives as well. Unlike, India that follows the system of Build, Operate and Transfer (BOT) for projects abroad, China does not transfer projects once completed but continues to operate them. This gives tremendous advantage for intelligence collection, as well as planning and execution of hybrid warfare strategy. Chinese missions too are packed with purportedly former PLA officers, some of whom may actually be serving. For example, a Counsellor-level official at the Chinese Embassy at New Delhi in 2014 admitted privately that he was a Brigadier of PLA.

Nuclear

China possesses WMDs including chemical and nuclear weapons. China's first nuclear test took place in 1964, and it tested the first hydrogen bomb in 1967. The tests continued until 1996, when China signed the Comprehensive Test Ban Treaty (CTBT). China acceded to the Biological and Toxin Weapons Convention (BWC) in 1984 and ratified the Chemical Weapons Convention (CWC) in 1997. Though China declared in 1997 that it had dismantled its 'offensive' chemical warfare (CW) programme, the US maintains China has an 'advanced' CW programme under cover of research and development. The number of nuclear warheads in China's arsenal is maintained state secret. The Federation of American Scientists in 2015 estimated China's arsenal having about 260 total warheads. According to some estimates, the country could 'more than double' the number of warheads on missiles that could threaten the United States by the mid-2020s.[11]

Considering that China's concept of 'Unrestricted Warfare' professes the use of both 'atomic' and 'terrorism', China promoting CBRN terrorism is very much a possibility, besides the use 'atomic' as part of hybrid warfare. A 1.5 kg Uranium mine recovered by the Indian Army in Assam during January 2015 could well have been supplied to insurgents by China.

Psychological Operations

China's considers psychological operations vital to hybrid warfare. For example, after the 1962 War, China withdrew to the North of the McMohan Line unilaterally. Till today, we in India are trying to understand why they did so. While China wanted to gain moral ascendancy, this action put a lot of psychological pressure on the minds of Indians. For close to 40 years after the war, India suffered from the "1962 Syndrome". What is this syndrome? In any action that India contemplated, the factor of how China will react to that action weighed in the minds of decision makers. This is an example of highest form of psychological warfare. From 1960 to 1985 China had offered a package settlement which implied that mainly the issue can be settled on the status quo with some adjustments. India proposed a sector by sector settlement with Eastern sector being the first. Starting from 1986, China's position started hardening as they started claiming areas south of the McMohan Line. After the signing of the Agreement on the Maintenance of Peace and Tranquillity along the Line of Actual Control in 1993, Confidence Building Measures in the Military Field Along the Line of Actual Control in the India—China Border Areas in 1996 and Political Parameters and Guiding Principles for the Settlement of the India–China Boundary Question in 2005, the then Chinese Ambassador to India made a statement in 2006 that China claims the whole of Arunachal Pradesh. By shifting its stance and using the media effectively, China has managed to keep India guessing and thereby gaining the psychological advantage.

Does China behave only with India in this manner? To answer this question, one has to look at its strategic behaviour in the recent past. From the way China has handled the East and South China Sea issues and the reaction of other countries after the Permanent Court of Arbitration's decision of 12 July 2016 on the South China Sea issue, it can be clearly seen that it has been able to coerce the other countries and moderated their behaviour. China's reaction to any action in the South China Sea weighs heavily on the other countries. The aggressive behaviour that China displays is part of the psychological warfare strategy that it has adopted and it is achieved through legal and media war fares. China justifies its claims by trying to legalise them through some historical records and employs all the media that is available to the country, i.e. print, visual, and cyber, to propagate its claims.

Global Times published an article on 27 September 2012 in which it quoted a fisherman named Xu Jianxing from Zhoushan as saying that local fishermen fished in waters within 12 miles of the Diaoyu (Senkaku) islands until the mid-1990s. Such news is catchy and attracts the attention on the local population who then supports China's claim to the Senkaku islands. It also uses such information to build the legal justification for its stance. When one critically analyses the PLA's official website, (english.chinamil.com.cn), one can see an effort to project the technological advancements and the capabilities of China's military more than the actuals. It serves two purposes. One, it influences the population favorably and second, it imposes caution on the adversary by conveying that the PLA is a better force.

A group of PLA analysts has created a typology of psychological warfare operations. By a study of number of case studies, they have classified them into coercive, deceptive, alienating, and defensive psychological warfare. What China is practicing now is coercive psychological warfare. By doing that, it tries to weaken the resolve of the adversary to enter into a conflict. This is in line with Sun Zu's teaching of winning a war without fighting. Incidentally, psychological operations are not new to the Chinese, dating back to 4,000 years. During the Tang dynasty, an oath was to be taken by everyone in its army to carry out propaganda. The aim was to attack enemy's strategy and diplomacy. The main principle was to control the hearts, minds and morale. The main idea was to focus on the enemy commander's decision-making skills and personal traits.

Hybrid Warfare Strategy

Hybrid Warfare strategy includes abetting insurgencies, playing Pakistan's jihadi card, cyber, outer space, conventional and nuclear.

CAPABILITIES 2030

Defence Spending

As per the IISS Military Balance 2017, Asian states together spent US $367.7 billion in 2016, up by 5.3 per cent when compared with the 2015 figure of US $349.1 billion. In 2012–16, Asian real-terms defence spending grew by 5–6 per cent each year. In 2016, China accounted for 39.4 per cent of this total spend. The projected defence spending by China this year is at $175 billion and SIPRI's estimate that it may be 55 per cent more than the official figures puts it upwards of $271 billion. China always deflects criticism over its defence expenditure citing: (1) it is in line with its economic growth and is still well below the US military spending, especially compared to the GDP ratio; (2) it is necessary given the increasingly complex security environment in China's periphery; (3) it needs to develop military capabilities through investment in high-tech weapon technology research. The focus of defence expenditure is also on developing high-technology defence in military and non-military enterprises that would equip their private industries to meet PLA's increasing demand on weaponry and equipment. SIPRI estimates that beyond year 2035, Chinese defence spending will overtake that of the US and take a sharp upward rise. See Figure 4.5.

Figure 4.5: SIPRI Forecast of Chinese Military Spending

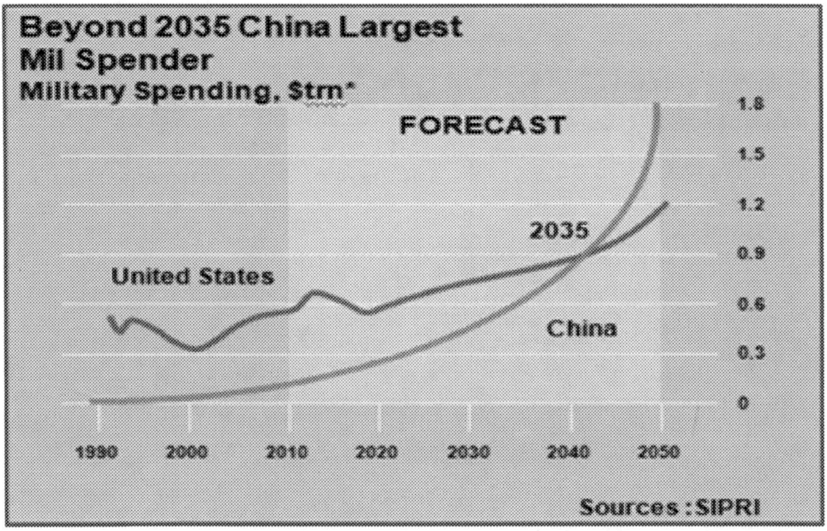

Higher Defence Organisation

Reorganisation of the PLA has been briefly discussed earlier. The CMC is China's highest military command and control organization, standing at the apex of the military (nuclear and conventional) chain of command and military-industrial complex. It commands a 2.3 million strong regular force, the People's Liberation Army (PLA); the 6,60,000 People's Armed Police Force (PAPF) and 8 million Militia. The CMC has 11 members, at the apex is the President and there are 10 members. All the members, less the Minister of Defence, are all from the military hierarchy. The PLA enjoys close proximity to the CMC and does not take orders directly from the state council, which comprises various ministers. Therefore, there exists *complete politico-military synergy in the National Command Authority. Such jointness is pervasive between the CMC and other organs of the military as also at the five Theatre Commands (post-reorganization of the seven military regions) where all the services and civil services work under a unified command structure* China's President Xi Jinping is the Chairman of CMC and Chairman of the Communist Party Politburo, the highest policy-making forum. Last year, Xi Jinping was also proclaimed C-in-C of

PLA, and thus enjoys total power. A good insight into the organization of the NCA and Military Area commands is covered by Dennis J Blasko in his book '*The Chinese Army Today, Tradition and Transformation for the 21st Century*. In this regard, the following organisational tree (Figure 4.6) is instructive, with jointness starting from the CMC percolating down to the Military Districts.

Figure 4.6: Organisation of CMC

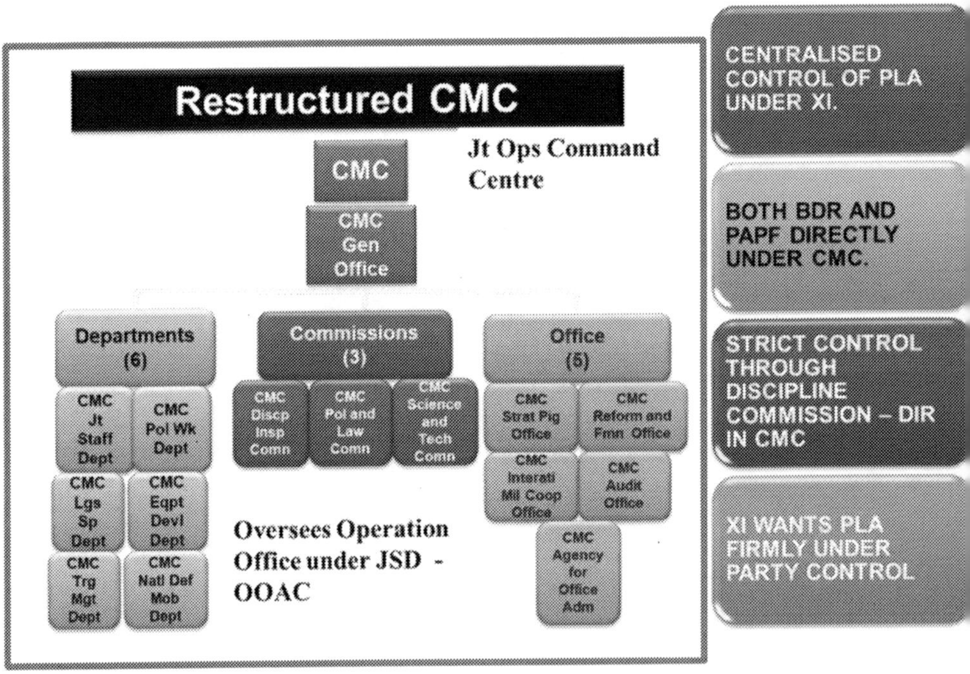

Defence Industry

Chairman Jiang Zemin was the one who initiated the Revolution in Military Affairs (RMA) in China. He and Hu Jintao, both with engineering background, were the driving force behind the technological modernisation of the PRC and the PLA. It was because of them that China concentrated on R&D, especially in 'niche' technologies and made technology a major driver of change. Though it has been a story of many ups and downs, the next two decades are expected to be crucial. China is benefitting from its selective investments in Science and Technology undertaken by the Ministry of Science and Technology (MOST), and having sponsored higher education for its students abroad, is also benefitting from the 'Reverse' Brain Drain. The contributions of the Chinese Academy of Sciences (CAS), Chinese Academy of Engineering (CAE) and the work being undertaken in its universities is significant and China is fast emerging as an important source of scientific papers and patents reflecting its growing scientific prowess. From a global innovativeness ranking of 24 in 2004, China has jumped to the sixth position in 2009, and targets to be fifth by 2020 and by 2040-50, attain technological parity with the US. In terms of an Arms exports, the PRC has already become the third largest exporting nation,[12] with nearly 35 per cent of her exports going to Pakistan.

China's Military Industrial Complex (MIC), which has emerged as largest in Asia, comprises more than a thousand State Owned Enterprises (SOE) and employs at least a million workers, several thousand scientists, engineers and technicians. The Chinese MIC is unique in the sense that it produces the full range of military equipment, starting from small arms to armoured vehicles to fighter aircraft to warships and submarines, in addition to nuclear weapons and ballistic missiles.

While reforms in the defence industry focused on re-organizing the R&D, its industrial base was integrated with the civil sector and selectively absorbed foreign technology. The National Defence Science, Technology and Industry Commission (NDSTIC) was made the coordinating body for both research and development as also for production and reports directly to the CMC's 'National Defence Industries Committee'. This was necessitated to break down the barriers between the defence and the industry. The NDSTIC, through its various trading arms like the China Xinshidai Cooperation, coordinates the procurement of foreign technology. In addition, large SOEs, like the China Northern Industrial Cooperation (NORINCO), have become part of this vast conglomeration. Apart from direct state funding, the NDSTIC also generated funds through direct arms sales for hard cash. The NDSTIC adopted a contractual approach and started, what is called a process of 'creative adaptation' by indigenising critical parts of foreign weapons systems and equipment and then developing them as 'reverse engineered' indigenous systems. The idea was to absorb technology, essentially from Russia and Israel and then innovate to make it a potent weapon system by what is called 'disruptive innovation'.

Since 1998, China has adopted a series of policies to revamp the structures and operations of the defence procurement system and reform operations of the defence enterprises. These were aimed at inculcating the principles of 'competition, evaluation, supervision, and encouragement' or what came to be called 'Four Mechanisms'. The aim was to centralize and standardize weapon procurement decisions while de-centralising defence-enterprise operations to increase initiative for efficiency, higher quality production and eventually innovation. This has shown positive results in the Missile, Ship-building, Military Aviation, and in the IT sectors. Apart from military R&D, some of the other 'dual-use' fields that the Chinese scientific faculty is actively engaged in and are expected to give the Chinese a 'generation leap' in the future are listed next:

- **Nano Technology and Nano Science**. The research in Nano technology in China is pioneered by the National Centre for Nano Science and Technology, Nano polis, Suzhou and the National Natural Science Foundation of China. In addition, at present there are approximately thirty institutions in China, engaged in basic Nanotechnology Research.
- **Space Systems and Means of Delivery**. The China Aerospace Science and Technology Corporation and the China Academy of Space Technology are the lead institutes for developing the space-based surveillance systems including electronic surveillance satellites and the China Academy of Launch Technology is for means of delivery. The BeiDou 2 series of satellites, a latest example, with effective protection against electromagnetic interference and attack and the Long March series of rockets are some of the technologies developed, which have made China self-reliant in space launching capability and enhanced the navigation, tracking and targeting capabilities of PLA.
- **Directed and Kinetic Energy Weapons Technology**. Programme 863 China's technological research and development programme has been closely tied to the operations of the General Armaments Department's Project 921 and COSTIND (now known as SASTIND) of the People's Liberation Army and is responsible for the development of the Directed and Kinetic Weapons Technology as part of its ASAT Weapons programme.
- **Nuclear Engineering**
- **Biometrics, Bio-technology and Bio-Medical Equipment**
- **Lasers and Optic-Mechanics**. Research Center of Laser Fusion at the China Academy of Engineering Physics at Mianyang is the lead institute for research in this field. In 2012, Shenguang 3 (Divine Light 3), a high-power super-laser facility was completed. The two strategic implications that emerge are that it may accelerate China's next-generation thermonuclear weapon development and advance China's directed energy laser weapons programme.
- **Materials**
- **IT and Telecomrelated Hard and Soft Ware**
- **Hypersonic Vehicle Technology Project**. The development of the Hypersonic Cruise Vehicle (HCV) or the Shenlong (Divine Dragon) space plane project is being done at the 10th Research Institute under the China Academy of Launch Technology and Qian Xuesen National Engineering Science Experiment Base in Beijing's Huairou district. The HCV developed

is capable of manoeuvring at greater than Mach 5 speeds and flying at near space altitudes.

Defence Cooperation

Pakistan. China is the strongest ally of Pakistan in the world and words like 'higher than the mountains, deeper than the oceans, stronger than steel, dearer than eyesight and sweeter than honey' are used repeatedly to describe this relationship very often. China and Pakistan have traditionally valued one another as a strategic hedge against India. Husain Haqqani, Pakistani ambassador to the US, stated in 2006, 'For China, Pakistan is a low-cost secondary deterrent to India; for Pakistan, China is a high-value guarantor of "security against Indi"'.[13] Since 1962, China has been a steady source of military equipment to the Pakistani Army, helping establish ammunition factories, providing technological assistance and modernizing existing facilities. China and Pakistan are involved in several projects to enhance military and weaponry systems, which include the development of the Chinese tailor made for Pakistan JF-17 Thunder fighter aircraft, K-8 Karakorum advance training aircraft, a training aircraft for the PAF based on the Chinese domestic Hongdu L-15, space technology, AWACS systems, Al-Khalid tanks, which China granted license production and made modifications based on the initial Chinese Type 90 and/or MBT-2000. China has helped Pakistan in launching communication satellite PAKSAT 1R, 57 optical satellite and high-resolution remote sensing satellite system to be launched in 2016. China is also providing GPS coverage to Pakistan and training Pakistani astronauts for space flights on board Chinese spacecrafts. The Chinese have designed advanced weapons for Pakistan, making it a strong military power in the Asian region. The armies have a schedule for organizing joint military exercises. The CPEC, commissioning of the Gwadar Port and access of Chinese navy to Pakistani sea ports have major strategic implications for India.

Myanmar. China has developed a major Rail–Road–Pipeline corridor from Kyaukpyu in Myanmar to Kunming in Yunnan. Though a commercial venture, it has the potential to assume a military dimension. The development, if any, such as deployment of communication or surveillance equipment at any of these places or in Coco Islands would merit a close watch in the coming decade. The potential of such assets for use by Chinese military needs examination. Any Chinese military presence in Myanmar will have serious implications for the military balance in the region. China is the most important supplier of military aid to Myanmar and maintains extensive strategic and military cooperation. Since 1989, China has supplied Myanmar with jet fighters, armoured vehicles and naval vessels, and has trained Burmese army, air force and naval personnel.

Bangladesh. The Bangladesh–China Defence Co-operation Agreement was signed in 2002, expanding strategic and military cooperation. Since then, China has emerged as a major supplier of arms to the Bangladeshi armed forces. It has supplied 65 artillery guns, 114 missile systems, 155 mm howitzers, and large cache of small arms and ammunitions. The Bangladesh army is in the process of procuring 44 Chinese MBT 2000 Main Battle Tanks (MBT) from China at the cost of 162 million dollars.[14] This is a significant purchase for a country that has a GDP per capita of 700 dollars. The Bangladesh navy (*Nou Bahini*) is collaborating extensively with the Chinese Navy (PLAN) in acquiring missile boats, torpedo boats, gunboats, and submarine hunters. With Chinese assistance, Bangladesh has built a missile launch pad near Chittagong Port. China's port investment includes a seaport in Bangladesh, which is a vitally important trade centre for Beijing. The new docking facility in Bangladesh, for example, came with an agreement that China could dock its naval fleet there as and when needed. Bangladesh is seeking Chinese assistance in developing road links, railway lines, the Chittagong port, and the deep-sea port in Sonadia Island. Myanmar and Bangladesh are developing road and rail links that would connect China's Yunnan Province with the Chittagong area of Bangladesh.

Sri Lanka. The handing over of Hambantota to China for 99 years by Sri Lanka under China's 'debt trap' policy is indicative of China's economic application of hybrid warfare. China had forged a strong military relationship with Sri Lanka. To support Sri Lanka's war with the LTTE, China supplied major military hardware, to include Jian-7 fighter jets, anti-aircraft guns, JY-11 3D air surveillance radars and other heavy weapons, which played a central role in Sri Lankan military successes against the LTTE. Pakistan too had supplied weapons to Sri Lanka during this period. Sri Lanka supports the 'One-China' policy without raising any questions on Tibet and other human rights issues. China has been expanding major infrastructure projects in Sri Lanka like the $1.5 billion flagship Hambantota Development Zone, which includes an international deep-sea container port, an oil refinery and an airport. A second new seaport has been promised by the Sri Lankans. Utilization of these ports by PLAN for dominating the IOR cannot be ruled out and needs to be continuously observed and assessed. China has also helped Sri Lanka in obtaining status of dialogue partner in the Shanghai Corporation Organization (SCO) that shows their growing understanding on wider issues.

Nepal. The new Oli-led government in Nepal is a strategic victory for China. China is fast developing communication infrastructure from Tibet into Nepal and is constructing a number of infrastructure projects, which have military implications. Of utmost concern is the increasing footprint of China in Eastern Nepal bordering the Siliguri Corridor. China has offered a 'no strings attached' military assistance primarily to wean Nepal away from India. Both countries have agreed to widen their defence and security ties and take forward training cooperation between their militaries. Nepal has pledged its support to China in strong terms on cracking down on any 'anti-China activities' on Nepali soil—a reference to the activities of Tibetans based in Nepal. The PLA has agreed to help set up two mobile hospitals for the Nepal Army and has stepped up both financial aid and training assistance to the Nepal Army. A large number of Nepalese military personnel undergo training in various PLA training establishments and there are reports that PLA is likely to establish a training establishment for the Royal Nepal Army in Kathmandu. China has surpassed India in terms of committing foreign direct investment (FDI) in Nepal. According to the latest statistics maintained by Nepal Rastra Bank (NRB), China has outdone India in terms of committing FDI in Nepal as well as in terms of projects in Nepal. The latest data put India on the fourth position in terms of the number of development projects pledged in Nepal and on the second position after China in terms of FDI, with China providing five times the FDI than India. Nepal has also signed a gas exploration deal with China in the Terai region, which opens the possibility of covert PLA deployment in proximity of the Siliguri Corridor.

Bhutan. Bhutan had been parrying Chinese overtures to settle the boundary issue through a package deal. China recognises the importance of Doklam Plateau vis-à-vis security of Chumbi valley and the Siliguri Corridor. However, post the 73-day standoff between India and China at Doklam, China has occupied North Doklam, developed fortified positions and made helipads. China's endeavour will be to establish diplomatic relations with Bhutan, connect it with Tibet by road and rail, commence trade and wean it away from India. The proximity of Doklam Plateau to the Siliguri Corridor has strategic implications.

Maldives. China has assiduously subsumed Maldives into its ambit again employing its debt trap policy. Not only has it obtained the Maldives–China FTA, Maldives already owes 70 per cent of its total external debt to China. Maldives policy from 'India First' has taken a total about turn. Given the geostrategic location of Maldives in the Indian Ocean, this has serious implications for India. China and Pakistan would like to ensure that President Yameen continues to remain in power beyond the next elections in Maldives. For this, all stops will be removed at the political, financial, military and ideological levels, latter even soliciting the service of terrorist-mullahs of Pakistan, monitoring teams of United Nations notwithstanding. *Ahmed Naseem, former Maldives Foreign Minister, had warned in April 2006 that* Maldives was looking to let the Chinese build a port at Gadhoo Island, people had already been evacuated from the region and that the Chinese were already building roads there. A Chinese Task Force (TF) centred on Maldives creates new complexities for India. Not without reason, Zhiyong of Shanghai Academy of Social Sciences says, China is promoting Maldives as a maritime pivot; Maldives could become supply base for Chinese military and civil vessels.

Russia. Chinese and Russian defence relations are at an all-time high. Russia contributes high-end weaponry and technology to China. During 2015, trade between China and Russia was about $68 billion while the projects for the next four years are pegged at $200 billion. China has been an active buyer of Russian defence technology. In November 2016, Russia announced the delivery of S-400 defence systems to China by 2020.[15] Beijing has also become the first state in the world authorized to buy the one of a kind system. According to media reports, the transaction amounted to around $3 billion. In 2016, China and Russia also held a massive eight-day joint exercise ('Joint Sea 2016') in the South China Sea with drills in the air, coastal and maritime zones of the disputed sea.

Peoples Liberation Army Ground Force (PLAGF)

There are 18 Corps sized Group Armies, divided among five Theatre Commands-Eastern, Southern, Northern, Western, Central. Within the Theatre Commands, divisions are being downsized into brigades. The International Institute for Strategic Studies (IISS) currently attributes the PLA Ground Force with nine active tank divisions consisting of a number of armoured brigades. The traditional structure of PLA divisions was estimated in 2000 as consisting roughly of three regiments—*tuan* 团—of the main arm, each of three battalions (营) plus support units, a fourth regiment of infantry (in an armoured division) or armour (in an infantry division), an artillery regiment, an anti-aircraft regiment or battalion, and signals, engineer, reconnaissance and chemical defence battalions or companies, plus combat service support units. A typical PLAGF armoured brigade has 4 tank battalions (124 main battle tanks)—each tank battalion has three tank companies (30 + one tank for the battalion commander), 1 mechanized infantry battalion (40 armoured personnel carriers), 1 artillery battalion (18 self-propelled howitzers)—three batteries of six guns each and one anti-aircraft battalion. There are eight active artillery divisions consisting of a number of artillery brigades. A typical PLAGF artillery brigade has four artillery battalions each with 18 guns in three batteries and one self-propelled anti-tank gun battalion (18 vehicles). Brigades are a relatively new formation for the PLAGF (introduced in the 1990s), the PLAGF plans to expand their number and rid itself of the massive, rigid formations of the Soviet model. As a step towards modernizing its army, this new system allows for smaller, cross-service arm battle groups of battalion size within a brigade to operate independently, increasing the

PLA's ability to respond to a rapidly changing battle situation. The areas of the five Theatre Commands are shown in Figure 4.7.

Figure 4.7: Theatre Commands (5)

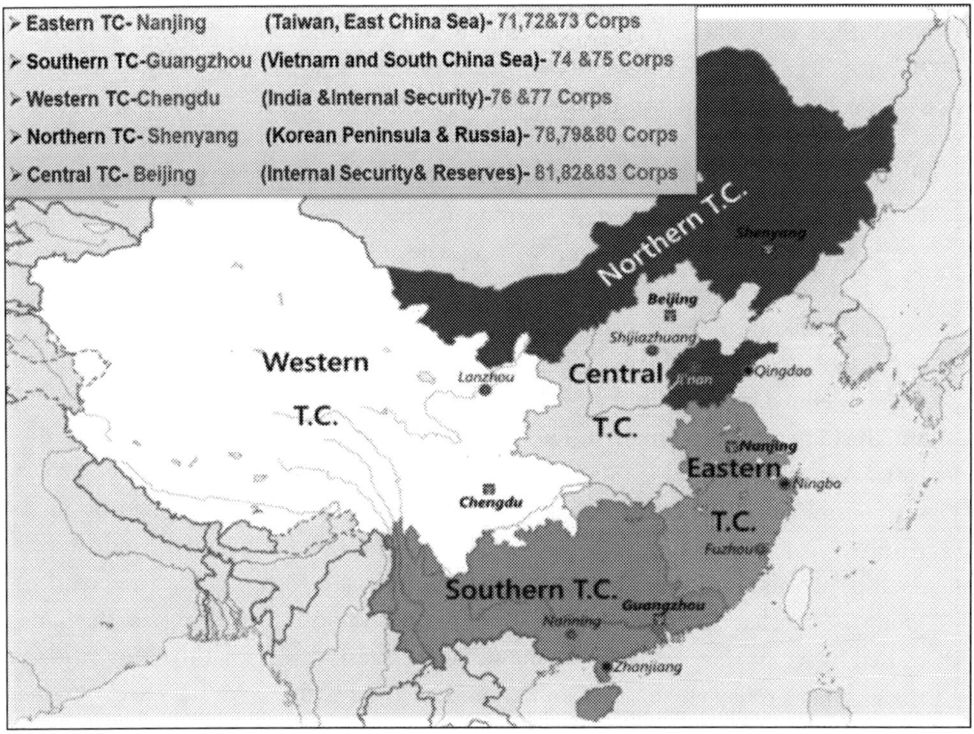

The Western Theatre Command (WTC) is responsible for China's borders from Myanmar to Afghanistan. It has the 13th Group Army, 21st Group Army and 47th Group Army integral to it, in addition to following reporting directly to the WTC: 1st Tactical Reconnaissance Bureau, 52nd and 53rd Mountain Infantry Brigades, 54th Mechanized Infantry Brigade, Mechanized Infantry Division ex Hotan, 'Red Army' Division ex Kuga, 8th and 11th Motorized Infantry Divisions, Artillery Brigade ex Urumqi and Army Aviation Brigade ex Korla. Aside from being supported by the Rocket Force and Strategic Support Force, WTC has the support of following PLAAF formations: 6th, 33rd and 37th Fighter Divisions, 36th Bomber Division and 4th Transport Division. Theatre Missions of the WTC include supporting People's Armed Police Force maintaining internal stability in restive Tibet and Xinjiang regions, and disaster relief requiring liaison with civilian organizations. The external responsibilities include responding to unrest in Central Asia under auspices of the Shanghai Corporation Organisation SCO. SCO-sponsored peace mission exercises have been held since 2005 and SCO forces have been trained for combined combat operations for responding to large scale unrest. Very significantly, the primary strategic direction of the WTC is India and the contested border regions, which implies India and Bhutan, since China has settled her borders with all other nations. Details of Chinese Military as given in Military Balance 2017 from the International Institute of Strategic Studies (IISS), London, are as per Appendix 'D' attached.

PLA Navy (PLAN)

In 1979, Deng Xiaoping called for 'a strong navy with modern combat capability'.[16] Liu Huaqing, a General of the PLA Army who served as the Commander of the PLA Navy from 1982 to 1988 and is sometimes described as China's equivalent of Sergei Gorshkov, conceptualised a three-step programme for modernising the PLAN, as follows[17]: by 2000, PLAN capable of exerting sea control out to the First Island Chain, defined by the Kurile Islands, Japan and the Ryuku Islands, the Philippines and the Indonesian Archipelago. This step currently translates into what is described by USA and others as China's Anti-Access/Area Denial (A2/AD) strategy; by 2020, sea control would be enforced out to the Second Island Chain, defined by the Kuriles, Japan and the Bonin Islands, the Marianas Islands, Palau, and the Indonesia Archipelago and by 2050, PLAN would operate globally, with aircraft carrier battle groups. China has clearly internalized that not only was the Century of Humiliation caused by its inability to deal with the seaborne threat, as also that the only viable threat it faces today emanates from the sea. Details of Chinese Military as given in Military Balance 2017 from the IISS are given in Appendix 'D'.

China's ship-building industry has demonstrated the ability to produce modern warships and submarines at an unmatched rate. Since the overwhelming majority of China's warships and submarines are built at state-owned yards, the present contraction in ship-building is unlikely to impact on their ability to continue turning out ships at this unprecedented rate. If anything, the rate may increase due to the need to keep the yards in business and ensure jobs and skills are not lost.

Seaborne Nuclear Deterrence. A submarine-based nuclear deterrent requires three basic attributes.[18] First, it must have operational stealth, making it difficult if not impossible to find and track. If it fails in this, the risk of its being eliminated by an adversary first strike becomes unacceptably high. Second, it must have a reliable long-range SLBM capable of striking the enemy at intercontinental ranges with a nuclear payload. Finally, a reliable and survivable C3 system must be in place, to enable the NCA to order retaliation after a first strike by the enemy. China's sea-based nuclear deterrence is based on the following:

- **Type 094 Jin Class SSBN**. First spotted in 2006, the Type 094 appears to form the current mainstay of the PLAN deterrent force. Four submarines are reported in service, each carrying 12 JL-2 SLBMs with range assessed as 7,200–8,000 km. An American ONI study indicates that the relative detectability of the Jin is greater than that of the Delta III Class fielded by the Soviet Union in the 1970s.[19] Projections indicate that up to five more submarines of this class may be built before China begins fielding the next-generation SSBILLION.[20] These must be tempered by other assessments that programme will be capped at five boats, to be followed by the Type 096 Tang class. The Jin has been assessed to be China's first credible sea-based nuclear deterrent and the first deterrence patrol by it was expected sometime in 2016. China is known to have VLF stations in Changde and Datong, permitting receipt of messages at depths of about 20 m.
- **Type 096 Tang Class**. Unconfirmed reports indicate that the Type 096 SSBILLION, armed with the JL-3 SLBM (range over 12,000 km) is already in service.[21] The eventual numbers to be fielded are, however, not known. From India's perspective, however, these numbers will become relevant only after India develops the ability to take out land-based Chinese nuclear missiles in a pre-emptive first strike. So long as India continues with its 'No First Use' policy, the China's SSBILLION force level remains irrelevant.

Expeditionary Forces. China's continued investment in amphibious forces is a clear indicator of her desire to develop an expeditionary and over-the-horizon amphibious assault capability, also usable for Humanitarian Assistance and Disaster Relief (HADR). A number of classes of amphibious platforms have been added to the fleet. Those that could pose a threat to India are as follows:

- **Type 071 Yuzhao Class Amphibious Transport Docks**. Displacing 25,000 tons, the Yuzhao class began entering service from 2007. Four have already been inducted, fifth is under construction and sixth is known to have been ordered. Each ship can transport one marine battalion, comprising 500–800 personnel and 15–20 amphibious armoured vehicles to a distance of 10,000 nm (18,520 km) at a speed of 18 knots, covering roughly 810 km every day. These can then be landed on all types of opposing coasts (the beach and its limitations have been removed from the equation) using four Yuyi class LCAC, each capable of transporting a 50–60 ton payload to a range of 165 nm (over 300 km) at a speed of 60 knots (110 km/h), and/or four Z-8 (Super Frelon) helicopters, each carrying 27 passengers to a range of nearly 550 nm (1,018 km), while the mothership itself remains over the horizon.

- **Type 072 Series**. The Type 072 began entering service in 1978 and still constitutes the core of PLAN amphibious capability, with 32 ships known to be in active service and at least two under construction. They are the traditional type of landing ship, requiring a suitable beach to be able to discharge assault forces. Each carries up to 10 tanks, or 500 fully armed troops, or a combination.
- **Others**. The PLAN also has Type 073 and Type 074 class Landing Ships. These are of comparatively smaller range, designed for assault on proximate targets, such as Taiwan. They have not been considered further in this paper.
- **Future Plans**. Reports indicate that China is building a 40,000 ton Landing Helicopter Dock (LHD), somewhat similar to USS America. The ship is expected to displace around 40,000 tons.[22]

Sea Control. The basic tool for sea control is the Carrier Battle Group (CBG) comprising aircraft carriers with integral aircraft and helicopters, destroyers, frigates, perhaps corvettes (light frigates), and logistic support vessels. It is the whole that makes the tool, not individual component parts, however big and expensive they may be. China's capability to exercise sea control is assessed as under:

- **Aircraft Carriers**. China acquired four aircraft carriers, first three for study. The fourth one, 'Varyag' ex Ukraine, arrived at Dalian Shipyard, China in March 2002, completed sea trials in August 2011, and was commissioned on 25 September 2012. Initially planned to be outfitted with 50 Russian Su-33 aircraft, but the deal fell through. The Shenyang J-15 (reverse engineered based on a prototype Su-33 bought from Ukraine) has been selected as the on-board interceptor. The first batch of domestically trained J-15 pilots was operationally certified in 2015 and the air wing of 24 J-15s was expected to deploy on board Liaoning in 2016.[23] Reports about construction of a second aircraft carrier have already appeared in the media. One writer has indicated its name will be 'Shandong' and a second carrier of this class will be built before graduating to an improved design. Shandong will also use ski-jump for launch of aircraft, but subsequent carriers could see a shift to catapult based launch systems, enabling use of much heavier aircraft. An unconfirmed report indicates that China has plans to build an 110,000 ton nuclear propelled super carrier.[24] There seems to be agreement that China will construct multiple aircraft carriers over the next 15 years,[25] with one analyst predicting the eventual fleet size to be at least seven, permitting the continuous deployment of two carrier battle groups.[26] However, there is no official indication of the numbers China will build. Capability-wise, air compliment of 'Liaoning' is expected to comprise 36 aircraft; 24 J-15 fighters, six Z-18F ASW helicopters, four Z-18J AEW helicopters, and two Z-9C rescue helicopters. The J-15 is presently capable of only air defence missions. This will likely limit the J-15's payload by as much as 10,500 lbs,[27] a substantial reduction in capability as no mid-air refuelling is available. China's lack of experience in aircraft carrier operations poses a substantial handicap unlike India, which has been operating a carrier since 1961.

Destroyers. China has inducted 15 new destroyers of increasing potency and sophistication since 2006 and today operates 27 of them. The most recent class, the Type 052 D (Luyang III) is being mass produced. Four ships have been commissioned with three being at different stages of sea trials. Four more have been launched and are fitting out and two more are under construction. Displacing 7,500 tons, they are fitted with a single-barrel 130 mm gun, a 64-cell vertical launch system capable of launching CY-5 ASW missiles (which delivers a lightweight torpedo to a range of 30 km); the CJ-10 Land Attack Cruise Missile (range > 1,500 km); YJ-18 or YJ-83 anti-ship cruise missiles (the former has a range of 290 nm and is similar to the Klub used by the IN, and can be used for land attack also; the latter has a much lower operational range); the HHQ-9 SAM (range 200 km); HHQ-16 medium-range SAM (range 35–75 km); and the DK-10A SAM (range 50 km+). Other weapons include short-range SAMs and CIWS and anti-submarine torpedo tubes. One helicopter is carried. A new design (Type 055) is under development, which may mount laser weapons. No information is available about the numbers to be built. However, assuming that the current accretion rate of about 1.8 ships per year will continue and the life of a destroyer is 30 years, *the PLAN would have a destroyer force of around 35 by 2030.*

- **Frigates**. The core of China's frigates is the Type 054 A (Jiangkai II Class); 22 of these have been commissioned in the last eight years, with at least three more in the pipeline. Their armament comprises a 32-cell VLS launcher for HQ-16 SAM (range 35-75 km) or the Yu-8, which delivers an anti-submarine torpedo to a range of 30 km; eight YJ-83 anti-ship cruise missiles with a range of about 200 km; CIWS; a 76-mm dual-purpose gun; anti-submarine rocket launchers and one helicopter. No information is available about future frigates once the Type 054A programme comes to an end next year. Assuming the current rate of accretion of about 2.5 ships per year will continue and considering their life to be 30 years, the *PLAN would have a frigate force of 65-70 frigates by 2030.*
- **Corvettes**. The smallest principal surface combatant in the PLA Navy, the Type 056 Corvette (Jiangdao Class) has seen virtually an explosion in

numbers, with 27 having entered service since 2013. Four shipyards are reported to be building them, churning out 8–10 ships per year. The ships are 90 m long, displace about 1500 tons and carry the short-range FL 3000N SAM, four YJ-83 anti-ship missiles, a CIWS, a 76-mm gun and torpedo tubes. They can stage a medium helicopter. *The current force level of 27 ships could jump to over 150 vessels by 2030, if the present rate of construction is maintained.*

- **Replenishment Ships**. The key to continued successful sea control by a CBG is its replenishment capability. Not only do escort vessels have to be refuelled frequently, the carrier engaged in flight operations consumes aviation fuel at an enormous rate and requires to be topped up every now and then. All CBGs thus include replenishment vessels. The PLAN inventory today comprises more than 15 fleet tankers, with the Type 901 Fuchi class of 40,000 tons about to commission.
- **Projected Capability**. Taking into account the requirements of refit and training, it is assessed that the *projected PLAN force level in 2030 will be more than sufficient to operate 2-3 CBGs anywhere in the Western Pacific and Indian Oceans.*

Sea Denial. So far as denying the Indian Navy (IN) the ability to operate in the Indian Ocean is concerned, China has three options: the use of proxies such as Pakistan; the use of submarines for SLOC interdiction as also to pose an existential threat to IN units at sea; and the use of mines. China will be influenced by Pakistani beliefs about the impact of their submarines on the IN. Two types of submarines could be used by China: nuclear propelled SSN, and the conventional submarine [modern versions equipped with Air Independent Propulsion (AIP)]. The big advantage SSNs have is their virtually unlimited range and ability to maintain high submerged speeds. PLAN SSN force comprises the following:

- **Type 091 Han Class**. Commissioned since 1974, three are still listed as 'active'. The Han class was known for its high radiated noise levels and poor radiation shielding, leading to health hazards for the crew. Her armament comprised torpedoes. This class could be considered part of a 'learning curve' for the Chinese submarine building industry.
- **Type 093 Shang Class**. Five boats of this class are reported to have entered service since 2006, with at least one more under construction. Apart from torpedoes, these are armed with vertically launched CJ-10 land attack cruise missiles with a conventional or nuclear payload delivered to a range of 1500–400 km (based on different reports) and a CEP of 10 m as well as YJ-18

land attack and anti-ship cruise missiles with a range of 290 nm, akin to the Klub used by the IN.

- **Type 095**. Type 095 is a proposed class of third-generation nuclear attack submarines with a substantially reduced acoustic signature, better sensors including active/passive flank array sonar, and towed low- and high-frequency sonar arrays. It could be used as an undersea escort for the PLAN CBG. One submarine of this class is reported to have been completed, but has not yet entered service.
- **Type 097 Qin Class**. There have been rumours about a fourth-generation attack submarine having completed development.[28] These are supposed to be of a revolutionary design using magnetic liquid for propulsion and capable of speeds of 100 knots (faster than any current anti-submarine torpedo). The absence of propellers and rudders is supposed to enable them to be absolutely silent. The same report goes on to say that construction may take another 8-10 years. The report cannot be verified.

As for conventional submarines, discounting older submarine classes including the Type 035 Ming and variants (all of which are at least 25 years old), China still has a force level of 40 modern submarines of the Russian Kilo and indigenous Song and Yuan classes, with five more under construction. The Song class entered service in 1998, while the Yuan class was first inducted in 2006. Both are armed with torpedoes and anti-ship missiles; the Yuan class also has AIP.

Projected Force Level. China has commissioned 2.9 submarines of various types per year since 1995.[29] Assuming a life of 30 years, this would translate into a steady state force level of 87 submarines of all types. Furthermore, about one in three of the 23 submarines commissioned by the PLAN since 2006 has been nuclear (SSN or SSBILLION). The conventional submarine force level by 2030 could, therefore, comprise around 58-60 conventional submarines, with the remainder being equally split between SSNs and SSBNs.

Mines. PLAN focus has been more towards access denial than sea control and significant underwater warfare capability has quietly been built up. Chinese strategists describe the mine as being easy to lay, difficult to sweep, possessing strong concealment potential, high destructive power, and posing a long lasting threat. Analysts assess the objectives of an offensive Chinese Mine Warfare strategy to be 'blockading enemy bases, harbours, and sea lanes; destroying enemy sea transport capability; attacking or restricting warships mobility; and crippling and exhausting enemy combat strength'. A tactically focussed Chinese doctrinal textbook declares, 'We must make full use of units that can force their way into enemy ports and shipping lanes to carry out mine-laying on a grand scale'. Assessments indicate that China possesses an inventory of as many as 500,000 mines of enormous variety with different manufacturers and designs: C-1 to C-6 ground mines, M-1 to M-5 and EM 52–57 ground mines, Piao 1-3 drifting mines, PMK 1 & 2 torpedo carrying mines, T-5 and Te 2-1 mobile mines, and the Type 500 and Xun-1 training mines, for ships/aircraft and submarines respectively. Given the doctrine and huge inventory, it would be somewhat naive to believe that China will not use mines for both offensive and defensive missions. On the other hand, mine warfare continues to remain among the most neglected disciplines for most Western navies, as also for the Indian Navy.

ISR

Maritime Patrol and AEW. The PLAN is also reported to be expanding its inventory of MR and AEW aircraft. The basic airframe used is the Y-8, a licence produced version of the ex-Soviet An-12.[30] More than 30 MR variants, designated Y-8 AF and Y-8 FQ, were reported in service in 2015. The AEW variant is designated as KJ-200 and at least three are reported in service with the PLAN.

Satellites

- **Surveillance**. China maintains that its Yaogan series of satellites, the 30th of which was launched on 15 May 2016, are intended for scientific experiments, crop assessment, land survey and disaster monitoring. Analysts, however, believe that these are high-resolution earth observation satellites carrying either electro-optical or synthetic aperture radar sensors, intended to boost China's anti-access/area denial capabilities and provide target information to the DF-21D ASBM.[31] A number of triple launches have been reported. These are thought to be ELINT satellites to triangulate the position of electronic signals transmitted by vessels, thereby enabling their location. Identification and exact location could thereafter be determined by a satellite with optical/SAR systems, enabling targeting by the ASBM.
- **Navigation**. The Chinese BeiDou navigational satellite system became operational in December 2012. It provides the users with precision navigation and time information, as well as the ability to receive short messages of up to 120 characters. China intended to expand it to provide global coverage by 2020, by when it is expected that the constellation will comprise 35 satellites.
- **Data Relay and Communication**. The Tianlian-1 constellation, comprising three satellites in a geostationary orbit, provides the PLAN with a real-time

data relay system with global coverage, enabling collection of real-time information on mobile targets. Applications for this in location and identification of naval units globally are evident. In parallel, a counter-space anti-satellite programme enables China to deny the same information to adversaries in times of conflict.

PLA Air Force (PLAAF)

The US Air Force's technological air power superiority over China is rapidly diminishing in light of rapid Chinese modernisation of fighter jets, missiles, air-to-air weapons, cargo planes, and stealth aircraft, according to analysts, Pentagon officials, and a Congressional review released several years ago.[32] The 2014 US-China Economic and Security Review Commission recommended that Congress appoint an outside panel of experts to assess the US-Chinese military balance and make recommendations regarding US military plans and budgets, among other things. Despite being released in 2014, the findings of the report offered a detailed and insightful window into Chinese Air Force technology, progress, and development, highlights of which were the following: (1) PLAAF had approximately 2,200 operational aircraft, nearly 600 of which are considered modern; (2) recent flights of prototypes of the Chinese J-20 stealth fighter, calling the aircraft more advanced than any other air platform deployed in the Asia-Pacific region; (3) Chinese were also testing a smaller stealth fighter variant called the J-31 although its intended use was unclear; (4) alongside the J-10 and J-11 fighters, the Chinese also own Russian-built Su-27s and Su-30s and were on the verge of buying the new Su-35 from Russia; (5) in addition to stealth technology, high-tech fighter aircraft, and improved avionics, the Chinese have massively increased their ability with air-to-air missiles over the last 15-years; (6) the Y-20 aircraft, a new strategic airlifter now being tested by the Chinese has three times the cargo-carrying capacity of the US Air Force's C-130. Some of these new planes could be configured into tanker aircraft, allowing the Chinese to massively increase their reach and ability to project air power over longer distances; (7) Chinese are believed to already have a number of road-mobile ICBMs capable of carrying nuclear weapons, while the DF-41 is reported to have as many as 10 re-entry vehicles.

Details of Chinese Military, as given in Military Balance 2017 from the IISS, are given in Appendix 'D'. The present PLAAF force levels along with projected force levels up to 2030 are given in succeeding paragraphs.

Fighters. Present total holdings: 890.

- J-7 (equivalent to MiG-21) (23 Regiments with 452 aircraft).

- J-8 (7 Regiments with 168 aircraft).
- Su-27 and its Chinese derivative J-11 (7 regiments with 43 Su-27, 23 Su-27UBK & 95 J-11). In addition, three additional regiments are under formation and would be equipped with J-11B/BS.
- China also signed a contract with Russia in November 2012 for purchase of 24xSu-35 aircraft with deliveries commencing from 2015 onward.[33] China may develop its own version of Su-35 later.
- J-20 and J-31 are also under development. J-20 is likely to enter the service by 2018 but because of complex fifth-generation technologies, limited number may enter service by 2030. J-31 is reportedly for export but some may be fielded by the PLAAF and maybe PLAN after 2025 mainly as its cost would be much lower than the J-20.

Fighter/Ground Attack. Total holdings: 415 plus.

- Su-30MKK (3 regiments with 73 aircraft).
- J-10 (based on Israeli Levi design) (200+ aircraft in 6 regiments).
- China reportedly has its own version of Su-30 (J-16) but with enhanced stealth features that will further enhance its strike capability.[34] With induction of J-20 and Su-35, the strike capability will be further enhanced and one should not be surprised to see a significant increase in the total inventory of multi-role aircraft. These multi-role aircraft would permit greater flexibility in operational planning and enable China to do more with lesser number of aircraft. It need not be said that China's 'throw weight' capability and with greater emphasis on PGMs weapon effectiveness would increase significantly in the coming years.

Bombers. Current holdings: 82 aircraft of all types.

- 6 Regiments of H-6A/E/H/K/M including one nuclear ready. H-6 is a derivative of TU-16 and has been in service for over three decades and should have been normally phased out as these aircraft would be vulnerable against modern air defence. Apparently, China intends to continue with these aircraft as it has embarked on their upgradation and modification for carriage of air launched cruise missiles that will enhance China's strike capability especially in South China Sea. YJ-10 cruise missiles with 2,000 km range will add to the value of these aircraft.
- China had expressed an interest in TU-22 supersonic bomber when India was contemplating their lease from Russia a few years back. However, nothing happened till end of 2012, when China showed its interest once again.

Some reports indicate that China may have already acquired this aircraft. It has been reported that aircraft would be armed with anti-ship cruise missiles and would be used in that role in South China Sea. The number of TU-22s, if acquired, is most likely to be limited and is unlikely to exceed 20 or thereabouts.

Transport Aircraft. The PLAAF has one airborne corps with three airborne divisions. For their airlift, the following aircraft collectively provide airlift of one airborne division in a cycle of 48 hours:

- IL-76 (10 aircraft in 1 regiment).
- Y-8 (40+ An-12 class aircraft in 3 regiments).
- Y-7 (40+ An-26 class aircraft in 3 regiments).
- China has been trying to acquire additional IL-76s from Ukraine and IL-476 from Russia.
- China flew the first flight of the Y-20 heavy transport aircraft of a class between C-130 and C-17 in January 2013. One should expect production of these aircraft within the next three to five years. The Y-20 is likely to serve as a mother platform for the Chinese tanker and AEW&C fleet.
- China can also rely on its large fleet of civil aircraft (around 800) that can be used to augment its strategic airlift capability as was demonstrated during evacuation of Chinese citizens from Libya.

Force Multipliers

- **Tankers.** China has 10 H-6U. It had placed an order for four IL-78s and 30 IL-76 from Russia but apparently the order was cancelled or has been deferred for reasons that remain unclear. It would not be surprising that China comes up with an indigenous tanker aircraft based on its Y-20 aircraft. Another option would be to modify C-919 civil airliner under development, which is supposed to enter service but Y-20 seems a better option. China must have a large fleet of tanker aircraft if it wants to have power projection capability.
- **AEW and C Aircraft.** The present holdings of 4 KJ-2000 and 4 KJ-200 are likely to increase by 2030 considering the multiple and multidirectional threats. Needless to say, one should also expect significant improvement in capabilities in this field.
- **UAVs and UCAVs.** China has large inventory of UAVs and has showcased a supersonic UCAV with a supersonic anti-ship cruise missiles aimed at targeting large aircraft carriers. China has also converted their fleet of retired

J-6s into unmanned attack fighters due to their manoeuvrability, high thrust-to-weight ratio and their suitability for close combat.[35] It is not clear how many of these aircraft have been modified and their role in which they would be utilized. Apparently, China would convert other retiring aircraft into unmanned aircraft as well.

Projected Force Levels. It is unlikely that PLAAF would increase its strength to 4,000 combat aircraft as was the case in 1960s and 1970s as this figure is not affordable. Currently, the average flying for pilots varies between 100 to 150 hours/year instead of the ideal and desirable 200 hours/year. It was assessed in the late 1990s and early years of decade of 2,000 that China would downsize to around 1,000 fourth/fifth-generation aircraft. The present inventory level is around 1,800 aircraft, including third-generation aircraft. There are additional 300 combat aircraft with the PL Navy. There would normally be a case for reduction in the total size of inventory, though it is unlikely that outstanding issues that China faces (like Japan, Taiwan, Philippines, South Korea, India, and most importantly the United States) would get resolved in the next 10–15 years. It is assessed that the PLAAF would maintain its present inventory level though its ageing aircraft would be replaced with modern and state-of-the-art, a combination of fourth- and fifth-generation, aircraft. Even if there is any increase, the total is unlikely to go beyond 2000 combat aircraft.

Aero-Engines. China faces major problem with aero-engine technology. Almost all its modern aircraft, including J-10, J-11 and JF-17/FC-1, are powered by Russian or Ukrainian designed engines—either bought outright or license-manufactured. China's J-31 stealth fighter reportedly flew with Russian RD-93 engines as did the first flight of J-20. China has been trying to develop high-performance aero-engines but has not had the requisite success. Chinese purchase of Su-35 was linked to its purchase of S-117 engines for its J-20 programme. Due to secrecy that surrounds Chinese defence industry, one is not sure how long would the Chinese continue their dependence on imports. China cannot become a front-line air power unless it masters aero-engine technologies and is able to meet her domestic and export customers' requirements. The problem is not restricted only to engines for combat aircraft but also its transport fleet—C-919 will have American engines while its Y-20's first flight was with Russian engines. Even if there is a break-through, it would take a few years before production is streamlined as integration of engines with the airframe is a long and time consuming process.

Aircraft Radars. China also has problem in developing Active Electronically Scanned Array (AESA) radar that has now become standard upgrade for the western fourth-generation combat aircraft and the standard equipment for fifth-generation fighters. There are some unconfirmed reports that J-15 has a Chinese-designed AESA radar; if true, this speaks high of the Chinese aircraft industry. In addition, there have been unconfirmed reports that Russia had supplied AESA radar for Russian-supplied Su-30MKK aircraft. If the reports are correct, it should assist China in finding a solution to its problems in the quest for the vital indigenous AESA.

Electronic Warfare. This is a grey area where no formal assessments are available about sophistication of the Chinese airborne electronic warfare suites. It has been generally accepted that the Americans and the European are way ahead of the Russians and since the Chinese have either Russian equipment or indigenous EW equipment based on Russian designs; one cannot make an accurate assessment of their efficacy in actual war scenario. Chinese will be keen to close the technology gap with the US. Whether Russia would help China in this regard is debatable.

Chinese Airfields. There are nearly eleven airfields[36] in and around Tibet from which the PLAAF can operate against India. Requisite infrastructure has been built at these airfields for round-the-year operation by combat aircraft. Most of these airfields have aircraft permanently deployed there. The exact capabilities of these airfields is not known but it is estimated that each of these should be able to house around 50–70 aircraft during operations. On one hand, China would be able to operate around 50–70 aircraft, including those staging through these bases, while on the other, these airfields will be saturated with aircraft and thus would offer themselves as lucrative targets for attacks. Further, air-to-air refuelling would be required, when operating from majority of these airfields for attack against Indian airfields and other targets implying need for large fleet of tanker aircraft to support air operations.

Air Defence. China lays special emphasis on air defence. It has, thus, built a formidable air defence that is difficult to penetrate. Important points in this regard are covered below:

- **Radar Coverage**. China has extensive network of radars throughout the country including Tibet; each of its MACs has at least one radar brigade. Most of these radars are of Russian origin or their upgraded and modernized indigenous versions. Among the radars, there are at least three over-the-horizon radars, which give the PLAAF the ability to detect aircraft and missiles (cruise and ballistic) at extended ranges.[37] China is also working on counter-stealth and counter-network radar technology.[38]
- **Surface to Air Missiles** (SAM). China reportedly has some 500 SAM

launchers and 16,000 anti-aircraft guns for air defence.[39] The PLAAF's SAM Corps has been operating the S-300 (NATO code name: SA-10 Grumble) family of SAM system since the mid-1990s. The S-300 missile system was regarded as one of the world's most effective all-altitude regional air defence system, comparable in performance to the US MIM-104 Patriot system. By 2008, PLAAF was operating a total of 160 S-300 launchers (32 S-300PMUs, 64 S-300PMU1s, and 64 S-300PMU2s) grouped into 10 SAM battalions (40 batteries)—a few more systems have been inducted since then. PLAAF reportedly has over 1,000 of these missiles. The acquisition of the S-300 system has significantly improved the PLA's capability of denying Chinese airspace to enemy air forces. The latest S-300PMU2 system gives the PLAAF limited ballistic missile defence capability for the first time.[40] The Chinese are reported to have their version of the missile called *Hongqi-15* (HQ-15)[41]; it is reported that only the missiles have been produced while rest of the systems continue to be imported. At least one such system (S-300PMU) has been deployed in Tibet since 2010. PLA and PLAN have their own air defence network. The number of SAM launchers and AA guns mentioned earlier are inclusive of their assets as well.

- **Passive Air Defence**. The Chinese literature on air defence lays special emphasis on passive air defence measures like dispersal of assets, camouflage and concealment and hardened shelters (including surplus ones) for aircraft and equipment. Though no hard intelligence is available on the subject but one should expect a large number of reinforced concrete blast pens on any airfield with many of them without any aircraft or with just dummy aircraft; the attacking pilot would thus be wasting his/her effort by attacking them.

PLA Rocket Force (PLARF)

Since 1985, Chinese missile forces, which are under the command of the Second Artillery Force (SAF) or Second Artillery Corps (SAC), have changed strikingly in character, shifting from a nuclear deterrent force based primarily on intermediate and medium-range missiles to a force of intercontinental- and medium-range nuclear forces combined with a powerful conventional missile arm capable of conducting precision attacks at a medium range. Further changes took place on the eve of 2016 as the SAF was re-commissioned as the PLA Rocket Force (PLARF) on 31 December 2015. PLARF was elevated from an independent branch to the fourth military service alongside the PLA, PLAN, and PLAAF. Though the decision to reconstitute the PLARF as a military service indicates the importance China puts on maintaining modern missile forces, at this point it seems unlikely that the PLARF's roles and responsibilities will differ substantially from the SAF.

China's 2013 defense white paper, supplemented with the current PRC Ministry of Defense explanation of the PLARF, provides more details available through open sources than the 2015 defense white paper. It described China's 2013 strategy for building and developing the PLARF as follows: PLA Second Artillery Force (PLASAF) is a core force for China's strategic deterrence. It is mainly composed of nuclear and conventional missile forces and operational support units, primarily responsible for deterring other countries from using nuclear weapons against China, and carrying out nuclear counterattacks and precision strikes with conventional missiles. Following the principle of building a lean and effective force, the PLASAF is striving to push forward its informationisation transform, relying on scientific and technological progress to boost independent innovations in weaponry and equipment, modernizing current equipment selectively by applying mature technology, enhancing the safety, reliability and effectiveness of its missiles, improving its force structure of having both nuclear and conventional missiles, strengthening its rapid reaction, effective penetration, precision strike, damage infliction, protection and survivability capabilities. The PLASAF capabilities of strategic deterrence, nuclear counterattack and conventional precision strike are being steadily elevated. The PLASAF has under its command missile bases, training bases, specialized support units, academies and research institutions. It has a series of 'Dong Feng' ballistic missiles and 'Chang Jian' cruise missiles.

When it comes to future force goals, China's 2015 defense white paper stated that the PLARF will strengthen its capabilities and remain vigilant in peacetime. The most extensive portion of the 2015 paper referring the PLARF was limited to the following statement: In line with the strategic requirement of being lean and effective and possessing both nuclear and conventional missiles, the PLA Second Artillery Force (PLASAF) will strive to transform itself in the direction of informationisation, press forward with independent innovations in weaponry and equipment by reliance on science and technology, enhance the safety, reliability and effectiveness of missile systems, and improve the force structure featuring a combination of both nuclear and conventional capabilities. The PLASAF will strengthen its capabilities for strategic deterrence and nuclear counterattack, and medium- and long-range precision strikes. China has a total of six missile brigades, located in the six regions of China, and each Brigade has either 3-3 or 4-4 subordinate entities. Along with this, it has training and storage brigade and testing sites.

The PRC Ministry of Defense website further explained PLARF force building in 2015 by stating: Following the principle of building a lean and effective force and going with the tide of the development of military science and technology, the Second Artillery Force strives to raise the informationisation level of its weaponry and equipment, ensure their safety and reliability, and enhance its capabilities in protection, rapid reaction, penetration, damage and precision strike. After several decades of development, it has created a weaponry and equipment system with both nuclear and conventional missiles, both solid-fueled and liquid-fueled missiles, different launching ranges and different types of warheads. PLARF's missile bases and deployments are as shown in Figure 4.8.

Figure 4.8: PLARF Missile Bases and Deployment

The US summarised Chinese missile developments in its 2016 DoD report[42] as follows: the Rocket Force, renamed from the PLASAF late last year, operates China's land-based nuclear and conventional missiles. It is developing and testing several new classes and variants of offensive missiles, including a hypersonic glide vehicle; forming additional missile units; upgrading older missile systems; and developing methods to counter ballistic missile defenses. The force possesses approximately 1,200 short-range ballistic missiles (SRBM) in its inventory. China is increasing the lethality of its conventional missile force by fielding the CSS-11 (DF-16) ballistic missile with a range of 800-1,000 km. The CSS-11, coupled with the already deployed conventional land-attack and anti-ship variants of the CSS-5 (DF-21C/D) medium-range ballistic missile (MRBM), will improve China's ability to strike not only Taiwan, but other regional targets as well. These ballistic missile systems are complemented by the CJ-10 ground-launched cruise missile (GLCM). The CJ-10 has a range in excess of 1,500 km and offers flight profiles different from ballistic missiles that can enhance targeting options. China's 2016 missile capabilities are depicted in Figure 4.9.

Figure 4.9: China's Missile Capabilities

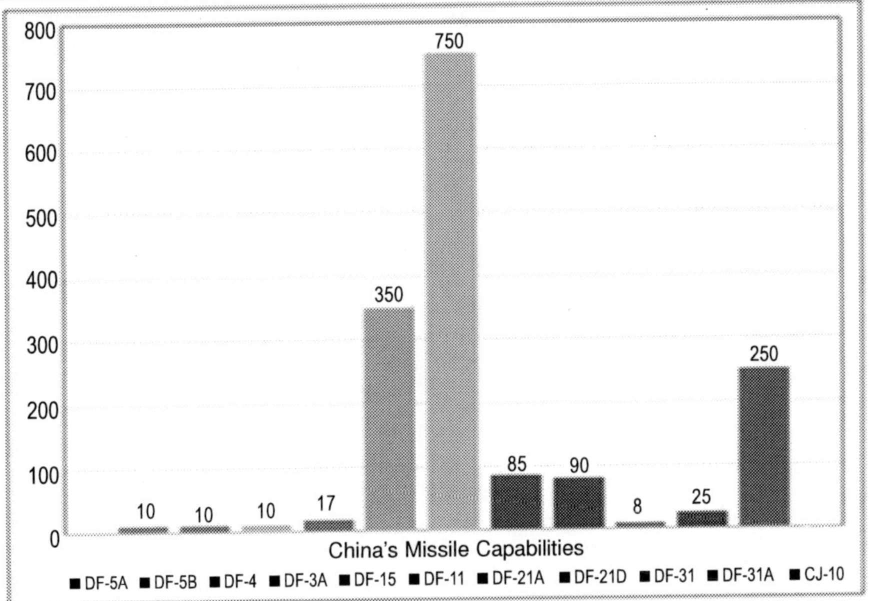

Source: "China Strategic Weapons Systems", Jane's Sentinel Security Assessment, March 3, 2016

Roughly 80 per cent of the current PLARF arsenal can conduct effective conventional missions and thus contribute to victory in non-nuclear Local Wars under Conditions of Informatisation. As the Figures show, the reason for this significant change has been the introduction of precision or near-precision strike SRBMs and Land-Attack Cruise Missiles (LACMs). The second major indicator of a shift in PLARF doctrine and capability is the significant growth in the relative size of the ICBM arsenal. Not only does the ICBM force increase in relative size from 5–12 per cent, but also much of the growth is due to modern DF-31 and DF-31A ICBMs. This trend may be an indication of a shifting priority from regional and Eurasian deterrence missions to intercontinental deterrence missions. Consequently, not only have the PLARF's equipment holdings revealed a shift from nuclear to nuclear and conventional missions, it is possible that the same equipment holdings also indicate a shift in the priority of nuclear deterrence missions. Expanding range of China's medium and intercontinental ballistic missile forces are as shown in Figure 4.10.

Figure 4.10: Expanding Range of Medium and ICBM Millile Force

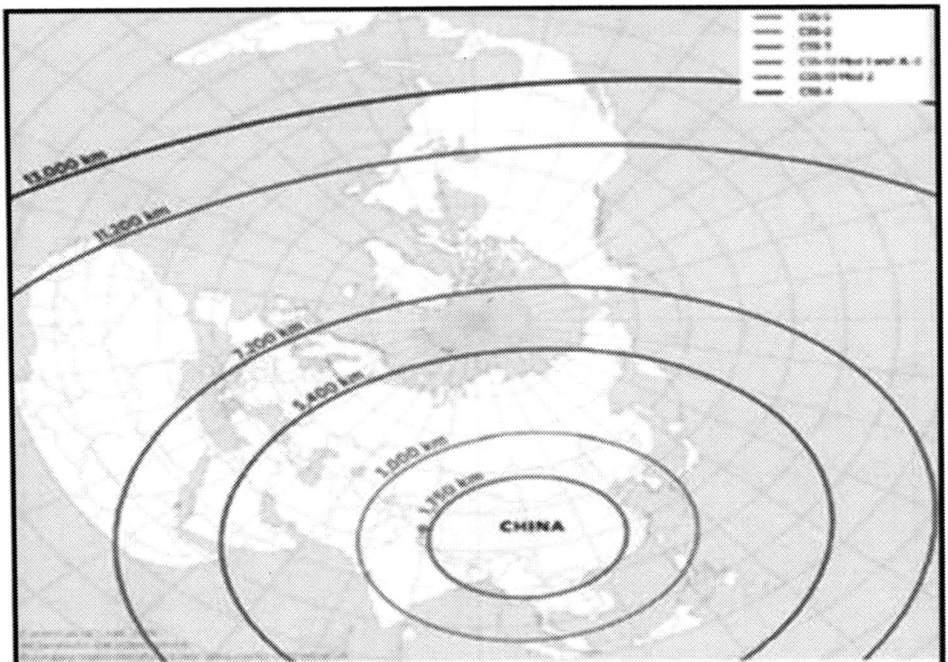

Source: DoD, Report to Congress on Military and Security Developments Involving the People's Republic of China 2016, April 24, 2016.

Nuclear Dimension

China requires both conventional and the nuclear missile forces to counter the adversary, conventional missiles to destroy enemy ability to wage war effectively, and nuclear weapons for offence–defence strategy of massive retaliation. Hence, China has developed a combination of missiles, intercontinental ballistic missile (ICBM) and intermediate-range ballistic missile (IRBM) for long ranges, plus short-range ballistic missile (SRBM) and the all-important Ground Launched Cruise Missile (GLCM) for shorter ranges. China is developing and testing several new classes and variants of offensive missiles, including a hypersonic glide vehicle; forming additional missile units; upgrading older missile systems; and developing methods to counter ballistic missile defence. China is developing new road mobile units with Multiple Independently Targeted Re-entry Vehicles (MIRVs) and penetration aids, while importance is being given to communication links, and better command

and control structures through training and joint manoeuvres with the other three services. China's force structure continues to be a mixture of land, air and sea assets. The following table below depicts its approximate numbers:

System	Missiles	Launchers	Estimated Range*
ICBM	75-100	50-75	5,400-13,000+ km
MRBM	200-300	100-125	1,500+ km
SRBM	1,000-1,200	250-300	300-1000 km
GLCM	200-300	40-55	1,500+ km

Note: Estimates reflect the PLA's ongoing modernization of its missile forces and in some cases may have increased.

Source: Department of Defence, Military and Security Developments Involving the People's Republic of China for 2016, April.

China is also making its conventional weapons lethal through precession strike missiles of short and medium range. Missiles DF-16 and DF 21C/D are for eastern and southern theatre to counter the regional threat emanating from Taiwan, and India. Its DF-21D MRBM, anti-ship ballistic missile (ASBM), is for the purpose of A2AD in the Western Pacific, to counter American ships and aircraft carriers. Further DF-26, the IRBM, has been developed in both the versions. Presently, China's conventional missiles can hit both first and second island chains in Western Pacific. China could have fully global precision strike capabilities by 2030. PLA emphasises using conventional missiles to 'strike first, strike hard, strike precisely, and strike rapidly' to 'seize the initiative' and quickly gain 'campaign control' in order to speed up the process of warfare leading to the adversary's quick capitulation. Goals of such attacks are to 'smash or weaken the enemy's military strength, to politically shock the enemy, to shake the [enemy's] willpower [to wage] war, to check the escalation of war, and to speed up the progress of war'. Therefore, the number of this missile force has increased tremendously since the 1990s.

China has the most active and diverse ballistic missile development programme in the world. It is developing and testing offensive missiles, forming additional missile units, qualitatively upgrading missile systems, and developing methods to counter ballistic missile defence. The trends in modernisation are as follows:

- Shift from silo base, liquid missile system, to road mobile, solid fuel, missile systems, for improving survivability.
- With largest conventional missile arsenal in Asia-Pacific. China has indigenously developed cruise missiles for achieving precision-strike, warhead penetration and accuracy.
- Increased survivability with a 5,000-km-long tunnel network and improving

PLAAF air defences. China has also increased the number of its SRBMs, and ground and air-launched land-attack cruise missiles (LACMs).

- PLARF has moved away from single-use launchers to re-loadable launchers, increasing stockpiles. While ICBM is primarily retaliatory in nature, SRBM (with an arsenal of 1,200 missiles) and 100 MRBM force is for surprise attack, i.e. to pre-empt the enemy's attack, and this strategy is especially meant to be used in a regional war scenario.
- China's is modernising both qualitatively and quantitatively its nuclear arsenal, which consists of 75-100 ICBMs, including silo-based DF-5A and Mod DF-5B with MIRV capabilities; the solid-fuelled, road-mobile DF-31 and DF-31A. China is also developing the long-range CSS-10 Mod 2, with a range in excess of 11,200 km. These are all for power projection. Apart from its long-range ICBMs, it also has its IRBMs/MRBMs where the DF-26 precision strike missile is mainly to counter threats in Asia-Pacific.
- China has strengthened its triad and continues to produce the Jin-class nuclear-powered ballistic missile submarine (SSBN). Four such submarines have been commissioned and another one is under construction. The Jin will eventually carry the CSS-NX-14 (JL-2) SLBM with an estimated range of 7,200 km. Together these will give the PLAN its first credible long-range sea-based nuclear capability and Jin SSBNs based at Hainan Island in the South China Sea would then be able to conduct nuclear deterrence patrols.
- China is continuing to develop its Ballistic Missile Defence (BMD). Presently, China's long-range SAMs have limited capabilities against ballistic missiles. However, it is believed that new home-grown radars, the JL-1A and JY-27A, will address this threat. China is also developing missile defence umbrella consisting of kinetic energy intercept at exo-atmospheric altitudes (greater than 80 km), as well as intercepts of ballistic missiles and other aerospace vehicles within the upper atmosphere.

Over the last decade, China has added more than 50 nuclear warheads to its ICBM forces capable of hitting the US mainland, and within another decade, the number could well exceed to 100. China has sufficient stockpile of fissile material to sustain this expansion, retaining a stockpile of military plutonium at an estimated 1.8 metric tons. Resorting to warheads drawing only on HEU (from its stockpiles of some 18 metric tons), would allow China to create some 600 warheads. A lot of research has also been going on in developing hypersonic vehicles and Ballistic Missile Defence. China will continue to develop new missile versions like the DF-5B, DF-31A, DF-41 etc. Some of these warheads would be capable of having MIRVs and other penetration aids. The trends of the missile force and the detailed growth of various missiles are given in the following tables:

Transition of Missile Force through the Years

Type of Launcher	1985	1995	2000	2010	2012	2016
LACM	0	0	0	54	54	54
ICBM	6	17	40	66	66	62
IRBM	60	60	30	2	2	6
MRBM	50	10	50	116	122	146
SRBM	0	–	60	204	216	189

Source: IISS, Military Balance 1985-2016, adapted by Anthony H. Cordesman and Joseph Kendall at the Centre for Strategic and International Studies.

Transition of Missile Force through the Years

	Missiles	1985	2000	2010	2016
ICBM	DF-4	4	20	10	10
	DF5A	2	20	20	10
	DF-5B	0	0	0	10
	DF-31	–	–	12	8
	DF-31A	–	–	24	24
IRBM	DF-3A	60	30	02	06
MRBM	DF-16	0	0	0	12
	DF-21A	0	50	80	80
	DF-21C	–	–	36	36
	DF-21D	–	–		18
SRBM	DF-15B	–	20	96	81
	DF-11A/M-11A	–	40	108	108
	DF-2	50	0	0	0
LACM	DH-10	0	–	54	54

Source: IISS, Military Balance 1985-2016, adapted by Anthony H. Cordesman and Joseph Kendall at the Centre for Strategic and International Studies.

The force structure has seen a remarkable increase in the number of conventional short/medium range missiles with an equally effective nuclear force of medium and long range ballistic missiles. The local war concept has made China increase its precision SRBMs and LACM that constitutes nearly 60 per cent of the PLARF arsenal. However, since the last few years the trend has stabilised and may not see a drastic increase in these numbers, but the new variations will be developed concurrently for replacing the older ones.

In order to strengthen counterforce and counter-attack capabilities, new variants of DF-31, like the DF 31-A and DF-41, and an offload TEL are being developed so that the weapons can be deployed from garrisons whose launch area would be difficult to identify. China's future aim will be to develop a range of niche technologies for countering US and other countries' ballistic missile defence systems, including manoeuvrable re-entry vehicles (MARVs), MIRVs, decoys, chaff, jamming, and thermal shielding, also to conduct training exercises featuring manoeuvre, camouflage and launch operations under simulated combat conditions for improving survivability.

Strategic Support Force

For long-term observers of the PLA's development, the fact that the Second Artillery Corps (SAC) was restructured as the PLA Rocket Force (PLARF) was not surprising. The establishment of the PLA Strategic Support Force (PLASSF), however, was a different story; to many specialists, the PLASSF represented a major break in tradition.[43] In addition, after China announced its establishment, media reports on the SSF have been scarce. The new service is veiled in mystery. According to official sources, the SSF will form the core of China's information warfare force, which is central to China's 'active defence strategic concept. This is an evolution, not a departure from, China's evolving military strategy. It is a culmination of years of technological advancement and institutional change. In the context of ongoing reforms, the creation of the SSF may be one of the most important changes yet. Consolidating and restructuring China's information forces is a key measure to enable a number of other state goals of reform, including reducing the power of the army, implementing joint operations, and increasing emphasis on high-tech forces.

Senior Chinese military experts regard PLASSF as a 'fifth service', not a 'military branch', which should be seen as an independent military service in its own right; composed of three separate forces or force-types, space troops, cyber troops, and electronic warfare forces; cyber force would be composed hackers focusing on attack and defence; space forces would focus on reconnaissance and navigation satellites; electronic warfare force would focus on jamming and disrupting enemy radar and communications and this would allow the PLA to meet the challenges of not only traditional warfare but also of new warfare centered on new technology. (Fig. 11)

Special Forces

Chinese Special Forces numbering an estimated 14,000 are specialised in rapid reaction combat in a limited regional war under high-tech conditions, commando operations, counter-terrorism and intelligence gathering. They are organised in a number of units and sub-units like Guangzhou Military Region Special Forces Unit established in 1988 and expanded in 2000 as first PLA special operations unit capable of air, sea, and land operations; Chengdu Military Region Special Forces

Figure 4.11: Operationalisation of PLASSF

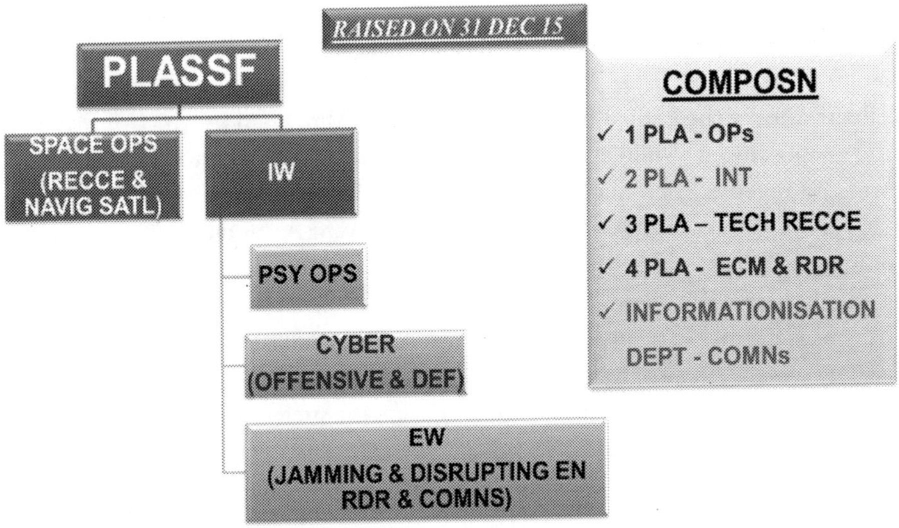

Unit established in 1992 and specialised in target surveillance, target designation, airborne insertion, sabotage, offensive strike, rescue, and has experimented new concepts, tactics, equipment including digitised army soldier system and high-mobility land weapon platforms; Beijing Military Region Special Forces Unit established in early 1990s and holds high-tech equipment including UAVs, modern demolitions, laser designators and laser dazzlers; Shenyang Military Region Special Forces Unit; Nanjing Military Region Special Forces Units (two of them); Lanzhou Military Region Special Forces Unit; Hong Kong Special Operations Company known as five minute Response Unit; and the Macau Quick Reaction Platoon. In conflict scenarios, Chinese Special Forces will likely be deployed in conjunction China's Airborne Corps. However, in non-war period Chinese Special Forces would be covertly deployed for information support operations, strategic surveillance, training, arming and advising dissident/terrorist/insurgent groups in target countries, and perception management.

Sub-Conventional

Though China keeps bandying about its peaceful rise, the fact is the opposite. The Maoists movements spawned globally during the era of Mao Tse Tung were insurgent movements centred on violence akin to terrorists. These included the Maoists movements in Burma (now Myanmar) and Nepal, the Khmer Rouge of Cambodia, the Japanese Red Army, and the Shining Path of Peru. In addition to the China-Pakistan sub-conventional nexus (being discussed in the next chapter), China has individually indulged in supporting and nurturing multiple proxy forces: Taliban in Afghanistan; using Pakistani proxies to further her own national interests; financing Kashmiri separatists and militants; arming and financing militants in India's northeast as well as Maoists; establishing and supporting Nepalese Maoists; lethally arming the United Wa State Army (UWSA) in Shan province of Myanmar and establishing the United Liberation Front of West, South, East Asia (ULFWSEA) bringing together nine major militant organisations of northeast India including the NSCN (K) and ULFA. Significantly, the ULFWSEA was established concurrent to Prime Minister Narendra Modi announcing the 'Act East Policy'. From all this, it should be evident that while both China and Pakistan have developed advanced sub-conventional capabilities and are using them proactively, India is woefully lagging behind in this sphere. This is a great strategically asymmetry especially since application of irregular forces has become the preferred mode of conflict and conventional forces cannot be very effective in eliminating such forces. That is the very reason we have continued to bleed internally because of proxy wars waged against us. We have failed to heed Chanakya who said, 'Do not be very upright in your dealings for you would see by going to the forest that straight trees are cut down while crooked ones are left standing'.

Capabilities of the PLAN have already been discussed above; however, note must be taken of the Merchant Marine of China. Counted on the basis of the number of ships registered under the Chinese flag, China's merchant marine, with 2,030 vessels registered in China, is the largest in the world. The total number of Chinese owned vessels, including those registered in other countries, is 3,567. If Hong Kong owned vessels are added to the list, the total goes up to 5,076. China is expected to account for 17 per cent of all global shipping by 2030. Chinese guidelines require all civilian shipbuilders to ensure that their new vessels are suitable for military use in an emergency.[44] These guidelines apply to all container, ro-ro, multi-purpose, bulk carrier and break bulk vessels, establishing requisite specifications and design requirements. Security of merchant fleet also provides the PLAN the cover needed to deploy anywhere in the world, as, for example, its deployment in the Gulf of Aden patrol since 2009. The Merchant Marine, therefore, can be used for slipping in task forces/detachments for sub-conventional operations.

PLA STRATEGIC SUPPORT FORCE

Cyber and IW

China's military doctrine supports Kinetic Warfare, Information Warfare which includes Cyber Warfare, Electronic Warfare (EW), Psychological Warfare, Space and Nuclear Warfare and it has selectively concentrated on 'lead ahead'[45] capabilities in niche areas like Command, Control, Communications, Computers, Intelligence, Surveillance and Reconnaissance (C4ISR), Aviation and Space. One of the main principles of the local wars concept is that information warfare (IW) will play a central role in future warfare.[46] The PLA believes that advantages in collecting, transmitting and processing information will lead to a decided advantage at the operational and strategic levels. The PLA's sustained modernisation efforts have driven transformation in the PLA, particularly in the development of a viable C4ISR capability. This has acted as a catalyst for acquiring integrated IW capability, which aims to effectively interfere with the adversaries networks while protecting own military and civilian networks and systems.[47] PLA has developed the Integrated Network and Electronic Warfare (INEW) doctrine to organise and structure its forces for gaining information superiority. INEW combines application of Computer Network Operations (CNO) and EW encompasses coordinated and simultaneous attack on the adversaries C4ISR networks and other key information systems/assets to gain information dominance. PLA's Science of Campaigns notes that one of the main roles of IW is to create windows of opportunity for other forces to operate without detection or with a reduced risk of counter attack by exploiting the periods of 'blindness', 'deafness' or 'paralysis' created by information attacks.

The strategic imperative for the PLA to operate in the electromagnetic domain is driving the formulation of new approach to IW termed as 'Information Confrontation' *(xinxiduikang)* that applies 'system of systems' operations theory to IW, viewing it as a macro system comprising discreet capabilities linked together under a single command structure and fully integrated into the overall campaign plan. PLA has raised the Blue Force IW units that carry out information confrontation missions in exercises to create a complicated jamming and network attack environment for units who are under training. Use of 'complex electromagnetic environment' is a regular feature in the PLA exercises wherein the blue force units target command and control networks via Computer Network Attack (CNA) or jamming critical communication nodes, thus preparing the units for realistic IW environment. It has also been reported that PLA arty units have developed 'soft kill' capabilities integrated into their fire support missions, suggesting a model that incorporates EW and CNA capabilities as 'organic' to the unit rather than solely relying on dedicated external INEW units for support.

Achieving information dominance is one of the key goals for the PLA at the strategic and campaign level. 'The science of military strategy' and 'the science of campaigns' both identify adversary's C4ISR and logistics system, networks as the highest priority for IW attacks. The aim being to combine paralysing CNO strikes on the enemy's command and control architecture combined with hard kill using missiles, airstrikes and/or Special Forces against critical installations or hardware. The Science of Campaigns states that IW must mark the start of a campaign and, if used properly, can enable overall operational success.

Space

In China's Space Dream, 'the dream of space flight is an important part of the strong country dream [and] the space dream is an important component of realising the Chinese people's mighty dream of national rejuvenation'.[48] To achieve this, China has created the PLARF discussed above. The necessity to develop space-based C4ISR systems is based on the requirement to develop 'power projection and precision-strike capabilities'. Space is an essential component in the development of long-range cruise missiles and anti-ship ballistic missiles for over-the-horizon attacks requires the ability to locate, track, and target enemy ships hundreds of kilometres away from China's shores, as well as the ability to coordinate these operations with units from multiple services. Remote sensing satellites provide intelligence on enemy dispositions and strategic intelligence before conflict begins. Communication satellites can provide global connectivity and can facilitate communications between far-flung forces. Navigation and positioning satellites can provide critical information on location and can improve the accuracy of strikes.

China is using space for the projection of both, the soft as well as the hard power. It is using space to not only monitor the Sea Lanes of Communications (SLOCs), coordinate humanitarian and counter piracy activities (as most of the C4ISR activities are dependent on Space) but also to monitor disputed maritime territories in South China Sea and East China Sea. China's A2/AD programmes rely on a mix of space-based systems including C4ISR and SATNAV (BeiDou) capabilities. China is relying on land and sea launch capabilities as well as sea-based systems that utilize 'Long View' space support ships to perform tasks like monitoring and tracking space vehicles—such as spacecraft, missiles, and rockets—while also coordinating and communicating with ground-based assets.[49] In this regard, the Chinese land-based DF-21D anti-ship ballistic missile (ASBM), along with the ship-based C4ISR capabilities, is of utmost significance, as it claims to counter the threat posed by the Americans in the Asia-Pacific region.

China's space-tracking vessels have successfully participated in full-range ICBM tests, submarine-to-shore guided-missile underwater-launch tests, communication-satellite launches, manned and unmanned space-vehicle launches, and an Antarctic visit. They have played a significant role in the development and testing of technologies and weapons. As for land-based assets, China has three satellite launch centers and stations; Jiuquan (Base 20), Dongfeng Space City, Xichang (Base 27), and Taiyuan (Base 25). The country is currently constructing a station in Wenchang (also known as Wenchang Space City and Wenchang Satellite Launch Center); additionally, it has two control facilities: an Aerospace Command and Control Center in Xi'an (also known as Base 26). The Aerospace Telemetry Oceanic Ship Base is a crucial ground station, as it tracks Yuanwang data on both commercial satellites and spacecraft. Also, China has overseas tracking stations in Karachi, Pakistan; Malindi, Kenya; and Swakopmund, Namibia. China's growing space capabilities translate into military capabilities affecting all aspects of conventional and nuclear targeting, ground-air-sea operations, precision conventional strike capacities, and missile defence. Also, China is also using its intelligence collection efforts to improve technological capacity.

PLA considers technological improvements to Command, Control, Communications, Computers, and Intelligence (C4I) systems essential to improve speed and effectiveness of decision-making, while providing secure and reliable communications to fixed and mobile command posts, and is fielding advanced automated command systems like the Integrated Command Platform (ICP) to units at lower echelons across the force.[50] These technical improvements have greatly enhanced the PLA's flexibility and responsiveness. The endeavor is thus to make the space capabilities more advanced, with special emphasis on: Satellite Communications (SATCOM); Intelligence, Surveillance Reconnaissance (ISR); Satellite Navigation (SATNAV); meteorology as well as manned, unmanned, and interplanetary space exploration. As of December 2015, China launched 19 SLVs carrying 45 spacecraft, including navigation, ISR, and test/engineering satellites that include Long March (LM)-6 (carrying 20 satellites) and the LM-11 'next generation' SLVs, also the launch of the BeiDou I1-S, an inclined geosynchronous orbit (IGSO) satellite.[51]

China has made efforts to gain a Ballistic Missile Defence (BMD) capability. New indigenous radars, the JL-1A and JY-27A, are designed to address the ballistic missile threat, with the JL-1A advertised as capable of precision tracking of multiple ballistic missiles. China is proceeding with the research and development of a missile defence umbrella consisting of kinetic energy intercept at exo-atmospheric altitudes (greater than 80 km), as well as intercepts of ballistic missiles and other aerospace vehicles within the upper atmosphere. China's ASAT test and procurement of Russia's S-400 air defense system has already been discussed above.

For counter-space capabilities, China is requires a wide range of capabilities to dissuade an adversary's tactical and strategic capabilities. These include developing 'direct-ascent anti-satellite missiles, co-orbital anti-satellite systems, computer network operations, ground based satellite jammers, and directed energy weapons'.[52]

PLA writings emphasise the necessity of destroying, damaging, and interfering with the enemy's reconnaissance and communications satellites, suggesting that such systems, as well as navigation and early warning satellites, could be among the targets of attacks designed to 'blind and deafen the enemy'.[53] China is also researching radio-frequency (RF) weapons that could be used against satellites. RF weapons using high-power microwaves can be ground-based, space-based, or employed on missiles to temporarily or permanently disable electronic components through either overheating or short circuiting. RF weapons are thus useful in achieving a wide spectrum of effects against satellites in all orbits. [54]

Doctrinal Thought

The Chinese military thinkers deem doctrine as fundamental, which encapsulates the perceived nature of war, purpose of military power and its relationship with other instruments of power. After an in-depth study of the wars in Kosovo, Iraq and Afghanistan, China has evolved new strategic and operational military doctrines. The main tenets of the strategic military doctrine are as follows:

- **Informationisation**. Informationisation entails the development of net-centric and knowledge-based capability to launch 'effect based' operations against a high-technology and modernised adversary. PLA's drive to Informationisation is based on the network-centric warfare (NCW) concept of the US, which involves translating an information advantage into a 'war fighting' advantage, characterised by knowledge of the commander's intent, self-synchronisation and increased combat power. A Command Automation system is described in the PLA Regulations as an *'Military Information System' that processes command and control, intelligence and reconnaissance (Recce), Early Warning and Surveillance, Communications, Electronic Counter Measures and other operational and information support capabilities with computers at its core.* It emerges that informationisation *clearly relates to the PLA's ability to adopt information technologies to command, intelligence, training and weapon systems.* This would include broad investments in new automatic command systems, linked by fibre-optic nets, satellite and new high-frequency digital radio systems.
- **Active Defence**. The 'active defence' doctrine is transformation from Mao's large-scale people's land-centric war to high-intensity, short-duration local war under informationised conditions. Though, 'Active Defence' can be taken as a manifestation of China's defensive outlook, this is only so at the strategic level and its employment is distinctively offensive at the operational and tactical levels. As put in perspective by the Chinese Academy of Military

Science (AMS), 'The guiding principle is passive in form, but it is initiative and active in content'. The operational method that is recommended is 'take defence at the beginning of the enemy's attack and actively take offensive actions to defeat the enemy after he gets exhausted'. David Shambaugh, the well-known Chinese scholar, has explained, 'The PLA doctrine of 'Active Defence' calls for forward positioning, frontier defence, engagement of the enemy at or over the border and potential engagement in conflict beyond China's immediate periphery.... This doctrine is essentially proactive and seeks to take the battle into enemy territory'. The steps proscribed for the execution of 'Active Defence' by the AMS in the Science of Strategy are reproduced next and it needs to be highlighted that they are in line with the stratagem's for war making as proscribed by Sun Tzu: make correct judgement of the situation; make full, secret and rapid war preparations, carry out smart camouflage and demonstration; launch attacks at unexpected time and location when the enemy is tired or careless; employ new weapons and new operational methods to win victory in surprise attacks; and consolidate and exploit fruits of victory when the initial battle is won. Active Defence, therefore, is characterised by proactive offensive operations with limited political objectives; heavy attrition on war waging potential of enemy in his own territory employing long-range artillery, SRBM and precision-guided munitions (PGMs), essentially being punitive action.

- **Oceanic Offensive**. There is a doctrinal shift from continental war to maritime strategic offensive capability aimed at securing the energy supply sources, trade routes (SLOCs) and to project maritime power. The operating of Oceanic Offensive is '*Anti-Access Strategy - aimed at preserving and maximising a country's strategic space through 'deterrence' exercised by 'strong military capability' that is intended to raise the costs of intervention for a potential challenger*'. China's A2/AD strategy or what the Chinese call 'Counter Intervention Operations' exemplifies China's concept of 'Active Defence'. The principle behind this concept and what has been defined as 'Active Strategic Counter Attack on Exterior Lines' (ASCEL) is an extension of China's Active Defence strategy. The A2/AD strategy aims to deny the US the capability to use the sea freely making it a 'No-Go' area, conversely, China can deny vital battle-space without physically controlling it—Sea Denial by other means. Under ASCEL, the Chinese are expected to take the initiative, achieve surprise and pre-empt the US by its 'key point' 'integrated' strikes which manifest as concentrated, multi-dimensional and multi-spectral attacks on combat, combat support, logistics and Theatre

Information Systems. ASCEL operations extend the scope of the strategy of 'Active Defence' from the 'Operational' to the 'Strategic' level.

Unrestricted Warfare. China's concept of 'Unrestricted Warfare' has been discussed in Chapter 1. The terminal aim is to undermine and/or to paralyse the enemy and forcing one's will on him. Because of this requirement, the PLA has included psychological, public opinion, and legal warfare also under its scope. This has expanded the traditional battle-space and permeated all spheres, traditional and non-traditional, thereby blurring the lines of conflict and makes the war 'omni-dimensional'. When seen in perspective within the traditional Chinese thinking, this meshes with Sun Tzu's strategy of 'subduing the enemy without fighting'. The kaleidoscope of options and their combinations as given by the authors is reproduced as below:

Multiplicity of Options for Waging Unrestricted War

Military	Trans-Military	Non-Military
Atomic Warfare	Diplomatic Warfare	Financial Warfare
Conventional warfare	Network Warfare	Trade Warfare
Bio-Chemical Warfare	Intelligence Warfare	Resources Warfare
Ecological Warfare	Psychological Warfare	Economic Aid Warfare
Space Warfare	Tactical Warfare	Regulatory Warfare
Electronic Warfare	Smuggling Warfare	Sanctions Warfare
Guerrilla Warfare	Drug Warfare	Media Warfare
Terrorist Warfare	Virtual Warfare (Deterrence)	Ideological Warfare

Source: Unrestricted Warfare by Qiao Liang and Wang Xiangsui, reproduced by CIA's FBIS and available at http://www.terrorism.com/documents/unrestricted/pdf.

As can be interpreted from the above, the range of options that could be generated make them omni-dimensional and reinforces the opinion that the struggle for victory will take place beyond the traditional battlefield. It is a modified concept whose scope and application goes beyond traditional limits (*pian zheng shi chao xian zuhe zhan*). Since the purpose is to reduce the possibility of mitigating actual combat, it can be considered as another way of 'cohesion' and resolving security issues. It needs to be noted that Ecological and Terrorist Warfare are listed under what the authors feel are legitimate military means. This has major implications as India is susceptible to both forms of attacks. The principles as espoused by the authors are listed next. Though they are self-explanatory, a brief amplification has also been added.

Principles of Unrestricted Warfare

Principle	Amplification/Explanation
Omni directionality	This is at the heart of the concept and is all pervasive
Synchrony	Conducting concurrent actions in different locations, spheres and domains
Limited Objectives	Focussed Approach on Achievable Objectives
Unlimited Measures	Adequate Measures and Means allotted to achieve the limited objectives
Asymmetry (Fei junheng)	A measure and the means to accomplish the objective
Minimal Consumption	Corresponds to the principle of war 'Economy of Effort'
Multi-Dimensional Coordination	Requires a structurally networked environment to coordinate and synergise the application of means
Adjustment and Control over the entire process	Requires a Real time system of feed-back for evolving and applying timely responses

Source: Unrestricted Warfare by Qiao Liang and Wang Xiangsui, reproduced by CIA's FBIS and available at http://www.terrorism.com/documents/unrestricted/pdf.

Assured Nuclear Deterrence. China's military nuclear programme has witnessed a steady transition from nuclear defence to minimum credible deterrence. The emphasis currently is on limited nuclear deterrence which entails enhancement in nuclear deterrence to 'assured and survivable' second strike capability. These have been discussed earlier.

Strategic Deception. Chinese are past masters in strategic, operational, and tactical deception. Chinese doctrinal material defines strategic deception as luring the other side into developing misperceptions and establishing for oneself a strategically advantageous position by producing various kinds of false phenomena in an organised and planned manner with the smallest cost in manpower and material. The two main drivers of China's strategic deception are enhanced Information Warfare and Asymmetric Warfare capability.

War Zone Campaign (WZC) Doctrine. PLA has formulated military doctrine for war fighting at operational level (level of Theatre of Operations) which PLA refers as War Zone. The WZC Doctrine involves a phased rapid yet calibrated raising of the conflict threshold and to force application while offering opportunity to the adversary to capitulate and seek negotiations prior to transcending to next phase in the escalatory ladder. Military destruction and annihilation is only a means; political capitulation of the adversary is the objective. The success of this doctrine is based upon preliminary lulling of the adversary into a state of complacency while the PLA upgrades its readiness levels. This preliminary phase, to be executed during peace time and over prolonged periods, is referred as '*External Calm & Internal Intensity* (ECII)'. Once the PLA's desired readiness levels are achieved and the geo-political situation is considered appropriate, the actual military campaign under a unified HQ (WZC HQ) would commence under the WZC Doctrine in three phases:

- **'Elite Forces and Sharp Arms (EFSA)' or *Jingbing Liqi*.** These forces are initially employed for indirect posturing by concentrated Pockets of Excellence (POEs) Forces and thereafter employment for Gaining Initiative by Striking First (GISF). Special Operations Forces (SOF) are employed to gain first-hand information of the battle, disrupt enemy build up and, in addition, to build up a presence with elite forces and make a political statement to the adversary to back off. The aim is political victory, and not territorial gain. If the adversary backs off, WZC is considered successful.
- **GISF**. If the adversary does not capitulate through EFSA measures, the next phase is prosecuted to gain the Initiative by Striking First (*Xianji Zhidi*) and by employing POEs Forces. The purpose is to prosecute a 'deep non-contact battle' through long-range precision strikes at the adversary's strategic and operational decision-making nodes, major military infrastructures, and mobility and logistical nodes. These are to be conducted synergistically with intense EW, cyber warfare and other asymmetric elements. The operational objective is to cause a decision paralysis and convince the enemy of the inevitability of military annihilation unless they capitulate and seek negotiations; it is often referred to as winning victory with one decisive strike.
- **Quick Battle to force Quick Resolution (QBQR)**. In the last phase, if the politico-military aims have still not been achieved, the PLA plans to fight a 'QBQR' or *Suzhan Sujue*. At this stage, the mobile formations such as the armour and mechanised infantry divisions are sent in for a quick and decisive result to force a final political resolution of the conflict.

The WZC appears to be a calibrated approach for prosecution of a military campaign under a rubric wherein the time lines are blurred and the escalation tightly controlled. It seeks an integration of means and ways to achieve the intended goals. The conceptual model is depicted in Figure 4.12.

Integrated Joint Operations (IJO) (Y*itihua lianhe zuozhan*)

Attributing the transition from Joint Operations (JO; *Lianhe zuozhan)* to 'Integrated Joint Operations (IJO), Nan Li observes that this was due to the evolution in

Figure 4.12: Phases and Escalation Matrix of WZC

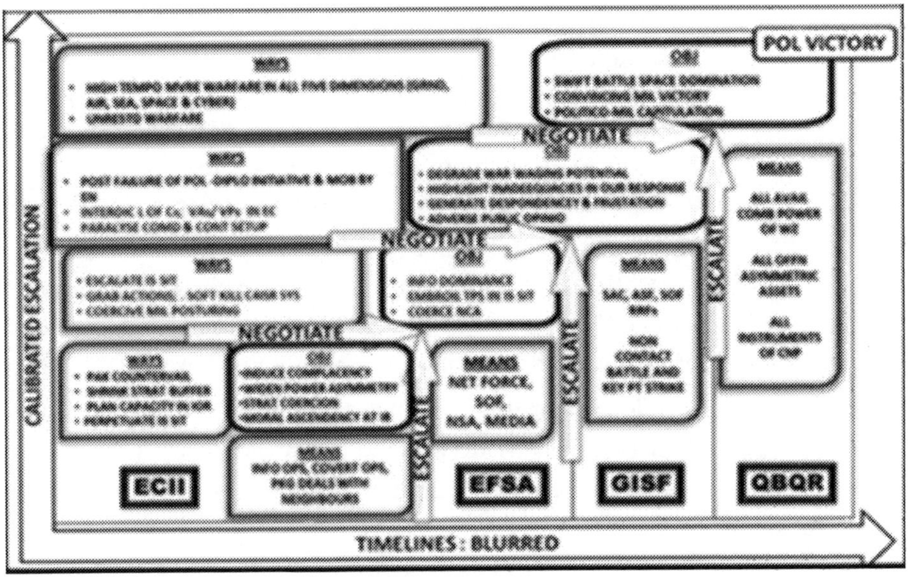

China's Military Research and Learning under Jiang Zemin, and was undertaken to further the institutionalised interests of the PLA. The dual-track modernisation–mechanisation and informationisation was to be operationalised through the concept of IJO. In essence, while JO emphasised on 'jointness' within the service, IJO seeks to achieve 'jointness' across the three services, the Local Forces and also with the civilian organisations. Though JO and IJO have many similarities as both involve two or more services operating under a Unified Command, there were major differences in their strategies and implementation. In addition, the separation between services has blurred as units have been enabled to perform multiple functions because of a higher level of situational awareness and enhanced operational capabilities. The differences between the two are tabulated as follows:

	Actor/Structure	Service Boundaries	Coordina-tion	Levels	Depth	Time	Effects
JO	Individual Service Structures, Hence, vertical by nature	Clear	Plan based	Campaign	Limited	Limited	Unit
IJO	Networked System, flat and short and horizontal	Blurred	Action based	All Levels	All Depths	All Times	System

The integrated systems approach facilitates non-linear targeting at greater depths by facilitating concurrent targeting of the tactical, operational, and strategic depths as it optimises information received for selection of targets, conduct of multi-dimensional saturation attacks by multiple means, and the ability to revisit the target-based real/near real-time 'Post Strike Damage Assessments'; facilitates better Situational Awareness; and battlefield transparency mitigates the disadvantages of night and facilitates closer battlefield engagements by optimising safety distances between opposing forces.

Chinese Operational Guidance. A critical study of *Art of War* by Sun Tzu, Military Thoughts of Mao and NDU publications namely 'On Campaigns' and 'Science of Military Strategy' bring out the following features of Chinese way of war fighting:

- **Strategic Coercion**. Acme of skill is to subdue enemy without fighting.
- **Centre of Gravity**. Enemy leadership and Enemy Strategy.
- **Thorough Preparation**. 'Fight no battle unprepared and without being sure of victory'.
- **Pre-emption**. 'And therefore those skilled in war bring the enemy to the field of battle and are not brought there by him'.
- **Guile and Subterfuge**.
  - 'The enemy must not know where I intend to give battle.... He must prepare in a great many places ... and when he prepares everywhere he will be weak everywhere'.
  - 'Never fight at a time and place where enemy expects in a way or style which he anticipates'.
- **Manoeuvre and Speed**.
  - 'Offensive should be like water which follows path of least resistance'.
  - 'Attack dispersed locations first, Concentrate, avoid attrition and strive for dislocation of the enemy strength'.
  - 'Paralyse first annihilate later'.
  - 'Offensive should be delivered with supernatural speed'.
- **Jointness**. Political, Military and Civil Integration, and Synergy.

Military Strategic Guidance. Study of abovementioned documents highlights four facets of military strategic guidance as under:

- Continuous resistance from the front to make the enemy passive.
- Continuous harassment in depth forcing the enemy to deploy a Rear Area Security (RAS) scheme.
- Strike from the flanks—effect an Outflanking Manoeuvre.
- Destruction of enemy operational energy centres by effect-based operations.

Military Diplomacy. China's military engagement with other countries seeks to enhance China's international presence and influence by improving relationships with foreign militaries, bolstering China's international and regional image, and assuaging other countries' concerns about China's rise. In 2012, senior military officials from at least 25 countries visited China. Senior PLA officials visited at least 33 countries. The PLA participated in UN peacekeeping operations (PKO), carried out humanitarian assistance and disaster relief work in Pakistan and conducted the second global goodwill voyage of the PLA Navy ZHENG HE training vessel. PLA leaders participated in various multilateral meetings, including the Defense Ministers' Meeting of the Shanghai Cooperation Organisation (SCO) and the Association of Southeast Asian Nations (ASEAN) Regional Forum Security Policy Conference. PLA participation in bilateral and multilateral exercises is increasing. In 2011 and 2012 alone, the PLA held 21 joint exercise and training events with foreign militaries, compared to 32 during the entire 11th Five-Year Plan period (2006-2010). These activities included military exercises with SCO members, naval exercises, ground forces training, peacekeeping, and search and rescue operations/missions. China also conducted joint training for operations other than war, including the 2011 COOPERATION SPIRIT humanitarian assistance/ disaster relief (HA/DR) exercise with Australia. China observed KHAN QUEST-11, a peacekeeping exercise in Mongolia—the first time it had done so. The PLA Navy conducted maritime exercises with Russia, Vietnam, and Thailand and counter-piracy exercises with France and the United States. The PLA Air Force (PLAAF) conducted unprecedented bilateral training during 2011, including its first bilateral air exercise with Pakistan and training with air forces in Belarus and Venezuela. In contrast, the PLA Air Force participated in only one bilateral exercise in 2012—an airborne training exercise with Belarus in November. PEACE MISSION 2012, conducted under the auspices of the SCO, did not include PLA Air Force participation as in the past, and instead focused on what SCO nations called 'counterterrorism' training, which more closely resembles training to suppress armed opposition within a member country.

Key Issues

- ✓ *China aims to emerge as a regional predominant military power by 2020 and a world military power by 2050.*
- ✓ *There has been a perceptible doctrinal shift in China's thinking and way of war fighting. The doctrinal tenants include Informationisation, Active Defence, Oceanic Offensive, Unrestricted Warfare, Assured Nuclear Deterrence and Strategic Deception.*

- ✓ *WZC is the operating doctrine for undertaking military campaigns in a conflict zone. The CMC's role in command and control of the WZC is pivotal.*
- ✓ *Reorganisation of the Chinese Military gives tremendous advantage of synergy, decision making and application of military power.*
- ✓ *China's strategic aims vis-à-vis India centre upon nudging India to accept subordinate role in Asia, hedge India's economy, shrink India's strategic space in South Asia and IOR, and realise own territorial gains.*
- ✓ *Strengthening Pakistan to countervail India and gravitational pull to India's neighbours is part of the strategy.*
- ✓ *China is abetting insurgencies in India and playing Pakistan's jihadi card against India and Indian interests.*
- ✓ *China's hybrid warfare is waged in all domains of civil and military, including cyberspace and space.*
- ✓ *Information warfare and psychological operations are vital aspects of China's hybrid warfare.*
- ✓ *A confident PLA is enhancing its military diplomacy, be it in conduct of joint training, participation in PKO, sale of military hardware to foreign countries or its role in counter piracy operations.*
- ✓ *The China–Pakistan nexus is expanding with the CPEC and China's entry in Gwadar Port.*
- ✓ *For Chinese, the acquisition of high-end technology is of prime importance, for which means do not matter. All resources of the state are and will be employed to get high-end technology.*
- ✓ *The focus of development of the defence industry will remain on the six sectors described in the chapter. The exact pace and direction of the Chinese Defence Industry can be assessed and tracked by closely following the six sectors.*
- ✓ *The boundary between the Civilian and Military industries will be blurred and the two will integrate and cooperate in developing and manufacturing a vast array of defence equipment.*

NOTES

1 China GDP Annual Growth Rate Forecast 2016-2020, Trading Economics, http://www.tradingeconomics.com/china/gdp-growth-annual/forecast.

2 'China Military Spending Quickens as Xi Seeks "World Class" Military', Bloomberg News, 5 March 2018, https://www.bloomberg.com/news/articles/2018-03-05/china-military-spending-quickens-as-xi-seeks-world-class-force.

3 Forest, Kaya and Sierra Rayne, 'China and Russia Combined Now at Military Spending Parity with US', 13 April 2016. http://www.americanthinker.com/blog/2016/04/china_and_russia_combined_now_at_military_spending_parity_with_us.html.

4 Zafar, Muhammad Saleh, 'Chinese Premier Vows to Support Pakistan at Every Forum', The News, 21 September 2016, https://www.thenews.com.pk/print/151751-Chinese-premier-vows-to-support-Pakistan-at-every-forum.

5 Kenny, Stuart, 'China and India: A "New Great Game" Founded on Historic Mistrust and Current Competition', Indo-Pacific Strategic Papers, September 2015, http://www.defence.gov.au/ADC/Publications/IndoPac/Kenny_IPS_Paper.pdf.

6 Malik, Mohan, 'China Unveils "The Kashmir Card"', *China Brief*, Volume 10, Issue 19, 24 September 2010, https://jamestown.org/program/china-unveils-the-kashmir-card/.

7 Laskar, Rezaul H, 'Nine Militant Groups of NE Form United Front with Chinese Blessings', Hindustan Times, 24 April 2015, http://www.hindustantimes.com/india/nine-miltant-groups-of-ne-form-united-front-with-chinese-blessings/story-6SuTFuFRymf27fSueYyoaP.html.

8 Kai, Boh Ze, 'Narco Diplomacy: Foreign Policy of the United Wa State Army', Mantraya Special Report, 27 January 2016, http://mantraya.org/narco-diplomacy-foreign-policy-of-the-united-wa-state-army/.

9 Green, Marcel A, 'China's Growing Cyberwar Capabilities', The Diplomat, 13 April 2015, http://thediplomat.com/2015/04/chinas-growing-cyberwar-capabilities/.

10 'China Rushing to Beat US in the Race to Space', Pakistan Defence, 19 February 2016, https://defence.pk/pdf/threads/china-rushing-to-beat-us-in-the-race-to-space.422675/.

11 Kistensen, Hans M and Robert S Norris, 'Chinese Nuclear Forces, 2011', 27 November 2015, http://www.tandfonline.com/doi/abs/10.1177/0096340211426630.

12 http://www.worldatlas.com/articles/world-s-largest-exporters-of-arms.html, accessed 26 April 2017.

13 Arora, Kamna, 'Two-Front War Against India Possible', Zee News, 23 October 2011, http://zeenews.india.com/exclusive/-two-front-war-against-india-possible_3375.html.

14 Moss, Trefor, 'Bangladesh Eyes China Arms', The Diplomat, 30 June 2011, http://thediplomat.com/2011/06/bangladesh-eyes-china-arms/.

15 'Russia to Deliver S-400 Air Defence Missile Systems to China Before 2020', defenseaerospace.com, 10 November 2016, http://www.defense-aerospace.com/articles-view/release/3/178669/russia-to-complete-s_400-deliveries-to-china-by-2020.html.

16 Cole, Bernard D, in "Reflections on China's Maritime Strategy: Island Chains and the Classics", published by US Naval War College, see https://www.usnwc.edu/Academics/Faculty/Derek-Reveron/Workshops/Maritime-Security,-Seapower,--Trade/Maritime-Working-Papers/cole-island-chains.aspx.

17 Tellis, Ashley J, 'India as a Leading Power', published by Carnegie Endowment for International Peace, April 2016.

18 Adapted from McDevitt, Michael, 'Does China Have an Effective Sea Based Deterrent', published by CSIS, see http://chinapower.csis.org/ssbn/.

19 'The PLA Navy: A Modern Navy with Chinese Characteristics', p. 22, accessed http://fas.org/irp/agency/oni/pla-navy.pdf.

20 US DoD Annual Report to Congress, 'Military and Security Developments Involving the People's Republic of China 2016', p. 26.

21 See, for example, Arthur Dominic Villasanta, in http://www.chinatopix.com/articles/96363/20160725/china-reveals-new-type-094a-nuclear-submarine-missiles-reach-usa.htm, and Brian Wang in http://www.nextbigfuture.com/2015/05/chinas-096-nuclear-sub-has-specs.html.

22 Sourced from 'China's Straight Deck Amphibious Assault Ship Confirmed by Official Information', 7 December 2015, http://www.china-arms.com/2015/12/chinas-straight-deck-amphibious-assault-ship-confirmed-by-official-information/.

23 Interview with Andrew Erickson, 'How Does China's First Aircraft Carrier Stack Up', CSIS, see http://chinapower.csis.org/aircraft-carrier/.

24 See https://www.rt.com/news/china-super-aircraft-carrier-634/, published 22 December 2013.

25 Annual Report to Congress, op. cit.

26 Holmes, James, 'Will China Become an Aircraft Carrier Superpower', *Foreign Policy*, 21 January 2016, see http://foreignpolicy.com/2016/01/21/will-china-become-an-aircraft-carrier-superpower/.

27 Interview with Andrew Erickson, op. cit.

28 See https://tiananmenstremendousachievements.wordpress.com/tag/097-submarine/.

29 O'Rourke, Ronald, 'China Naval Modernisation: Implications for US Navy Capabilities – Issues for Congress', CRS, 23 December 2014, p. 13.

30 From 'The PLA Navy: New Capabilities and Missions for the 21st Century', US Office of Naval Intelligence, 2015, p. 19.

31 Peri, Dinakar, 'Yaogan Satellites and Chinese ASBM Capability', http://www.claws.in/images/journals_doc/653652095_DinakerPeri.pdf.

32 http://www.businessinsider.com/china-is-diminishing-the-uss-air-power-superiority-2014-12?IR=T.

33 http://www.scmp.com/news/china/article/1099368/pla-signs-preliminary-deal-24-russian-su-35-jet-fighters, accessed 3 January 2013.

34 http://www.deagel.com/Combat-Aircraft/J-16_a002954001.aspx.

35 http://chinesemilitaryreview.blogspot.in/2013/01/chinese-j-6-unmanned-aerial-combat.html.

36 Kashgar, Korla, Yarkand, Hotan, Cherchen (Qiemo) and Gardzong opposite Ladakh, http://www.defence.pk/forums/indian-defence/138148-chinese-airfields-encircle-ladakh.html#ixzz2JGx2Ph7p. According to Indiandefence.com, there are seven airfields which can take on SU-27 aircraft. Gongar, Pangta, Linchi, Hoping and Gar Gunsa are other airfields in Tibet.

37 http://www.ausairpower.net/APA-PLA-IADS-Radars.html#mozTocId663922, accessed 3 January 2013.

38 At IDEX in February, 2011, China released details of the meter-wave (VHF) HK-JM and HK-JM2 radars, both mobile and with detection ranges of 330 and 500 km, respectively. The radars could cue more accurate tracking systems. China also unveiled the DWL002 ground-based electronic surveillance measure system, which could be deployed as a passive coherent-location radar, using long-range broadcast signals to detect non-emitting targets.

39 http://www.sinodefence.com/airforce/default.asp, accessed 3 January 2013.

40 Sinodefence.com, dated 8 May 2008.

41 'HQ-9/-15, and RF-9 (HHQ-9 and S-300) (China), Defensive Weapons'. Jane's Strategic Weapon Systems, 29 November 2012, http://articles.janes.com/articles/Janes-Strategic-Weapon-Systems/HQ-915-and-RF-9-HHQ-9-and-S-300-China.html.

42 US DoD Annual Report to Congress, Military and Security Developments Involving the People's Republic of China 2016, https://www.defense.gov/Portals/1/Documents/pubs/2016%20China%20Military%20Power%20Report.pdf.

43 https://sinodefence.com/pla-strategic-support-force/.

44 Lei, Zhao, 'New Rules Mean Ships Can be Used by Military', China Daily, 18 June 2015, http://www.chinadaily.com.cn/china/2015-06/18/content_21036944.htm.

45 Capabilities for Computer Network Operations and Cyber Espionage by Northrop Grumman Corporation, March 2012.

46 Chinese Military Modernisation and Force Development, July 2012, Burke Chair Study, csis.org.

47 Capability of the PRC to conduct Computer Network Operations and Computer Network Exploitation. US-China Economic Security Review Commission by Northrop Grumman, 16 October 2009.

48 Pollpeter, Kevin, 'China Dream, Space Dream: China's Progress in Space Technologies and Implications for the United States', US-China Economic and Security Review Commission, 2 March 2015.

49 US DoD Annual Report to Congress, op. cit.

50 Ibid.

51 Ibid.

52 'China's Space and Counterspace Programs', 2015 Report to Congress, US-China Economic and Security Review Commission, November 2015, http://origin.www.uscc.gov/sites/default/files/annual_reports/2015%20Annual%20Report%20to%20Congress.PDF.

53 US DoD Annual Report to Congress, op. cit.

54 Pollpeter, op. cit.

5

PAKISTAN–CHINA HYBRID WARFARE COLLUSIVITY

General

Kautilya, in his treatise, the 'Arthashastra' had outlined for the Mauryan emperor a model of international conflict and alliances that provides a framework for understanding the geographic determinants of Pakistan's contemporary international conflicts and alignments. Basically, it read, 'the enemy of my enemy is my friend, and the friend of my enemy is my enemy'. A king, observed Kautilya, will always find a bordering state hostile, and should seek an ally to the rear of that hostile state. Likewise, this enemy state will seek an ally on the other side of the king, and so too will those states seek allies likewise. It was the first articulation of the maxim 'the enemy of my enemy is my friend'. It is this fact which is at the center of the Sino-Pakistan military nexus, a comprehensive strategic relationship that has been a part of South Asia's geopolitical landscape for over 50 years. So far as Pakistan is concerned, India seeks hegemony on the subcontinent, and Pakistan's existential imperative is to confound that hegemony. Likewise, China's grand strategy posits that the United States seeks global hegemony—and India is America's ally in that quest. Thus, the strategic interests of both the countries converge and lay the foundation for the nexus described as 'higher than Himalayas, deeper than the deepest ocean and sweeter than honey'. Often, politicians on both sides describe each other as Iron Brothers. Until now, the nexus had a negative connotation to it i.e., contain India's rise; however, CPEC has added a positive element to this relationship which is likely to impinge on our security calculus.

The China–Pakistan collaboration and cooperation in all spheres has been comprehensive and has stood the test of time. India has somewhat inimical relations with both China and Pakistan including unsettled border issues. Therefore, their collaboration as also collusivity can only have adverse strategic implications for India. For decades, Beijing's secretive ties with Islamabad have run closer than most formal alliances. Founded on a shared enmity with India, China's backing to Pakistan has gone so deep that it was willing to offer the ultimate gift from one state to another: the materials that Pakistan's nuclear scientists needed to build the bomb. Pakistan acted as China's backdoor during its years of diplomatic isolation, the bridge between Nixon and Mao, and the front-line in Beijing's struggles with the Soviet Union during the late stages of the Cold War. Now, Pakistan is a central part of China's transition from a regional power to a global one. The country lies at the heart of Beijing's plans for a network of ports, pipelines, roads and railways connecting the oil and gas fields of the Middle East to the mega-cities of East Asia. Its coastline is becoming a crucial staging post for China's take-off as a naval power, extending its reach from the Indian Ocean to the Persian Gulf and the Mediterranean Sea. Penetration by Pakistan's intelligence services into the darkest corners of global jihadi networks are a vital asset to China as it navigates its growing interests in the Islamic world, and seeks to choke off support for the militant activities that pose one of the gravest threats to China's internal stability.[1]

Symbiotic Relationship

The China–Pakistan relationship is mutually beneficial; if it was one sided or more favourable to one of the nations, it would have withered. The fact that it has stood the test of time is indicative that both counties have gained from this semi-alliance. Pakistan is perceived by China to be its gateway to the Islamic bloc of countries. It helps to trap India within South Asia rather than permit it to emerge as a challenger to China. Pakistan also fulfils Chinese aspirations to gain a land route to the Indian Ocean obviating its Malacca dilemma. Through Pakistan, China also attempts to gain influence in the Af-Pak region and monitor the extra regional presence in Afghanistan. At the same time, China wants influence to limit Pakistan's role in any possible support to the ETIM. Pakistan also helped China gain access to USA as a backdoor intermediary during the early turbulent years of its existence. In addition, Pakistan also provided China access to some Western weaponry and equipment which could then be copied by its manufacturers. On the other hand, Pakistan has found an all-weather ally in China which supports it in all forums. China creates the two-front dilemma for India reducing Indian threat to Pakistan. China has been generous in transfer of technology as also direct military aid. However, its most significant help is in the field of nuclear and missile technology, which Pakistan may not have been able to master on its own. China has repeatedly come to rescue of Pakistan in terms of economic aid. However, the extent of Chinese economic support to Pakistan is debatable and in terms of trade, it may well be China which benefitted more. China also vetoes any resolution in Security Council which goes against Pakistan, Masood Azhar being a case in point. The recent precondition of accepting Pakistan also, in case of Indian entry to the Nuclear Suppliers Group (NSG), underscores the level of Chinese support to Pakistan.

Early Relations

Sino-Pak relations were in a dormant state in 1947. India, in fact, perceived itself to be the closest ally of PRC. India was among the first countries to grant recognition to PRC in 1949. Nehru repeatedly extended a hand of friendship to China. China on the other hand viewed this relationship differently, perceiving India to be the most powerful country in South Asia, which may challenge China's rise in future. The Chinese, therefore, followed a policy of containment right from the beginning. Chinese priority was a complete control over its frontier territories of Tibet and Xinxiang. In fact much of China's strategic thinking was shaped by Mao who believed that a rising nation must continue to push against its frontiers. This thinking was partly shaped by his experiences of the Century of Humiliation as also the Chinese civil war. Tibet as also the Southern boundary of Tibet constituted one such frontier. Therefore, China was not content only with the annexation of Tibet but also wanted to push further southwards. But China being weak militarily did not want to be openly hostile towards India. They thus needed the benign Sino-Indian agreement of 1954. Nehru's visit to China in 1954 also brought to fore irreconcilable differences between India and Pakistan. Pakistan thus entered long-term strategic calculus of China as the only country which can balance India.

India in those years remained oblivious of this Chinese design. In fact, consequent to Chinese occupation of Tibet, India accepted that Tibet is a part of China. This state was possibly driven by beliefs of the then Prime Minister Nehru as also the first ambassador to China, KM Panikkar. Despite clear warnings of China's devious intentions towards India by Home Minister Sardar Patel to Nehru, latter continued to view China to be a long-term Indian ally. Surprisingly, initially the Pakistani leadership was not well disposed towards China as they clearly were worried about Chinese territorial ambitions. The Pakistani tilt, in this period, was decidedly towards USA. Post the Chinese annexation of Tibet, the Central Intelligence Agency's (CIA) covert operations to train the Tibetan guerrilla force for an uprising in Tibet against the PLA were directed from Peshawar. India, on the other hand, provided the sustenance for PLA in Tibet in terms of food grains. During the visit of Ayub Khan to India on 24 April 1959, he proposed for a joint strategy for defence against China which was refused by Nehru. Pakistan also tried to develop cordial relations with USSR at this stage but without much success. The Bandung conference in 1955 did normalize Sino-Pak relations to some extent but not to the extent of turning it into an alliance. Strangely, the Karakoram highway was started by the Chinese in 1959, the exact year that Ayub Khan's proposal was rebuffed by Nehru and also the year when Dalai Lama fled to India. Thus, the highway is indicative of the long-term strategic calculus of China. The road was opened to public in 1979 concurrent to USSR invading Afghanistan.

Period Post 1962 Sino-Indian Conflict

Year 1962 proved Pakistan correct in terms of China's threat from the North—same as was warned by Sardar Patel explicitly in his letter to Nehru on 7 November 1950. This proved to be the turning point in Sino-Pak relations. The shift was accentuated by three factors. First, by this stage Sino-Soviet friendship was falling apart and China needed new friends. Second, by befriending Pakistan, the Chinese hoped to counter-veil India and also grow closer to USA. Pakistan also realized that it cannot wish away China being their neighbour. Third, and the last reason, was that the Indian defeat in 1962 brought to fore the urgency of settling the border issue with China. Post-1962, Pakistan went on to normalize its relations with China and after illegally ceding the Shaksgam Valley resolved its border problems with China in 1963. China similarly understood and condoned Pakistan's reasons for joining SEATO/CENTO. Pakistan thus shifted its position from being sceptical about China to becoming its ally. In fact, by settling and demarcating the border with China, Pakistan also somewhat legitimized its illegal occupation of POK and the Northern areas. Thus, seeds of Chinese intervention in the J&K dispute were sown at this stage. Chinese were cautious about making any statement on J&K till 1962 as they were concerned that India may similarly comment about Tibet. However, in 1964, they made statements about ill treatment of Muslims in J&K, signalling their support for Pakistan's position.

In 1964, Chou en Lai visited Pakistan and used Pakistan to message USA about its intentions regarding the ongoing conflict in Vietnam. He stated that China does not want a conflict in South East Asia, but will retaliate only if bombed and will then use its full might at point of choosing. In this manner, China tacitly condoned US involvement in Vietnam. Thus, use of Pakistan as an intermediary between China and USA was established in late sixties and early seventies. This process was taken further during the Nixon era, when Pakistan facilitated a number of high-level secret negotiations between China and USA, finally resulting in UN recognition of China as a permanent member of the Security Council in 1972. The worsening of Sino-Indian relations was also partially co-terminus with deteriorating China–Soviet relations. This is a little vexing as by this stage India was not very close to Soviet Union.[2]

China's Nuanced Support

Despite the all-weather friendship which was developing between China and

Pakistan, the Chinese support to Pakistan was not unconditional. Pakistan realized that USA would not be underwriting all their security concerns with respect to India. In fact, the US had militarily helped India in the 1962 war. Post-1962, Pakistan perceived that China could now militarily support them against a common foe in India. This hope was belied in 1965 war wherein China provided only verbal support to Pakistan. Mao then asked Pakistan to be prepared to wage a long-drawn guerrilla war against India. Similarly, even in 1971, despite of all the help that Pakistan was providing to China, the latter refused to bail out Pakistan militarily from East Pakistan. The reasons for such Chinese behavior may well have been their internal political compulsions as also the fact that the Chinese armed forces were not very strong. China was also actively seeking the permanent seat in UN Security Council in 1971, which it would not have risked by unprovoked military action against India. Even during the Kargil Conflict, Pakistan was heavily banking on the Chinese support which did not really materialize except for few isolated statements.

Strategic Engagement: 1971–1990 and Beyond

This period was defined by the Soviet expansion in Afghanistan and the peak of Cold War. Presence of Soviet troops in Afghanistan made Pakistan a frontline state for both USA and China. China funneled arms to the Afghan mujahedeen through Pakistan. China truly became the strategic ally of Pakistan extending its military hardware, monetary support as also the ultimate gift of nuclear and missile technology. At the same time, China used Pakistan to get closer to USA against USSR. In fact USA clandestinely propped up China as a counter weight to the USSR. Later, the Tiananmen incident in 1989 did weaken the US-China relationship to some extent but post-1991, after breakdown of the Soviet Union, US continued its economic relationship with China in the process making it an economic superpower. China and Pakistan friendship also continued. Chinese support to Pakistan after its nuclear explosion was indicative of the degree of friendship and alliance between the two countries. However, like before, Chinese support to Pakistan remained nuanced during the Kargil Conflict.

The China Dream

The China Dream[3] (*Zhôngguómèng*) is a term popularized after 2013, within Chinese socialist thought, that describes a set of personal and national ideals in the People's Republic of China and the Communist Party of China. It is used by journalists, government officials, and activists to describe the role of the individual in Chinese society as well as the goals of the 'Chinese nation'. The One Belt, One Road Initiative (OBOR)[4] was accordingly launched with great fanfare as part of this China dream. OBOR has over a period of time become the signature initiative of XI Jinping. He has attached certain personal credibility to its success. CPEC is a part of this OBOR initiative. CPEC is somewhat different from other alignments of OBOR, in that the alignment is over extremely difficult terrain and through disputed territory. Both nations have chosen to push for it in spite of obvious legal as well as physical hurdles. Clearly, CPEC fulfills geo-economics as well as geostrategic needs of both nations. Their close relations naturally made Pakistan a prime contender for the CPEC. Gwadar is the culmination point of CPEC where the OBOR and the Maritime Silk Route (MSR) converge.

Gwadar is located at a strategic point and control over Gwadar provides enhanced expeditionary capabilities to the Chinese Navy. Gwadar in times to come is likely to become a strategic naval base for PLAN. The relationship, based on the shared common animosity towards India, further gains from CPEC as it enhances the physical connectivity between the two nations. Moreover, Pakistan's economy desperately needs the infusion of Foreign Direct Investment (FDI) for its infrastructure, primarily its power sector. China also made a new regional monetary system by announcing the formation of the China-led Asian Infrastructure Investment Bank (AIIB). This posed a direct challenge to International Monetary Fund (IMF) as also Asian Development Bank (ADB) that had Western/Japanese domination. Many projects under CPEC are to be funded through AIIB funds thereby earning revenue for the Chinese. Some of the investments had interest rates as high as 6 per cent which have, however, been since reduced to 1–2 per cent in most cases. Even investments by private Chinese companies were secured by China by seeking sovereign guarantees from Pakistan for repayments.

Crux of Collusivity

There are no value systems in the Sino-Pakistan collaboration. It is purely based on the same strategic security concerns and necessity. It is an all-weather strategic partnership with a common destiny. The Free Trade Agreement (FTA) of 2003 and the Treaty of Friendship, Cooperation, and Good Neighbourly Relations in 2005 further cemented the relations between the two countries. In this treaty, China reaffirmed the status of Pakistan as a strategic ally, whereas Pakistan restated its One China stance. Present Chinese security concerns are mainly in the East in the South China Sea, East China Sea, and USA. The principle objective of China is to win wars for which they have recently reorganized the PLA. China has realised that expeditionary capabilities were key to the success and economic rise of Western nations in the previous century. China is therefore keen to emulate the same model for which it needs allies. China has been seeking a land access to the Indian Ocean to boost its presence there. Countries which can make this possible are Pakistan and Myanmar. China has, therefore, tried to develop friendly relations with them, Pakistan being the most successful story. The coastline of Pakistan today offers the opportunity to China to give a strategic reach to the PLAN. China also has problems in the province of Xinjiang. It is one-sixth of China's land mass; however, it is important due to being home to its nuclear Industry, being the largest gas producer and second largest oil producer. Its network of communications enables China to access wealth of Central Asia. China believes that Pakistan plays an important role in Xinxiang. China projects Pakistan as a friendly Islamic country. Pakistan gives access to China to the larger Muslim/Islamic community and does not criticize China's iron hand policy on Muslims in Xinjiang. China in the garb of security will also be able to deploy PLA troops on Pak soil.[5] This gives it a strategic edge in Afghanistan, Pakistan, as also against India. Troops also provide China traction against any endeavors by Pakistan Army to provide support to East Turkestan Islamic Movement (ETIM). The Chinese footprint in the Indian Ocean is indirectly supported by CPEC. In summation, Sino-Pak relations have weathered the vagaries of time and have emerged even stronger. Pakistan has become China's Israel in a manner of speaking. The relationship is symbiotic with both countries benefitting from it. The strategic objectives of both, China and Pakistan in being such a relationship, are summarised in Figure 5.1.

Figure 5.1: Contemporary Strategic Objectives

	CHINA	PAKISTAN
Strategic	✓ Success of BRI ✓ Access to IOR ✓ Mitigate Malacca Dilemma ✓ Countervail India	✓ Access to Eurasia ✓ China Stakeholder in Kashmir Dispute ✓ Countervail India
Economic	✓ Invest over Capacity of China's Enterprises Abroad and Seek New Markets ✓ Diversify Transportation of Energy Corridors	✓ Revival of Economy and Infrastructure Development ✓ Mitigate Power Deficit ✓ Ensure pre-eminence of Pak Army within Pakistan
Technology	✓ Proliferation of Military Hardware, Nuclear and Missile Technology	✓ Source of Military Technology and Nuclear Deterrence
Politico Diplomatic	✓ Increase Influence in Persian Gulf & Islamic World ✓ Pakistan as a Satellite/Proxy State	✓ Protection of China's veto Power ✓ Alignment in Afghanistan ✓ Access to Central Asia
Security	✓ Combat ETIM (Islamic State?) ✓ Two front Collusive Hybrid Threat	✓ Two front Collusive Hybrid Threat

MANIFESTATION OF COLLUSIVE THREAT

Strategic Dimensions of Karakoram Highway (KKH)

British Viceroy Lord Curzon had said that 'Gilgit is one of the northern gates of India, through which a would-be invader must advance, if he advances at all'. It was because of this vulnerability that for hundreds of years, militaries on the southern side of the Karakoram-Himalaya guarded their mountain passes to safeguard the subcontinent as well as commercial sea-lanes, which extended from Australia to Western Europe. KKH has given China an easy access to the Strait of Hormuz and the Suez Canal; China termed the highway a 'strategic investment'.[6] It has provided China with a short and safe link through its western provinces to the Arabian Sea. For this purpose, it constructed feeder roads and linked its highway system with the KKH. For instance, the feeder road built eastward through the Shaksgam, Raskam, and Shimshal Valleys (originally part of J&K), linked Gilgit with Hotan, which is an important military base situated at the cross-section of Tibet-Xinjiang Highway and the Hotan-Golmud Highway.[7] The Hotan-Golmud Highway links Xinjiang to Qinghai province and central China. It reduces the distance between Gilgit and Golmud to almost half, while bypassing the longer Urumuqi-Kashgar Highway. Golmud, once a salty marshland, is currently one of the largest goods transit points in western China, a strategic military HQ, and the national petrochemical base. Likewise, the feeder road stretching along the southern rim of Xinjiang connects Gilgit with Aksai Chin and reduces the distance between both regions by more than 800 miles.[8] Such interventions have helped to connect military complexes in West Tibet to Xinjiang and Pakistan.

KKH has enabled Pakistan to access Gilgit-Baltistan (GB) and the north-eastern valleys of North-West Frontier Province (NWFP). It was a strategic move to extend its internal communication and transportation networks to these areas and exert physical presence to counter the Indian claim over Gilgit-Baltistan and Afghanistan's claim to NWFP. Thus it helped Pakistan consolidate control over occupied territories and its resources, as well as parts of NWFP along POK; sustain military trade with China; and integrate the people of these regions with the Pakistani mainland. With Chinese help, Pakistan also expanded the network of feeder roads and bridges in the strategic peripheral valleys of GB, which also included converting AT tracks to jeep-able roads in the villages along the LoC.[9]

This not only helped Pakistan strengthen its defences near LoC but also increased the ability of its troops to mobilize swiftly and deeply into Ladakh and the Kashmir valley. Likewise, feeders along Qala Panja, Mintaka and Wakhjir Passes provide a direct connection between Gilgit-Baltistan and Afghanistan and Tajikistan. Chinese have also built bridges; for example, the Shigar Bridge provides an alternate supply line to Siachen and Shaksgam sectors in Baltistan. The bridge helped sustain Pakistani presence in the Nubra-Turtuk sector during the Kargil War, when supply routes to Chorbat, Saltoro, Masherbrum and Hushe valleys came under intense Indian attack. It is therefore amply clear that the road connectivity in the region built with Chinese assistance has military connotations as the prime motive.

The interdependency which both nations achieved through the Karakoram corridor has also allowed China to use Pakistan as its security front and as a low-cost but high- efficiency deterrent against India. The 1966 Sino-Pak accord enabled Pakistan to access Chinese weapons through the KKH. Chinese military contributions have helped Pakistan sustain its wars on its eastern front and continue a low-intensity conflict along the LoC. According to Press Trust of India (PTI), Tass and Pravda, China used the KKH as a secret corridor for arms smuggling, which enhanced its military strength along the Indian border, and enabled it to station specialists in POK, perhaps to keep a close eye on the developments in the region as a whole and J&K in particular. Further, Chinese personnel also trained the Gilgit Scouts to fight in the Ladakh sector. As a quid pro quo, Pakistan used KKH to supply high-tech weapons including unexploded American missiles from the Afghan jihad theatre to China for reverse engineering. See Figure 5.2 also.

Figure 5.2: Connectivity Opposite Ladakh

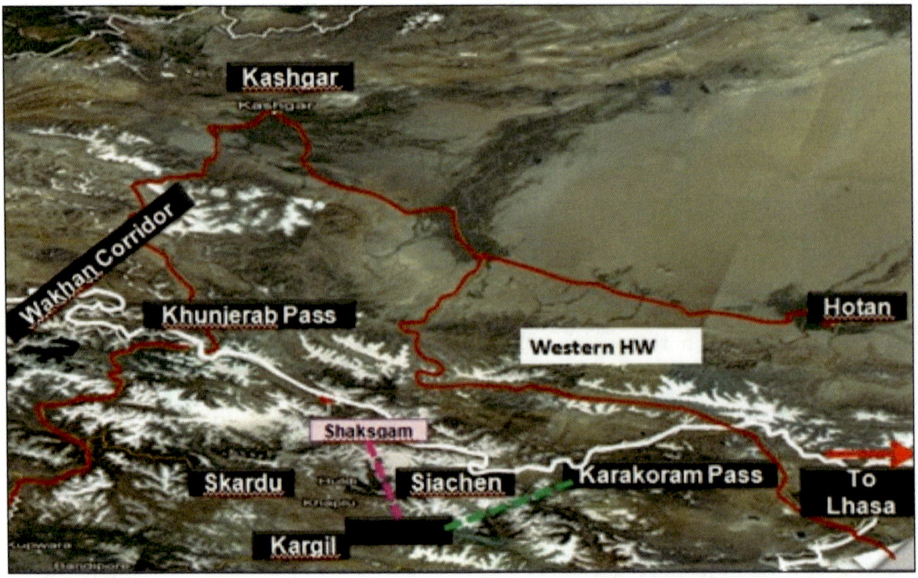

It is assessed that CPEC, once completed, will further assist in conduct of military operations in a two-front war scenario. The Corridor Development Plan envisages construction of 19 tunnels, which will be dug out on the road stretch between Hunza and Khunjerab Pass. The construction staffs for this patch are composed entirely of Chinese nationals. Gilgit-Baltistan is highly suitable as a storage base for high-value military weapons like missiles and tunnels enhance such capability. Among them, one major tunnel will pass under Khunjerab Pass, which is also known as the gateway to India, or China's Khyber Pass. Called the Friendship Tunnel, the Chinese claim it as a significant milestone in the Sino-Pak relations, as it will provide all-weather access and revolutionize inter-regional travel and freight carriage. What is also of great significance to us is that KKH has been built to take heavy vehicles and possibly tanks with mustering points for the convoys. The gains to both the countries are therefore strategic in nature and also accrue military advantages in a possible conflict with India. KKH will facilitate movement of military supplies, deployment of heavy armament and troops in a conflict situation with either or both countries and this collusivity will pose strategic decision dilemmas to the Indian military commanders particularly in Northern Command. Thus, Karakoram Highway and its proposed expansion that provides connectivity to both our hostile neighbours poses a major security challenge.

Strategic Dimensions of CPEC

China's defence white paper of 2015 has stipulated that PLA should be able to protect the Chinese interests anywhere in the globe and also be able to shape the international environment.[10] The main strategic objectives of the PLA are to safeguard China's national sovereignty, national security, and territorial integrity, and support China's peaceful development. The white paper provides a clear confirmation that the PLA will continue to expand its range of operations and capabilities. Concomitantly, President Xi Jinping announced major reforms for PLA on 3 September 2015. Of particular interest for India is the West Zone, which merges the erstwhile Lanzhou and Chengdu Military Regions (MRs). Comprising more than half China's land area, 22 per cent of its population and more than one-third of China's land-based military, the newly constituted West Zone represent a strengthened military formation. The merger of the Lanzhou and Chengdu MRs will improve joint planning, coordination and operations. Incorporation of the Qinghai region in the West Zone will facilitate the rapid induction and deployment of high-altitude acclimatized and trained troops into Tibet and across Ladakh. Establishment of the West Zone also reveals China's increased and abiding military interest in the region in addition to facilitating focus on threats in Xinjiang and Tibet as well as Afghanistan. Equally pertinent is the appointment of General Zhao Zongqi, till recently Jinan MR Commander, as Commander of the new West Zone. His credentials indicate he was handpicked for this post. The China's military strategy to achieve its strategic missions is 'active defence' and local wars under 'informationised' conditions. 'Active defence' means that China is willing to counter threats pre-emptively, even outside China's sovereign territory.[11] It also lays down the concept of prosecuting War Zone Campaigns which envisages achieving the end-state with minimum effort and at the lowest level of the escalatory matrix/ operational continuum. This runs from the Domination-cum-Deterrence (DCD) phase to Gaining Initiative by Striking First (GISF), concluding in the Quick Battle Quick Resolution (QBQR) phase, through measured application of military force. The abovementioned developments indicate that China is better poised to achieve its military objectives in Ladakh in a two-front collusive war with India.

Gwadar—Future PLAN Base

Gwadar port is situated in the South-Western Arabian sea coast in the Gwadar district of Baluchistan. It has acquired the status of centre piece as a gateway of Strait of Hormuz, a global key oil supply route. The port has a potential to become a strong Sino-Pak military base to check and monitor India's influence in Indian Ocean, Arabian Sea, Persian Gulf, and the future of any Indo-US strategic cooperation. When completed, it will be a great strategic asset for Pakistan as an alternative port as the Karachi Port has been under a continuous threat of blockade by India in the past. On the other hand, Gwadar port being 470 km away from Karachi is less vulnerable to any such Indian threat. Gwadar Port has become a milestone in Pak-China military and strategic cooperation. The port of Gwadar is also a part of the China's String of Pearls Strategy. The port will be complemented with a modern air defence unit, a garrison, and a first-rate international airport capable of handling airbus service.

Chinese submarines, both nuclear and conventional, have been foraging in the Indian Ocean in past months—even in close vicinity of the Andaman and Nicobar Group of Islands. NASA recently released photo of a Chinese SSBN docked at Karachi last year. Gwadar not being on any trade route is unquestionably coming up as a Chinese SSBN base. Gwadar must also be seen in conjunction with Pakistan's Jinnah naval base at Omara in Baluchistan that provides docking and repair facilities for submarines and warships and is to be connected to the CPEC, in addition to PLA's military base planned at Jiwani. Gwadar, Jiwani, Omara and Karachi will provide PLAN and Pakistani Navy domination over the Arabian Sea and eastern opening of the Persian Gulf. In view of the prevailing situation in Pakistan, it may not be politically feasible for Pakistan to openly allow China to set up naval or a military base on its soil; however, it is widely believed that CPEC will make Chinese naval presence in Gwadar a necessity.

Politico-Diplomatic Dimensions

China and Pakistan established diplomatic relations in 1951, making Pakistan one of the first Islamic countries as well as the second country in South Asia after India to establish diplomatic relations with China. The two countries have remained strong allies ever since. The closeness of the relationship between the two countries can be seen from major bilateral interactions over the years. Pakistan played a crucial role in the ice-breaking visit of US National Security Adviser Henry Kissinger to China in 1971, and was one of only two United Nations (UN) member countries (along with Cuba) to support China following the Tiananmen Square incident of 1989.[12] The two countries enjoy close cooperation in areas such as trade, borders, and their militaries, meaning that Pakistan has a unique status among China's many diplomatic allies.[13] Although China–Pakistan relations have always been friendly, past cooperation between the two countries was mostly at the political and military level and had not extended to the comprehensive social, economic, and cultural exchange relations of today. This new phase in relations started in May 2013 with the visit of Chinese Premier Li Keqiang to Pakistan and the official proposal of the concept of the 'China-Pakistan Economic Corridor'. Subsequently, there was an exchange of visits between leaders and officials from both countries, including the visit of Pakistani President Mamnoon Hussain to China in February 2014 and Pakistani Prime Minister Nawaz Sharif's subsequent visit in April 2014 which involved intensive consultations over the proposal. Finally, during Chinese President Xi Jinping's visit to Pakistan in April 2015, the proposal was officially finalised.[14]

China's view of Pakistan should be seen from the perspective of international politics, taking into account Pakistan's interlocking relationships with the US, China itself, and the Arab world. Following the military interventions in Afghanistan in 2001 and Iraq in 2003, the efforts of the US to re-establish the regional order in the Middle East suffered a major setback. The financial, material, and human costs gradually eroded domestic support for military intervention in the region and, following the rise of Islamic State in 2014, there was a strong wave of public opinion in the US advocating withdrawal from the Middle East[15] with US peacekeeping efforts in Afghanistan and military and political support for Pakistan coming under increasing scrutiny. Because of this, the US has played the role of mediator for Chinese involvement in Afghanistan, generally welcoming China's enhanced role. This trend reflects US concern that if efforts to reconstruct the order in Afghanistan are not sustained, there will be a power vacuum in Afghanistan, causing the Taliban, the Islamic State, and even pro-Pakistan militants to carve up political power. Therefore, if China can effectively share the burden with the US and exert influence over Pakistan, it should be sufficient to stabilize the current political situation in

Afghanistan.[16] However, China's development across a range of areas has been the subject of increasing international attention in recent years. China is widely considered to be an "emerging power" that may threaten the US in the future.[17] Therefore, China's strategic relationship with Pakistan must be understood from an international strategic perspective, specifically the interlocking geopolitical relationships between China, the US, India, and Russia. In addition, the struggle between Western and Islamic civilization in the context of developments in the Middle East following the 9/11 attacks, in particular the global spread and diffusion of terrorism, are also crucial factors in China–Pakistan relations. At the same time, the aggressive Chinese moves in Western Pacific and challenges it is throwing to US supremacy will likely change US perceptions of China's role in the Af-Pak region.

Economic Dimensions

Economic trade between Pakistan and China is increasing at a rapid pace and a free trade agreement has been signed. Military and technological transactions continue to dominate the economic relationship between the two nations. On 26 April 2015, 'China Mobile' announced $1 billion of investment in Pakistan telecommunication infrastructure and training of its officials within a period of three years. The announcement came a day after China Mobile subsidy Zong emerged as the highest bidder in the 3G auction, claiming a 10-MHz 3G band license, qualifying for the 4G license. As mentioned above, during the visit of Chinese President Xi Jinping to Pakistan in April 2015, the CPEC proposal was officially finalized including the signing of 51 Memorandums of Understanding (MoUs) between the two countries, the inauguration of eight projects, and the launching of five joint energy projects. Aside from the familiar infrastructure and energy projects, this new phase of relations between the two countries also included social, economic, technological, and even cultural cooperation. For example, the two countries have organized bilateral exchanges in radio and television. The Industrial and Commercial Bank of China set up a branch in Lahore, Pakistan's second city; the ministries of science and technology in the two countries jointly established the China-Pakistan Joint Cotton Bio-Tech Laboratory; Pakistan's University of Modern Languages (NUML) and Xinjiang University jointly established the NUML International Center of Education, and the China Culture Center in Pakistan has been established.[18]

Sun Weidong, China's ambassador to Pakistan, said in July 2016,[19] 'achievements from China-Pakistan cooperation projects are focused on four areas: energy projects, transport infrastructure, Gwadar Port, and industrial cooperation'. Major energy projects include construction of a 300-MW solar power plant by Chinese company

Zonergy, and work has already started on more than half of the remaining sixteen planned energy projects. In terms of transport infrastructure, reconstruction and upgrade works of the KKH within Pakistan are underway, and the construction of the Karachi-Lahore Motorway also started this March for the development of Gwadar Port, on 11 November 2015, Pakistan handed over 280 hectares of land-use rights to a Chinese company for a term of 43 years, and construction on new facilities is already underway. Finally, Chinese projects in Pakistan under the CPEC already employ more than 6,000 Pakistani workers, showing that the close relationship between China and Pakistan has already moved from the policy announcement to the project implementation stage. The amount of funds involved, the depth of the exchanges, and the number of people participating is unprecedented in relations between the two countries.

Chinese companies are in talks to snap up more businesses and land in Pakistan after sealing two major deals. Chinese companies are looking mainly at the cement, steel, energy, and textile sectors, the backbone of Pakistan's $270 billion economy.[20] A Chinese-led consortium recently took a strategic stake in the Pakistan Stock Exchange, and Shanghai Electric Power acquired one of Pakistan's biggest energy producers, K-Electric, for $1.8 billion. At the stock exchange signing ceremony, Sun Weidong, China's ambassador to Pakistan, said the deal 'embodies the on-going financial integration' between Chinese and Pakistani markets.[21] China's steel giant Baosteel Group is in talks over a 30-year lease for state-run Pakistan Steel Mills. Islamabad and Beijing are discussing the next phase of CPEC: how to build Pakistan's industry with the help of Chinese state-owned industrial giants. Plans are being drafted for special economic zones which would offer tax breaks and other benefits to Chinese businesses. But even before zones are established, Chinese investors are scoping out land deals; some just want 500 acres of land to set up shop.[22] Oxon is in talks with two state-run Chinese companies and a wealthy Chinese businessman to purchase and develop land for high-end residential and commercial properties in prime markets like Lahore, Karachi and Islamabad.

But not everyone is excited by China's growing role in the Pakistan economy, including trade unions, who say Chinese companies' alleged mistreatment of local workers in Africa in the past had alarmed them.[23] And doing business may not be easy for newcomers. Security remains a concern despite a drop in Islamist militant violence, and in the World Bank's ease of doing business index, Pakistan ranks 144 out of 190 countries.

Military Dimensions

The strategic dimensions of KKH, CPEC and Gwadar port have already been discussed above. The military gains to both the nations are immense and are elucidated in subsequent paragraphs.

Military Hardware. Pakistan came to rely on China for weapons and military equipment almost immediately after losing the Indo-Pak War in 1965. It is also to be noted that USA had stopped the military supplies to Pakistan after this war. Ever since, theirs has been the single most important military alliance that either of the two nations has had since the late 1950s. Pakistan and China have cooperated quite closely across the entire spectrum of military and security affairs ever since. Though both nations' military establishments are dominated by the heads of their armies, but to a noteworthy degree, the Sino-Pakistan friendship has (in terms of conventional arms) been of greatest benefit to the two air forces. The relationship is secretive in nature and is dominated by intelligence agencies besides the Army. Military arms supply is one of the cornerstones of the deepening nexus and is aimed directly at blunting the edge that India enjoys in conventional war waging capabilities against Pakistan.

Air Force. The current fleet of the Pakistani Air Force includes Chinese interceptor and advanced trainer aircraft, as well as an Airborne Early Warning and Control radar system used to detect aircraft. Beijing and Islamabad had agreed in 1999 to co-develop and produce the JF-17 Thunder a single engine multipurpose fighter jet. Its maiden flight was conducted in 2003. Pakistan hopes that these aircraft will replace most of its older fighters and certain other aircraft. Pakistan hopes to build and assemble an increasing percentage of these at home, both for its own use and for export. At the 2015 Paris Air Show, Pakistan claimed it had sealed a deal to export a JF-17 to a third nation (reported to be Myanmar) and was in discussions with 11 other countries for the same. The prospect of Pakistan becoming a supplier, rather than merely a purchaser, of advanced fighter aircraft would represent a major victory for Pakistan's military and air force. China has not only contributed technology to the effort but has also reportedly sought to open doors to friendly states in Africa, Asia, and Latin America. The K-8 Karakorum light attack aircraft was also being coproduced. In 2009, Pakistan signed a deal to purchase 36 of China's more advanced fourth-generation fighter, the J-10. Observers have noted that Pakistan's two unmanned aerial vehicles, the purportedly indigenous Burraq and Shahpar models, bear an uncanny resemblance to China's Rainbow CH-3. Burraq was first inducted in November 2013 and was deployed in combat for the first time during counterinsurgency operations in the Federally Administered Tribal Areas (FATA) in September 2015.

Navy. In a significant arms sale, China announced the sale of eight Type 039B/041

Yuan-class submarines to Pakistan in Apr 2015; worth anywhere from \$2-–\$4 billion, with delivery dates unspecified. Type 041 class is a 3,600 ton diesel electric attack submarine, fitted with AIP and equipped with the YJ-82 anti-ship cruise missile, Yu-4 passive homing and Yu-8 active and passive homing torpedoes. The ability to launch SLCMs in the form of the Pakistani Babur land-attack cruise missile (LACM) would enable Pakistan to achieve assured nuclear second-strike capability. The availability of as many as eight submarines with SLCM capability will allow Pakistan to complete its nuclear-strike triad.[24] China has also supplied F-22P Zulfiqar class frigate, a modern system, equipped with eight AShM, two triple-cell ASW torpedo launchers and a short-range surface-to-air missile (SAM) system (of up to 5 km). Pakistan Naval Ship Aslat, the fourth frigate, was launched in Karachi in May 2013. Pakistan is also acquiring six Harbin Z-9EC ASW helicopters from China. The Z-9 is a Chinese license-built variant of the French AS365 Dauphin utility helicopter. The Z-9 EC can be equipped with an ET-52C torpedo (a Chinese-built derivative of the Italian A244-S light torpedo), enabling its host frigate to engage a submarine that is too far for its own ASW torpedoes (or to help it engage multiple submarines simultaneously in its vicinity). China has also provided design for Azmat-class patrol boats which are built locally at Karachi Shipyard and Engineering Works Limited (KSEW) under a transfer-of-technology agreement. It is a heavier ship (at 560 tons) with top speed of 30 knots (KSEW) and can be armed with eight 180-km range C-802A AShMs and is equipped with Type 347 fire-control radar and twin 30 mm forward mounted guns. It is a complete package in as far as small littoral combat ships are concerned.

Army. The most distinguished feature of this military cooperation is its continuity and durability. Between 1965 and 1968, China provided Pakistan with a considerable amount of war materiel, including at least 160 × T59 medium tanks and 124 × MiG 19 jet fighters. China also assisted Pakistan in raising three infantry divisions soon after the war. The Heavy Industries Taxila (HIT), the largest military industrial complex, was founded in 1971 with Chinese support. It is here that the Al Khalid main battle tank was jointly developed by China and Pakistan that was marketed for export as MBT-2000. China has also supplied 122 mm Towed Gun, Type 347G Fire Control Radar and Anti-Tank Missile Bakhtar Shikan. Recently, Pakistan has inducted Chinese HQ-7B Short Range Air-Defence System (Pakistani FM-90) to counter aerial targets including cruise missiles.

Benefits to China. China has benefitted from the Western technology which Pakistan has transferred covertly. During the later stages of the Cold War, much of this covert technology transfer was tacitly permitted by the US, as a way of promoting its own budding relationship with Beijing and putting pressure on the Soviet Union.

For example, in 1982, the CIA warned that if the AN/ALR-69 radar warning system was sold to Pakistan, as part of the F-16 fighter jet package, then Pakistan would transfer this sensitive technology to China. However, US went through with the sale, and in the seven years that followed, China, Pakistan, and the US worked hand in glove to support the anti-Soviet mujahidin in Afghanistan. Once the Cold War ended, so too did the US wink-and-nod policy toward Pakistan's transfer of Washington's technology to Beijing. These transfers, however, have continued ever since. Perhaps, the highest-profile episode of suspected US aviation technology transfer to China by Pakistan happened in 2011 following the US raid at Abbottabad to kill Osama bin Laden; US intelligence accused Pakistan granting China technical access to the downed Black Hawk helicopter, permitting them to take samples of the aircraft's skin, which contained state-of-the-art stealth technology. SIPRI has reported that just over half of Pakistan's weapon imports from 2010 to 2014 came from China and 30 per cent from the US. Pakistan emerged as China's largest arms customer, accounting for 41 per cent of Beijing's exports during the same period.

Space Cooperation. The first agreement to enhance cooperation in Space technology was signed between the two countries in 1991. China has contributed a great deal to support Pakistan in the development of RAKSAT-IR (Pakistan's communication Satellite), an upgraded version of PAKSAT-1. A landmark in the manufacture of RAKSAT-IR was signed in October 2008. Besides this, the defence organizations of the two countries have reiterated their efforts to continue their cooperation in space technology. China has successfully launched RAKSAT-IR on 11 August 2011, from its Xichang Launch Center in Sichaun Province. The satellite, has 15-year-long life cycle, covers televised information broadcast, relays signals and transmits cyber data (to televisions and radio channels, Internet and cable networks) from across three continents of Asia, Europe and Africa. The satellite has in-built monitoring features controlled through the Satellite Ground Station (SGS) that Pakistan set up with China's help. It will provide strategic advantages to Pakistan's armed forces besides Pakistani scientists gaining first-hand experience by working alongside Chinese counterparts. In any military conflict in the region, there is every possibility that the two strategic partners will collaborate to share surveillance capabilities and exchange intelligence.

Asymmetric/Coercive Dimensions

The proactive use of proxy forces both by China and Pakistan have been discussed in previous chapters. Pakistan's ISI is linked with some 15 regional and international terrorist organizations including ISIS, Al Qaeda, Taliban, LeT, JeM, LeJ, HuM, Sipah-e-Sahiba, IM, SIMI, Muslim militant groups in our northeast, PFI etc. China has access to Pakistani proxies, exploits links with insurgents in India and also has patronised terrorist organizations like the United Liberation Front of West South East Asia (ULFWSEA) and the United Wa State Army (UWSA) in Myanmar. ULFWSEA has been specifically established by Chinese intelligence to target India. These combined sub-conventional forces pose immense strategic challenge to India ay the sub-conventional level since we have not developed effective deterrence to proxy wars being waged against us past several years. But other than the sub-conventional, China's prowess at the asymmetric and coercive levels would be applied against India in tandem with Pakistan, and in accordance with the Chinese concept of 'Unrestricted Warfare', application of which will be based on the following:

- **First**. Omni-directional observation, design and utilization of all forms of kinetic and non-kinetic defence capabilities and factors, one example being the financing and support of crime, addiction, corruption, arms transfers, illegal smuggling, and the corruption of public and governmental institutions across the board. Every conceivable avenue of approach is used encompassing the entire network of a society's relationships.
- **Second**. Synchronise actions taking place at the same time across the depth of the entire 'theatre'; orchestrated or turned on and off like a rheostat as circumstances in any particular theatre warrant.
- **Third**. Aim is not to destroy the adversary and its military or government or necessarily those of any other state but rather to weaken them and prevent their ability to restrict the aggressor's activity.
- **Fourth**. In pursuit of the limited objectives that are within the reach of the active network waging this kind of war and within that framework of limited goals the attacking force should pursue 'unlimited measures'; unrestricted employment of measures that are restricted only to the pursuit of those objectives.
- **Fifth**. Asymmetry, operations conducted in ways contrary to enemy expectations or understanding of the balance of symmetry.
- **Sixth**. Waging war with the least necessary expenditure of resources; minimal consumption.
- **Seventh**. Coordination and allocation of all forces, military and otherwise, that can be mobilised, to accomplishment of the task at hand and realisation of the objective in question; multi-dimensionality.
- **Eighth**. Continuous adjustment and control of the entire process in dynamic fashion, using all the instruments of warfare and of national power towards accomplishment of the objective.

Information Warfare (IW). IW in the context of 'unrestricted warfare' does not refer only to the disabling of physical infrastructure, e.g., electricity grids, power plants, etc. like the well-known Stuxnet virus used against Iran's nuclear programme but rather, as defined by Russian and Chinese authorities alike, to a much broader concept. For example, in 2009, First Deputy Chief of the Russian General staff, Alexander Burutin stated that IW is not only essential in disabling command control (C2) structures of military establishments, but more importantly the essence of contemporary information attacks lies in altering the outside principles of societal structure and the life of society with the help of information expansion. This can be done by imposing onto the citizens' moral norms and cultural traditions that are foreign to them. Similarly, Chinese military forces have been trained since 2003 in what China calls Public Opinion Warfare, 'a concept that seeks to support combat operations efforts by strengthening public support, demoralising foes, and building international support through innovative tactics employing mass media'. In other words, this form of IW, like unrestricted and strategic hybrid warfare, recognises no limits to the scope of its activity. The entire socio-economic-cultural-political-informational-military space of the targeted country is fair game. Chinese strategists believe that IW or one or another form of this political warfare (also using IW) is US strategy and is being used against them. Worse yet, incautious American analyses claiming that they employed such a strategy to effectuate regime change in Serbia in 2000 will only lend further credence to such views. Thus, analysts now believe that regime change in unfriendly states can be accomplished through largely non-violent means, or a combination of these low-level forms of violence, plus subversion, and IW as described here. Indeed, some Russian analysts maintain that this is how US took down the Soviet Union. In discussing these eight pillars we must always remember that they are being deployed simultaneously and in tandem with IW as part of an overall strategic approach.

Deep Coalition. A de facto deep coalition, instead of being limited to nation-states as in the Gulf War alliance, might consist, for example, of three nation-states, 14 civil society organizations, a narcotraficante here or there, a couple of private corporations with their own self-interest at stake, an individual speculator, and who knows what other components.[25] The deep coalition involves players at many levels of the system. It is multi-dimensional with all these groups operating all the time, in continuous flow—multiplying, fissioning, and then fusing into others, and so on. Such a system is based less on 'balance of power' relations among major nations than on the ability to configure the right combination of players at every level. More important than the balance of power is the 'power of balance'; the ability of a major state to keep its senses in the midst of this turbulence, and to match its economic and military capabilities with high-level knowledge resources. This idea of 'deep coalition' is present in all but to name in Unrestricted Warfare, with its repeated references to the political role played by non-state actors ranging from credit rating agencies to Norco-mafias, and its emphasis on the 'civilianisation of war' thesis: Precisely in the same way that modern technology is changing weapons and the battlefield, it is also at the same time blurring the concepts of who the war participants are—non-professional warriors and non-state organisations are posing a greater and greater threat to sovereign nations.[26] Faced with warfare in the broad sense that will unfold on a borderless battlefield, it is no longer possible to rely on military forces and weapons alone to achieve national security in the larger strategic sense, nor is it possible to protect these stratified national interests. Obviously, warfare is in the process of transcending the domains of soldiers, military units, and military affairs, and is increasingly becoming a matter for politicians, scientists, and even bankers.

ALTERNATE SCENARIOS—COLLUSIVE CAMPAIGN AGAINST INDIA

The changed geopolitics of GB and Gwadar has brought about a paradigm shift of monumental proportions in the entire strategic calculus about J&K. The presence of Chinese personnel has added to the complexity of the security dynamics in the region and so have the reports that Pakistan is actively considering a proposal to lease the region to Beijing for 50 years.[27] Moreover, the law now permits PLA to be deployed outside the national boundaries for protection of Chinese assets in OBOR. A study of the geo-strategic importance of the region comprising GB, Saltoro Ridge, Shaksgam Valley and Aksai Chin will highlight the enormity of the military threat that India faces in an eventuality of a two-front collusive war. GB located to the immediate west of Saltoro Ridge is part of PoK with majority Shia population. The Shaksgam Valley immediately to the North of Saltoro Ridge has already been ceded to China by Pakistan illegally. Xinjiang lies to the immediate North of Sakshgam. Aksai Chin which is occupied by China lies to the South East of Sakshgam Valley. The Nurba Valley and Ladakh leading to J&K are hemmed in on three sides by Baltistan, Sakshgam Valley and Aksai Chin. If the proposal to lease the GB area comes through, then all the three areas right up to Xinjiang will be under Chinese control. Saltoro Ridge acts as a separator between Pakistan (GB) and China. Its capture will jeopardise the security of Nubra Valley and Ladakh which will have an adverse effect on the security of entire J&K.

Factors

The following dimensions have been considered towards examination of collusive threat:

- Dimensions of Sino-Pak collusivity: It's a symbiotic relationship.
- Strategic dimensions of KKH.
- Strategic dimensions of CPEC.
- Politico-diplomatic dimensions.
- Economic dimensions.
- Military dimensions including asymmetric/coercive dimensions.

Sino-Pak Strategic Objectives vis-à-vis India

The discussions of dimensions of the Sino-Pak collusivity that lead to the combined strategic objectives of China-Pakistan vis-à-vis India are enumerated as under:

- Keep India confined to South Asia through asymmetric and hybrid means, nudging India to accept subordination to China.
- Expand joint power asymmetry and indirect posturing in POK-Pakistan to force India give up designs for capturing POK.
- Hedge India's economic rise asymmetrically while ensuring availability of Indian markets to China.
- Shrink India's strategic space in South Asia/IOR through gravitational pull to smaller states, weaning them away from India.
- Undermine and curb India's role in Afghanistan.
- Dominate Arabian Sea—posing indirect challenge to Indian Navy and India's SLOCs.
- Perpetuate two-front collusive hybrid threat dilemma including destabilizing India from within to realize own territorial claims, as possible.
- Scuttle India's entry into Nuclear Suppliers Group (NSG) and UNSC till Pakistan is given concurrent entry.
- Reduce India's influence in Iran, as possible.

Threat Manifestation

From the Indian security perspective, it is pertinent to emphasise that there exist a number of potential drivers which can lead the three countries in a coercive/conflict situations. These drivers are as follows:

- **Border Issues**. On the Eastern side, a forward military posturing in Tibet to quell internal unrest could lead to creeping assertiveness at the LAC. Border transgressions and incursion in unheld/lightly held claimed areas could spiral into local skirmishes with potential to escalate further. On the Western front, routine cross-border firing, infiltration, jihadi strikes etc. have all the potential to escalate into a conflict.

- **Security of CPEC**. CPEC is the strategic gateway of China to the Arabian Sea. It's a flagship programme of China with regional strategic implications. Any obstruction from India to scuttle smooth implementation of the CPEC has the potential to up the ante against India.
- **Tibetan/Dalai Lama Issue**. Any unrest in Tibet could escalate into militancy with a potential to exacerbate with contentious succession of Dalai Lama. These developments can perpetrate China's suspicion of an Indian hand in Tibet thus propelling it to adopt a hardened stand vis-à-vis India.
- **Role of Pakistan**. Pakistan is highly susceptible to its internal pressures and at the same time roguish enough to provoke India to exercise its military option. Enhanced secessionist activity in Baluchistan and movement for creation of a 'Greater Pakhtunistan' increase the threat of balkanisation of Pakistan. Post CPEC, a weakened Pakistan or its military defeat at the hands of India will seriously impinge on China's strategic objectives in the region. Therefore, in any future Indo-Pak conflict, the possibility of China coercing India or even to open the Northern front in the long run cannot be ruled out.
- **Strategic Brinkmanship in IOR**. Security of its SLOCs in the IOR is a matter of serious strategic concern for China. Post-CPEC, the increased movements of PLAN in the IOR is bound to cause consternation for India. The possibility of the two sites contesting for domination of locations, resources and influence will increase. This increased strategic brinkmanship could lead to naval stand-off/accidental skirmishes.
- **Water Issue**. Indus, Satluj and Brahmaputra River flow from Tibet to India and further to Pakistan. The Indus Water Treaty (IWT) on water sharing exists between India and Pakistan but China is not a signatory of any water sharing treaty and can divert the waters at these rivers to serve its water stressed northern provinces. The most contentious issue is that of likely damming of Brahmaputra at the Great Bend in Tibet. Any tampering of these rivers would run the risk of impacting the flow of water to India and also cause ecological and environmental problems. India will be highly sensitive to Chinese attempts to divert or misuse these waters. The water dispute can therefore became a contributory cause to deterioration of relations between the two countries.
- **Indo-US Strategic Partnership**. China perceives India as part of 'Grand

Encirclement Design' being weaved by the US to contain that country. Growing Indo-US-Japan-Australia partnership, conduct of joint military exercises (land, sea and air), and involvement of Japanese companies in the development of Northeast etc. will be viewed as anti-China. This factor combined with related politico-diplomatic spats could increase the chances of conflict.

Based on these triggers, by design any one of them, either Pakistan or China, could push the current situation up the escalatory ladder or it could be a result of series of accidental flare-ups or strategic miscalculations. In the event of India-Pakistan conflict, China would support Pakistan with unrestrained war material, its assets in space, cyber, electromagnetic domain, its plethora of cruise missiles and unmanned vehicles, and by keeping the pressure on Chinese front with threat of troop's insertion by vertical envelopment. Similarly, Pakistan is expected to tacitly up the ante on the Western front in case of any escalation between India and China. Before elucidating the alternate scenarios, one needs to examine the on-going situation, which is the state of Non-contact Coercion.

Scenario I (Ongoing Situation): Non-contact Coercion

Presently, India is being coerced by the nexus in all domains (politico-diplomatic, economic, military, social etc.) with the following milestones:

- ✓ Tension exists all along the LoC with regular attempts for infiltration and frequent ceasefire violations.
- ✓ The Doklam standoff and Chinese occupation of North Doklam has added new complexity in Sino-Indian relations.
- ✓ On the LAC too there are periodic incursions, a recent one being in Tuting region where China constructed 1.25 km road across LAC in three feet snow.
- ✓ Low intensity terrorist strikes in and around the Valley.
- ✓ Fuelling tensions in the Valley through public propaganda and exploitation.
- ✓ Growing Chinese footprints in India's immediate neighbourhood.
- ✓ Growing Chinese maritime activities in the IOR.
- ✓ Cyber espionage.
- ✓ Increasing trade deficit with China.
- ✓ China backing Pakistan by blocking India's proposals at the UN to declare Jaish-e-Mohammed (JeM) chief Masood Azhar listed as a global terrorist.
- ✓ Blocking India's entry into the UNSC and NSG.

- ✓ China renaming six districts in Arunachal Pradesh and not recognising it as a part of India.

Cost/Risk/Gain Analysis. This is the ongoing scenario. There is no major financial impact on Pakistan/China. China is achieving its aim through Pakistan to keep India tied down with sub-conventional routine activities. In view of the level of threats, no international interventions are being made. Pakistan military is consolidating its position by diverting the internal attentions to the actions in the valley. The scenario is 'most likely' to persist.

Implications for India. The options for India are limited as India has not developed effective and credible deterrence to sub-conventional threats. The 'surgical strikes' is being seen as no more than a one-time signal. China-Pakistan would continue to test India's resolve and depict India as a 'soft' state. From the present situation, the scenarios can only move up the escalatory ladder. There is no indication, whatsoever, of any let off from the current state of Non-contact Coercion.

Scenario II: Coercive Muscle Flexing

With an aim to prevent any credible response/strategic posturing by India to the existing scenario, the scenario of coercive muscle flexing by China and Pakistan in collusion can manifest from short to medium term in continuum. The salient features of the scenario would be as follows:

- ✓ It will develop incrementally over time.
- ✓ It will involve enhancement of all activities of the ongoing scenario and will include activities in all domains.
- ✓ In addition, Pakistan declares GB as its fifth province and may lease out parts of the province to China in the garb of CPEC projects or SEZs.
- ✓ Creeping assertiveness including border intrusions and transgressions.
- ✓ Attempt will be made to undermine Indian influence in buffer states of Nepal and Bhutan, Bangladesh, Myanmar, Sri Lanka and Maldives.
- ✓ Gradually strengthen Pakistan as countervail and undermine India's strategic interests in Afghanistan.
- ✓ There will be covert moral and material support to Indian Insurgent Groups (IIGs) including NE insurgent groups and Maoists along Nepal border.
- ✓ Hardened stand on Tibetan issue and playing bogey of southern Tibet.
- ✓ Leverage water issue.
- ✓ There will be demonstration of disruptive technological capabilities to subdue Indian policy makers.

- ✓ Aggressive indirect forward posturing by China along our Northern borders and India Ocean Region (IOR) in the garb of training or IS duties.
- ✓ Increased air exercises, UAV activity, and vehicular traffic on strategic highways.
- ✓ Cyber sabotage against critical infrastructure/projects.
- ✓ Enhanced IW operations to propagate India's mishandling of J&K, NE, and other socio-political fissures.

Cost/Risk/Gain Analysis. In the instant case, the Sino-Pak nexus is not likely to incur major setbacks and can continue with its unrestricted growth as well as maintain its diplomatic posturing in the international arena. Further, since there will not be any large-scale overt operations, the risk of international intervention and retaliation is minimal. Hence this scenario will be seen to have desired outcome of keeping India tied down with least cost and risk for China/Pakistan. But by incremental efforts and wooing of India's immediate neighbours, China will be able to tie India down not only in trying to respond to China's tactics but also handle enhanced Pakistan's covert actions. The nexus will thus be able to keep India preoccupied and tied down within the region, thereby inhibiting it from exerting any strategic posturing beyond it and hence will enjoy optimal gains. To keep India subdued, the chances of this scenario playing out are 'High'.

Implications for India. The scenario will create a dilemma for India with regard to its response to such coercive and covert tactics. Indian response would expectedly be subdued for not having developed adequate proactive capabilities at the sub-conventional level and for fear of escalation. The following are the likely impact on India:

- ✓ The scenario will undermine India's status as regional power.
- ✓ If India fails to respond adequately, it will be projected as a 'Soft State' susceptible to Coercion.
- ✓ India will remain embroiled in fighting internal/regional conflicts.
- ✓ Indian plans to take back POK would be diluted with China becoming third party in the POK dispute.

Scenario III: Coercion to Conflict

India's response to the earlier scenarios has the risk of pushing the coercive situation up the escalatory ladder towards the conflict zone. In case of subdued Indian response which is conducive to the objectives of the nexus, the coercive scenarios are likely to persist. However, should India exhibit resolve to challenge the coercion and handle the challenges with a credible response and resolute strategic posturing, the

China-Pakistan collusivity is likely to intensify with the potential to escalate from coercion towards conflict, in short to medium term, in continuum. The salient features of the scenario would be:

- ✓ Pakistan abetted terrorist strikes against Indian assets in Afghanistan.
- ✓ ISI engineered terrorists' attacks on religious sites, financial institutions and public places in India.
- ✓ Contamination attacks by 'jihadis' at public places.
- ✓ Escalation at the LoC and intrusions in lightly held/unheld sectors.
- ✓ Forward military posturing.
- ✓ Abetment of separatist movement in Kashmir valley and subversion of people.
- ✓ Engineering violence in Tibet and blaming India for it.
- ✓ Engineering fatal attacks against Dalai Lama or senior members of Tibetan government in exile.
- ✓ Declaration of successor of Dalai Lama either by Dalai Lama himself or by the government in exile in case of death of Dalai Lama or by the Chinese government, which leads to mass protests in India and Tibet and blaming India for abetting uprising.
- ✓ Intrusions and clashes at the border.
- ✓ Stand-offs in the IOR.
- ✓ Cyber-attacks against India's critical infrastructures.
- ✓ Attack in space on Indian satellites.

Cost/Risk/Gain Analysis. This case will be an escalation from the previous scenario and the cost per se would be low and is not likely to cause any significant setback to the nexus in terms of its growth as well as its international standing. The nexus will thus be able to keep India preoccupied and tied down to exert any strategic posturing in the region and hence will enjoy optimal gains.

Implications for India. In this scenario, India will face a dilemma with regard to its response, whether to keep it subdued or risk pushing the scenario to a limited conflict. India is likely to face embarrassment in case it fails to respond adequately to the situation and thereby adversely affect its regional standing and international recognition. On the other hand, there is bound to be tremendous internal pressure on the Indian government to respond credibly and adequately to such moves. However, a resolute Indian response carries the risk of pushing the envelope into a limited conflict.

Scenario IV: Collusive Support with Direct Military Intervention

An interventionist military collusion could come about in different scenarios as under:

- ✓ Pakistan led or China led.
- ✓ Either state may take advantage of an adverse situation for India brought on by the other.
- ✓ It could be part of a grand design between China and Pakistan to bring India down to its knees.

Historically, full scale activation of a second front has never occurred despite the collusion being in place since the 1960s. However, in view of the updated military infrastructure development in Tibet, and in GB and presence of Chinese troops in POK, the possibility of a two-front war cannot be ruled out. Each one of these scenarios is explained in subsequent paragraphs.

Pakistan Led Scenario. In this manifestation, China is unlikely to participate overtly unless it sees some gains for itself. Otherwise, it would not be in its best interest. In such a situation, a major offensive by China is unlikely. That would hurt its global image and scare many friendly neighbours. But on Pakistan's insistence, China provides support to Pakistan. Such support could be in following forms:

- ✓ During hostilities, it may enhance Pakistan's weapons and equipment reserves, force regeneration, and war duration capability. Support in the nature of high-end technological weapons and equipment can become a major advantage for Pakistan.
- ✓ Make moves to tie down our forces in the North and East by moving extra forces in Tibet; aggressive patrolling by the Chinese leading to provocation and minor clashes; major/minor fire assaults, and intrusion of Indian airspace. India's dual-tasked formations would then not be available for deployment against Pakistan. Our offensive capability on the Western front would then be affected adversely.
- ✓ Activate the Siliguri Corridor through proxy forces.
- ✓ China's potent cyber warfare capability, shared with Pakistan, can cripple India's crucial networks, including strategic forces assets, command and control systems, air defence, and civil support structures like the railways, civil aviation, power grids, banking sector, and so on. It can impact India's deterrence and war fighting capability very adversely.
- ✓ China can support Pakistan's strategy to shape the world opinion against India, in the UN and other world forums.

- ✓ China could exploit India's internal fault lines and instigate ethnic strife, particularly in the northeast. It would result in diversion of India's war effort.

China Led Scenario. In a China-led manifestation, there may be an attempt to seize Tawang or other territory along the LAC with an aim to teach India a lesson. China may initiate a limited conventional war to achieve the objective. It would have to take into consideration likely escalation into the nuclear, aerospace, and maritime domain. In any such conflict situation, China is unlikely to bank on the Pakistani collusion or participation, but Pakistan could try to exploit such a situation on the Line of Control (LoC) or international border. It could make diversionary moves in Kargil or Siachen, which will result in our formations based in Ladakh having to 'look' both ways. Pakistan could also upgrade proxy war in J&K.

Cost/Risk/Gain Analysis. Since the aims are limited, with theatre-specific operations, with the covert assistance of the other party, the cost per se would remain low and no major setback is likely to the nexus in terms of its growth. Though a limited conflict is likely to recalibrate the regional balance, it faces low risk of international intervention/rebuke. But the gains will be high because such actions could cause substantial setback to India in terms of its growth profile as well as its stature as a regional power.

Implications for India. In this scenario, India will again face the dilemma with regard to its response in terms of whether to keep the conflict limited to the region or escalate it to wider areas. There would be tremendous pressure on India to balance its response on two fronts. India is likely to face political, diplomatic, and military embarrassment in case it fails to respond adequately to the situation. India would be at risk to lose its regional standing among its immediate neighbours and internationally. However, a befitting reply from India carries the risk to escalate the limited conflict into a full scale war.

Scenario V: Himalayan Plunder (Full Scale War)

This scenario would emerge as a result of non-capitulation of India in previous scenarios and could play out in medium to long term. In this, China-Pakistan could activate the entire LAC, LoC, and IB in a theatre-wide military conflict with incremental and protracted build-up of their forces and would be characterised by the following:

- ✓ Major PLA deployments in POK-Pakistan precede the scenario.
- ✓ Increased PLAN presence/movement in IOR including in close vicinity of Andaman and Nicobar.

- ✓ China challenges legality of Andaman and Nicobar being Indian Territory.
- ✓ China reiterates claim on major portions of Arunachal Pradesh, as South Tibet.
- ✓ Proxy war pan India (including northeast and in Siliguri Corridor) will be fully activated, preceded to or simultaneous with conventional attacks.
- ✓ Use of TNWs by Pakistan/(China???) cannot be discounted.
- ✓ Would have concurrent battles running at strategic/operational/tactical level.
- ✓ The conflict will encompass maritime, cyber and outer space, and nuclear dimensions.
- ✓ Could also involve Bhutan, Nepal, Bangladesh, and North Myanmar.

Cost/Risk/Gain Analysis. China is likely to suffer high cost in terms of its economic growth as well as its regional and international image as a peaceful and developing nation capable of being a global power. The Sino-Pak nexus faces a very high risk of international criticism, intervention, and isolation. India, on the other hand, could get support and sympathy both, regionally as well as internationally. As India would be the main sufferer, it could legitimately 'hurt' maritime interests of China and Pakistan in the Indian Ocean and even review its No First Use (NFU) of the nuclear doctrine to send warning signals to both countries. Since the aim is only to keep India subdued and strategically restricted, the gains from such an effort would be 'sub optimal' for the nexus.

Implications for India. This is the worst case scenario that will test India and its strategic partnership to their utmost limits. In this scenario, though India will face adverse effects in terms of its economic growth, denial of any outright victory to China would lead to a stalemate which in turn can boost India's regional standing.

China's Paradox

Despite the interlocking economies of the US and China, China knows that its rise to become a 'Great Power' can only be contested by the US. China is also aware that attack on Taiwan would likely invite action by US and allies because capture of Taiwan would facilitate Chinese nuclear submarines to quickly submerge in deep waters ports of Taiwan which is a sanctuary against attacks because of topographical conditions in the South China Sea (SCS). Further, it would facilitate China's future aim of deploying SSBNs in the Pacific Ocean. On the other hand, capture of Indian Territory along the Himalayas would be unlikely to invite US actions similar to an attempt to annex Taiwan, especially with America's multiple global engagements including the China-Pakistan-Russia-Iran conflict of interests against US-NATO-Indian interests in Afghanistan. China would like to test the Indo-US Strategic

Partnership that it abhors without many disadvantages to her. Should China, and by extension Pakistan, succeed in annexing parts of Indian Territory, it would (1) snub the Indo-US Strategic Partnership, with corresponding signals to American partnerships elsewhere; (2) diminish America's stature as a super power and global player; (3) force India into submitting to a China-Centric Asia; (4) confine India within South Asia, never to challenge China economically or otherwise again and (5) raise China's stature in the world arena and facilitate attainment of 'Great Power' status.

Activities that Need Monitoring

Security of CPEC. A day after Xi Jinping's visit, the Inter Services Public Relations (ISPR) wing of Pakistan Army had tweeted that Pakistan would raise a Special Security Division for CPEC which would comprise of nine Army Battalions and six Wings of Civil

Armed Forces and this division would be commanded by a Major General.[28] By February 2016, the news of the establishment of a Special Security Division (SSD) commanded by Major General Abid Rafique in Rawalpindi army headquarters came to light. An ISPR press release noted that the then Army Chief, General Raheel Sharif had visited the SSD and 'emphasized the need to ensure a peaceful environment to be able to push all the planned developmental projects'. He also said that the army was 'totally aware of all campaigns against the Corridor and vowed that the security forces are ready to pay any price to turn this long cherished dream into reality'.[29] Two months later, participating in a seminar on the 'Development of Baluchistan and Economic Corridor in Gwadar', he informed the audience that 'a 15,000-strong dedicated force is already in place under the ambit of Special Security Division for the CPEC'.[30] He went on to claim that 'this year, we will move cargo from heartland China to Gwadar and beyond, fulfilling our dream'. There were other reports of China planning to raise a special force and station it in Pakistan to protect its workers, which could reach a figure of about 30,000 as the projects get implemented in full swing.[31] Against this backdrop, on May 16, 2016, the then Army Chief, Raheel Sharif, visited Beijing and assured provision of full security to projects under CPEC. However, soon afterwards on 30 May 30, there was a road-bomb attack on a Chinese engineer and his driver injuring both of them in Karachi. The attack was claimed by Sindhi nationalists and a note written in Sindhi recovered from the place of attack said, 'As a rising imperialist power and supporter of Pakistan's cause we consider China equivalent to Punjab', and 'We will oppose every anti-Sindh project including the China-Pakistan economic corridor'.[32] However, security concerns remain, despite reports of surrender by Baluch rebels and success of operation Zarb-e-Azb against the Pakistani Taliban.

Joint Patrolling. In a first, PLA and Pakistan's border police force carried out a joint patrol along their shared border.[33] While China has been patrolling the region since 2014, this is the first time that the two armies have carried out a joint patrol in the region. It is interesting to note that the area of the patrol, identified as the 'China-Pakistan border', is the frontier region of Pakistan occupied Kashmir—an area claimed by India as an integral part of its territory.

Joint Military Exercises. The PLA is presently focused on developing the capability to execute large-scale, complex joint operations. This includes greater realism during exercises, improved core service capabilities, strengthened strategic campaign training, and execution of long-distance manoeuvres and mobility operations. Exercises in western China focused on high altitude operations, with special emphasis on using space-based reconnaissance.[34] China and Pakistan have a long history of conducting joint military exercises. The two militaries seem to have achieved high degree of inter-operability, joint planning, and intelligence sharing. The Pakistani Navy and the PLAN held their first-ever exercise in the East China Sea from 31 December 2015 to 1 January 2016. Commodore Bilal Abdul Nadir of the Pakistani Navy in an interview with the 'Global Times', a Chinese state-run newspaper, described the exercise as 'very significant', noting that they would 'enhance the interoperability and cohesion between the two navies'.[35] Likewise the two Air Forces conduct Shaheen series of joint exercises, the latest exercise featured fourth-generation fighter jets and bombers as well as airborne early warning and control (AEW&C) aircraft. During April 2016, Pakistan and China showcased their all-weather friendship with the launch of one of the biggest joint military exercises in decades. According to the Inter-Services Public Relations, the war games that began on 11 April 2016, near Jhelum, followed speculation over whether China will step in to fill the economic, military and diplomatic void if Pakistan's relationship with the US further deteriorated. Pakistan and China also conduct exercises joint planning, intelligence sharing and functioning from joint operation centres. It can therefore be concluded that the two militaries seem to have achieved a high degree of interoperability and overcome many differences in the outlook to defence strategy and joint planning due to differences in the background/history of the two militaries.

Future Prospects

From analysis of the above, it may be assumed that China is now engaged in an unprecedented close bilateral cooperation with Pakistan across a range of areas. From a domestic, regional, or international political perspective, China has shown a willingness to continue strengthening its relations with Pakistan. Aside from India, regional powers such as the United States, Arab countries, and Iran are positive about China taking responsibility for maintaining regional order in Afghanistan and Pakistan. Therefore, for the foreseeable future, China-Pakistan relations as well as the expansion of Chinese influence in Central and South Asia will develop further as China pursues the 'One Belt and One Road' initiative; gradually replacing the US dominated status-quo. Following his rise to power, Xi Jinping has made major adjustments to China's international strategy. China is no longer prepared to play a passive and low-key role, and has sought great power status consistent with its own strength that can influence the international system. With the current situation in Afghanistan and Pakistan, China is intent to take on responsibility for filling the power vacuum in a way that appears generally acceptable to the parties involved.

Key Issues

- ✓ *China's entry in POK has made India's western front vulnerable, and raised possibilities of a two-front collusive hybrid attack, also employing state as well as non-state actors opening a third front within India.*
- ✓ *OBOR was launched in accordance with the China Dream and the CPEC is part of the OBOR initiative.*
- ✓ *CPEC ending up at Gwadar (future PLAN base) is China's strategic highway to India Ocean with adverse security implications for India.*
- ✓ *Pakistan's coastline provides PLAN with strategic reach.*
- ✓ *China-Pakistan interdependency through KKH allows China to use Pakistan as her security front and as a low-cost, high-efficiency deterrent against India.*
- ✓ *Combined China-Pak strategic objectives revolve around keeping India confined to South Asia and restrict India's strategic space in South Asia and IOR.*
- ✓ *Military gains of the China-Pakistan relationship are immense to both nations.*
- ✓ *The relationship at the asymmetric level is of great value in exercising coercion against India.*
- ✓ *As part of 'unrestricted warfare', China employs 'deep coalitions' that can consist of nation-states, civil society organizations, drug mafias, private corporations, individuals and others, with all these groups operating all the time, in continuous flow—multiplying, fissioning then fusing into others, and so on.*
- ✓ *Multiple scenarios can be envisaged of joint China-Pakistan military campaigns against India ranging from non-contact coercion, to coercive muscle flexing and beyond for annexing segments of Indian Territory.*
- ✓ *India would do well to examine the various collusive China-Pakistan scenarios, which can become real if the aggressive China-Pakistan moves remain unchallenged and China's all-round aggression remains uncontested at the global level.*

NOTES

1 Small, Andrew, 'The China-Pakistan Axis: Asia's New Geopolitics', London: C Hurst & Co Publishers Ltd, 2015.
2 Ibid.
3 'Chinese Dream', Wikipedia, the Free Encyclopedia, 4 June 2016, https://en.wikipedia.org/w/index.php?title=Chinese_Dream&oldid=72372946.
4 'One Belt, One Road', Wikipedia, the Free Encyclopedia, 4 August 2016, https://en.wikipedia.org/w/index.php?title=One_Belt_One_Road&oldid=732943554.
5 Panda, Ankit, 'Pakistan Army Seeks Greater Authority Over China-Pakistan Economic Corridor Administration', The Diplomat, 18 August 2016, http://thediplomat.com/2016/04/pakistans-army-seeks-greater-authority-over-china-pakistan-economic-corridor-administration/.
6 Ispahani, Mahnaz Z., 'Roads and Rivals: The Political Uses of Access in the Borderlands of Asia', Ithaca, NY: Cornell University Press, 1989, p. 197.
7 These valleys are under illegal Chinese occupation and belong to Gilgit-Baltistan of J&K.
8 Aksai Chin is the Chinese occupied part of Ladakh (J&K); Isapahani, op. cit., 190, 202 & ff.
9 One such bridge linked Muzaffarabad and Uri with Pakistani towns of Balakot and Mansehra and enabled Pakistani troops to reach to forward military posts in AJK (Ispahani 1989, p. 192).
10 http://www.chinadaily.com.cn/china/2015-05/26/content_20820628_2.htm.
11 Naravane, Manoj, 'War Zone Campaign Doctrine: A Revisit', http://www.claws.in/images/journals_doc/SW%20i-10.10.2012.71-79.pdf.
12 Yaxin, Shen, 'China-Pakistan Relations in Xin Jinping's Eye', People's Daily Online, 17 April 2015, http://politics.people.com.cn/n/2015/0417/c1024-26862088.html, retrieved 23 July 2016.
13 Hao, Zhan, 'Why Is the China-Pakistan Relation Unique in the World?', Beyondnewsnet, 22 April 2015, http://beyondnewsnet.com/20150422/16557/, retrieved 23 July 2016.
14 Ping, Su and Kao Yi, 'Intensive Talks between Chinese and Pakistani Business Communities', BBC China, 19 April 2015, http://www.bbc.com/zhongwen/trad/world/2015/04/150419_china_pakistan_deals, retrieved 23 July 2016.
15 Trofimov, Yaroslav, 2015, 'America's Fading Footprint in the Middle East', *The Wall Street Journal*, 9 October 2015. http://www.wsj.com/articles/americas-fading-footprint-in-the-middle-east-1444411954, retrieved 23 July 23 2016.
16 Feldman, Dan, 'Successes and Challenges in Afghanistan and Pakistan', Remarks, Special Representative for Afghanistan and Pakistan, United States Institute of Peace, 5 August 2015, http://www.state.gov/p/sca/rls/rmks/2015/245767.htm, retrieved 23 July 2016].
17 Bijian, Zheng, 'China's "Peaceful Rise" to Great-Power Status', Foreign Affairs, 2005, 84(5), pp. 18-24.
18 Haider, Irfan, 'Details of Agreements Signed During Xi's Visit to Pakistan', Dawn, 20 April 2015, http://www.dawn.com/news/1177129/details-of-agreements-signed-during-xis-visit-to-pakistan, retrieved 23 July 2016.
19 Weidong, Sun, 'Interview: The Progress of the China-Pakistan Economic Corridor Goes Well', Xinhua News, 24 June 2016, http://news.xinhuanet.com/world/2016-06/24/c_1119108622.htm, retrieved 23 July 2016.
20 'Chinese, Pakistani Businesses Build Ties as Beijing Splurges on "Silk Road", Dawn, 3 February 2017. http://www.dawn.com/news/1312472.
21 Ibid.
22 Ibid.

23 Ibid.

24 Khan, Bilal, 'Is it Finally the Pakistan Navy's Turn', Quwa, 3 October 2015, http://quwa.org/2015/10/03/is-it-finally-the-pakistan-navys-turn/.

25 Blank, Stephen, 'The Chinese Concept of "Unrestricted Warfare": Global Competitors Up the Ante', Second Line of Defense, 11 April 2014, http://www.sldinfo.com/the-chinese-concept-of-unrestricted-warfare-global-competitors-up-the-ante/.

26 Ibid.

27 'China's Road & Belt Initiative: Indian Perspective', http://www.vifindia.org/article/2016/may/19/chinas-road-and-belt-initiative-indian-perspective.

28 Press release of ISPR on 21 April 2015, https://www.ispr.gov.pk/front/main.asp?o=t-press_release&date=2015/4/21.

29 Press release of ISPR on 19 February 2016, https://www.ispr.gov.pk/front/main.asp?o=t-press_release&date=2016/2/19.

30 'Pakistani Army Chief Assures Full Security for CPEC', *Xinhuanet*, 13 April 2016, http://news.xinhuanet.com/english/2016-04/13/c_135274538.htm.

31 'Chinese Army Spotted Along Line of Control in Pakistan-Occupied Kashmir, Say Sources', *Times of India*, 13 March 2016, http://timesofindia.indiatimes.com/india/Chinese-army-spotted-along-Line-of-Control-in-Pakistan-occupied-Kashmir-say-sources/articleshow/51380359.cms. This unconfirmed report suggested that China was contemplating to raise three division of about 30,000 soldiers for this purpose.

32 'Chinese Engineer and Driver Injured in Karachi Separatist Bombing', *The Guardian*, 30 May 2016, https://www.theguardian.com/world/2016/may/30/chinese-worker-driver-injured-karachi-bombing-claimed-separatists.

33 'Joint Patrol Along China-Pakistan Border', People's Daily, http://en.people.cn/n3/2016/0721/c98649-9089345.html.

34 US DoD Annual Report to Congress, op. cit., http://www.defense.gov/Portals/1/Documents/pubs/2016%20China%20Military%20Power%20Report.pdf.

35 Panda, Ankit, 'A First: China and Pakistan Conclude Naval Exercise in East China Sea', The Diplomat, 4 January2016, http://thediplomat.com/2016/01/a-first-china-and-pakistan-conclude-naval-exercise-in-east-china-sea/.

6

CHALLENGES AND IMPLICATIONS FOR INDIA

Concurrent to the rise of China's 'Comprehensive National Power' (CNP), President Xi Jinping has made major adjustments to China's international strategy, of which the China-Pakistan relationship is an important pillar. The China-Pakistan relationship will continue to strengthen and expand in the foreseeable future. PLA's entry into POK gives China the strategic pivot to influence the Indian Ocean, India, and Afghanistan, aside from expanding towards Central Asia in conjunction with its 'One Belt and One Road' initiative. China has stepped up its presence in POK even as it has begun to question implicitly our sovereignty over J&K. It sees no contradiction between its stand on Oil and Natural Gas Corporation's (ONGC) oil exploration in a Vietnamese block in the South China Sea on the ground that it is disputed area and its involvement in projects in POK, including strategic ones with military implications for India. POK is becoming key, geo-politically, to China's access to the Arabian Sea through Gwadar as well as its penetration into Afghanistan, with connectivity to Central Asia, in partnership with Pakistan. $ 62 billon CPEC is a step in this direction. China's increasingly strong presence in this region will act as a bulwark against the extension of India's power and influence westwards.

In a geostrategic environment where conflict continues to persist between advanced militaries and their substandard adversaries, either rogue states or terror cells, the latter have been forced to develop asymmetric ways of challenging the superior with the inferior. As much as the US had hoped it could defeat extremist elements using sophisticated weapons and other advanced technologies, the supposed superiority of network-centric warfare proved insufficient against irregular forces. As Robert Kaplan has explained, terrorists and their crude tactics fall on the low end of asymmetric strategy. In the case of China and Pakistan, both nations are successfully exploiting irregular forces individually as also in synergised fashion. This provides the capability to open a third front against an adversary, which is already being applied to India over past several years.

China wants to be the dominant power in Asia and aspires to be to leading world power. Pakistan on the other hand is still struggling to become a nation state and is facing myriad problems, many of them of its own making. It has realised that it can exploit its geo-strategic location to its advantage and is the ultimate security rentier state. China-Pakistan strategic nexus, therefore, advances the national interests of both the countries. Pakistan wants to have parity with India; China wants to be the dominant power in the region. Pakistan wants to limit India's regional as well as global role by blocking us westwards so that we don't have easy access to Afghanistan and Central Asia; China wants to confine India to South Asia, keep us entangled in the sub-continent so that we are unable to fully exert our influence in the rest of Asia and beyond, giving China space and time to entrench its influence there without having to face competition from India. Pakistan is determined to confront India and China is intent on giving Pakistan the means and the confidence to continue this confrontation. China has transferred nuclear and missile technology to Pakistan, neutralising us strategically in South Asia and limiting our capacity to dominate our neighbourhood because of our size and potential. We now have the problematic situation of having two nuclear powers on our borders, with both collaborating with each other to put constraints on India.

While it was assessed in the past that the continued success of its economic expansion will allow China in the coming decades to take a much more assertive geopolitical posture projecting force far beyond its borders, it was generally opined that Taiwan will remain the primary focus for Chinese policymakers, and while ensuring Taiwan does not entertain ambitions of secession from the mainland, PLA military planners will also be forced to concern themselves with defeating US military that remains committed to the defence of Taiwan.[1] In fact, a US view is that US and China may go for war over the South China Sea (SCS) within the next decade.[2] However, China's omni-directional approach through her OBOR initiative and the MSR, particularly the CPEC, has opened the avenue for China to effectively influence the Arabian Sea in not too distant a time-frame.

Addressing the National Defence College at New Delhi in 2008, the then External Affairs Minister (later President) Pranab Mukherjee had stated, 'Today's China seeks to further its interests more aggressively than in the past, thanks to the phenomenal increase of its capacities after thirty years of reforms'. That was over nine years back and China has made giant strides in defence technology since then, especially in the fields of space, battle at sea, air, cyberspace, and electromagnetic domains. PLA has concluded that attacking information systems could offset capabilities of the adversary like the US, Taiwan, India, and Japan. China had conducted an anti-satellite test in 2007, has acquired aircraft carriers and missiles for its SSBILLIONs, developed capability to severely disrupt C4ISR, manoeuvrability re-entry vehicle (MaRV) technology, hypersonic platforms, and the like. China would have reverse engineered the recently captured American Unmanned Underwater Vehicle (UUV). In addition, China has an impressive array of 'Assassin's Mace' weapons, some which may be shared with Pakistan or deployed with the PLA in POK. In February 2017, China reportedly tested a new version of a missile that can carry up to 10 nuclear warheads, signalling a major shift in its nuclear capability as Beijing gears up for a possible military showdown with the US under the Trump Presidency.[3]

India's security dilemmas are particularly acute. It is facing two hostile powers on its frontiers, Pakistan and China, and both cooperate with each other to threaten its security. Both countries occupy large tracts of Indian Territory acquired through aggression and claim additional Indian Territory. All in all, while there is agreement on a cease-fire across the LoC in J&K and Agreements to maintain Peace and Tranquillity and observe CBMs across the LAC with China, the basic situation is unstable, holding the potential of a conflict. Beijing has been wary of the growing warmth in India-US ties. As India seeks to establish a new partnership with the US that can give us the strategic space, China is countering it with an equivalent gesture towards Pakistan, be it support in NSG or blocking India's bid at the UN to ban JeM chief Masood Azhar, the mastermind of the Pathankot terror attack. It is also the biggest supplier of arms and missile technology to Pakistan.

National Security

Since India has not articulated a national security strategy, the general undestanding of national security is restricted to 'military' security. Therefore, the response mechanism is looked at within the ambit of the spectrum of conflict. This is a major policy failure when faced with hybrid war. Scrutiny of conflicts and major incidents, which have occurred over the past decade, indicate that military threat is often no longer the only major factor affecting national security. Traditional factors like territorial disputes, nationality conflicts, religious clashes etc. are increasingly becoming more intertwined with grabbing resources, contending for markets, controlling capital, trade, sanctions and other economic factors, to the extent that they are even becoming secondary to these factors. The phenomenon of 'deep coalition', as discussed in Chapter 5 as part of China's 'Unrestricted Warfare', is a combination of kinetic and non-kinetic measures inclusive of non-state actors, narcotic mafias, and the like. Therefore, the wars are borderless and identities of the war participants ambiguous.

Since, hybrid war is not waged against the military but the whole nation as such, it is no longer possible to rely on military forces and weapons alone to achieve national security in the larger strategic sense, nor is it possible to protect these stratified national interests. Obviously, warfare is in the process of transcending the domains of soldiers, military units, and military affairs, and is increasingly becoming a matter for politicians, scientists, and even bankers. Today we see a global series of 'unrestricted' wars. These wars are global and bring together states, terrorists, insurgents, bankers, high- and low-ranking government, judiciary, customs, police, and security officials in many countries in loose overlapping networks that target national interests, allies, partners on multiple, simultaneous and dynamic fronts, not all of which actually involve the direct use of violence. These forms of subversion and of unrestricted war could involve drug running, money laundering, bribery and corruption of high-placed officials, shady business deals, use of banks to evade sanctions, various forms of gun running, also but not necessarily in conjunction with the evasion of sanctions, and the proliferation of WMDs using any or all of these means. Therefore, when examining challenges to our national security, these must be weighed against the entire gamut of national security, major components of which are depicted in Figure 6.1.

Figure 6.1: Components of National Security

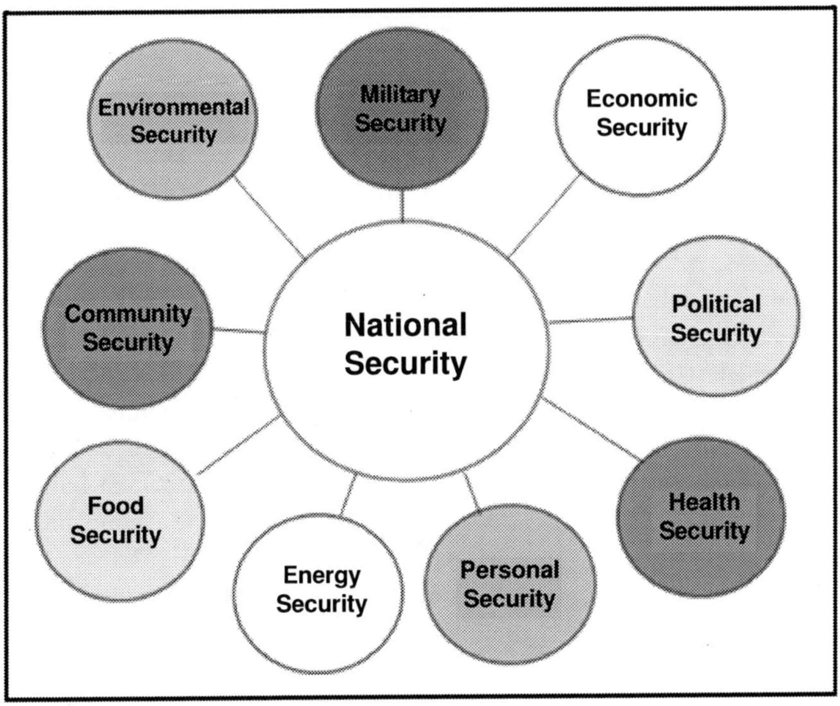

Military Security

'Military Security' implies the capability of a nation-state to defend itself, and/or deter military aggression. Alternatively, military security implies the capability of a nation-state to enforce its policy choices by use of military force. Traditionally, military security was the earliest recognized form of national security, which continues to be the general belief in India. The term 'military' generally refers to Armed Forces or the Army, Navy and Air Force of a country but the ministry or department of defence too is integral part of defence. However, in India, unlike any other country in the world, there are no military professionals in the Ministry of Defence (MoD)—only bureaucrats who are generalists. The military are authorised to use deadly force and weapons to support the interests of the state and, some or all of its citizens. The task of the military is usually defined as defence of the state and its citizens, and the prosecution of war against another state. Military policy (also called defence policy) is public policy dealing with international security and the military. It comprises the measures and initiatives that governments do or do not take in relation to decision-making and strategic goals, such as when and how to commit national armed forces.

The Military has defined a military strategy but this has been worked out in absence of a National Security Strategy (NSS). MoD has no institutionalised set-up for strategic thinking and policy formulation. Resultantly, we are without a NSS which should be the basis of a Comprehensive Defence Review (CDR). It is these two essentials on which our defence procurement in short, medium, and long term should be based. A Tri-Service Doctrine exists but cannot be implanted in the absence of Tri-Service structures. The higher command structures are archaic and do not have military professionals, including in the MoD and the National Security Advisory Board (NSAB). Despite recommendations by the Kargil Review Committee and the follow-up Group of Ministers (GoM) Report, headed by then Deputy Prime Minister and Home minister LK Advani, to appoint a Chief of Defence Staff (CDS), this action has not been implemented to date. As a result, the much-needed Revolution in Military Affairs (RMA) and synergy within the military is lacking. There are indications of some cosmetic changes in the offing with a CDS or a permanent Chairman of Chiefs of Staff Committee (COSC), but without giving him operational powers. Media also indicates Theatre Commands in the offing with the Theatre Commanders reporting directly to the Defence Ministry but with a MoD manned only by bureaucracy, decision-making will remain in deficit. There are indications that military officers may be appointed to some middle-level posts in the MoD, but that would not make much difference either.

Not only have defence allocations been poorer, three successive defence budgets have been negative in actual terms. Besides, no nation can be militarily strong without adequate capacity in meeting defence requirements indigenously. India continues to import some 70 per cent of its defence needs. The CAG has pointed out in many of its reports that most of the defence products of the governmental defence-industrial complex are sub-standard and overpriced. There is not enough investment in defence R&D and the annual budgetary defence allocations continue to be negative in actual terms. The critical deficiencies have been ballooning and mass criticalities like, in ammunition and ageing aircraft, are grave concerns. The 'Make in India' initiative has been foundered horribly by Dr Subhash Bhamre, MoS (Defence Minister) who has put forth the following shortcoming in MoD through a presentation to the Prime Minister during December 2017: tendency to find faults rather than facilitate the process; entire 'Make in India' policy in the defence production sector continues to languish due procedural delays, without taking off in any concrete manner; arms procurement process dogged by multiple and diffused structures without single-point accountability, duplication of processes, avoidable redundant layers doing the same thing again and again, delayed execution, no real-time monitoring and no project-based approach.

Dr Bhamre's forthright presentation rightly projected that Armed Forces continue to view MoD's Acquisition Wing 'as an obstacle rather than a facilitator' and pointed to the need for a 'tectonic change' in mind-set of the ministry's officialdom, also stressing that the tendency to accept delays should be unacceptable. But the 'tectonic change' in the mindset of MoD officials cannot come without inducting military professionals into MoD and DRDO, military being the lone user in latter. It is for these reasons that the FDI in defence sector from 2014 to end 2017 has been a measly Rs 1.17 crore. Defence manufacturing by DRDO versus privatization needs to be seriously examined in keeping with global trends; DRDO to concentrate on R&D with commercialization left to private industry; to include privatization of defence PSUs and OFB. This will also help DRDO concentrate developing technologies for asymmetric advantage. Whatever 'Make in India' takes off, major industrial, acquisition, and fiscal structural problems will continue to limit the potential of Indian military reform. Besides, the indigenous arms industry will remain heavily reliant on foreign partners. The capability gap between the PLA and the Indian Military is widening exponentially. The poor state of our indigenous defence production encourages asymmetric actions by our adversaries.

India has been subject to proxy wars since past three decades but we have not established effective deterrence against it. Pakistan is upping the ante and succeeding in its 'thousands cut policy'. Chinese media says India's actions in Kashmir can stir up Muslim organisations in northeast, even as Pakistani terror attacks in Pathankot,

Gurdaspur, Pampore, Uri, Nagrota, Samba drew no comments from China. In fact, China is already stoking insurgencies in our northeast to relieve pressure on Pakistan by India. Post the killing of Burhan Wani, there has been heavy exchange of artillery fire, while violence has gone up in J&K with the population increasingly involved in stone pelting at security forces. We have suffered scores of casualties including officers. It is difficult to accurately gauge how many casualties Pakistan has suffered during the same period. However, even though Pakistani military personnel would have been killed and wounded by our actions, bulk of the terrorists killed are the gutter-level riff-raff who are radicalised and flush on narcotics, even though Pakistan mixes regulars with terrorists. That is why it is a highly low-cost option for Pakistan. Apparently, we have no clear cut policy on J&K; our handling of Hurriyat separatists and the stone-pelters is indicative of this. Significantly, despite Article 370, around 4000 Rohingya Muslims have been permitted to settle in the Jammu region. Such a development must be seen in the background of Pakistan's ISI and Asim Umar, Al Qaeda's South Asia (AQIS) chief, himself a Pakistani national, calling for Rohingya Muslims to take up arms because of developments in Myanmar—Buddhist-Rohingya clashes.

Figure 6.2: India-China-Pakistan Strategic Asymmetry

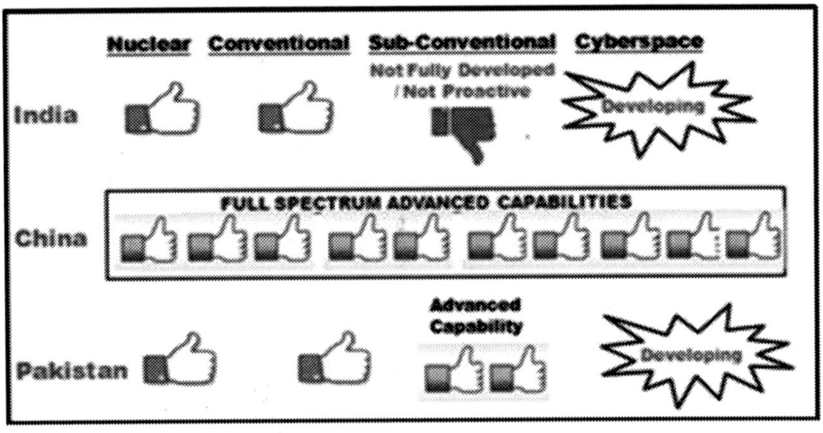

The above strategic asymmetry (see Figure 6.2 also) adversely affects India. Pakistan and India are both developing capacity in cyberspace but Pakistan has the advantage of close cooperation of China. Both in China and the US, it is the PLA and the US Military that is spearheading respective cyber-warfare programmes but in India, the military has been kept away. As per media reports, government has deferred the establishment of the Cyber, Aerospace, and Special Forces Commands as recommended by the Naresh Chandra Committee, on grounds of 'first create capabilities and structures for such operations before going for such expansion'.

But the question is if capabilities and structures already existed, these commands would not be required. India has Special Forces (SF) numerically almost at par with the US Special Forces (USSF) but India is not employing them at the strategic level on politico-military missions, whereas, Special Forces are central for establishing deterrence against proxy wars. Sure we executed the 'surgical strike' and the same may be repeated too. But they are no panacea for subduing the aggressive China-Pakistan strategic nexus unless sustained covert operations are launched at strategic level. Aside from bridging gaping strategic voids in equipping, major effort has to be made towards ensuring the security of our installations. Findings of the study post the terror attack on IAF's Pathankot base will need urgent follow-up. The army post at Uri had just a cattle fence and no thermal imager when attacked.

Speaking to the media on the occasion of Army Day 2017, Chief of Army Staff General Bipin Rawat stated that while two-front war is possible, of the 73 all-weather roads required along the border with China and 14 strategic railways needed along the two-fronts, railway lines exist on paper and only 22 of the 73 roads have been completed over a decade after they were identified. So, the state remains pathetic, for which MoD can't absolve itself of blame. In May 2015, then MoS (Defence) had stated that MoD has set itself a deadline of 2017 to complete infrastructure projects in Sikkim and Arunachal Pradesh, and by 2018 put the infrastructure in Arunachal Pradesh and the Northeast in place, but not much progress has been made.

Despite hostile neighbours, India has consistently failed to adopt the 'One Border, One Force' policy. Sensitive areas like the Depsang Plains and Chumar in Eastern Ladakh where Chinese have been making repeated intrusions are manned by the Indo-Tibetan Border Police (ITBP) who have not been placed under command of the local Army formation because of turf wars. They report to their Director General and the Ministry of Home Affairs (MHA), which is a lopsided arrangement. Similarly, our border with Nepal is manned by the Sashastra Seema Bal (SSB) but they do not man any defences, just widely dispersed 'nakas' (posts) under the concept of 'open border'. This gives free access for sub-conventional activities. Pakistan exploits this avenue for infiltrating terrorists, fake Indian currency, smuggling, narcotics, and the like. Our Prime Minister has publicly stated that recent train accidents have been the handiwork of Pakistan while the NIA reports say that Pakistani nationals have been coming across the India-Nepal border for organizing such sabotage. Like the ITBP, the SSB reports to their headquarters at Delhi and the MHA. The concept of 'open border' should not mean that no defences need to be manned. This open border also must be viewed with the expanding Chinese presence in Nepal, Chinese rail link planned with Nepal, links between the Nepal Maoists (who are Chinese surrogates) with Indian Maoists, and availability of North-South communications in Nepal that could be exploited by China to enter the Siliguri Corridor. Logically, all Central Armed Police Forces (CAPF) manning the borders should be placed under command of the local military formations and then the MoD instead of MHA. It is for similar reasons that the Indian Coast Guard (ICG), established on 18 August 1978, that protects India's maritime interests and enforces maritime law over the territorial waters of India including its contiguous zone and Exclusive Economic Zone (EEZ) has been placed under the MoD and not MHA right from its inception.

To summarise, India's military security is adversely affected because of the following major factors:

- ✓ Void of national security strategy, from which should flow the military strategy.
- ✓ Critical voids; for example, ageing aircraft and issues like ammunition shortfalls would pose a risk to the military on the battlefield.
- ✓ Lack of military professionals in higher defence set-up, particularly in the MoD and National Security Advisory Board (NSAB).
- ✓ Void of CDS, lack of synergy within military and lack of RMA.
- ✓ Abysmal indigenous defence production capacity resulting in continued imports to meet 70 per cent of defence needs and in some cases sub-standard indigenous products at prices higher than commercially available products
- ✓ In adequate defence allocations; successive defence budgets have been 'negative' in actual terms.
- ✓ Major industrial, acquisition, and fiscal structural problems will continue to limit the potential of Indian military reform.
- ✓ Indigenous arms industry will remain heavily reliant on foreign partners.
- ✓ Lack of effective deterrence to proxy war despite facing years of cross-border terrorism.
- ✓ Lack of cohesive policy on J&K.
- ✓ Widening capability gap between PLA and Indian Military – China's 'Assassin's Mace' inventory being case in point.
- ✓ Consistent lowering of status, pay, and emoluments of military personnel.
- ✓ Lack of 'One Border, One Force'; CAPF deployed in portions including open border between India and Nepal that is being exploited by Pakistan and China.
- ✓ Poor border infrastructure and lack of focus to improve it.
- ✓ Unresolved borders.

Economic Security

India is the sixth largest economy in the world measured by nominal Gross Domestic Product (GDP) and the third largest by purchasing power parity (PPP). GDP growth in India stood at 7.2 per cent (2014), 7.6 per cent (2015), 7.0 per cent (2016), and 7.2 per cent in the last three months of 2017. GDP per capita forecast for 2017 was $1,852 (nominal) and $7.224 (PPP), while GDP per capita rank was 140th (nominal) and 122nd (PPP).

However, the good news is that *India is likely to regain the position in 2018 with growth expected to accelerate to 7.3 per cent in 2018 according to the World Bank's Global Economic Prospects published in January 2018*. At the same time, it is good to maintain focus on various factors at international and national levels that affect economic growth. It is interesting to note that capital formation in India declined in three straight quarters 'before' demonetisation[4], industrial activity contracted for eight out of the 14 months between November 2015 and December 2016.[5] All in all there are several factors that periodically affect the Indian economic growth[6] and these include:

- **Capital flows and Stock Exchange Market**. India has had a very steady flow of capital from both foreign and local investors. In addition to this, the country also has a thriving stock market and this has helped it gain capital. With this amount of capital, India has less to worry about in case the GDP rates fall. This is because its currency can still get overvalued given its steady flow of capital.
- **The RBI Ranks**. The currency of India largely depends on the rankings by RBI. The RBI is in charge of managing the balance of payments for India. Slight changes in the RBI assessments can have a huge impact on the currency of India and lead to either over assessment or under rankings of the country's economy.
- **Global Currency Trends of Economically Powerful Countries**. India like many other countries has economic and currency links with powerful countries such as US, UK, Japan, Canada and others. When the currencies of these countries are undervalued, India's currency is also likely to depreciate. On the other hand, an appreciation of these currencies has similar effects on India's currency. These global currency trends therefore influence India's economic growth.
- **Political Changes**. Political setup in India also influences its economic growth. A change in the country governance often leads to changes in economic policies especially with regard to importation and exportation of

goods and services. Political changes also impact on the tax rates and may affect the investment climate which ultimately influences the economic growth rate of the country.

- **Energy and Oil**. India imports oil in large quantities. This is an essential commodity and it affects India's economic growth rate. When crude oil prices in the world market fluctuate, India's currency cannot remain stable. High oil prices result in high inflation rates hence overvaluing of India's currency.
- **Demographics and Poverty Rates**. India is one of the most populous countries in the world and economists predict that its population will rise by over 300 million by 2030. In as much as this population growth may be good in terms of larger markets, it is costly to maintain and can only be fruitful if India puts in place measures to provide its citizens with social, educational and economic needs. Otherwise poverty rates which are already high will increase with this population and drag the economic growth rate of the country.

Of the above factors, demography and poverty will continue to affect seriously. Historically, conquest of nations has made conquerors rich through plunder, access to new resources and enlarged trade by controlling a conquered nations' economy. In today's complex system of international trade, characterized by multi-national agreements, mutual inter-dependence, availability of natural resources etc., the freedom to exercise choice of policies to develop a nation's economy in the manner desired invites economic security. Economic security today forms, arguably, as important a part of national security as military security. Creation and protection of jobs catering to defence and non-defence needs are vital to national security. Third-world countries are less secure due to lack of employment for their citizens. There is little focus in India on population control and even though job creation is being factored in, the rate of population growth may offset the jobs being created. The lack of management of social change and lack of governance is the reason of multiple insurgencies. These are being exploited by our enemies especially because India has failed to establish effective deterrence against it. Consequently, India's expenditure on internal security is heavy. Beginning with the spike in budgetary allocation to the MHA in 2009-10 following the Mumbai terror attacks of November 2008, the MHA has been witnessing a steady increase in its allocations over the years.[7] In the last three years too, allocations have increased from Rs. 61,401.78 crore in 2014-15 to 65,651.10 crore in 2015-16, and to 73,406.37 crore in 2016-17. For the financial year 2017-18 as well, this upward trend has persisted with allocations reaching Rs. 83,823 crore, a hike of around 11.5 per cent over that of the previous year. Budgetary provisions have been pegged at over Rs 92,600 crore for 2018-19, a hike of 10.5 per cent over 2017-18

One of the serious internal security threats that the country has been grappling with, for more than a decade, is Left Wing Extremism (LWE). At present, 106 districts in 10 states are affected by LWE.[8] Since the Central Reserve Police Force (CRPF) is the primary force deployed in the LWE-affected states, the Government in 2009, sanctioned funds for raising 39 additional battalions of the CRPF. As a result, the CRPF has been receiving the highest allocations in successive budgets since then.[9] In the previous fiscal year, the force received Rs. 16,228.18 crore, which has been increased by another 1635.35 crore to Rs. 17,868.53 crore for 2017-18. Of the sanctioned 39 battalions, 26 have been raised till 2016 and the remainder is to be raised by 2018-19. However, little has been done to dominate the 72,000 km^2 Dandakaranya Forest where the LWE have free run.

The budgetary allocation for internal allocation includes expenditures on various Security Related Expenditure (SRE) schemes, border management, and Comprehensive Integrated Border Management Systems (CIBMS) along the India-Pakistan border on pilot basis, border guarding forces, Integrated Check Posts (ICPs), Border Area Development Programme (BADP), police modernisation and the like. The Intelligence Bureau (IB), which in recent years has been augmenting its strength, has also received an allocation of Rs. 1,577 crore, an increase of 11 per cent from the previous year.[10] In the overall context, while the accent has been on expansion of the CAPF and Police Forces, modernisation of these forces has been lagging.

The relationship between economics and security has become more complex globally but the volatile neighbourhood of India and the China-Pakistan anti-India nexus compound this complexity. Planners need to understand that an economy is made up of people making millions of individual decisions. The economic fundamentals are important but they are not enough. Understanding the interplay between economics and security can make huge differences. Economists should do more to anticipate problems caused by security. Military planners need to take more account of the economic effects of their actions. More needs to be invested in bringing economic and security planning together. The economic and security problems of fragile and conflict affected areas may seem insignificant to many but they can become home to far greater problems. India does not appear to have found the right mix between economy and security as may be gleaned from the discussion on military security above. Inadequate focus on defence and security can retard economy and development in the event of conflict.

Political Security

The Human Development Report 1994 of the United Nations Development Programme (UNDP) uses 'political security' as one of the seven main categories of threats to 'human security', the seven categories being economic, food, health, environment, personal, community, and political.[11] Political security is the defence against any form of political oppression. It is concerned with whether people live in a society that honours their basic human rights. There is convergence of views that a degree of participation by 'all' in legitimate decision-making processes of a society, under and protected by rules of stable laws, would result in political security (a dependent variable in a desired state of affairs). Also, there is a broad scope of governing activities, or features, to be considered as associated with the concept, from voting and separation of powers to the accountability of elected individuals and bureaucrats, from the protection of human rights and government stability to access to economic benefits. There is serious shortfall in accountability of elected representatives and bureaucrats in India, the roots of which can be found in the 1993 Vohra Committee Report wherein it established the nexus between governmental functionaries, political leaders and others with various mafia organisation and crime syndicates, enabling development of significant muscle and money power to operate with impunity, but finally opining that 'leakage about the linkages of crime syndicate to senior government functionaries or political leaders in the states or at the centre could have a destabilising effect on the functioning of Government'. So, naturally there was no follow-up to this report.[12] As for participation by 'all' in legitimate decision-making processes of a society, this is generally lacking in insurgency areas including J&K where the Panchayats have little powers and access to funds.

Political security is about the stability of the social order. It is closely allied to military security and societal security. Other components in a framework for national security while addressing threats to sovereignty, maybe referent objects like transnational/within groups of political importance including tribes, minorities, religious organisations.[13] Diplomacy, negotiation and other interactions form the means of interaction between the objects. This is relevant to India's northeast where many insurgent groups are both sides of the border. The LWE problem too is largely connected with tribal and in some cases their forest rights. The lack of homogeneity in the Indian population causes division between different sections of the people based on religion, region, language, caste and race. This has led to the rise of political parties with agendas catering to one or a mix of these groups. Parties in India also target people who are not in favour of other parties and use them as an asset. Some parties openly profess their focus on a particular group. The narrow focus and vote bank politics of most parties, even in the central government and central legislature, side lines national issues such as economic welfare and national security. Moreover, internal security is also threatened as incidences of political parties instigating and leading violence between two opposing groups of people is a frequent occurrence.

Finally, there is the issue of 'reservations'. The Constitution had indicated that reservations should not go beyond 10-15 years. However, this has been encouraged and expanded to disproportionate levels due to vote-bank politics. The primary objective of the present-day Indian reservation system is to enhance the social and educational status of underprivileged communities and thus improve their lives, but ironically reservations are not applied to those who are below the poverty line (BPL) but done on the basis of Scheduled Tribes (ST), Scheduled Castes (SC) and Other Backward Classes (OBC). This has created a lopsided situation where many individuals and families despite having become millionaires and got high-placed jobs continue to enjoy reservations unlimitedly at the cost of other BPL families. At the same time, there are endless demands by segments of the society to be included in the SC, ST, OBC category, some engaging in violent agitations causing immense damage to government and private property.

Human Security

As mentioned above, the UNDP's 1994 Human Development Report defining 'Human Security' argues that the scope of global security should be expanded to include threats in seven areas as under:

- **Economic Security**. Economic security requires an assured basic income for individuals, usually from productive and remunerative work or, as a last resort, from a publicly financed safety net. In this sense, only about a quarter of the world's people are presently economically secure. While the economic security problem may be more serious in developing countries concern also arises in developed countries as well. Unemployment problems constitute an important factor underlying political tensions and ethnic violence.
- **Food Security**. Food security requires that all people at all times have both physical and economic access to basic food. According to the UN, the overall availability of food is not a problem; rather the problem often is the poor distribution of food and a lack of purchasing power. In the past, food security problems have been dealt with at both national and global levels. However, their impacts are limited. According to UN, the key is to tackle the problems relating to access to assets, work and assured income (related to economic security).

- **Health Security.** Health Security aims to guarantee a minimum protection from diseases and unhealthy lifestyles. In developing countries, the major causes of death traditionally were infectious and parasitic diseases, whereas in industrialized countries, the major killers were diseases of the circulatory system. Today, lifestyle-related chronic diseases are leading killers worldwide, with 80 per cent of deaths from chronic diseases occurring in low- and middle-income countries. According to the UN, in both developing and industrial countries, threats to health security are usually greater for poor people in rural areas, particularly children. This is due to malnutrition and insufficient access to health services, clean water and other basic necessities.
- **Environmental Security.** Environmental security aims to protect people from the short- and long-term ravages of nature, man-made threats in nature, and deterioration of the natural environment. In developing countries, lack of access to clean water resources is one of the greatest environmental threats. In industrial countries, one of the major threats is air pollution. Global warming, caused by the emission of greenhouse gasses, is another environmental security issue.
- **Personal Security.** Personal security aims to protect people from physical violence, whether from the state or external states, from violent individuals and sub-state actors, from domestic abuse, or from predatory adults. For many people, the greatest source of anxiety is crime, particularly violent crime.
- **Community Security.** Community security aims to protect people from the loss of traditional relationships and values and from sectarian and ethnic violence. Traditional communities, particularly minority ethnic groups are often threatened. About half of the world's states have experienced some inter-ethnic strife. The UN declared 1993 the Year of Indigenous People to highlight the continuing vulnerability of the 300 million aboriginal people in 70 countries as they face a widening spiral of violence.
- **Political Security.** Political security is concerned with whether people live in a society that honours their basic human rights. According to a survey conducted by Amnesty International, political repression, systematic torture, ill treatment or disappearance was still practiced in 110 countries. Human rights violations are most frequent during periods of political unrest. Along with repressing individuals and groups, governments may try to exercise control over ideas and information.

Since then, human security has been receiving more attention from the key global development institutions, such as the World Bank. However, it is opined that the concept has been manipulated and transformed considerably since 1994 to fit organisational interests.[14] This is quite true in the backdrop of the human rights violations by China in Xinjiang and Tibet grossly ignored, as also Pakistani genocide in Baluchistan.

The human security approach can be usefully applied as a policy measure in India to reinforce successes in the social and economic spheres so that the possibility of dissatisfaction turning into violent opposition and internal conflict is minimised. In 2012, the Indian government stated 22 per cent of its population is below its official poverty limit.[15] The World Bank, in 2011 based on 2005's PPPs International Comparison Programme, estimated 23.6 per cent of Indian population, or about 276 million people lived below $1.25 per day on purchasing power parity. The World Bank proposed revisions in May 2014, to its poverty calculation methodology and purchasing power parity basis for measuring poverty worldwide, including India. According to this revised methodology, the world had 872.3 million people below the new poverty line, of which 179.6 million people lived in India. In other words, India with 17.5 per cent of total world's population had 20.6 per cent share of world's poorest in 2011.[16] As of 2014, 58 per cent of the total population were living on less than $3.10 per day.[17] According to the *Modified* Mixed Reference Period (MMRP) concept proposed by World Bank in 2015, India's poverty rate for period 2011-12 stood at 12.4 per cent of the total population, or about 172 million people, taking the revised poverty line as $1.90.[18] The Asian Development Bank estimates India's population to be at 1.28 billion with an average growth rate, from 2010-2015, at 1.3 per cent. In 2014, 49.9 per cent of the population aged 15 years and above were employed. However, there are still 21.9 per cent of the population who live below the national poverty line.[19]

India also has a sizeable chunk of children out of school, people without access to primary health care, and those suffering from hordes of diseases. India is racing against time. The Millennium Development Goals are still far away. But the government has taken a series of policy measures which, 'if pursued meticulously', could take it nearer the goals. The Mahatma Gandhi National Rural Employment Guarantee Act (MGNREGA) has been promulgated and the scheme put in motion. With the right to information (RTI) Act, now in place, and the promotion of e-governance and 'Digital India' is progressing in a big way, India appears to be on the cusp of a new revolution. A law which casts direct accountability on a public service officer for non-performance is also in place but it is the implementation of all these measures in true letter and spirit that is the crux. The government has lined up a series of measures to transform rural India. Implementation of minimum wage laws, crop and livestock insurance, and an improvement in rural credit are high on the agenda. But unless a sound monitoring system and grievance redress mechanism are put in place, India will still be chasing a chimera—as has been the case with many of its well-conceived schemes like 'education for all' and 'health for all'.

India continued to rank low in the Human Development Index (HDI), 130th in the 2014 UNDP report.[20] India's 2014 HDI of 0.609 is below the average of 0.630 for countries in the medium human development group. This clearly shows the considerable distance that India will have to go before it can rank among the better-off nations. In terms of the global crime index[21], India stands at 66th position in 125 countries with a crime index of 43.96. Poor population to police ratio and delayed justice and inappropriate laws contribute to high crime rate. For example, majority of rapes are being committed by juveniles, yet the law permits punishment to them which can well be considered 'mild', with many repeat offenders in this category. *Ironically, India slipped one place from 130 to 131 among 188 countries in terms of human development in the 2016 Human Development Report (HDR) released by UNDP in March 2017. India's HDI value of 0.624 placed it in the 'medium human development' category alongside countries Congo, Namibia and Pakistan but third among the SAARC countries, behind Sri Lanka (73) and Maldives (105), both of which figure in the 'high human development' category.*

Energy Security

Energy plays an important role in the national security as a fuel to power the economic engine.[22] The modern world relies on vast energy supply to fuel everything from transportation to communication, to security and health delivery systems. Michael Ruppert has claimed that for every calorie of food produced in the industrial world, ten calories of oil and gas energy are invested in the forms of fertilizer, pesticide, packaging, transportation, and running farm equipment.[23] Threats to energy security include the political instability of several energy producing countries, the manipulation of energy supplies, the competition over energy sources, attacks on supply infrastructure, as well as accidents, natural disasters, terrorism, and reliance on foreign countries for oil.[24]

India's fragile energy security is under severe pressure from its rising dependence on imported oil, regulatory uncertainty and opaque natural gas pricing policies, small pool of skilled manpower and poorly developed upstream infrastructure and dependence on fossil fuels as the dominant source of energy in the near future.[25] Coal, oil and natural gas are the most important sources of primary energy in India. Inadequate domestic supplies of these hydrocarbons are forcing the country to increase its import bill. The supply of natural gas as well, which was expected to alleviate our energy security from the new domestic fields, remains well below projections. Of late, driven by accelerated capacity addition in power generation and decline in domestic coal production, India's imports of coal have risen (Figure 6.3 refers).

Figure 6.3: Coal Imports by India

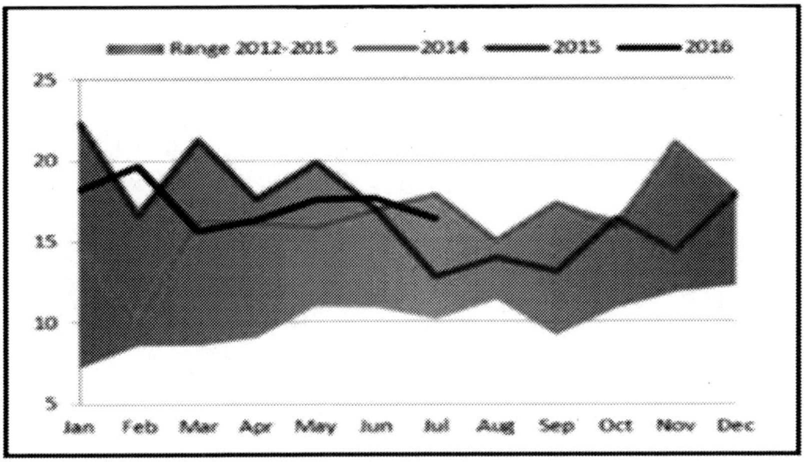

To meet the growing energy demand over the next few years, India will have to enhance its energy security by procuring energy supplies at affordable prices. While the country has surplus refining capacity and is an exporter of petroleum products, major investments will have to be made in the domestic upstream industry and to acquire hydrocarbon reserves abroad. Currently, there is a move towards a diversified fuel basket, together with a focus on efficient exploration and consumption of energy resources, is needed. Additionally, key areas of action are:

- Accelerated development of energy infrastructure.
- Human resource development.
- Technological upgrade.

A more conducive policy environment coupled with an effective regulatory regime is, without doubt, the basis for accelerated growth of domestic energy resources. Energy security needs integrated action by all stakeholders. With a population of one billion, around 300 million Indians still lacked access to electricity as of 2014.[26] But this statistic only told part of the story. The UN claimed that more than two-thirds of India's population still relied on biomass (wood) and dung-based fuel to meet their energy needs for cooking. About a quarter of the country lacked access to the electrical grid, but India is still fourth-largest energy consumer in the world, after China, the United States, and Russia. The 2014 report also said that in the last decade, India has nearly doubled its electricity consumption on a per capita basis. The growth is remarkable. Since India consumed only about 500 kWh at the turn of the century, the nation still has a long way to go. At 917 kWh per capita, India remains far off the global per capita average of 2,600 kWh.[27]

Significantly, India has a hydropower generating capacity of 39,491 MW, represented only 18 per cent of the country's installed capacity in 2013; hydropower production stood at 113,626 GWh, 11.8 per cent of India's total electricity generation capacity. According to a FICCI report,[28] India is endowed with rich hydropower potential to the tune of 148 GW (which would meet a demand of 84 GW at 60 per cent load factor), potentially making it one of the most important sources to meet the energy security needs of the country. As of 2013, 13 GW of hydropower was under construction. But with all 13 GW completed, India still will have tapped only about 33 per cent of its potential. In comparison, Canada and Brazil have achieved 69 per cent and 48 per cent, respectively. Hydropower's percentage of installed capacity in India has been in continuous decline since 1966, when it was 46 per cent of the country's installed capacity.

What must be acknowledged is that our energy security is intricately entwined with our military security, even as it fuels our economic growth. Not only would the energy installations within the country like nuclear power plants, refineries, storage and pipelines be targets for sabotage and hybrid warfare, security of our SLOCs will remain of vital importance. All this will require catering for adequate military security.

Environmental Security

South Asia is faced with serious environmental insecurity. The region faces rising sea levels and regularly experiences coastal flooding with heavily populated and arable-land-rich coastal areas. Additionally, it is highly vulnerable to glacial melting. The Western Himalayas, which provide water supplies to much of South Asia, have experienced some of the most rapid melt in the world. Natural resource deficiencies are also high. South Asia houses nearly a quarter of the world's population, yet contains less than 5 per cent of its annual renewable water resources. Water availability plummeted from over 21,000 cubic meters per capita in the 1960s to about 8,000 in 2005. According to estimates, some of the region could face water scarcity (per capita water availability under 1,000 cubic meters) by 2025.[29] In South Asia, water shortage imperils food security and health, but also livelihoods, because farming and fishing are dominant sectors. Energy is similarly lacking in South Asia. The World Bank has ranked its electricity grid as one of the world's worst. Millions of South Asians do not have electricity—including 400 million in India alone.

India is a microcosm of the region's environmental insecurity. According to the Center for Global Development, nearly 40 million people in India (more than in any other country) are at risk of dying from rising sea levels by 2050.[30] Another estimate is that because of rising temperatures, India's agricultural productivity could fall by 30 per cent to 40 per cent by 2080.[31] India has over 20 per cent of the world's population, yet only 4 per cent of its water. About 25 per cent of Indians (250 million people) lack access to clean water. So extensive is India's water consumption that users are raiding groundwater supplies with abandon. According to the World Bank, India is the world's most voracious consumer of groundwater. A US study in 2009 found that groundwater levels fell by 4 cm per year between 2002 and 2008 in three north-western states, including Punjab.[32] A similar story prevails with energy. India's economic growth has sent demand skyrocketing, and estimates peg India as the world's third largest energy consumer by 2030.

While climate vulnerability and resource constraints have received heightened attention in recent years, their ties to stability and national security often goes unaddressed, example being the LWE in eastern and central reaches of India, which happen to be the locations of the country's chief reserves of coal, India's most heavily consumed energy source. The basic drivers of the insurgency are tied to natural resource constraints. The fruits of heavy resource extraction, mainly coal, often fail to reach local communities, fuelling grievances among poor villagers that the Maoists exploit to spark recruitment.[33] Intensive coal mining in these areas also displaces locals and creates toxic living conditions for those who stay, further strengthening the insurgency.

The external manifestations of links between India's resource woes and security are discernible in ties with Pakistan. While India provides water to Pakistan under the Indus Water Treaty, far more than global norms based on the size of the basin, however, Pakistan contends that hydropower projects on these rivers amounts to India stealing Pakistan's share of water. Such accusations become a security matter when they emanate from the likes of the Laskhar-e-Taiba (LeT), in order to attack India. Another external example of India's resource security links is its relationship with China. Since India lacks energy supplies at home to fulfill its immense demand, it is taking its search for energy abroad. This can bring it into fierce competition with China, whose growing regional and global presence is driven, to a great extent, by its own search for natural resources.[34] Some security analysts have depicted the Bay of Bengal and its significant deposits of natural gas as a future source of Sino-India conflict. China has secured a major natural gas deal with Myanmar and may conclude one with Sri Lanka soon. Water too is a key factor in border tensions between India and China. These tensions centre around one of the region's rare water-rich areas, particularly Arunachal Pradesh state. China, like India, suffers from water insecurity. The North China Plain, one of China's core breadbaskets, is acutely water-scarce, with per capita availability of only 225 cubic meters per year. The strategic significance of Arunachal Pradesh, therefore, goes beyond the issue of territory. Finally, India has grave concerns over Chinese dam building on Tibetan Plateau Rivers including the Brahmaputra.

Climate change could also aggravate India's external security concerns. Existing water-related tensions with Pakistan and with China would likely worsen. However, perhaps the most serious threat would emerge from Bangladesh,[35] which is extremely vulnerable to climate changes which will likely cause major flooding and agricultural losses in the coming decades. Millions of environmental refugees may stream across the border into north-eastern India, a tense region with separatist tendencies. India, therefore, must (1) integrate resource considerations into security policy and planning; (2) improve own resource governance and (3) develop demand-side conservation-based policies that better manage resources that are precious, but not yet scarce. These would make environmental and security manageable, even as climate change can hardly be reversed.

CHALLENGES

China-Pak Nexus. The Sino-Pak nexus is based on common enmity with India. Currently, China and Pakistan are both inimical in their attitude to Indian interests in the region. Chinese lodgement in GB, the CPEC and China's presence in Gwadar has adverse strategic impact on India's national security. If India continues to lag behind China in its economic as well as CNP growth then the existing nexus would grow stronger and further marginalise India's status in the region. Conversely, potential growth of Indian economy and its CNP would pave the way for better bilateral engagement with China resulting in more interdependence and reducing the trust deficit. Apart from economic, other common areas for cooperation would be terrorism, energy, climate change issues and reforms related to international monetary institution. Such interdependence would weaken the Sino-Pak nexus. Faltering Pakistan economy/internal situation could further accelerate weakening of Sino-Pak nexus and result in better Sino-Indian cooperation. Such a scenario would enable India a greater role in the region and enhanced influence on its neighbours.

Jihadi Terrorism. The global jihadist movements inherently religious, centred on

Islam. Given the ethnic and religious character of the South Asian region, entire South Asia suffers from such movements and the trend is likely to continue even beyond 2025. Pakistan continues to use 'Jihadi' terrorism as an instrument of state policy to wage proxy war against India. Post the increased operations against ISIS in Iraq-Syria and recapture of part Mosul, ISIS cadre's migration to Af-Pak region is inevitable. The ISIS reportedly has made its first strike in India during March 2017. Asim Umar, AQIS chief has also given calls to strike India. In the Kashmir Valley, radicalization and violence has gone up after the killing of terrorist Burhan Wani, with rural areas also affected in some five districts of J&K. With China, Pakistan, Russia, and Iran backing Taliban, the situation in Afghanistan is deteriorating, which is not in India's interest. All these trends, if not managed, will embroil India in its internal security dilemma, impede its growth and thereby, its capability to influence events at the strategic levels. Combative capabilities and strategies would be needed to combat the global war on terrorism.

Geopolitical Containment by Proxy. China has on a sustained basis, propped up Pakistan politically, economically and more importantly, militarily, to contain India as well as erode her competitive politico-economic-military advantage in Asia. It has also been stepping up military and economic engagement with India's immediate neighbour's—Bangladesh, Nepal, and Sri Lanka. Beijing's broad-based military cooperation agreement with Dhaka, Bangladesh's first military accord with any country has four apparent objectives: to bring Bangladesh into the Chinese strategic orbit; to gain naval and commercial access to the strategically important port of Chittagong; to connect Bangladesh with Myanmar; and to secure a doorway to India's vulnerable North-East. Far from moderating Indian fears, Beijing's deepening ties with India's neighbouring states are of increasing concern over Chinese activities. China's rising power has become the single biggest cause of qualitative change in the geopolitical landscape. China is unlikely to shy away from investing more resources into activities and capabilities antithetical to Indian interests and security.

China's String of Pearls. China's incremental efforts to build a 'string of pearls' along the Indian Ocean rim symbolize Beijing's desire for a fourth strategic corridor that would create a challenge to India from the South. China seeks to assemble this 'string of pearls'—a term first used in a report for the Pentagon by US defence contractor Booz Allen Hamilton—through forward listening posts, naval-access agreements and Chinese-built harbours stretching from Pakistan and Sri Lanka to Bangladesh and Myanmar. The Chinese interest in the Indian Ocean rim extends to the Seychelles. Refer to Figure 6.4.

Figure 6.4: China's Interest in IOR

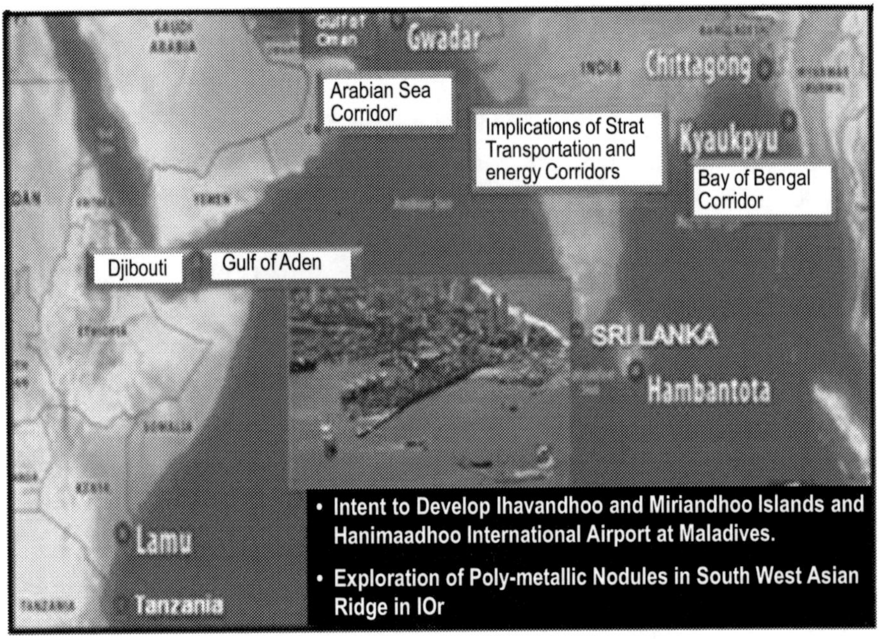

Border Disputes. India has border disputes with both, China and Pakistan. A Border Defence Cooperation Agreement (BDCA) was signed with China in October 2013 while with Pakistan a ceasefire agreement exists since Nov 2003. There have been transgressions by China on the LAC and frequent ceasefire violations by Pakistan on the LoC. Such a game of brinkmanship is likely to persist till such time India develops suitable defence and deterrence capabilities. China's position is unlikely to change in the foreseeable future. On the one hand, stakes are high for Indian troops to ensure status quo until the final resolution of dispute, yet, on the other hand, the Chinese through, diplomatic posturing and the PLA on ground, continue to repeatedly question the status quo. The probability of a local military aggressive posturing spiralling into a major military conflict also remains high. Of course, going by the Chinese strategic culture, a trigger could well be engineered by them to exercise military option to seek Indian capitulation. At the same time, such development is directly linked to the state of Indian economy. Should India not be able to sustain economic growth, then the gap with China would widen further and thus embolden China, along with Pakistan, to increase its cross-border activities and conflict.

India-China Military Asymmetry. China's military modernisation along with capacity building, infrastructure development in Tibet, and forays into the Indian

Ocean pose serious challenges to India's security. According to Pentagon's 2016 China Military report, China is aggressively pursuing military modernization. India on the other hand is grappling to replace its military's obsolete weapons and weapon systems, in addition to making available to its armed forces cutting-edge mobility, weapons and equipment. However, India doesn't appear to have found the right balance between economic development and security. Neglect of the military over past years and two consecutive 'negative' defence budgets in India (including for the current financial year) have all led to the military asymmetry between the Indian Military and the PLA widening as summarised in Figure 6.5.

Figure 6.5: India-China Military Comparison

Units	India	China
Manpower Available	616000000	75000000
Active Military Personnel	1325000	2335000
Active Military Reserves	2143000	2300000
Aircraft (All Types)	2086	2942
Hellicopters	646	802
Attack Hellicopters	19	200
Attack aircraft (Fixed Wing)	809	1385
Fighter Aircraft	679	1230
Trainer Aircraft	318	352
Transport Aircraft	857	782
Serviceable Airports	346	507
Tank Strength	6464	9150
AFV Strength	6704	4768
SPG Strength	290	1710
Towed Artillery	7414	6246
MLRS Strength	292	1770
Merchant Marine Strength	340	2030
Major Ports/Terminals	7	15
Fleet Strength	295	714
Aircraft Carriers	1	1
Submarines	14	68
Frigates	14	48
Destroyers	10	32
Corvettes	26	26
Mine Warfare Craft	6	4
Patrol Craft	135	138

Source: globalfirepower.com

Disruptive Technologies. Military asymmetry is not just a game of numbers, as seen in the illustration above. Presently, China has an edge in the field of disruptive military technologies vis-à-vis India and is also covertly aiding Pakistan in such technologies. Failure of India to develop and field such technologies would result in further increasing the existing gap and thereby allow China to not only dominate India but the entire South Asian region as well. Such growing discrepancy would also embolden Pakistan to increase its asymmetric activities against India. However, with the efforts of our scientists there is a likelihood of major breakthroughs in the field of missiles, robotics, laser, direct energy weapons and cyber warfare. In doing so, we must also optimize our strategic partnerships with countries like US, Japan, and Israel. Such a development would reduce Chinese supremacy and result in India emerging as a technological power in the region. Reducing gap with China would enable India to play integrative role more proactively and prominently in the region.

Energy Competition

- In Asia, energy is increasingly intertwined with geopolitics; as a result, energy and security are inseparable. With competition for the world's oil and gas resources sharpening, Asia faces the spectre of a 21st century version of an energy-related Great Game in which India and China are the major players. China has been aggressively seizing energy-related opportunities overseas. Beijing persuaded Myanmar's military junta in 2006 to sell China gas from the partly Indian-owned A-1 and A-3 offshore blocks via a planned 2,380 km pipe line to Yunnan. Myanmar took India unaware by signing a MoU with China's state-run PetroChina in early 2006 to supply gas to China from the partly Indian-owned fields over a 30-year period. The loss of Burmese gas to China put Indian plans of importing gas from Myanmar via a pipe line through Bangladesh, to nought.
- Beijing also has aggressively sought oil and gas contracts in Iran, which is now the largest supplier of foreign oil to China, delivering 14 per cent of China's total oil imports. China has planned a 386-km oil pipe line from Iran to link up with the Atasu-Alashankou line laid between Kazakhstan and Xinjiang. China's state-owned oil company, Sinopec (also known as China Petrochemical Corporation), signed a $100 billion deal in October 2004 to buy 10 million metric tons of liquefied natural gas (LNG) from Iran annually over a 25-year period. In exchange, Sinopec secured a 51 per cent stake in the giant Yadavaran oilfield in Iran's South, leaving a minority 20 per cent stake for a consortium of Indian companies led by the Oil and Natural Gas Company (ONGC) Videsh Limited.
- Cash-rich China has shown time and again that the country can nimbly

> outmanoeuvre India in bids for energy contracts in third-world countries. Aggressive competition in this field can surely trigger active hostilities as China's internal security and stability depends on the continued growth of its imported energy-fuelled economy.

Economy as a driver impacts India and China predominantly in South Asia. As on date, the Chinese economy has slowed down whereas India is claiming a growth rate of 7 per cent and World Bank forecasts Indian economy will grow at 7.3 per cent in 2018. However, In the event of success of OBOR and MSR plus continuity in economic growth, China will dominate the South Asian region thereby marginalizing India, leading to a China Centric South Asia. At the same time, an economically buoyant India will have desired appeal to attract other South Asian economies in an integrative framework, thus driving the regional countries away from China's sole influence. While it may take some time for India to reach its zenith in terms of economic growth, with a steady upward trend, India would gradually be able to balance existing Chinese superiority through increasing mutual understanding with China.

Open Borders. We have a 1,751 km border with Nepal, 699 km with Bhutan, 1,643 km with Myanmar, and 4,096 km with Bangladesh where mainly an 'open border' is followed despite the fencing along the Indo-Bangla border. Unchecked movements astride these borders assist hybrid warfare by our enemies in the form of illegal migration, move of terrorists, arms, narcotics, fake Indian currency, etc. In a written reply to a question Minister of State for Home, Kiren Rijiju, stated in the Rajya Sabha on 17 November 2016 that there are around 20 million (2 crore) illegal Bangladeshi migrants staying in India. While 'open borders' under the Free Movement Regime (FMR) imply movement without visa, it must be incumbent upon both countries astride international borders to evolve a mechanism wherein the movement is channelised and free-flow of terrorists, insurgents, weapons, narcotics, fake currency, etc. is blocked.

Internal Security. India has to deal with multiple insurgencies, Left Wing Extremism (LWE) being the biggest fault line. These insurgencies provide an asymmetric battlefield for our enemies to exploit, which they are doing. There are 39 banned organizations in India. In addition, there are many other organizations in India that have the potential for active terrorism, the Kerala-headquartered Popular Front of India (PFI) being one example. The PFI was established after Al Qaeda and LeT footprints were discovered in Kerala during 2005. Five PFI cadres were caught in Kupwara few years back attempting to cross over to POK. There is photographic evidence of PFI cadres in combat uniform undergoing arms training in jungles of

Kerala. Then there is also the problem of radicalization by the ISIS, Indian Mujahiddeen, etc. who use the internet and social media for radicalization and recruitment. Mumbai Police had reported in April 2013 that the Girls Islamic Organization (offshoot of Jamat-e-Islami Hind) that runs 40 High Schools and 2 Junior Colleges in Maharashtra was training girls for Jihad. India needs to deal with the internal security problems and insurgencies in a cogent and comprehensive manner. External support, including funding to insurgents and terrorists organisations, needs to be ruthlessly stamped out. The recent agreement with Nagas to lift the blockade of Manipur is good beginning. Similarly, other insurgencies need to be tackled in comprehensive fashion. The LWE must be given special attention keeping in mind: Pakistan's ISI had arranged training in IEDs/explosive for a core group of LWE with the LTTE; as early as 2005, LWE were found using ammunition with Pakistan Ordnance Factory markings; Stratfor warned in 2008 that ISI was forging alliance with the LWE, and media reports of SIMI training 500 LWE cadres in 2008.

Managing Social Change. India presently constitutes 17.3 per cent of world population, implying every sixth human being on earth is Indian. At current annual growth rate of 1.58 per cent, our population will cross 1.53 billion in few years from now surpassing China. Today, 50 per cent of our population is 25 years and below; 65 per cent is 35 years and below. Conversely, most countries are struggling with bulk population on wrong side of 60 years. A total of 72.2 per cent of our population lives in 6,38,000 villages and 27.8 per cent in 5,480 towns and cities. We have the largest illiterate population in the world. Thomas Friedman says, 'India is the sole country of 21st Century with abundant youth power', but it is a question of how we handle this youth power. Today, there are some 40 million illegal weapons (of total 73 million globally) circulating within India with an annual illegal trade of $4 million. These include the crude locally manufactured plus the sophisticated ones with terrorist and insurgent organizations bought on the world market and being supplied by both China and Pakistan. In December 2010, in a single district of Bihar (Munger District), the police seized 65 illegal weapons. As per the World Drug Report, India consumes some 11 tons of heroine annually. Presently, India is ranked 81st in the CPI (Corruption Perception Index) in Transparency International's Global Corruption Perception Index 2017, and 131st in HDI. The state of malnutrition in children remains pathetic. We have some 4.5 crore unemployed, 90 per cent of which are youth. All these socio-economic factors also contribute to insurgencies. So it is a question of how effectively India can manage social change, a vital part of which is effective governance and administration, in order to rise as a global player.

IMPLICATIONS

National Security

The challenges to India's national security are numerous, as can be gauged from the above. The enormity of these challenges is much more when viewed from the aspect of both China and Pakistan trying their utmost to stymie India's growth, using all available asymmetric means. India's problem is not only to progress its economy and development but this has to be done in an environment of stiff collusivity by China and Pakistan. What India needs is inclusive growth in face of expanding threats. Therefore, India needs to look beyond basing national security on military security, even as defence has remained a neglected sector over the years. Also, the notion that by establishing a booming economy, threats to national security will vanish or diminish is misnomer. If this was indeed true, then Japan as an economic giant would not have faced any threats. Therefore, India must define a cohesive national security strategy, affix national security objectives and embark on a timed road map for omni-directional growth; the foremost requirement is formulating a comprehensive national security strategy that must also include internal security.

Military Operations

China poses the most potent military threat to India and, given the nuclear, missile and military hardware nexus between China and Pakistan, future conventional conflict in Southern Asia could be a two-front war. Over and above this is the sub-conventional component of the China-Pakistan ongoing hybrid war, to which India has made little effort to establish effective deterrence. If this asymmetry is not bridged, China and Pakistan will jointly continue to destabilize India, raising the levels infinitely. Bridging the India-China military asymmetry including in disruptive technologies is as important. It needs little emphasis to state that neglecting these issues will seriously affect our military operations. A military strategy without a cohesive national security strategy and comprehensive defence review is of little value. However, considering that both China and Pakistan have repeatedly displayed ambiguity, deceit and backstabbing, operations by the Indian Military must be planned as a 'Devil's Advocate', catering for the worst case scenario in order to not get surprised.

Key Issues

- ✓ *Pakistan is determined to confront India and China intent on giving Pakistan the means and the confidence to do so.*
- ✓ *China's omni-directional approach through OBOR-CPEC and MST opens avenue for China to effectively influence the Arabian Sea.*

- ✓ *India has not articulated a national security strategy, the general undestanding of national security being restricted to 'military' security.*
- ✓ *China's concept of 'deep coalition' is all inclusive of political and role played by non-state actors, mafias and others.*
- ✓ *Our MoD and higher defence organizations need urgent restructuring.*
- ✓ *Military has critical voids; lacks jointness; and defence allocations are inadequate.*
- ✓ *70 per cent of defence needs still being imported.*
- ✓ *No effective deterrence to proxy wars.*
- ✓ *Poor border management and border infrastructure.*
- ✓ *Challenges to India include: China-Pak nexus, jihadi terrorism, geopolitical containment by proxy, Chinese 'string of pearls', border disputes, military asymmetry vis-à-vis China including in disruptive technologies; energy competition; economic competition; open borders; internal security and managing social change.*
- ✓ *Challenges India faces have serious implications for national security and military operations.*
- ✓ *India must define a cohesive national security strategy, affix national security objectives and embark on a timed road map for omni-directional growth.*
- ✓ *Considering past history of ambiguity, deceit and backstabbing by China-Pakistan, our military operations must cater for worst case scenario.*

NOTES

1 Sayers, Eric, 'China's Asymmetrical Strategy', The Weekly Standard, 26 December 2007, http://www.weeklystandard.com/chinas-asymmetrical-strategy/article/15628.

2 Bannon, Steve, 'We're Going to War in the South China Sea . . . No Doubt', The Guardian, 2 February 2017, https://www.theguardian.com/us-news/2017/feb/02/steve-bannon-donald-trump-war-south-china-sea-no-doubt.

3 'China Tests Missile That Can Carry 10 Nuclear Warheads: Report', The Tribune, 3 February 2017, http://www.tribuneindia.com/news/world/china-tests-missile-that-can-carry-10-nuclear-warheads-report/358517.html

4 Jain, Dipti, 'Was the Indian Economy "Healthy" Before Demonetisation?', Live Mint, 17 February 2017, http://www.livemint.com/Politics/P87C89as66H11KefFnba9J/Was-the-Indian-economy-healthy-before-demonetisation.html

5 Ibid.

6 Ibid.

7 Das, Pushpa, 'India: Internal Security Budget 2017-2018 – Analysis', Eurasia View, 22 February 2017, http://www.eurasiareview.com/22022017-india-internal-security-budget-2017-2018-analysis/

8 Ibid.

9 Ibid.

10 Ibid.

11 The seven categories of human security are economic, food, health, environment, personal, community and political; see UNDP (1994: 22.40).
Katoch, Prakash, 'Demonitization: India Can't Win Its Black Money War by Going Soft on Political Parties', First Post, 17 December 2016, http://www.firstpost.com/india/demonetisation-india-cant-win-its-black-money-war-by-going-soft-on-political-parties-3161200.html

12 Katoch, op. cit.

13 Security: A New Framework for Analysis, Lynne Rienner Publishers, 1998, p. 239 (ISBN 978-1-55587-784-2).

14 Tadjbakhsh, S, 'Human Security in International Organizations: Blessing or Scourge?', *The Human Security Journal*, Volume 4, Summer 2007. Archived 15 February 2010, at the Wayback Machine.

15 'Number and Percentage of Population Below Poverty Line', Reserve Bank of India, 2012, Retrieved 4 April 2014.

16 Donnan, Shawn, 'World Bank Eyes Biggest Global Poverty Line Increase In Decades, *The Financial Times*, 9 May 2014.

17 Poverty & Equity Data Portal. *povertydata.worldbank.org*, Retrieved 11 February 2016.

18 'India's Poverty Rate at 12.4% in 2011-12', *Business Standard*, 6 October 2015, Retrieved 14 July 2016.

19 Asian Development Bank (nd), *Poverty in India*, Retrieved 21 November 2016, https://www.adb.org/countries/india/poverty.

20 'India Up 5 Spots, Ranks 130th in Human Development Index: UNDP', *Times of India*, 14 December 2015, http://timesofindia.indiatimes.com/india/India-up-5-spots-ranks-130th-in-Human-Development-Index-UNDP/articleshow/50170343.cms.

21 Crime Index for Country 2017, https://www.numbeo.com/crime/rankings_by_country.jsp.

22 'Sino-Indian Cooperation in the Search for Overseas Petroleum Resources: Prospects and Implications for India', *Emeraldinsight.com*. Retrieved 2010-06-01.

23 Ruppert, Michael, Event occurs at 27:50. There are ten calories of hydrocarbon energy in every calorie of food consumed in the industrialized world.

24 'Power plays: Energy and Australia's security'. Aspi.org.au. Retrieved 2015-11-14

25 Key issues impacting the Indian oil and gas sector, EY.

26 Pedesen, Chris, 'Flipping the Switch: A Look at India's Future Energy Demands', Energy, 20 October 2014, http://breakingenergy.com/2014/10/20/flipping-the-switch-a-look-at-indias-future-energy-demands/

27 Ibid.

28 'Hydropower in India: Key Enablers for a Better Tomorrow', FICCI, http://www.pwc.in/assets/pdfs/publications/2014/hydropower-in-india-key-enablers-for-better-tomorrow.pdf.

29 Kugelman, Michael, 'India's Environmental Security Challenge: Water, Coal, Natural Gas, and Climate Change Fuel Friction', New Security Beat, 23 November 2012, https://www.newsecuritybeat.org/2012/11/indias-environmental-security-challenge/.

30 Ibid.

31 Ibid.

32 Ibid.

33 Ibid.

34 Ibid.

35 Ibid.

7

INDIA'S STRATEGY AND CAPABILITY SCAN

General

Sino-Pak cooperation's main motivating factor has been the common enmity with India and Chinese efforts to contain India's strategic space within South Asia. China will continue to seek containment of India by its military, nuclear, diplomatic cooperation with Pakistan and its growing military profile across the strategic sea lanes of India's Indian Ocean neighbourhood. The relationship has, for years, adversely affected the strategic interests of India and has pinned down India with perpetual 'two-front' dilemma. The nexus is also responsible to aggravate India's internal security situation by supporting asymmetric efforts through terrorism and insurgencies across India. Pakistan strives to balance India's conventional supremacy through asymmetric means and nuclear brinkmanship but with China's lodgement in POK and Gwadar, together with the CPEC, the dual front dilemma has magnified. The asymmetric and irregular warfare application by both, China and Pakistan has the potential of a three-front dilemma unless corrective steps are taken by India. Therefore, in the construct of a collusive scenario, there exists a tangible combat asymmetry with Sino-Pak on one side and India on the other. India, however, retains a competitive edge in deterrence capabilities in the IOR, which can be further augmented through strategic partnerships. For India to maintain favourable strategic balance in the region, it would be incumbent to enhance its hybrid warfare capability.

National Security Strategy

National Security Strategy (NSS) is an integral part of a nation state's quest to safeguard her national interest. National aims, interests, and objectives drive the security and military policies and strategies of a country. However, it is a strange paradox that India, an emerging power, aspiring to be a regional power, does not have a formal 'national security strategy'. Consequently, 'contingency-driven adhocism', derived from individual inclinations of the leadership and the bureaucracy of the day, can describe India's response to most security crises. An Indian 'NSS', in the current context, must not only deal with threats to our strategic autonomy and the external military threats to the nation, it must also deal with internal threats, threats to our core values, and other non-traditional threats that face the nation. It must also take into account that external and internal threats need to be countered not only by the armed forces and other elements of hard power, but also require political and diplomatic means to deal with them. Further, the NSS must also aim to achieve our national aspirations in the domestic, regional and global contexts, in a time-bound manner. These goals would include achievement of non-traditional aspects of security like economic and human development, which contribute to human security, as well as aspects like energy and environmental security.

In India, it is not only the thinking that military security alone constitutes national security, but the problem also lies in not acknowledging the changed nature of conflict, beyond conventional war, in nuclear backdrop. Equally significant is the continuing deficit of strategic culture, aptly described by former Foreign Secretary Kanwal Sibal in saying,[1]

> We courted military defeat in 1962 at China's hands because our assertive political positions were not backed by credible military strength.... What would explain our unwillingness to recognise the depth of these threats even today and take appropriate steps to build our defences politically and physically? Pakistan uses the instrument of terrorism against us but we think that we can bring this to an end through dialogue. We let Kashmiri separatists meet Pakistani leaders in Delhi and Islamabad.... We let China dictate management of our bilateral relations. China allows itself to question India's territorial integrity but we hesitate to respond to its provocations. We have procrastinated in building adequate defence capability.... Inordinately slow in developing our strategic programmes. Our failure to build an indigenous defence manufacturing base shows the fragility of our strategic thinking. We have reduced our defence expenditure to 1.7 per cent of GDP in the last budget.... That we produced Chanakya almost 2400 years ago is not sufficient ground to claim that today's India possesses a strategic culture.

An overarching flaw in India's higher defence setup is the lack of military professionals, as the system of 'case by case' advice has proved grossly ineffective. On the military side, the result is that the Services are left to define the threats they believe the country faces and accordingly they appear to be preparing to fight three different wars against three different enemies.[2] India was one of the first countries in the world to integrate officer training at the NDA and the Staff College but everything else seems to be contributing to service rivalries. The problem is exacerbated by the lack of military expertise in the political and bureaucratic class.

According to Sunil Dasgupta and Stephen P. Cohen, several retired defence secretaries they spoke with, during the course of writing their book *Arming without Aiming*, reported that it was not until their second or third postings in the ministry that they had acquired a sense of competence in the field.[3] Indian defence badly needs reform, but the recommendations of several high-powered committees, including those headed by Arun Singh, Naresh Chandra and the irreplaceable K. Subrahmanyam (Kargil review), remain ignored by several governments. India needs to begin at the beginning, with a clearer vision of the role of the military and use of force in the country's rise as a great power.[4]

Articulation of India's 'NSS', and consequent 'national defence policy', must take into consideration the following: the need to preserve our strategic autonomy, territorial integrity, and core values; the security-related developments in the global and regional environments; the external and internal threats which impact the nation; our capabilities in relation to our threats and the capabilities of our adversaries; the need to contribute towards regional and global security and our strategic relationships with other countries. It should be noted, however, that India's capability development agenda and goals will invariably face challenges of budget constraints, resulting in the 'guns versus butter' debate at every stage. Nonetheless, as an overarching factor, it must be kept in view that the economic, developmental, and aspirational goals of the nation cannot be achieved unless there is peace, stability and security in the country.[5]

National Security Objectives

India needs a cohesive NSS, which should be structured by the National Security Advisor. Within this, the national security objectives must be carefully drawn up if the NSS is to be achievable. As a country's national security objectives are normally derived directly from its national interests, India's major national security objectives should comprise the following:[6]

- ✓ Maintaining the territorial integrity of India's borders on land, sea and air, as defined by law and enshrined in the Constitution, including the defence of India's island territories.
- ✓ Defending India's coastline against aggression and infiltration, and ensuring the security of Indian personnel and assets such as ships and oil rigs operating in the Exclusive Economic Zone (EEZ).
- ✓ Resolving the territorial and boundary disputes with China and Pakistan on favourable terms through negotiations in an early time-frame. In this context, as the territory occupied by the Chinese on the Aksai Chin Plateau in Ladakh and by the Pakistanis in Pakistan occupied Kashmir is required

to be regained in accordance with two separate parliamentary resolutions, building a national consensus to resolve both territorial disputes through a negotiated settlement should be an important political objective.

- ✓ Protecting the lives and property of India's citizens, including during insurgencies and against acts of terrorism.
- ✓ Maintaining effective nuclear deterrence against the use or the threat of use of nuclear weapons against India.
- ✓ Protecting critical infrastructure and military command and control systems against cyber-attack from State and non-State actors and developing offensive cyber operations capabilities to deter such attacks.
- ✓ Ensuring the security of India's energy sources, refining facilities and modes of transportation, especially the security of oil and gas fields, ships transporting oil and gas and, where necessary, oil and gas pipelines within India and abroad.
- ✓ Undermining the China-Pakistan nexus and reducing the salience of the Pakistan army in Pakistan.
- ✓ Responding to China's hybrid hegemony in conjunction own strategic partners.
- ✓ Ensuring through diplomatic means and in conjunction with strategic partners that India will not be required to fight a simultaneous two-front war with China and Pakistan.
- ✓ Providing a stable and peaceful external security environment in India's area of strategic interest to facilitate unimpeded socio-economic development and the free flow of trade; this may involve military intervention, singly or in conjunction with strategic partners, when India's vital national interests are threatened.
- ✓ Creating and sustaining an effective capability for Out of Area Contingency (OOAC) operations through military intervention, when necessary, to ensure peace and stability in the Indo-Pacific and the security of the global commons; freedom of navigation in the sea lanes of communication, air space, cyber space and outer space.
- ✓ Being prepared to provide security and other assistance to the Indian diaspora on foreign soil.
- ✓ Acting vigorously against narcotics traffickers and small arms smugglers and disrupting their linkages with terrorist organisations.
- ✓ Bringing to speedy justice both overseas and local perpetrators of terrorist strikes in India and against Indian assets anywhere.

- ✓ Preventing the destabilisation of friendly countries in India's area of strategic interest and providing military and other assistance when requested by them.
- ✓ Leveraging relations with strategic partners, including through defence cooperation, to deter conflict and manage crises, and engaging with organisations such as the ASEAN Regional Forum and the Shanghai Cooperation Organisation to launch cooperative security initiatives, while preserving India's strategic autonomy.
- ✓ Promoting cooperation and understanding with neighbouring countries and implementing mutually agreed confidence-building measures to prevent crises through miscalculation.
- ✓ Pursuing security and strategic dialogues to address key challenges before the international community.
- ✓ Following a consistent and principled policy on nuclear disarmament and international security issues based on universality, non-discrimination and equal security for all.
- ✓ Working dynamically to achieve the goal of self-reliance (70 per cent indigenous content) in defence procurement by 2025. The indigenous manufacture of microchips, the basic building block of ICT products, must be a national priority.
- ✓ Investing appropriately in the development of high-end defence technologies in conjunction with strategic partners to gain an edge in combat capabilities over military adversaries.
- ✓ Developing a proactive strategic culture by exposing all students in schools and colleges to understanding basic threats and challenges to national security and the measures necessary to overcome these. All government training institutions must also educate their trainees about national security issues by devoting a portion of the syllabus to the subject.

Military Strategy

A military strategy, essentially, must flow from a national defence strategy, which in turn must be a subset of the NSS. With regard to 'defence of India's national territory and resources from an external threat', the related national security strategy issues which must be addressed by a national defence policy, are as follows:[7]

- ✓ Maintain credible military deterrence against potential adversaries.
- ✓ Defend our national and territorial interests on land, sea, air, space and cyber space.
- ✓ Physical guarding and/or surveillance of land, air, and maritime borders,

island territories, off-shore assets and trade routes, especially disputed borders, for early detection of intrusions or threats, if any.

- ✓ Maintain a tri-service rapid response capability to respond to security challenges during war and peace.
- ✓ Ensure a fool-proof and well-coordinated intelligence mechanism to provide early warning of threats, both external and internal.
- ✓ Prevent attacks in the cyber and information domains against own defence and civilian networks and capabilities.
- ✓ Build up/strengthen a strong military technology base and related indigenous capability for manufacture of arms/ammunition/equipment to enhance self-reliance and prevent external pressures during crises.

Other aspects related to India's national security where the military is mandated to take necessary action are as follows:[8]

- ✓ Protect national interests against internal threats like terrorism (including nuclear terrorism), insurgency and militancy with a view to negate secessionist and related destabilising efforts.
- ✓ Promote and protect the core values of democracy, secularism, freedom, unity and human rights as enshrined in our Constitution by value-based ethics and practices as well as providing aid to civil authority, when requisitioned.
- ✓ Maintain close surveillance and monitoring of the internal security situation in areas of heightened threat.
- ✓ Maintain rapid response capability against terror strikes/hostage taking, involving multiple agencies, both police and military, including the National Security Guard (NSG) and Special Forces (SF).
- ✓ Promote peace and stability in the region through cooperative economic development backed by diplomatic initiatives for resolution of disputes and conflicts.
- ✓ Promote regional cooperation and coordination for early detection of regional/transnational cross-spectrum threats, to neutralise the same in a timely and proactive manner.
- ✓ Provide Humanitarian Assistance and Disaster Relief (HADR) support in the region, when required/requested.
- ✓ Contribute towards selective capacity-building in the military domain among neighbouring and other friendly countries.
- ✓ Neutralise anti-Indian efforts/propaganda by potential adversaries/inimical elements.

- ✓ Promote/protect diaspora interests in the region and the world.
- ✓ Establish strong and mutually beneficial relations/strategic partnerships with other countries, and regional/global security groupings, including the United Nations, through defence cooperation, anti-piracy, counter-terrorism and peacekeeping activities.
- ✓ Promote security interests at the global level, including coordination of security, intelligence and cyber issues.

It is imperative that our NSS must integrate the national defence policy. As mentioned above, the national defence policy should be derived from the NSS, and should form an integral part of the national security policy. The primary role of the armed forces is to defend territorial integrity, preserve core values enshrined in the Constitution and protect the strategic autonomy of the country by deterrence or waging war.[9] The secondary roles include providing assistance for maintenance of internal security and restoring law and order, providing troops and resources for humanitarian assistance and disaster relief and participation in UN peacekeeping, foreign defence cooperation activities and OOAC when so directed by the government.[10] Hence, in keeping with the defence-related issues of the NSS, the national defence policy must incorporate issues as given in succeeding paragraphs.

Issues Related to Military's Primary Role. These are as enumerated next:

- ✓ **Deterrence Against External Threats**. Preventing war by maintaining credible military deterrence against potential adversaries is the primary role of the armed forces of a nation. This is achieved by ensuring a strong and modern military capability in the nuclear, conventional, counter-sub-conventional, cyber and space realms, backed by appropriate military and nuclear doctrines, combined with optimum preparedness to take to war at appropriate notice. The desired capabilities would take note of the existing and future military capabilities of potential adversaries, their doctrines and the likelihood and nature of conflicts. Actual preparedness would factor in prioritisation, based on budget allotment and related constraints.
- ✓ **Capability to Undertake Military Operations Successfully**. In case so directed by the government, the armed forces must defend our national and territorial interests on land, sea, air, space and cyber space by waging war. In this regard, the armed forces should be always well trained and prepared to respond proactively, when directed, to any threat from our potential adversaries. War, if undertaken, must be prosecuted swiftly and terminated on terms favourable to our country and armed forces. This would entail defending our territorial integrity, capture of territory, and destruction of

the war-waging potential of the adversary, as also capture of prisoners of war, for post-war negotiations from a position of advantage.

- ✓ **Guarding of Disputed Borders During Peace-Time**. Physical guarding and/or surveillance, including technological surveillance of disputed land, air, and maritime borders like the Line of Control (LoC), Actual Ground Position Line (AGPL) and Line of Actual Control (LAC), to detect intrusions, if any, at the earliest and take action to restore the status-quo ante. In case of war, the defence of other (undisputed) borders, if attacked or threatened, would automatically devolve on the armed forces.
- ✓ **Maintenance of Tri-Service Rapid Response Capability**. India, as an emerging power, must maintain a tri-service rapid response capability to respond to security challenges in the operational, internal security and regional domains during peace and war, with capabilities to respond speedily to threats to our offshore island territories and other economic interests. Though it essentially entails better tri-service preparedness for air and sea transported operations by Army/Special Forces units and formations, it would also provide capability for OOAC and HADR in a peace-time scenario, when called upon to do so.
- ✓ **Effective Intelligence Mechanism**. There has been a number of cases of serious intelligence failures, the most prominent being the fiasco in Kargil in 1999. A fool-proof and well-coordinated military intelligence mechanism needs to be ensured, incorporating inputs of all the intelligence agencies and resources, to provide early warning of threats, both external and internal.
- ✓ **Cyber Security**. Cyber threats are growing exponentially, both in terms of the numbers and sophistication of attacks. There is a need to maintain a dynamic, proactive cyber security capability to prevent cyber-attacks against own defence as well as civilian networks and capabilities, while cooperating with external agencies on the wider issues of cyber defence.
- ✓ **Self-Reliance in Defence**. As long as we are dependent primarily on imports for our weapons, equipment, and ammunition, we are vulnerable to being held hostage during times of war in terms of availability of items and spares, as also the cost of these items. Thus, it is of prime importance to our defence capability that we build up/strengthen indigenous capability for manufacture of arms/ammunition/equipment to enhance self-reliance and prevent related external pressures during crises.
- ✓ **Protection of Defence Establishments**. In recent years, terrorist modules from across the border have attacked our defence establishments on a number of occasions, causing casualties, mostly among security personnel and

innocent civilians. The primary responsibility for protection of defence establishments and a 'first-tier' counter-terror response is of the unit/ establishment itself and the individual Service concerned. Specially trained Quick Reaction Teams (QRTs) and Defence Security Corps (DSC) units form the backbone of such response. The local Army formation, if available, is responsible for the second-tier response. Special Forces units are called upon as third-/fourth-tier responders. Military units are required to prepare adequately, in terms of training, equipping and periodic reconnaissance, to respond speedily and effectively against terror strikes.

✓ **Armed Forces at the Forefront of Harnessing Technology.** The armed forces have the strategic need and the structural capacity to drive technology missions in a number of niche areas. Hence, there is a need to incentivise all the wings within the armed forces to remain at the forefront in harnessing technology with a view to achieve strategic advantage vis-à-vis our adversaries as well as optimisation in military capability. Service design bureaus and technology boards must be strengthened so that they can work in concert with our research and manufacturing agencies.

Issues Related to Military's Secondary Role. These are as listed as follows:

✓ **Internal Security.** The armed forces, especially the Army, are required to play a substantial role in internal security matters, i.e. to protect national interests against internal threats like terrorism (including nuclear terrorism), insurgency, and militancy in various parts of the country, with a view to negate secessionist and related destabilising efforts. Such threats could be externally sponsored or home grown, or a combination of both. Raising of Rashtriya Rifles (RR) units has provided specialist capabilities in this field to the Army. Consequently, the Army has been able to stabilise the situation quite effectively in the hinterland areas of J&K. Army formations and units are also playing an important role in ensuring stability in the north-eastern states affected by insurgency. However, once the situation is stabilised, efforts to resolve the problem politically must be given the requisite attention by the government so that the Army is relieved of its internal security duties and can return to training commitments related to its primary role.

✓ **Preserve Core Values.** The armed forces play a crucial role in the promotion and protection of the core values of democracy, secularism, freedom, unity and human rights as enshrined in our Constitution by their value-based ethics and practices. They also assist in countering threats to these core values by providing aid to civil authority in times of need.

✓ **Restoration of Law and Order When Requisitioned for the Purpose.** The armed forces are mandated to provide 'aid to civil authority' in case of breakdown of law and order or in case of a heightened threat. In such cases, if the local police, central armed police and paramilitary are not available or found to be incapable of regaining control of the situation, the Army may be requisitioned to restore public order. To that extent, military units need to maintain close surveillance and monitoring of the internal security situation in areas of heightened threat, so that they are able to intervene speedily and effectively. In the case of terror attacks in civilian areas, the Army, if available, can be requisitioned by the local civil authority for a counter-terror response.

- ✓ **Defence Cooperation with Friendly Foreign Countries**. Military diplomacy and defence cooperation have been found to be effective tools for developing good relations with other countries. Training of military personnel, conduct of combined exercises, gifting of weapons and equipment, provision of logistic support, visits by senior officers, etc. are tools available to the military to promote or strengthen bonds with other countries as also for capacity building among friendly countries. The Indian military has proved very adept in this role and must be increasingly employed in defence cooperation activities and conduct of defence dialogues to build strategic partnerships with select countries, in pursuit of our national interests.
- ✓ **Humanitarian Assistance and Disaster Relief**. Though the National Disaster Management Authority (NDMA) is the primary authority mandated for HADR in the country, the Indian armed forces invariably end up being the first responders, due to their geographical spread in the country and their expertise in the field. Provision of HADR support within the country and in the wider regional context, when required/requested, has enabled India to project its military prowess in a benevolent and humane manner. It has also enabled building bridges with the affected population in militancy affected areas, as happened during the floods in J&K in 2014.
- ✓ **UN Peacekeeping Operations**. Right from the initial stages, the Indian military has been at the forefront of UN peacekeeping activities. Indian peacekeepers enjoy a good reputation and are sought by the United Nations not only for their exemplary neutrality and high levels of professionalism but also for their high behavioural standards and people-friendly approach towards the local population in the strife-torn areas of their deployment. The Indian Army has made major contributions towards capacity building in the field of UN peacekeeping by training military peacekeepers from other countries and providing instructors, when required. India must

continue to participate in UN peacekeeping and remain a beacon for high professional and behavioural standards. All the agencies concerned must ensure proper administrative and equipment back-up so that the peacekeepers are able to carry out their duties in an optimal manner without having to keep looking over their shoulder all the time.

- ✓ **Role in Anti-Piracy Operations**. The Indian Navy made a stellar contribution towards eradicating the threat of piracy along the global sea lanes of communication and trade routes by joining the regional and international collaborative effort in this regard. The Indian Navy will have to continue to participate in collective efforts, under the aegis of the United Nations, to secure the global commons, whenever required to do so.
- ✓ **Evacuation of Beleaguered Diaspora**. The Indian Air Force and Indian Navy have increasingly been playing a crucial role in evacuating our diaspora, who suddenly come under threat due to deteriorating security conditions, e.g. in Libya and Yemen in recent years. Safe and timely evacuation becomes a dire necessity, keeping in view the expanding numbers of Indians seeking employment all over the world, even in the strife-torn areas of West Asia and Africa. The Indian military will have to be prepared for such interventions/ evacuations at short notice.
- ✓ **Global Counter-Terror Response**. Keeping in view the possible terror threats to the global commons, including the threat of nuclear terrorism, it is increasingly possible that the UN will have to play a more decisive role in dealing with the evolving threats in this domain. Given its rising profile in the global security arena, India will have to be prepared for requests for active participation in such collective efforts. The Indian military, with its vast experience in counter-terror operations, is ideally suited to play a participatory role in such efforts, in case the government perceives such participation to be in India's national interests.

The military has a tri-service military doctrine but it has not been derived from any defence policy at the national level. Besides, the tri-service doctrine in its present avatar also cannot be implemented in absence of tri-service functional commands and a Chief of Defence Staff (CDS) at the apex.

Western View of War in Sub Continent

Western think tanks in recent years have expressed fears of war in the sub-continent going nuclear. According to Stratfor, India and Pakistan's military strategies could lead to greater insecurity in the region. Nuclear weapons, particularly, TNWs that are launched on the battlefield, have been introduced into India and Pakistan's military calculations, causing both sides to re-evaluate their policies.[11] Originally, India's unofficial military doctrine, Cold Start, relied on rapid, flexible conventional military operations to strike Pakistan while avoiding a protracted war that could increase the likelihood of nuclear retaliation. But Pakistan countered by developing a tactical nuclear response that made the prospect of large-scale fighting too risky for New Delhi and Islamabad. Nevertheless, India has sought alternate forms of deterrence against Pakistan's asymmetric tactics. Using more limited military strikes, or 'surgical deterrence', India will decrease the chances of a wider conflict erupting. Still, escalation will remain an underlying risk. The salience of Stratfor is threefold: (1) *introducing TNWs into India and Pakistan's military calculations will make operations using large-scale conventional forces less desirable; (2) India will modify its strategy to account for its growing need to use limited military strikes, narrow in scope and duration, to avoid a potential nuclear exchange and (3) India's so-called 'surgical deterrence' strategy will be less likely to trigger a wider war with Pakistan, though escalation will remain a risk. At the same time, Stratfor assesses that while Pakistan has invested heavily in the development of TNWs* to compensate for the widening divide between its military strength and that of India; these TNWs increase the chance of deterring a full-scale invasion from India but simultaneously increase the chance of a devastating nuclear exchange.[12] Besides, they also provide no real way for the Pakistani military to seize disputed territory.

Capability Audit

Pakistan's military establishment is said to be 'very concerned' about the conventional military modernisation programme of India.[13] As the IISS published its annual 'Military Balance 2016' report in February 2016, Ben Barry, former brigadier in the British army who works with the military-strategic communities in India and Pakistan, said they (Pakistan) are very concerned about India's conventional military modernisation, and that Pakistan was particularly concerned with India acquiring advanced weapons systems like Apache helicopters, C-130 Hercules aircraft and T-90 tanks. The India-US nuclear deal too remained a matter of concern in Islamabad. Military Balance 2016 detailed various initiatives taken by India to encourage FDI and private sector participation in defence, including the 'Make in India' policy that aims to strengthen the indigenous defence-industrial base through measures that include reforming India's FDI cap. It, however, pointed out that industrial-capability limitations and bureaucratic obstacles have hampered a number of promising initiatives.

In terms of overall combat capability, the Indian Military is at a disadvantage against the PLA, and it's not even about number comparisons, for example, how can one equate an 1000-ton corvette with an 8000-ton destroyer even though they both count as one warship? This will remain true as long as China is able to indigenously produce almost all weapons and equipment for its military (even lower quality in some cases) while India remains the top arms importer in the world.[14] There is no way a nation will win a modern large-scale military conflict without the support of a highly capable indigenous industry. In case of war, India would be hard-pressed to quickly resupply the forces with advanced weaponry like Su-30 or T90 if they can't be mass manufactured in Indian factories; even local assembly is not quick enough (because the parts will have to be imported). In the worst case, if Russia or European nations refuse to provide these to India due to China's political and/or economic influence, how do the Indian forces keep on fighting? Even in smaller conflicts, the fact that the aircraft are 'non-renewable' will in some degree affect the strategy/tactics employed, hence limiting the force's overall combat efficacy.

Even in peace time, reliance on foreign weapon manufacturer means that India will almost never acquire the most advanced weaponry, no matter how much money they are willing to spend.[15] In contrast, because of arms embargo on China 20 years back, Chinese weapon manufacturers now have the technology and resource to develop things like 5th-generation stealth fighters (which is at lease comparable to, if not as good as, Russia's T-50), anti-ship ballistic missiles (the only types in the world), hypersonic weapons (which the US and Russia models are also only in testing phase) and so on. With China pouring money into weapon development and Russia's poor economic condition, it is not impossible that in the future even Russia will have to look up to the Chinese in certain areas. Therefore, in the current condition, it is perceivable that the gap between China and India in terms of weapon technology will get even wider. It is easy to believe that the Indian soldier has better morale than the PLA albeit there is no evidence of this, but morale is also linked with what generation the war equipment of both sides belong to.[16] Morale counts for little if one side has stealth fighter that can shoot down the opponent with long-range missiles before it even appears on the opponent's radar screen, which is a highly likely scenario in air-dominated modern regional conflicts. The disparity in military hardware between India and China is larger than it appears due to India's heavy dependence on imports and negligence of indigenous industry; to make matters worse for the Indian side, China seems to be near the end of the technology-accumulation phase (20-30 years) and new waves of advance hardware are starting to come out (J20, Y20, Wu14, etc). Assuming conditions of China remains constant, the situation will keep getting worse for India for at least next two or three decades.

At the same time, if we compare the nuclear arsenal of both India and China, though China has a larger number of devices, the stockpile of both nations is enough to almost wipe out the other from its existence. After going through all the military balance, considering above facts and carefully assessing future prospects, it can perhaps be surmised that though India is outnumbered by the Chinese in many aspects of armaments, equipment and manpower, still, India is capable of holding its own if the two nations are actively engaged in a war. One major shortcoming, however, is China's superior connectivity to the North Eastern parts of India and Ladakh and its capability of rapid mobilisation of troops. India doesn't enjoy this luxury and this can adversely affect India's defence of Sikkim, Ladakh and Arunachal Pradesh in the scenario of an attack. This also needs to be viewed in context of China having increased defence capabilities and deploying more troops along the Indian border and bases in Pakistan, as warned by the Pentagon in May 2016.[17]

But India will certainly not be a pushover. Significantly, China is most worried about the manner in which the Indo-US defence partnership is progressing, including the US-India Defence Technology and Trade Initiative (DTTI) through which American and Indian officials have discussed sharing technology and boosting business ties between the two countries' defence industries. That US discussing the possibility of sharing technology to help New Delhi build its first domestically produced aircraft carrier INS '*Vishal*' through DTTI under the auspice of the 'Aircraft Carrier Working Group' is also being keenly watched by China. China has expressed concern about Indian plans to deploy BrahMos missiles close to the border. In 2014, the 'Vikramaditya' aircraft carrier, Fifth Generation Fighter Aircraft (FGFA), BrahMos anti-ship missile, Kolkatta-class destroyer, and Arihant-class Ballistic-missile submarine were listed as five Indian weapons of war that China should fear.[18] However, of these, while four are progressing, the FGFA is still on the drawing board whereas China has fielded its stealth fighter. Also in 2014, views were aired of the five Chinese weapons of war that India should fear, which included[19] ***WU-14 Hypersonic Weapon System, Future Chinese Carrier, Second Artillery Corps (now renamed Rocket Force), DH-10 Cruise Missile Family and Chengdu J-20 Fighter.* In February 2017, these same five weapons of war have been reiterated as something that China would use to 'crush' India.**[20]

Strategic Deficits

Lack of Strategic Vision. As highlighted below:

✓ Nehru's nonalignment was based on his personal convictions on how he saw India and its future. He said, 'I can understand some of the smaller countries of Europe or some of the smaller countries of Asia being forced by circumstances to bow down before some of the greater powers and becoming practically satellites of those powers.... But I do not think that consideration applies to India . . . India is too big a country herself to be bound down to any other country, however big it may be'.[21] He also mentioned in the Parliament, 'Let us not be frightened too much of the military might of this or that group. I am not frightened and I want to tell it to the world on behalf of this country that we are not frightened of the military might of this power or that. Our policy is not a passive policy or negative policy'.[22]

- ✓ However, Nehru loathed the military that resulted in the crushing defeat of 1962 at the hands of China. Nehru also ignored the clear warnings of Sardar Patel on 7 November 1950 about Chinese irredentism and communist imperialism and that for the first time, after centuries, India's defence has to concentrate itself on two fronts simultaneously.[23]
- ✓ Under Indira Gandhi's regime, India's strategic vision was based more on the regional and international system of the 1960-1980s, the Cold War, Indo-Pak War of 1971, US support to Pakistan and the growing China-Pakistan relationship. Under these Prime Ministers, the Cold War influenced India's security discourse and subsequently its vision. External threats were seen as being the primary sources of insecurity. Military security became synonymous with national security; building a strong and powerful military apparatus was seen as essential to safeguard India's security interests. Nuclear weapons were seen as a symbol of power and providing a security guarantee.
- ✓ Late K Subrahmanyam had mentioned in early 1990s, "it is one of the strange ironies of the situation that in spite of this criticism being voiced for well over a decade, and the country having gone through two major wars and a border skirmish, there has been no effort to study the reasons underlying this state of affairs, and to suggest concrete remedial steps.[24]
- ✓ India's strategic vision did undergo change after the nuclear tests. However, this was largely shaped on collective economic development and a 'peaceful periphery', but this is not shared by all – definitely not by Pakistan and China. The emergence of non-state actors/state sponsored terrorist organisations challenging the state has serious implications for social stability in the region, in turn affecting India's security. India's regional strategic vision is no more limited strictly to the South Asian region. Today it considers Central Asia, West Asia, Southeast Asia, and China as a part of its extended neighbourhood in Southern Asia.
- ✓ India's global strategic vision is based on shaping a new international order that includes the US, European Union, China, Russia, Japan, and India. Some of the issues that India faces are not limited to its immediate or

extended neighbourhood, but are international in nature. Terrorism, proliferation of WMDs, energy security, and environmental threats are significant international issues that India needs to tackle at the international level.[25] India needs to expand its strategic space, increase autonomy of our decision making, contribute to the emergence of an international order that is conducive to the pursuit of its national interests, in pursuit of which India is seeking new strategic partnerships including with the US. But the bottom-line remains that India still does not have a cohesive national security strategy.

Economy and Defence Budget. Relevant issues are as described next:

✓ The Parliamentary Standing Committee on Defence slammed the Government on 9 March 2017 through its report tabled in Parliament on Demands for Grants for 2017-18, for its adhocism, casual and lackadaisical approach saying it would adversely affect the country's defence preparedness as well as hit the morale of the armed forces. Media may enjoy using the term 'slammed' but ironically, this committee, like all other committees, is just an advisory body not akin to the Senate Armed Forces Committee of the US, to whom the US Government is answerable, which should be the case in any democracy. Highlights of this report include the following: in terms of modernization demands for FY 2017-2018, the Army, Navy, and Air Force have only received 60 per cent, 67 per cent, and 54 per cent respectively; only Rs 86,488 crore has been earmarked for modernization from the total defence outlay of Rs 2.74 lakh crore—what makes matters worse is bulk of this capital will be used to pay 'committed liabilities' of earlier arms contracts instead of new projects; Army received only Rs 25,254 crore against its demand of Rs 42,500 crore, and with committed liabilities of Rs 23,000 crores it leaves only Rs 2,254 crore for new projects—which is likely to affect both modernization and operational preparedness; IAF that should have a 458-aircraft force by 2027 is making do with just 235 aircraft at present, with many of them on their last legs; huge deficiencies in authorised and existing levels of ships, submarines and aircraft, and the Committee had asked government to provision at least another Rs 13,000 crore additional capital for modernsation. Ironically, the Defence Budget 2018-2019 also remains 'negative' in actual terms.

✓ India somehow has not been able to strike the appropriate balance between economic development and national security. With predictable difference of opinions, any coherent national security strategy must have a long-term thought process and vision, the basis for which is strategic culture. We do not have a national security strategy and while we desire global status, we take decisions in the cloistered confines of the MoD and MoF, which is hardly appropriate.

Socio-Political Fault Lines and Internal Security. Issues are elucidated next:

- ✓ South Asia is the most populous region in the world. The total population of the region in 2001 was 1,441 million. Growth rates of the countries are not uniform, which has security implications for the region. The HDI too varies, which together with economic prosperity and development, induces migrations. Then there are the varied population growth rates and ethnic similarities and affiliations on both sides of borders, some of which are open. Against the background of the militant assertion by some sections of hard-core Islamist groups, South Asia also hosts the largest number of Muslims (about 450 million) in the world compared to any other region. Except for a small proportion of them who live in Afghanistan, Maldives, Myanmar, Nepal and Sri Lanka, almost the entire community is shared between Pakistan, Bangladesh and India, in that order. Pakistan is the second largest Muslim country in the world after Indonesia, a position earlier held by Bangladesh. Ironically, however, global Muslim politics is dictated by events in West Asia, more particularly, the Arab world.[26]
- ✓ All nations in the region, including India, display symptoms of societal disharmony, which if not contained at the appropriate time, can lead to insurmountable integration crises in the future. As far as India is concerned, the problem can emerge primarily from three directions: communal, centre-state divergence, and intra-state and inter-state disparities.[27] This brings us to the fundamental question about the sanctity of political institutions. So long as the institutions of governance are above sectarian motivations, all communities repose faith in them. The rules of the political game are well known and everybody knows the limits. But sectarian politics by definition has the potential to destroy this fabric. This appears to be somewhat changing in India as seen by elections in some states in India, especially in the case of Uttar Pradesh.
- ✓ But India has its own share of multiple insurgencies some of which have external support but the primary reason still remains lack of governance. While religious fundamentalism in some districts of J&K is being fanned by Pakistan, India is also a target of the ISIS and Al Qaeda. The Central Government is all-powerful and the Governor is supposed to be the watchdog of central interest but on the crucial question of law and order, the Central

Government is virtually powerless even when larger constitutional commitments are in question.

✓ Growing regionalism, which would inevitably lead to sub-regionalism in due course, would wreak havoc in the peripheral regions of the country like Kashmir and the North East.[28] The disparity among the regions of J&K and Ladakh, in the State of J&K, in terms of development aid and investment has often led to acrimony and to demands for the trifurcation of the State into three units. The Northeast provides a peculiar amalgam of centrifugal and centripetal forces, which creates political complexities of which the growth of insurgency is just one symptom. While the 6th Schedule of the Constitution deals with the tribal areas, the Panchayat System (73rd Amendment) deals with the non-tribal areas. But Arunachal Pradesh, though tribal, is not covered by the 6th Schedule; in 1972, NEFA became a Union Territory and named as Arunachal Pradesh, later becoming a State in 1987.

✓ Then there is the rural-urban divide of the country. As the economy gets more and more polarised, the rate of migration of the rural poor to urban centres is bound to accelerate causing all kinds of urban tensions. Urbanisation per se is indicative of political development, but that kind of urbanisation connotes transformation of rural societies into urban centres on account of economic and social developments. The rural migration-fed urban growth, however, brings in its train societal tensions such as crime and inter-communal disharmony.[29] Managing social change is one of the biggest challenges for India, coupled with population growth, rising unemployment and the need for good governance.

Lack of R&D and Defence Industrialisation. The relevant issues are as follows:

✓ In 1995, Dr Abdul Kalam (later President) headed a review committee that set the target to achieve 70 per cent indigenisation in defence production by 2014. We are still importing over 70 per cent defense equipment. Target of 70 per cent indigenization has been now shifted to 2020, which is unachievable. Our DRDO (50 labs), DPSUs (9) and OFs (42) have total employee strength of 1,80,044 (annual budget was Rs 10,610 crore in 2013-14) but have been meeting below 30 per cent of defense needs with many items sub-standard. There is little accountability—no answers when the target of 70 per cent indigenisation by 2014 was laid in 1995, why there were no periodic reviews/corrections, this despite joint secretaries of MoD on all boards of DRDO-PSU-OF. CAG reports of last four years reveal: DRDO has wasted crores for reinventing the wheel when commercial off-the-shelf (COTS) items were available; at times, research is stopped altogether after spending crores or eventually COTS equipment purchased; equipment developed is either substandard or have extended deadlines and additional budgets; bulk of projects undertaken are without MoD clearance, as per one report only 10 per cent projects had sanction; sub-standard and costlier equipment is being provided to armed forces when cheaper and better COTS equipment is available; corruption and nepotism is rampant in higher echelons and there is exodus of qualified scientists; DRDO imports older, foreign technology under the guise of joint development and is promoting foreign firms without the mandatory formal Transfer of Technology (ToT) agreement.

- ✓ India is probably the only large country in the world which is overwhelmingly dependent on external sources for its defence requirements. According to *Stockholm International Peace Research Institute* (SIPRI), India continues to remain the world's largest arms importer, accounting for 14 per cent of the global imports in the 2011-2015 time-frame; this is yet another indicator of the country's enduring failure to build a strong domestic Defence Industrial Base (DIB).[30] India's arms imports remain three times greater than those of China and Pakistan. Its biggest suppliers are Russia, the US, Israel and France. After India, China ranks second in the global arms import list with 4.7 per cent, followed by Australia (3.6%), Pakistan (3.3%), Vietnam (2.9%) and South Korea (2.6%). China used to top the imports chart earlier but has gradually built a stronger DIB over the last couple of decades to even emerge as the world's third largest arms exporter after the US and Russia.
- ✓ This dependency on arms import is a stark reminder of how far India is from the objective of substantive self-reliance in defence production that it has aspired to since the early days of independence. However, all is not lost. The 'Make in India' (MII) initiative launched by the Modi Government offers a ray of hope. Under the initiative, 25 sectors including defence manufacturing have been identified to revive India's industrial growth and more importantly propel the nation as a global manufacturing hub.[31] If the objectives of the MII are to be realized in the defence manufacturing sector, the government needs to address some pressing issues that have hindered India's drive for self-reliance. In terms of R&D in defence sector, Indian investment is miniscule. The MII initiative cannot be achieved without a strong R&D base in the private sector. The Defence Procurement Procedure–2016 (DPP 2016) has focused on indigenisation and encouraging private sector participation, with all acquisition categories mandating ToT and

increasing indigenisation. This will be impossible without a strong and deep R&D eco-system whose key components are equipment and physical infrastructure, skilled technicians, qualified researchers (PhDs, engineers), a robust intellectual property (IP) regime, access to long-term, low-cost capital and comfort on getting orders. Besides, despite the push by the Prime Minister, the red tape has not permitted much ease of doing business.[32]

Higher Defence Organisation and Jointness. Defence of India has been grossly neglected despite mounting threats. As per the 'Rules of Business' of GoI, the Defence Secretary (not the Defence Minister) is responsible for defence of India and the Services HQs are 'Attached Offices' as was during British rule. Successive governments have actually used the Defence Minister for culling out money through defence deals and even surrendering part defence budget. Bureaucrats of MoD have little knowledge of matters military and continue in generalist fashion. MoD has no institutionalised set up for strategic thinking and policy formulation. Resultantly, we are without a National Security Strategy that should be the basis of a Comprehensive Defence Review. It is these two essentials on which our defence procurement in short, medium, and long term should be based. The lack of required focus on R&D, military modernisation, management of border defence, pathetic border defence infrastructure, poor defence-industrial complex, and most importantly, the un-strategic culture are all centred on 'generalist' bureaucrats ruling the roost. The military is kept largely out of strategic military formulations and policy making. Appointment of a CDS is stymied perhaps on the premise he may become too powerful or have direct contact with the political authority, whereas the most important issue is that without the CDS there is little synergy between the three Services. Not only has the media been permitted to tarnish the image of the defence forces, extraordinary efforts are being made by MoD to hit at morale of the soldiers as well. One example is continuing appeals by MoD against emoluments of war widows and disabled in civil courts despite directions of the Prime Minister to curb such practice. Significantly, this is giving the Government and the BJP a very bad name but bureaucrats are unconcerned. HQ Integrated Defence Staff (IDS) was raised with the aim that it would be part of the Ministry of Defence (MoD) but it has come up as a separate HQ, which defeats the very purpose. Present media reports indicate that government is in the process of identifying some 'middle-level' posts in MoD that could be manned by military officers, but that is hardly any reorganisation worth the name.

Lack of Asymmetric Warfare Strategy. The relevant issues are given next:

✓ Henry Kissinger writes in his book *World Order: Reflections on the Character of Nations and the Course of History*, 'The Arthshastra sets out, with dispassionate clarity, a vision of how to establish and guard a state while neutralising, subverting and (when opportune conditions have been established) conquering its neighbours. The Arthshastra encompasses a world of practical statecraft, not philosophical disputation. For Kautilya, power was the dominant reality. It was multidimensional, and its factors were interdependent. All elements in a given situation were relevant, calculable, and amenable to manipulation toward a leader's strategic aims. Geography, finance, military strength, diplomacy, espionage, law, agriculture, cultural traditions, morale and popular opinion, rumours and legends, and men's vices and weaknesses needed to be shaped as a unit by a wise king to strengthen and expand his realm—much as a modern orchestra conductor shapes the instruments in his charge into a coherent tune. It was combination of Machiavelli and Clausewitz. Use of terrorism has been recorded since the 1st century. Kautilya obviously appreciated this being waged by a country's neighbours. It is an irony that while Henry Kissinger derives strategic culture from the Arthshastra, we have failed to do so.

- ✓ India is lagging woefully in asymmetric warfare, particularly at the proactive sub-conventional level vis-à-vis Pakistan and China. We have much catching up to do in terms of cyberspace as well compared to China. This strategic asymmetry is all the more pronounced because the sub-conventional segment and use of irregular forces has become a strategic asset in furthering national interests, over waging conventional war, leave aside nuclear power that will remain a deterrent. Operation 'Parakram' should have been proof enough that conventional power by itself is no panacea to irregular threats. During Parakram, Musharraf kept taunting India to cross the LoC and upped his nuclear sabre rattling. India's inability to establish irregular deterrent has led Pakistan to high levels of arrogance and obduracy in continuing terrorist attacks in India.
- ✓ National Security Strategy should aim at the creation of national and international political conditions favourable to the protection or extension of vital national values against existing and potential adversaries. Unfortunately, not only we have not defined a national security strategy we have never even discussed how to go about establishing credible deterrence to Pakistan's proxy war despite being subjected to terrorism for over three decades. We have failed to acknowledge the strategic significance of sub-conventional warfare. In today's world you cannot guard your house without patrolling the streets no matter what barricading you do. Maloy K Dhar,

former Joint Director IB, in his book *Open Secrets – India's intelligence Unveiled* wrote,

> I continued to advocate for an aggressive and proactive counter and forward intelligence thrust against Pakistan. My voice was rarely heard and mostly ignored.... The Pakistani establishment is a geopolitical bully. The best response to blunt such a bully is to take the war inside his home. India has allowed itself to be blackmailed by Pakistan even before it went nuclear. The sabre rattling of 'coercive diplomacy', which is nothing but sterile military power, cannot convince the Islamist Pakistani Establishment that India can take the border skirmishes inside their homes and hit at the very roots of the jaundiced Islamist groups.

Why the US has managed to secure itself post-9/11 is not only because of homeland security, but also because US Special Forces (USSF) are operating in 200 countries including India.

✓ While we may revel as a nation in the much quoted 'surgical strikes' against terrorist launch pads in POK, this is no panacea. What India needs is continuous special operations at the strategic levels. Unless we develop requisite response to hybrid wars by our enemies, we will continue to be at the receiving end. Reliance on conventional response and diplomacy can hardly suffice.

Poor Border Infrastructure. As mentioned earlier, this needs to be viewed in context of China having increased defence capabilities and deploying more troops along the Indian border, and bases in Pakistan, as warned by the Pentagon in May 2016.[33] Lack of border infrastructure also translates to lack of administration in border villages. Conversely, better communications enables China to influence the villagers, assisting them with rations, fuel, money, which in turn facilitates smuggling and cultivating sources. China also encourages trans-border marriages that help perception management and infiltration. We may be deploying BrahMos in support of our forces but China's superior connectivity to the North Eastern parts of India and Ladakh and its capability of rapid mobilisation of troops can adversely affect India's defence of Sikkim, Ladakh and Arunachal Pradesh in case of conflict.

SWOT Matrix

India's main objective is to retain and consolidate a favourable strategic balance in South Asia while both China and Pakistan are endeavouring to limit India's strategic space in South Asia and the IOR. To this end, it is important that India develops formidable capabilities to fulfill the expectations of its smaller neighbours and thus reduce China's increasing influence on these nations. In the preceding chapters, the 'trend lines' of the key determinants of Pakistan and China have been discussed in detail. It is pertinent to highlight that the strategic balance in the region will be determined by the strategic outlook, objectives and interaction of three main players, i.e. Pakistan, China, and India. India's neighbours are crucial in terms of their alignments with either China or India or to maintain equidistance (balancing one against the other). Similarly, any extra-regional power is unlikely to get embroiled into any contentious scenarios. Hence, it is important to highlight in detail, the Strengths, Weaknesses, Opportunities and Threats (SWOT) of Pakistan, China and India. Based on the analysis, the strategies that India should adopt have been listed out. The SWOT matrix for each country is as follows:

Pakistan

INTERNAL		EXTERNAL	
Strengths	**Weaknesses**	**Opportunities**	**Threats**
Geo-strategic location	Economy	Democratic aspirations	Balkanisation of Pakistan
Professional armed force	Military domination in governance	Rapprochement with India	Radicalisation
Strong Int network	Ethno-regional fault lines	Demographic dividend	–
Nuclear status	Water security	Strategic gateway to CAR & Arabian sea	–
Strategic alignment with China	Energy security	–	–
Diplomatic support from OIC	Low Human Development Index	–	–
Asymmetric capabilities	Corruption	–	–

China

Strategic culture	Oceanic geographic restraint	To be a pre-eminent Asian power	US 'Pivot to Asia' strategy
Ethno-linguistic homogeneity	Over-dependence on international markets	To re-shape global monetary institutions	Threat to SLOCs
Economy and defence budget	Energy import dependence	–	Global recession
Higher direction of war & jointness	Internal security	–	–
Industrial base and R&D	War fighting experience	–	–

INTERNAL		EXTERNAL	
Strengths	**Weaknesses**	**Opportunities**	**Threats**
Nuclear edge	Strategic mistrust	–	–
Space & cyber warfare capabilities	–	–	–
Informationisation	–	–	–
Sino-Pak nexus	–	–	–
UN Veto power	–	–	–

India

Geo-strategic location	Socio-political faultlines	Demographic Dividend	Collusive 'Two Front' Threat
Democracy & soft power	Lack of strategic vision	Leverage IT potential	Asymmetric threats
Op experience of Armed Forces	Economy & defence budget	Strategic swing status	–
Strategic deterrence	Governance deficit	–	–
Youth bulge	Internal security	–	–
	Lack of asymmetric warfare strategy	–	–
	Lack of R&D and defence industrialisation	–	–
	Higher defence organi-sation and jointness	–	–

In order to widen its strategic space in South Asia and IOR for enhancing its regional power status, it is extremely important for India to rein in anti-India stance of Pakistan and neutralise the growing strategic nexus between China and Pakistan. Issues that especially impact the region with respect to Pakistan, China and India are elucidated in subsequent paragraphs.

Issues Relevant to Pakistan

✓ **Strengths**

- **Geo-strategic Location**. Pakistan is at the geo-strategic cross-roads of South Asia, the Middle East, Central Asia and China. The strategic location affords Pakistan an advantage as a 'Gateway' to the Arabian Sea, Afghanistan and Central Asia as also dominate the SLOCs.
- **Professional Military**. Pakistan has the sixth largest military in the world, which is well trained and equipped in the regional context. Military

leadership is strong and effective. It can effectively ward off threats to national security from within or outside as well as effectively participate in joint military operations with allies and the UN.

- **Strong Intelligence Network**. The intelligence community under the ISI is among the best in the world. This allows Pakistan to play a proactive and dominant role in any emerging security calculus in the region and also leverage its competency with extra regional powers.
- **Nuclear Status**. Pakistan's growing nuclear capability is an effective tool of strategic deterrence configured in Pakistan's military posturing against India.
- **Strategic Alignment with China**. Pakistan has maintained a strong strategic alignment with China primarily with mutual aim to continuously keep India in a 'two-front dilemma'. The CPEC and Gwadar have further strengthened this ant-India nexus.
- **Diplomatic Support from OIC**. Pakistan has a privileged status in the Organisation of Islamic Cooperation (OIC). In terms of population, it is the OIC's second largest member. Being the only Muslim country with nuclear weapons, having the sixth largest standing military force and a large labour workforce working in various Muslim countries play a role in its prominence. Pakistan enjoys active diplomatic support from other Islamic nations and has always used OIC as a platform to gather support on the Kashmir conflict against India.
- **Asymmetric Capabilities**. Pakistan has always adopted asymmetric warfare approach in its strategic construct against India. Asymmetric warfare has been an integral part of Pakistan's state policy since its independence. It has well-developed capabilities to prosecute proxy wars and unleash terrorist strikes. Pakistan's war-fighting doctrines seek to fuse conventional warfare with asymmetric warfare, what has come to be known as 'Hybrid Warfare'.

✓ **Weaknesses**

- **Economy**. Pakistan remains stuck in a low-income, low-growth trap, though the GDP rose to 4.24 per cent in 2015, from the previous year. Decades of internal political disputes and low levels of foreign investment have led to slow growth and underdevelopment in Pakistan. China's $46 billion investment in the CPEC is considered a bright spot by Pakistan but this may well be a debt trap, besides turning Pakistan into a subset of China. Though the CPEC is supposed to create 7,00,000 jobs for Pakistanis, Pakistan's population is also rising at an annual rate of 2.07

per cent. Therefore, the prognosis of Pakistan's economy in the coming decade looks grim.

- **Military Domination in Governance**. Pakistan Army has governed the state directly for more than half of its history and governed indirectly from behind the scenes for the balance period, especially controlling key areas of governance such as India/US/Afghanistan specific foreign policy, nuclear policy, security/defence as well as nuclear safety issues. Due to its long stints in power, it has systematically subverted the civil institutions.
- **Ethno-regional Fault Lines**. Pakistan's population comprises of 97 per cent Muslims (Sunni 77 per cent and Shia 20 per cent) and only 3 per cent minorities including Hindu, Christians and others. Despite a predominantly Muslim state, there exists serious fissiparous and separatists tendencies such as:
    - Saraiki movement in the heartland Punjab due to the economic divide within Punjab and the alleged domination by Punjabis.
    - Secessionist movement in Baluchistan towards the establishment of an independent state of Baluchistan separate from Pakistan and Iran.
    - In Sindh, there is a strong divide between the Punjabis, Pathans and the Urdu-speaking Mohajirs leading to estranged relations and the demand for separate Sindhudesh and Pashtunistan.
- **Water Security**. As per the Indus Water Treaty (IWT) of 1960, Pakistan receives water from the three western rivers of the Indus basin, namely Indus, Jhelum, and Chenab. These rivers flow into Pakistan from the state of J&K in India and irrigate Punjab and much of other fertile areas of Pakistan. The IWT is highly favourable to Pakistan. As per the hydrological survey, Pakistan is likely to witness severe water shortage due to receding water table. This will have an adverse effect on the power and agriculture sectors. In the event of Pakistan turning into a failed or a rouge state, India can effectively exploit this critical vulnerability of Pakistan by seeking renegotiation of the treaty or in certain circumstances, abrogating it altogether.
- **Energy Security**. Pakistan is heavily dependent on import of energy resources from the Middle East along the SLOCs passing through the IOR. Pakistan's energy import is bound to increase in the coming decades. Any conflict in the IOR and India's domination over the SLOCs will effectively compound Pakistan's energy dilemma.
- **Low Human Development Index (HDI)**. As per UNDP's Human

Development Rankings (HDI) 2015,[34] which are based on the composite statistic of life expectancy, education and income indices, Pakistan is ranked 'Low' at 147 out of 188 countries. Comparatively, both China and India scored medium HDI rankings placed at 90 and 130, respectively. The World Economic Forum's Global Competitiveness Index 2016-2017 Rankings placed it at 122 among 138 nations.[35] Poor governance and rising aspirations of the young generation may result in severe social unrest and mass protests in Pakistan.

- **Corruption**. The rampant corruption in the civil bureaucracy and the government has led to loss of faith of the population in the system.

✓ **Opportunities**

- **Democratic Aspirations**. The fate of civil politics in Pakistan died young with death of father of the nation, Mohammad Ali Jinnah. Presently, the political class and segments of civil society have got together to seize the political space from the military and restarted a democratic political process. In the last elections, Pakistan has got its second successive democratically elected government. The civilian government now has the opportunity to focus on internal reforms with respect to its economy, law and order situation, and foreign relations. With these parameters, the economy may improve, democracy may stabilise and there may be coherence in government policies.
- **Rapprochement with India**. There is an emerging perception among younger Army officers that America and not India is currently the main cause of Pakistan's woes. Pakistan's military doctrine also highlights 'terrorism' as the biggest threat and not India. Even during the recent elections, 'anti-India' sentiments were not focused on. The Pew Research Center's Global Attitudes Project titled 'Pakistani Public Opinion Ever More Critical of U.S.' of Jun 2012[36] has brought out that 'despite these negative sentiments, 62 per cent of Pakistanis say it is important to improve relations with India. And roughly two-thirds support more bilateral trade and further talks to try to reduce tensions between the two nations'. Therefore, a window of opportunity exists for the Pakistani establishment to make sincere efforts towards rapprochement with India for mutual benefits.
- **Demographic Dividend**. The country has one of world's youngest populations with a median age of 18 years. 59 per cent of total population is young men and women below the age of 25 and about 67 per cent of total population is below the age of 30. The current rate of 4.1 births per

woman is set to carry Pakistan's youth bulge well beyond 2025. The sheer numerical strength of Pakistan's upcoming generations implies that the direction in which the critical mass of this segment chooses to push the country will inevitably become the destiny of Pakistan. The opportunity exists for the government to invest in educating and providing the job opportunities to this young generation to convert the 'youth bulge' beneficially to drive its economic activities.

- **Strategic Gateway to CAR and Arabian Sea**. Pakistan's location affords it an advantage of being a frontline state providing a gateway to land locked Afghanistan, CAR and Xinjiang to the Arabian Sea. Its centrality in the subcontinent makes it an important player in the implementation of energy projects like TAPI/IPI and power energy grid to South Asia. Pakistan needs to convert this advantage into an opportunity to become a conduit for transfer of energy from the energy rich region of CAR to energy deprived nations of South Asia and beyond. However, peace and stability within Pakistan would be the prerequisite for this.

✓ **Threats**

- **Balkanisation of Pakistan**. This threat exists in case the democratic government fails to tackle the social pressure caused by rising population and urbanisation as well as its inability to rebuild the weakened state institutions and failure to pursue pragmatic economic policies leading to economic collapse. The resultant deteriorating law and order situation could result in mass protest akin to 'Arab Spring' or separatist movements in Baluchistan, Sindh, GB, and the Durand Line dividing Pashtuns could be exploited by the extremist elements leading to greater violence and paralysis in the functioning of the weak coalition government and may result in Balkanisation of the nation. In such a situation, the Army may get tempted to step in.
- **Radicalisation**. Pakistan in recent years has experienced several waves of political violence, essentially related to various forms of sectarian, ethnic, tribal and global jihadi movements. The core of much of the tension and violence experienced by the country is the result of the relationship between the state and religion and the role and place that Islam assumes in Pakistan's society. Among those blamed for the sectarian violence in the country are mainly Sunni militant groups such as the Lashkar-e-Jhangvi, Sipah-e-Sahaba, Tehrik-i-Taliban Pakistan and members of Shia militant groups such as Sipah-e-Muhammad Pakistan. The grip now held by the fundamentalist narratives on the mindset of Pakistani society

will be best countered by effective governance and a state with a modern vision and persuasive narrative of its own.

Issues Relevant to China

✓ **Strengths**

- **Strategic Culture.** China's strategic culture is an outcome of its historical legacies and precepts enunciated by Sun Tzu and other strategic thinkers and these continue to guide its policies and shape its strategic outlook in all of China's national and international endeavours. The Chinese leadership has a clear and well-articulated vision for the future from where flow its long-term national interests and strategic objectives. The leadership has clearly identified the first quarter of the 21st century (up to 2025) as a period of strategic opportunities and the next 25 years for 'Strategic Expansion' to become a global power. Smooth leadership transition and strong resolve have made it possible for China to achieve its goals in a time-bound manner and in many instances it has surprised the world by succeeding in its endeavours much before the proscribed time lines.
- **Ethno-linguistic Homogeneity**. An overwhelming majority of the population in China is Han and they speak the Mandarin language, though some societal stratification exists due to economic imbalance. The non-Han population living in the strategic buffers is just about 7 per cent and China is carrying out 'Hanisation' of its buffers as part of a well-calibrated social re-engineering programme. Therefore, despite its size and ethno-linguistic diversity, China can be considered a homogenous polity, especially when compared with India.
- **Economy and Defence Budget**. Economy is the main determinant of China's CNP and is a critical driver for the PLA's military modernisation. Despite the global meltdown, China's economy has maintained a growth rate of approximately 7 per cent that implies that China's military modernisation programme is expected to continue as planned, and going by the trends, its defence spending is likely to surpass that of the US.
- **Higher Direction of War and Jointness**. There exists very good synergy between the party, various organs of the Government, CMC and the PLA in China. The reorganisation of the PLA has placed total power in President Xi Jinping who is also C-in-C of PLA and Chairman of the CMC also controlling all militias. Jointness is promoted in military doctrines, concepts and logistics that are rehearsed during military

exercises. The PLA (Armed Police) and PLA (Militia) are controlled by the CMC and work in tandem with PLA and this is a major operational advantage that the PRC enjoys over India. All Border Guard Divisions are under the command of PLA. The capability to conduct 'Joint Integrated Operations' is a battle winning competitive edge.

- **Industrial Base and R&D**. Chinese companies and the government are investing heavily in R&D. In 2011, China overtook Japan to become the world's second biggest spender on industrial R&D, trailing only the US. China has developed its long-term S&T programmes in the form of 'Science and Technology in China: A Roadmap to 2050'. China desires to match the US levels of technical prowess by 2050. Though this is difficult, this might manifest if the US is unable to rebound economically.
- **Nuclear Edge**. The trends in PLA's Rocket Force and Strategic Support Force indicate a miniaturised and reliable strategic nuclear strike capability with an arsenal comprising solid fuel ballistic missiles with extended ranges and multiple war heads. Also, the force structure has a phenomenal number of conventional short-/medium-range missiles. The local war concept has made China increase its precision SRBMs and LACMs that currently constitute nearly 60 per cent of the SAC arsenal. All this gives China a major strategic competitive edge.
- **Space Warfare**. Chinese space capabilities rank just behind the USA and Russia. China has more than four times the satellites in orbit compared to India. It can launch much heavier satellites in geo-stationary orbit while India has just acquired the capability. China has been launching more satellites than any other country for the last few years. With a greater number of satellites, its dependence on satellites for military communication, reconnaissance, and navigation is higher than that of India. China has also demonstrated its anti-satellite capabilities.
- **Cyber Warfare**. China has already emerged as a cyber-super power and has shown both the propensity and display of refined skills to undertake cyber espionage as well as sabotage. These capabilities are blended with its military strategy which seeks employment of cyber weapons as a non-contact asymmetric means employed during all stages of the campaign. China has mastered the art of launching cyber-attacks against critical infrastructure using guile and subterfuge.
- **Informationisation**. China has taken bold strides in the application of IT in the C4ISR system and has achieved credible capability to network sensors and shooters for Effect Based Operations (EBO).

- **Sino-Pak Nexus**. China enjoys strategic congruence with Pakistan and it is expected to continue to play the Pakistan card against India. In the event of India-China conflict, Pakistan is likely to play a role of China's proxy and perpetuate India's 'Two-Front Dilemma'. It would do its best to pin down Indian military on the Western front as also enflame the internal situation in India and this would help the Chinese in creating asymmetric ascendency over India.
- **UN Veto Power**. China's rising economic clout and military power is complemented by her 'veto power' at the UN Security Council. China has adroitly leveraged its veto power to prevent impositions of economic and trade sanctions against particular states which serve China's strategic objectives in the global power play. China also effectively blocks India's entry, as a permanent member, into the UN Security Council.

✓ **Weaknesses**

- **Oceanic Geographic Restraint**. China is geographically constrained in the East and the South China Sea and is surrounded by a web of countries that contest China's maritime claims and concurrently enjoy defence alliances with the US. The US, together with these countries, is well postured to exploit China's critical vulnerability, i.e. domination of SLOCs and compounding China's Malacca Dilemma. The restive non-Han strategic buffer shares strategic frontiers with China's competitors namely, India and Russia. To an extent, China is trying to overcome this through the CPEC and availability of Gwadar, Omari and Karachi naval bases to dominate the Arabian Sea.
- **Overdependence on International Markets**. China's overdependence on the international market and unrestrained manufacturing sector expose it to the risk of falling in the vortex of the international recession whereby with the slowing of the international market, China's economy is bound to plummet. In 2011, China felt the impact of the global financial crisis, especially due to the European debt crisis and the US economy's weak recovery and as a result its economic performance was barely satisfactory during the period.
- **Energy Import Dependence**. China will become the biggest importer of hydrocarbon resources from the world market. Bulk of these resources will flow through the Eastern as well as the Western SLOCs. Therefore, security of SLOCs in the East China Sea, Malacca Strait and in the IOR will remain China's critical vulnerability. Any fragile security scenario in the Western Pacific and/or IOR will adversely affect China's economy.

- **Internal Security**. China's internal security concerns pertain to socio-economic inequality, relative sense of deprivation faced by the economically disadvantaged majority population and the restive non-Han strategic buffer. Ageing population, demographic shifts, non-traditional security threats, inadequacy of energy and water resources and a perceived cultural invasion exacerbates China's internal security dilemmas. The US 'Pivot to Asia' strategy, possibility of the secessionism of Taiwan and the potent threat to its SLOCs are perceived as the major external security challenges. It also faces secessionist movements in Xinjiang, Inner Mongolia and Tibet. These are fault lines which can be exploited by India.
- **War Fighting Experience**. The PLA has limited and only theoretical knowledge of war fighting under modern and high-tech conditions. Since 1979, when it fought against a militarily-weak Vietnam, it has marginally validated its doctrines and concepts, and seen the efficacy of its weapons and equipment against a strong, modern and networked military.
- **Strategic Mistrust**. China is envied by the international community for its economic rise but despised for its authoritarianism, oppressive policies and opportunistic alliances with dictatorial regimes, human rights and overbearing attitude towards its smaller neighbors. The world at large mistrusts China.

✓ **Opportunities**

- **Pre-eminent Asian Power**. China currently enjoys the regional power status in Asia and with its growing economy as well as military potential it is in direct competition with the US. Though it is difficult to precisely predict the outcome of growing competition and conflict between the US and China, it is very clear that the US is experiencing declining hegemonic power in the world. China's sustained economic growth and military modernisation are posing a serious challenge to the US as a pre-eminent Asia-Pacific power. If this trend continues and the US witnesses a relative decline, then China will emerge as the pre-eminent power in Asia-Pacific and a leading global player.
- **Re-shaping Global Monetary Institution**. China has been growing at about 9 per cent per annum and its goods and services are rapidly rising in quality and value albeit the global slowdown has also now affected China's growth. China has replaced the US and European controlled 'international financial institutions' (the IMF, World Bank, the Inter-American Development Bank) as the principle lender in Latin America.

China continues to lead as the prime investor in African energy and mineral resources. China has replaced the US as the principal market for Saudi Arabia, Sudanese and Iranian petroleum and it will soon replace the US as the principal market for Venezuela petroleum products. Today China is the world's biggest manufacturer and exporter, dominating even the US market, while playing the role of financial life line as it holds over $1.3 trillion in US Treasury notes. Thus, there exists the opportunity for China to influence the global monetary institutions as well as create an alternate global currency to dollar.

✓ **Threats**

- **US 'Pivot to Asia' Strategy**. In the Chinese strategic thinking, the US is viewed as the fundamental obstacle to China's continued ascent in global politics. The US arms transfer to Taiwan and the seeming centrality of the Taiwan question in the Asia calculus of the US continues to be an important threat for China. Apart from Taiwan issue, China sees the US as a threat for many reasons. It is seen as a facilitator for the creation of China containment policy in Asia. American relations with Japan and South Korea, its military engagement with Southeast Asia and its growing relationship with India are all seen as part of a greater strategy to reduce China's strategic space. The US has been raising the human rights issue of China. This has been viewed in Beijing as interference in China's internal matters and an effort to destabilise the country domestically.
- **Threat to SLOCs**. Currently 83 per cent of Chinese energy imports transit through IOR and the SCS. Energy, being the driver of Chinese economy for sustaining double-digit growth of its GDP, remains intricately dependent upon these SLOCs remaining free of disruption. Any hostile presence of regional and extra-regional navies in the IOR and in the China Seas makes Chinese energy supply routes extremely vulnerable to disruption.
- **Global Recession**. China's economy, which is mainly manufacturing and export oriented, is hugely dependent on the demand in international market. The global economic crisis, in the past, has exacerbated the problems for China within its rapidly growing economy. Any recession in the global market remains a potential threat to the Chinese economy.

Issues Relevant to India

✓ **Strengths**

- **Geo-strategic Location**. The geo-strategic location of India in the centre of South Asia and at the head of IOR affords it the advantage of overlooking world's major energy and trade routes. The Himalayas on the Northern borders provide a formidable defence line that denies China any deep ingress into the Indian Territory.

- **Democracy and Soft Power**. India is world's largest democracy with vibrant democratic institutions, voluntary armed forces, an active media and a historical culture that has strong religious and moral beliefs. The world admires India's pluralistic culture, democratic credentials and robustness of its judicial and financial institutions. India also enjoys a considerable soft power appeal. Further, the advantage of the widespread knowledge of the English language and ability of its diaspora to easily adapt to other cultures make Indians more acceptable in the international arena.
- **Operational Experience of Indian Armed Forces**. India Armed Forces have rich and live operational experience. Besides, it enjoys the advantage of handling modern and state-of-the-art military equipment during the simulated joint exercises conducted with some of the most advanced militaries in the world.
- **Strategic Deterrence**. India declared itself a nuclear state in 1998. Surrounded by nuclear powers on its either side, being a nuclear-powered state affords it the strategic deterrence capability.

✓ **Weaknesses**

- **Socio-political Fault Lines**. Even though India takes pride in its 'Unity in Diversity', the country remains beset with serious fault lines: geographic, linguistic, caste, ethno-religious, and economic and in a way, the political system remains hostage to these restraints. The divisive political culture, fragile nature of coalition politics, uncertainties related to leadership transition, ideological divergences, etc. hamper nationalistic decision making and the ability to take a long-term view of India's future destiny.
- **Lack of Strategic Vision**. India is known to be a pacifist and reactive nation with an intrinsic defensive mentality. It has yet to evolve a comprehensive grand strategy or even lay down strategic policy guidelines in the pursuance of national interests which otherwise are enshrined in the Constitution. India's strategic objectives and policies are found to be inarticulate and dithering, especially when faced with making difficult choices. The politico-bureaucratic establishment is shy of indulging in strategic issues and remains content with routine matters and maintaining the status quo.

- **Economy and Defence Spending**. The Indian economy after showing great promise had plummeted to about 5 per cent GDP growth before showing recent recovery. The relative gap between India and China is therefore large and is growing. Even if Indian economy recovers fully, the Chinese economy will still be four/five times larger than that of India. Similarly, India's defence spending will also remain four/five times less than that of China. The Indian defence budget increase over the previous year barely caters for inflation. Undoubtedly, this will impact defence acquisitions.
- **Governance Deficit**. As per UNDP's Human Development Rankings (HDI) 2015, India is ranked at 138 out of 188 countries. Corruption in India is a major issue and adversely affects its economy. The causes of corruption in India include excessive regulations, complicated taxes and licensing systems, numerous government departments each with opaque bureaucracy and discretionary powers, monopoly by government controlled institutions on certain goods and services delivery, and the lack of transparent laws and processes.
- **Internal Security**. India's internal security scenario continues to be complex and varied. The domestic dynamics of India's internal security are reflected in its socio-political milieu, the main feature of which is its diversity in terms of variety of castes, ethnic groups, fundamentalism and religious beliefs and customs and traditions, with different manifestations of culture, all operating in a dynamic environment. While problems will intrinsically rest on domestic roots, external factors will play a major role in aggravating these. Threats due to Islamic extremism and terrorism, Left Wing Maoist insurgency (LWE), ethnic fundamentalism, and small arms proliferation loom large on the horizon. Maintenance of internal security is one of the biggest challenges facing the country.
- **Lack of Asymmetric Warfare Strategy**. India not only has asymmetries in the space, cyberspace, and electromagnetic domains with respect to China, it also faces unconventional warfare including terrorism. China in conjunction with Pakistan is working towards creating an Afghanistan-like situation in the Indian hinterland. India lacks credible deterrent against irregular/unconventional warfare to break the China-Pakistan anti-India nexus.
- **Lack of R&D & Defence Industrialisation**. One major cause of inefficiency in the pursuit of self-reliance in military equipment has been

the state-run monopoly in the defence industry. Even though India's military arsenal is of better quality in comparison to China, the weakness lies in the fact that there is disproportionately high import dependence. Few defence industries as well as research agencies which India has are all public sector undertakings (PSU) and their performance till date has been far from satisfactory. Low investment in R&D and non-performing defence industries are India's major weaknesses.

- **Higher Defence Organisation and Lack of Jointness**. In India, there exists not only a politico-military disconnect, this is exacerbated by a hardened layer of civil services in between. The Service Chiefs are not part of the apex decision-making body and the Service Headquarters are totally subordinated to MoD. Intra- and Inter-Service integration is sub-optimal at all levels of command. Para Military Forces (PMF) lack desired compatibility with the military in operational capacities and generally functions outside the control of the military and MoD. Even among the three Services, there is a complete lack of jointness at all levels.

✓ **Opportunities**

- **Demographic Dividend**. The youth segment of India's population is growing rapidly and is projected to do so for the next 30 years. Today, more than half of India's population is under the age of 25, with 65 per cent of the population under 35. By 2020, India's average age will be just 29 years, in comparison with 37 in China. This trend will confer a significant competitive advantage upon India, provided India utilises this opportunity by ensuring education, skills enhancement and succeeds in creating the appropriate employment opportunities for its young population.
- **Leverage IT Potential**. India is a leading IT nation. There exists a major opportunity for India to leverage its IT potential to its advantage.
- **Strategic Swing Status**. The US considers India as a lynchpin of its Asia Pivot Strategy. Japan, South Korea and Vietnam also find India as a natural ally and a potential countervail to China. India has a strategic window of opportunity to develop multi-dimensional strategic partnership(s) with its neighbours and likeminded countries and to evolve a collective security framework. Such a strategic orientation can help India in balancing China's hegemony in South Asia in particular and Asia in general.

✓ **Threats**

- **Collusive 'Two-Front' Threat**. India's external security concerns primarily relate to the unresolved border problem with China and possible conflict scenarios with Pakistan over J&K. Thus, India faces a daunting 'Two-Front Collusive Hybrid' threat on its Western and Northern frontiers. In a conflict scenario with any one of the adversaries, the covert support of the other is a certainty. The challenge will be much bigger should such mutual support become overt and India is actively challenged on both the fronts simultaneously. Currently, India is not optimally prepared for a collusive 'two-front' scenario.

- **Asymmetric Threats**. India has, in the past, experienced asymmetric warfare in the form of insurgency, militancy, terrorism and other forms of violence. Thus, asymmetric threats have encompassed both military and non-military dimensions exploiting the security vulnerabilities of the country. While the 'proxy war' sponsored by Pakistan as well as the insurgencies in the North East are likely to continue, other asymmetric threats are also likely to manifest in the future. Some of these are:
    - Cyber warfare targeted at our IT industry, financial networks, and electricity grids and also the security of command and control networks.
    - Threats to the Indian economy through physical or cyber targeting of financial institutions or by manipulation of the stock markets.
    - Propaganda targeted at the minds of the people to undermine their faith in the political leadership and institutions.
    - Drug trafficking aimed at eroding social structures and also as a source for funding terrorism.

SWOT Analysis

China is pulling India's neighbours into its gravitational pull and in conjunction Pakistan wants India's growth stymied and constrained within South Asia. India needs to weaken the China-Pakistan anti-India nexus and build confidence and trust among its neighbours. But in order to succeed in its endeavours, India first needs to put its own house in order. The roles envisaged for India in the region are:

- ✓ Be a regional pivot of economic integration.
- ✓ Be the net security provider; both in terms of equipment as well as training.
- ✓ Be the leading power for disaster management.
- ✓ Be the provider of viable and stable governance model.

For India to fulfil the above expectations, its first need to achieve the following:

- ✓ Internal cohesiveness.
- ✓ Revival of economic growth.
- ✓ Enhance its R&D and technology base.

✓ Reduction in import dependency by enhancing indigenisation for its military and security hardware, by creating a level playing field for private industry.

Strategies for India

The grand strategy recommended to be adopted by India and its multiple nuances are discussed in the subsequent chapter. However, the strategies which India needs to follow, in order to leverage its strengths to exploit the opportunities, to overcome the weaknesses and to mitigate the threats based on above SWOT analysis, are elucidated as under:

✓ **Maximise Strengths**

➢ **Geo-strategic Location and Democratic Appeal**. These two attributes will enable India to maximise its politico-diplomatic influence among remainder South Asian countries. The geo-strategic centrality of India with borders with all other countries and India being the most vibrant democracy and economic power are the attributes that can be gainfully harnessed to induce a positive gravitational pull to integrate the regional economies and promote democratic culture.

➢ **Geo-strategic Location and Strong Military**. These strengths, with adequate consolidation and strategic configuration, will enable India to not only achieve a credible deterrence against China and Pakistan but also become a 'Net Security Provider' to smaller neighbouring countries to meet traditional as well as non-traditional threats and challenges. A concerted effort is needed in this regard and this will depend on state of India's economy. Poor economic growth will hinder flow of funds for such efforts.

➢ In addition, a pre-eminent maritime and aerospace capability in the IOR will enhance India's stature as a viable countervail to an assertive China.

➢ Maximisation of the above stated strengths will add traction to India's image as a Strategic Swing State.

✓ **Eradicate Weaknesses**. India's weaknesses stem mostly from its internal dynamics such as socio-political fault lines, lack of inclusive growth, governance deficit, energy security and import dependence of military hardware. These weaknesses can be mitigated by undertaking wide ranging policy, structural and procedural reforms and creating effective mechanism to ensure timely implementation of the enunciated policies and programmes.

✓ **Exploit Opportunities**

➢ India can ill-afford to let its demographic dividend go astray. Revival of economy, affordable yet high standards of education, improved healthcare, enabling skills, creation of job-orientated growth, etc. are 'Sine quo Non' to transform our youth bulge into a demographic dividend.

- India is an acknowledged IT power. This leverage, combined with proficiency in English language, can be harnessed to transform India into a regional and IT global knowledge hub.
- The above two with some other initiatives can be consolidated to make India as an alternate global manufacturing hub.

✓ **Mitigation of Threats**

- **'Two-Front' Collusive Hybrid Threat**. A strong deterrence capability against China and Pakistan is a 'Sine qua Non'. Proxy wars in the North-eastern states and in J&K need to be effectively neutralised to deny our adversaries any opportunities to fuse conventional threats with the internal security threats.
- **Asymmetric Warfare**. Proxy wars, terrorism, cyber espionage and sabotage, proliferation of fake currencies, spread of criminal activities, use of disruptive technologies in the outer space, etc. have emerged as the most potent tools of coercion and weakening of a target nation state. India is quite vulnerable to these threats. Therefore, India must develop credible defensive and offensive asymmetric warfare capabilities.

✓ **Strategies Against Pakistan and China**

- Pakistan is highly susceptible to ethno-regional fault lines. China faces similar challenge in Xinjiang and Tibet. India should create a broad spectrum 'Non-Contact' warfare leverage to exploit these weaknesses.
- On water issue, India enjoys leverages against Pakistan but is vulnerable vis-à-vis China. There is a need to devise a strategy to pressurise Pakistan on this premium resource, while at the same time persuade China to behave as responsible stakeholder in sharing of global commons.
- India, China, and Pakistan rely heavily on the SLOCs in the IOR for trade as well as for import of energy resources. A formidable naval capability by India would therefore be the best way in achieving a favourable strategic balance in the region.
- China's strategic forays in South Asia along three axes: (1) Xinjiang-Pakistan-Bay of Bengal, (2) Kunming-Myanmar-Chittagong and (3) 'String of Pearls' in the IOR, need to be balanced by India. To this end, success of India's 'Connect Central Asia' policy, 'Act East' policy and proactive engagement with Myanmar, Bangladesh, Maldives, and other IOR littorals is paramount to maximise our options and consequent

politico-economic and diplomatic influence. In this endeavour, Iran and Myanmar assume critical importance.

The US Factor

US would continue to remain an important player in South Asia. Containment of China's influence in the IOR, proliferation of nuclear weapons, terrorism, security of SLOCs, etc. are the abiding interests of the US that coalesce with India's strategic objectives. A great scope, therefore, exists for India and the US to coordinate strategic partnership at multiple levels. However, India should remain cognisant of the US interests vis-à-vis China as well as Pakistan and accordingly moderate its expectations and cooperation with the US. An astute and sophisticated politico-diplomatic approach would be needed to engage the US.

Key Issues

- ✓ *Focal point of Sino-Pak cooperation is enmity with India, aimed at containing India's strategic space within South Asia.*
- ✓ *Military asymmetry, and proxy forces of China-Pakistan has potential to pose three-front dilemma.*
- ✓ *Presently, India retains competitive deterrence capabilities in IOR.*
- ✓ *India doesn't have cohesive NSS and doesn't acknowledge changed nature of conflict beyond conventional war in nuclear backdrop.*
- ✓ *India's higher defence setup lacks of military professionals.*
- ✓ *Services are left to define threats and prepare to fight accordingly.*
- ✓ *Military Strategy flowing from the NSS must include defence of national and territorial interests and maintaining credible deterrence against potential adversaries on land, sea, air, cyberspace and space, aside from many other issues like promoting India on the world stage.*
- ✓ *India must achieve self-reliance in defence and futuristic/disruptive technologies.*
- ✓ *India's strategic deficits include lack of strategic vision; emerging economy with inadequate defence budget; socio-political fault-lines and internal security; small R&D and defence-industrialisation; higher defence organization and jointness and lack of asymmetric warfare strategy.*
- ✓ *SWOT analysis of Pakistan, China and India leads to the strategies that India should adopt.*
- ✓ *India should maximise its strengths, eradicate weaknesses, exploit opportunities and mitigate threats.*
- ✓ *Both China and Pakistan are highly susceptible to ethno-regional fault lines.*

India should create a broad spectrum 'Non-Contact' warfare leverage to exploit these weaknesses.

- ✓ *India has leverages against Pakistan on water but is vulnerable vis-à-vis China. India needs a strategy to pressure Pakistan and persuade China to behave as responsible stakeholder in sharing.*
- ✓ *Formidable Indian naval capability is best for achieving favourable strategic balance in the region.*
- ✓ *India's 'Connect Central Asia' policy, 'Look East' policy and proactive engagement with Myanmar, Bangladesh, Maldives and other IOR littorals is paramount to maximise options.*
- ✓ *Astute and sophisticated politico-diplomatic approach is required to engage the US in backdrop of the US-China and US-Pakistan equations.*

NOTES

1 Sibal, Kanwal, 'Adrift Without a Strategic Culture', India Today, 12 March 2013, http://indiatoday.intoday.in/story/national-security-nuclear-age-armed-forces-british-rule-security-threat-china-military/1/257472.html.

2 Dasgupta, Sunil and Cohen, P Stephen, 'How Not to Deal with Defence Corruption', Indian Express, 2 April 2013. http://indianexpress.com/article/opinion/columns/how-not-to-deal-with-defence-corruption/.

3 Ibid.

4 Ibid.

5 Campose, Phillip, 'India's National Security Strategy: Imperative of Integrating Defence Policy', CLAWS Journal, Winter 2016.

6 Kanwal, Gurmeet, 'Why India Needs a National Security Strategy', rediff.com, 17 June 2016, http://www.rediff.com/news/column/why-india-needs-a-national-security-strategy/20160617.htm.

7 Campose, op. cit.

8 Ibid.

9 Ibid.

10 Ibid.

11 'In India, a Military Strategy Guided by Precision', STRATFOR, 6 October 2016, https://www.stratfor.com/sample/analysis/india-military-strategy-guided-precision

12 Ibid.

13 Sonwalker, Prasun, 'Pakistan "Very Concerned" at India's Military Modernisation', *Hindustan Times,* 9 February 2016, http://www.hindustantimes.com/world/pakistan-very-concerned-at-india-s-military-modernisation/story-JOrnmwTnk8B6CJ3vfrGhnJ.html.

14 India vs China Military Power Comparison | Indian Army vs Chinese Army | Full Documentary, World Military Channel, 18 August 2016, https://www.youtube.com/watch?v=yyRROSl5SSM.

15 Ibid.

16 Ibid.

17 'China Has Deployed More Troops Near Indian Border: Pentagon', *The Indian Express,* 14 May 2016, http://indianexpress.com/article/india/india-news-india/china-has-deployed-more-troops-near-indian-border-pentagon-2799965/.

18 Mizokami, Kyle, 'Five Indian Weapons of War China Should Fear', *The National Interest*, 21 June 2014, http://nationalinterest.org/feature/five-indian-weapons-war-china-should-fear-10714.

19 Mizokami, Kyle, 'Five Chinese Weapons of War India Should Fear', *The National Interest*, 28 June 2014, http://nationalinterest.org/feature/five-chinese-weapons-war-india-should-fear-10774.

20 Mizokami, Kyle, '5 Super Weapons China Would Use to Crush India in a War', *The National Interests*, 6 February 2017, http://nationalinterest.org/blog/the-buzz/5-super-weapons-china-would-use-crush-india-war-19332.

21 Nehru, Jawaharlal, India's Foreign Policy, New Delhi, 1966, p. 80.

22 Gopal, S, *Selected Works of Jawaharlal Nehru, Second Series*, Volume Five, New Delhi: JN Memorial Fund, 1987, p. 499.

23 Sardar Vallabhbhai Patel's letter to Jawaharlal Nehru on 7 November 1950, not only deploring Indian Ambassador KM Panikkar's action but also warning about dangers from China, http://www.friendsoftibet.org/main/sardar.html.

24 Subrahmanyam, K, 'Academic Contribution to National Security Policy Formulation in India', The Institute for Defence Studies and Analyses Journal, January 1969, 1 (2), p. 82.

25 Invariably these issues are identified as core in terms of India's global concerns in various statements and speeches by political leaders and foreign ministry officials. See Speech by Foreign Secretary Shivshankar Menon on 'India and International Security' at the International Institute of Strategic Studies, http://meaindia.nic.in/speech/2007/05/04ss01.htm; and 'India and the Emerging World Order', Address by Shyam Saran, Foreign Secretary of India at IISS, London, 25 May 2006.

26 Ghosh, Partha S, 'Towards a Better Understanding of Indian Islam', *Status of Islamic Studies in India: An Overview*, New Delhi: Japan Foundation, 2003, pp. 1-18. For a critical rejoinder to the article, see Shahabuddin, Syed, 'Open Letter to Dr. Partha S. Ghosh: Understanding Islam in the Modern World', *The Milli Gazette*, New Delhi, 1-15 January 2004. Also see, Ghosh, Partha S, 'Intellectuals Analyse, Extremists Penalise: Limits of Textural Explorations', *Islam in Contemporary World: Some Indian Perspectives*, New Delhi: Japan Foundation, 2004, pp. 1-14.

27 Ghosh, Partha S, 'Socio-Political Trends in Southern Asia Security Implications for India', http://www.satp.org/satporgtp/publication/faultlines/volume17/Article2.htm.

28 Ibid.

29 Ibid.

30 Pandit, Rajat, 'India Remains World's Largest Arms Importer, with 14% of Total Share', *Times of India*, 22 February 2016, http://timesofindia.indiatimes.com/india/India-remains-worlds-largest-arms-importer-with-14-of-total-share/articleshow/51095168.cms.

31 Laxman, Beharam K, '"Make in India" for Defence: A Roadmap', Institute of Defence Studies and Analyses, 5 February 2015, http://www.idsa.in/policybrief/MakeinIndiafor Defence_lbehera_050215.

32 Mathur, Dhiraj, 'Unlocking Defence R&D in India – Do We Have the Skill?', *First Post*, 8 April 2016, http://www.firstpost.com/business/unlocking-defence-rd-in-india-do-we-have-the-skill-2715650.html.

33 'China has Deployed More Troops Near Indian Border: Pentagon', *The Indian Express*, 14 May 2016, http://indianexpress.com/article/india/india-news-india/china-has-deployed-more-troops-near-indian-border-pentagon-2799965/.

34 'Pakistan Ranked 147th on HDI', The News, 26 January 2016, https://www.thenews.com.pk/print/93753-Pakistan-ranked-147th-on-HDI

35 Khan, Mubarak Zeb, 'Pakistan Rises to 122nd in Global Competitiveness Rankings', *Dawn*, 28 September 2016, https://www.dawn.com/news/1286493.

36 http://www.pewglobal.org/2012/06/27/pakistani-public-opinion-ever-more-critical-of-u-s/.

8

GRAND STRATEGY TO MITIGATE COLLUSIVE THREATS

Background

From the preceding chapters, it stands out clearly that a militarily powerful and assertive China, its growing anti-India nexus with rabidly hostile Pakistan, and their combined potential pose formidable hybrid threats to India's vital interests. Pakistan's radicalisation and proxy forces will continue to be exploited by China against India and Indian interests in Afghanistan, in India's neighbourhood, and elsewhere in the foreseeable future. The spectrum of threats encompass both, traditional threats under a nuclear overhang and hosts of non-traditional threats of asymmetric nature. A dispassionate 'Net Assessment' of India and China power balance reveals that China's Comprehensive National Power (CNP), particularly its military component, surpasses that of India and the power gap between the two countries is bound to grow. Given the strategic mistrust between the China-Pakistan combine versus India, nature of disputes, and dynamics of competition, the possibility of conflict between the two Asian giants cannot be ruled out given that both Chinese and Pakistani objectives against India are increasingly coalescing. At the same time, it must be acknowledged that China is and will continue to be the driving force against India, with Pakistan playing China's subset. India's Comprehensive National Development (CND) is predicated on sustainable peace and comprehensive security, and conflict(s) would prove regressive. It is therefore, imperative that India formulates a coherent and comprehensive strategy to deter conflicts and if conflicts become unavoidable, terminate these on favourable terms. That notwithstanding, India should be cognisant of growing power asymmetry in China's favour or by extension in China-Pakistan's, and in the light of that examine choices and explore strategies to deal with that country. While it is prudent to 'build strength and bide time', hybrid warfare is an ongoing affair which must have responses at multiple levels to enable establishing effective deterrence. It is, therefore, essential to examine the strategic nature of future conflict and evolve a strategy accordingly.

Global Strategic Trend 2040

'Global Strategic Trend 2040' is a comprehensive view of the future, produced by a research team at the Development, Concepts and Doctrine Centre (DCDC) of UK.[1] According to this study, the locus of global power will move away from the US and Europe towards Asia. This shift, coupled with the global challenges of climate change, resource scarcity, and population growth, is likely to result in a period of instability in international relations, accompanied by the possibility of intense competition between major powers. The US is likely to remain the pre-eminent military power although, in political, economic, and military terms, it is likely to be increasingly constrained as others grow in influence and confidence. However, the rise of individual states, such as China, should not be considered a certainty given the nature and magnitude of the challenges they face, nor should their eventual influence be over-estimated. There will be several states and institutions competing for regional and global influence, cooperating and competing within the international community. Distribution and access to energy, food, and freshwater resources will be uneven, and local and regional shortages will occur, increasing the likelihood of societal instability and of disagreement between states and providing the triggers that may ignite conflict.

The global defence and security implications listed in the above study, as relevant to this study, are summarised as under:

- ✓ Incidence of armed conflict is likely to increase underpinned by; an unstable transition to a multi-polar world that allows old and new state rivalries to emerge; widespread global inequality that heightens associated grievances; population increases; resource scarcity; and the adverse effects of climate change that combine to increase instability and the increased importance of ideology.
- ✓ Future conflict will remain unpredictable and violent. Its character will continue to evolve and present new challenges. While technology will remain important, people are likely to provide the asymmetric edge when responding to both expected and unexpected challenges, if invested in and empowered through decentralisation.
- ✓ The differences between state, state-sponsored and non-state adversaries will blur. The range of threats will diversify, as technology and innovation opens up novel avenues of attack and adaptive adversaries exploit opportunities.
- ✓ Soft power will increasingly be utilised to facilitate the achievement of political goals. All elements of power are likely to be wielded by a broader spectrum of actors and agencies, including organised criminal, terrorist and

insurgent groups; degree of combining hard and soft power as effective statecraft will determine ability to achieve strategic objectives. It is unlikely that the military instrument alone will be decisive.

- ✓ The chemical, biological, radiological and nuclear (CBRN) threat from state and non-state actors is likely to increase; terrorist attacks using chemical, biological and radiological weapons are likely, as are mass-casualty attacks using novel methods. The likelihood of nuclear weapons usage will increase.
- ✓ Multilateral military activity to protect globalisation, including protection of global supply chains and space-based infrastructure from physical and virtual disruption, is likely.
- ✓ The changing balance of power is likely to deter military intervention by major powers outside their spheres of influence; when intervention becomes unavoidable, actors will seek to distance themselves by use of proxy forces, cyber-attack, as well as covert and clandestine methods. Persistent complex problems will require the integration of all levers of state power, both across government and among partners and allies.
- ✓ There will be an increasing range of political, legal, ethical and financial imperatives to build relationships with like-minded partners.
- ✓ Control and access to hydrocarbons will remain important and major powers are likely to use their defence forces to safeguard supplies. Conflicts over food and water resources are possible.
- ✓ Climate change will amplify existing social, political and resource stresses, shifting the tipping point at which conflict ignites, rather than directly causing it. Climate change is likely to increase the frequency, scale and duration of humanitarian crises. It is also likely to change patterns of migration, making border security an ongoing concern, especially in the developed world.
- ✓ Support to states suffering from instability will require interoperability between a wide range of joint and coalition military forces, other arms of state, and non-state actors, including international institutions, NGOs and contractors.
- ✓ Conflict will remain focused on influencing adversaries, neutrals and those at home, whose perceptions will be vital.
- ✓ Radicalisation, extremism and terrorism will continue to generate threats. Network technologies will provide new opportunities for group formation. Many threats will operate trans-nationally, requiring ongoing cooperation and multinational interoperability between security services to provide an effective response.

- ✓ Potential adversaries, both state and non-state, will leverage high-technology niche capabilities and employ innovative concepts of operation. Regional powers armed with precision-guided missiles and anti-access technologies, such as submarines and sophisticated surface-to-air missiles, will make traditional power projection strategies more costly.
- ✓ Advances in robotics, cognitive science coupled with powerful computing, sensors, energy efficiency, and nano-technology will combine to produce rapid improvements in the capabilities of combat systems.
- ✓ Defence production is likely to become increasingly internationalised and most states will lack guaranteed access to industrial surge capacity during times of escalating tension. Weapons themselves are likely to become more portable, more widely available and easier to use.
- ✓ Increasing dependence on Information and Communications Technology (ICT) and reliance on space-based assets to receive or transmit information across the electromagnetic spectrum will maintain the importance of cyber security. Cyberspace will be widely exploited by all types of actors, but the effects of their actions are likely to vary. Attribution, intent, and legitimacy of cyber-attacks will all be disputed.
- ✓ Strategic shocks will occur, although their character and detail remain unpredictable. Complex interconnected and interdependent systems will be subject to systemic risk and the potential of cascading failures.
- ✓ Success in future conflict, especially against adaptive and agile adversaries, will require a shift away from kinetic to influence activity, underpinned by a greater understanding of the enemy. This understanding will require more emphasis on intelligence gathering, cultural awareness, individual and collective training, and focused comprehensive approaches.

Lessons from Global Strategic Trend

Closer examination of 'Strategic Trend 2040' has following major lessons for India: (1) war is no longer exclusive military affair; (2) war is dirty without any rules and uses total comprehensive national power; (3) India has been at war all these years even as the political hierarchy perceives conventional conflict as war and (4) conventional forces and diplomacy are no match against hybrid warfare. India has been following a foreign policy based in idealism while a cross-section believes that idealism has no place in making of foreign policy. But the argument is not that idealism should not be a stand-alone factor, but that the costs of always following an inward-looking policy may be that much higher, which is what India has been following. Therefore, the most effective foreign policy for any country, whatever its weight, is one that balances realism and idealism—that in effect makes idealism realistic.[2] But if idealism has its limits, the substitute is not a unidimensional brand of foreign policy realism either. A foreign policy that is founded only on hard-headed realism is a policy that can all too readily descend into cynical indifference, with results that may not be palatable later. Successful foreign policy options that are exercised have a necessity to reflect domestic opinion and must be based on a principled and judicious mixture of both, idealism and realism.[3]

Grand Strategy Options for India

Closer examination of 'Strategic Trends 2040' and the rapidly changing global dynamics, particularly in South Asia, leads to the following analysis:

- ✓ Hybrid war is the new normal and will remain so in foreseeable future.
- ✓ Coping with hybrid wars in conventional manner combined with diplomacy is not sufficient.
- ✓ The China-Pakistan anti-India nexus is set to expand.
- ✓ China's noose of 'string of pearls' is tightening with PLAN vessels and marines posted in ports of Indian Ocean.
- ✓ In addition to PLA, Chinese weapon platforms would be deployed in POK starting with Gwadar and GB.
- ✓ With Russia having joined China's orbit, possibility of PLA tank divisions moving to POK on pretext of guarding CPEC and Gwadar Port cannot be ruled out, all bridges along CPEC built for tanks passage being one indication.
- ✓ India may not be full military alliance partner of the US but the attendant circumstances on which the US-India Strategic Partnership evolved was the 'China Threat' factor which cannot be denied.[4]
- ✓ The new US-China tussles for supremacy is concomitant to India's military imperative for upgrading its war preparedness and to fill the voids in its military inventory.
- ✓ China can be expected to use India as a pressure point against the US even without any military provocation since China feels best to first target countries close to USA like Japan and India.[5]
- ✓ China's challenge to India gets magnified with the China-Pakistan axis getting substantially reinforced as a result of geopolitical changes China views adversely. With Chinese support, Pakistan would adopt more provocative and adversarial postures against India.
- ✓ India needs to realise that the 'Pakistan Threat' to India in recent years is

being fuelled more by China. China is the major, potent and long-range threat to India; hence, no scope exists for Indian diplomacy to dilute the 'China Threat' and the now China-added 'Pakistan Threat' to India.[6]

✓ The US would continue to be the pre-eminent military power in future and can be expected to contest China's rise that go against US national interests. To this end, it is likely to employ hybrid means to stymie Chinese expansionism without conventional 'boots on ground', less the high seas.

A key lesson for Russia from the use of force in both Ukraine and Syria is that these actions have brought Moscow back to the diplomatic top table. For Moscow, this underscored the utility of military force as a coercive tool.[7] The messaging apparent in its employment of military power, meanwhile, met its narrative of a once-again powerful state able to deploy capabilities previously only held by the West. One concern for the international community lies in how this attitude towards the use of force may be perceived by other states, and whether it may embolden them to deploy military force. There is also a risk for the West in terms of whether its responses are sufficiently firm or united. China, watching the power play in Ukraine and being a backdoor participant in Syria, is employing a more subtle way of employing military force, as is visible in POK, particularly in the Gwadar Port.

There is no doubt that strategic determinants of India's foreign policy would tend to dominate the economic determinants albeit India already is an economic power and an attractive destination for FDI. But given the evolving threat scenario, exercising strategic restraint in the asymmetric and hybrid arena would be detrimental to our national interests. India already figures substantially in the geopolitical calculus of major powers as never before. There is the issue of the US-Pakistan relationship but given that US is also friend of Iraq, what has happened to the latter is for the world to see. India also needs to meet the challenge in devising diplomatic initiatives to offset Russia's tilt to Pakistan and creating a complex strategic challenge for India in South Asia. Given all the considerations discussed herein, the plausible strategic choices that India has are as follows:

✓ **Option I: Concentrate on Economy and Development**. India needs to develop and become economically strong. However, we have a volatile neighbourhood, including China and Pakistan that have developed an anti-India nexus. In addition, there are insurgent groups within India that are being externally supported and armed. Successive Indian Prime Ministers have been stating that there is enough space for India and China to grow together but ironically China believes there cannot be 'two suns', and therefore aims to limit India's strategic space and, consequentially, economic rise.

- ✓ **Option II: Stronger Bonding with America**. The Indo-US strategic partnership could have been exploited but for the unreliability of the US, going by past history. To top this, President Trump himself is proving to be quite unpredictable. Moreover, the support to Pakistan by the US administration, including the CIA, has not undergone 'much' change. America's stance on Iran too is hardening which may adversely affect India's Chahabar project, linking Chahabar with Afghanistan and beyond with the International North-South Transportation Corridor (INSTC). Even defence manufacture collaboration with the US has the danger of sanctions at the critical moment in the future. In addition to the unreliable track record and ambiguous policy of US, it is not likely to adequately address the China-Pakistan anti-India nexus. Therefore, this option has inherent dangers.
- ✓ **Option III: Weaken and Balkanise Pakistan**. The success of this option would be strategically advantageous to India, including possibly opening the land route to Afghanistan and facilitating operationalisation of the TAPI and IPI pipelines. However, China, US and Saudi Arabia will likely oppose such a move. Besides, such an option cannot be executed by India alone even with limited support of Afghanistan and Iran. Most importantly, given the Chinese strategic interests in Pakistan, this will result in more assertiveness/aggression by China.
- ✓ **Option IV: Establish Multiple Deep Coalitions, Retain Strategic Autonomy**. This strategic choice is predicated on the core belief that the US and allies plus strategic partners are concerned about the China-Pakistan-North Korea axis, Chinese expansionism in Indo-Pacific, and without going to war would like to neutralise such threat, even through controlled implosions in these countries without damaging western and global economies. The question remains whether the US and its allies will allow China free run to the Arabian Sea through Pakistan. The Al Qaeda was raised to deny Soviets in Afghanistan an oceanic front. In this case too, high instability could be engineered through sub-conventional forces. The current US move to destabilise Iran and the killing of Chinese nationals by ISIS (CIA sponsored?) in Baluchistan perhaps are indicative of this. However, in the cost–benefit analysis, the points that merit critical examination are: (1) will the US and allies make such a move without attracting blame, timing of such move, and is the emergence of ISIS in Af-Pak already sign of this; (2) will China be deterred from such move and seek rapprochement with India, or, will China's hostility to India rise since India and Afghanistan will invariable draw blame; (3) will US risk its relations with China if there is a

standoff between India and China? While disrupting the China-Pakistan nexus is in India's interest, India's role in such move in partnership with US and allies, and strategic partners will, out of necessity, have to be highly discreet, covert and totally ambiguous. In this option, India should develop 'deep coalitions' with the US and its allies and strategic partners, East Asian and ASEAN countries, Russia and Central Asian Republic(s) to further its own national interests, in addition to making determined effort to develop CNP and attain credible deterrence while interlocking combining collaborative security and economic interests. This is essentially a co-optive strategy without disturbing the Indo-US Strategic Partnership. While for a rising India, this should be a preferred choice, the key determinants common to all choices are CND, proactive diplomacy and credible deterrence. These elements are elucidated in the recommended strategic response.

Recommended Grand Strategy

> **The arrow shot by an archer may or may not kill a single person; but intrigue, devised by wise men, may even kill those who are in the womb.**
>
> ***—Chanakya***

Developing 'Establishing Deep Coalitions (at multiple levels) while Retaining Strategic Autonomy' should be the preferred strategic response for India without affecting the growing India-US partnership and strategic partnerships with other countries. Continued engagement with Russia too is important, which appears to be happening already in some measure with engagements at various levels: discussions on joint development of the Fifth Generation Fighter Aircraft (FGFA), though stalled temporarily; joint production of Kamov helicopters under 'Make in India'; visits of Prime Minister (PM) and the National Security Advisor (NSA) to Russia; visit of Russian Naval Chief to India, Russia inviting India for six-nation talks on Afghanistan and India's participation in the Six Plus One talks on Afghanistan being some examples. As for the overall strategic response, the key determinants common to all choices are CND, proactive diplomacy and credible deterrence.

Asymmetric warfare threats can manifest against entire political, social, military and financial fabric of the country. Targets could be anything: nuclear facilities, dignitaries, mass transit systems, harbours, military institutions and installations, religious and public places, demographic invasion, ethnic cleansing, financial institutions, support to anti-nationals, electronic and cyber warfare, drugs, counterfeit currency, etc. Not many are aware that in 1950s, China covertly introduced a particular strain of African locust in Ladakh that wiped out the entire crop in the region. Hence, requisite responses need to be developed with effective military strategy to include environment of high-intensity insurgency, militancy, and terrorism. This warrants re-orientation and a shift of emphasis from predictability to surprise; conventional threats to multiple complex challenges; nation state threats to networked non-state/state-sponsored adversaries; conventional deterrence to tailored deterrence; reactive to preventive to proactive action; crisis response to shaping the environment; threat based to capability based; routine planning to rapid adaptability; static defence to mobile expeditionary operations; battle ready to battle hardened; single/multi-service to multi-agency; vertical structure to horizontal integration; input (efforts) to output (results) and military response to inter-agency response.

Non-traditional threats, through sub-conventional warfare, are far greater than conventional and the entire society is likely to be the battlefield. Therefore, there is need to identify objectives for application of national power, assigning specific role, tasks and resources to deal with this complex issue which has little visibility. The need to have appropriate apex for control requires is vital. Response to an asymmetric threat has two facets: defensive and offensive (proactive). Defensive measures imply identifying the threat and instituting measures to negate the same so that the enemy is not able to exploit them. But the most effective method of fighting asymmetric war is offensive (proactive) approach: effective placement of measures in advance, which can be activated when considered necessary. The cardinal rules for countering asymmetric threats are as follows: all means military or non-military can be employed, preferably latter; employ unlimited means against limited objective; proactive action at multiple plains; avoid strengths of adversary and strike soft targets; objectives selected should create huge psychological impact; organisation to command multidimensionality and content adjustments and regain control of the whole process. The instruments of response available are diplomacy, intelligence agencies, law enforcement organisations, conventional forces and special forces. The latter are being employed world over to optimise national interests, as force multipliers to state power, and as deterrence. It also must be understood that credibility of deterrence can only be established through selective demonstration. The planes available for forging asymmetric war on the adversary are diplomatic warfare, financial warfare, resource warfare, electronic warfare, cyber warfare, 4GW, ideological warfare, etc.

In hybrid warfare, adversary perceptions are a function of three variables[8]: (1) who the adversary is, identity, values, fears, aspirations, goals, objectives, strategy, doctrine, and capabilities; (2) decision over which influence and deterrence is desired, for example, whether they would use nuclear weapons and (3) circumstances in which the decision is being made. Deterrence activities must be dynamic as also reactive (quid pro quo), because adversary perceptions will shift over time. This is quite complex because of growth in the range and nature of the threats and challenges that deterrence planning needs to accommodate. The rise of non-state/state–sponsored non-state threats, less discrete and immediately attributable capabilities (including biological, cyber and information/influence capabilities) and deliberately asymmetric doctrine and operations at the state level all combine to skew and complicate the relative comfort of balanced nuclear deterrence.[9] In attempting to deter adversaries, the most problematic targets for alliances are non-state actors. Their values, objectives and means differ from those of state actors, while they might not possess the physical dependencies that make states more susceptible to deterrence messaging and influence. Apart from the straightforward challenge of determining exactly who these groups are, their lack of identifiable structure brings greater uncertainty over how their decision-makers perceive the costs, benefits, and consequences of restraint regarding the actions to be deterred; there is undoubtedly a significant asymmetry in the stakes that either side may perceive. These actors also differ markedly in their susceptibility to efforts to credibly threaten to impose costs on their behaviours. In contrast to traditional state actors, deterrence of non-state actors is frustrated by an almost total lack of well-established means of communication between them and the state wishing to deter them. They are also the most threatening to the social fabric of those they oppose and they are probably the least threatened by traditional high-end military deterrence.

The aim of our grand strategy should focus on the following, for which deep coalitions would be of vital assistance:

- ✓ Unhindered economic growth.
- ✓ Maintain territorial integrity.
- ✓ Avoid conventional conflict as far as possible.
- ✓ Create deterrence against and weaken China-Pak nexus.
- ✓ Protect Indian interests abroad including in Afghanistan.
- ✓ Deter Chinese Naval bases coming up in IOR.
- ✓ Open land access to Afghanistan-CAR.
- ✓ Cripple China's aggressive moves by forcing it to look inwards in conjunction with strategic partners.
- ✓ Emerge as a global economically and militarily strong nation.
- ✓ Generate effective global response to nuclear terrorism.
- ✓ Protect SLOCs and freedom of Global Commons.

In developing deep coalitions to deter irregular warfare and use of proxies by

China and Pakistan against India, the problem areas that remain are as follows: (1) US so far had not bothered to target Pakistan-sponsored terrorist organizations like Lashkar-e-Taiba (LeT) and JEM that have been undertaking terror attacks against India, and now in Afghanistan too. This despite Ashley Tellis recommending to the US in 2012 that 'the only reasonable objective for the United States in this context must be the permanent evisceration of these groups (terrorist groups based in Pakistan) specially al-Qaeda and LeT, which threaten American interests directly, with Pakistani cooperation if possible, but without it if necessary', pointing out that it would be gross error to treat terrorism facing India as simply a problem for New Delhi alone, and that the LeT leadership has on numerous occasions singled out the Jewish community and the United States as being among the natural enemies of Islam;[10] (2) because of instability, Myanmar has not acted against northeastern insurgent camps based in Myanmar; (3) there has been global inaction against the China-Taliban nexus despite Taliban being all Muslims and Chinese genocide in Xinjiang; (4) similarly, China has created a lethal proxy in the all Buddhist United Wa State Army despite its genocide in Tibet and suppression of Tibetan culture and (5) purported Russian and Iranian support to Afghanistan that could be inimical to Indian interests.

Notwithstanding the above, the US and allies can hardly ignore the strategic implications of Chinese entry into Pakistan including Gwadar and Jiwani, and in Maldives coming up as PLAN SSBN bases, and China establishing oceanic front(s) in the IOR. China has numerous targetable vulnerabilities where pressure can be applied while Pakistan has so many vulnerabilities that one can literally pick and choose. The China-Pakistan-North Korea axis poses so much threat to the West that they are unlikely to remain bystanders, even as war would be avoided. That is where deep coalitions will be beneficial to India, simultaneous to progressing own CND.

Focus Areas of Grand Strategy

While detailed policy recommendations are given in the next chapter, focus areas for developing the recommended strategic response are as under:

- ✓ Define a comprehensive National Security Strategy (NSS).
- ✓ Undertake Comprehensive Defence Review (CDR).
- ✓ Enunciate clear policy to deal with the China-Pakistan nexus.
- ✓ Revamping national security architecture and higher defence organisations.
- ✓ Initiate all-inclusive military jointness.
- ✓ Streamline national security planning process.

- ✓ Effective mitigation of internal security challenges.
- ✓ Build requisite cyber warfare capability.
- ✓ Effective border control.
- ✓ Develop credible deterrence for collusive hybrid threats.
- ✓ Maximise influence in strategic neighbourhood.
- ✓ Develop multiple deep coalitions (not necessarily in conjunction with same countries) that would
  - ➢ Deter and weaken China-Pak nexus.
  - ➢ Exploit China-Pakistan fault lines.
  - ➢ Deter Pakistan from generating terror.
  - ➢ Stabilize Afghanistan and counter Pakistan's proxy war.
  - ➢ Protect Indian interests in Afghanistan and elsewhere.
  - ➢ Open land access to Afghanistan-CAR.
  - ➢ Deter PLAN bases in IOR.
  - ➢ Protect SLOCs and freedom of Global Commons.
  - ➢ Controlled implosion of China to deter its aggression.
  - ➢ Establish declared global response to nuclear terrorism.
  - ➢ Develop 'Assassin Mace' weapons and collective response to China.

Key Issues

- ✓ *Militarily powerful and assertive China, its growing anti-India nexus with rabidly hostile Pakistan and their combined potential pose formidable hybrid threats to India's vital interests.*
- ✓ *Given the China-Pakistan strategic mistrust with India, possibility of conflict cannot be ruled given coalescing objectives of China and Pakistan.*
- ✓ *Imperative for India to formulate strategy to deter conflicts, and if unavoidable, terminate these on favourable terms.*
- ✓ *Global Strategic Trend 2040 point to increase in unpredictable, violent armed conflicts; blurring of state, state-sponsored and non-state adversaries; novel methods of attack exploiting technology; more use of soft power; increased CBRN threat; indirect intervention through proxy forces, cyber-attack, covert means; continuing radicalisation, extremism and terrorism and success in future conflict requiring shift from kinetic to influence activity based on greater understanding of enemy, in turn requiring better intelligence gathering, cultural awareness, individual and collective training, focused comprehensive approaches.*
- ✓ *India has been at war all these years albeit political hierarchy perceives conventional conflict as war.*

- ✓ *Conventional forces and diplomacy is no match to hybrid war.*
- ✓ *India's foreign policy based in idealism but costs of inward-looking policy are that much higher.*
- ✓ *US-China tussles for supremacy is concomitant to India's military imperative for upgrading its war preparedness and to fill the voids in its military inventory.*
- ✓ *China can use India as pressure point against US even without military provocation.*
- ✓ *US can be expected to counter Chinese expansionism without conventional 'boots on ground'.*
- ✓ *Developing 'Deep Coalitions to offset the China-Pakistan Nexus' at multiple levels should be the preferred strategic response for India without affecting existing strategic partnerships.*
- ✓ *Aim of India's grand strategy should be unhindered economic growth; retain territorial integrity; avoid conventional conflict as far as possible; create deterrence against and weaken China-Pak nexus; protect Indian interests in Afghanistan and elsewhere; deter Chinese naval bases in IOR; open land access to Afghanistan-CAR; cripple China's aggressive moves by forcing it to look inwards; generate effective global response to nuclear terrorism and protect SLOCs.*

NOTES

1 'Global Strategic Trends – Out to 2040', Development, Concepts and Doctrine Centre (DCDC), Ministry of Defence, Government of UK, https://www.gov.uk/government/uploads/system/uploads/attachment_data/file/33717/GST4_v9_Feb10.pdf.

2 Kalha, Ranjit Singh, 'The Dynamics of Preventive Diplomacy', New Delhi: KW Publishers, 2014.

3 Ibid.

4 Kapila, Subhash, 'India's Foreign Policy Challenges 2017 Analysed', South Asia Analysis Group, Paper No. 6205, 16 December 2016, http://www.southasiaanalysis.org/node/2100.

5 Ibid.

6 Ibid.

7 'Russia's Use of Military Force as a Foreign Policy Tool: Is There a Logic?' http://www.ponarseurasia.org/node/8728.

8 IISS Military Balance 2017.

9 Ibid.

10 Tellis, Ashley, 'The Menace That is Lashkar-e-Taiba', Carnegie Endowment for International Peace, 13 March 2012.

9

POLICY RECOMMENDATIONS

Do not be very upright in your dealings for you would see by going to the forest that straight trees are cut down while crooked ones are left standing.

—Chanakya

India's pre-eminence in the region is critical to its status as an Asian power and an important global player. However, India faces a number of internal and external challenges which, if not addressed, will seriously impact the country's vital interests. Domestically, the next decade can truly be described as the 'decade of risks; to steer India towards sustainable growth aligned with the aspirations of its people; socio-economic fault lines and low Human Development Index (HDI) being major issues that need to be addressed. Economic well-being, access to energy resources, sufficiency of water, and technological advancement are some of the key attributes of Comprehensive National Development (CND). India continues to face the rising spectre of LWE, simmering insurgencies, proxy wars, and pan-India terrorism (including nuclear terrorism), thus making internal security a formidable challenge. India's volatile neighbourhood further complicates India's national security calculus. China's economic and military rise, growing assertion at the LAC, forays into South Asia and IOR, strategic nexus with Pakistan including military cooperation, gravitational pull towards other South Asian countries are some other critical drivers with potential to alter the strategic balance in South Asia to India's disadvantage. Adding to the alarming scenario is growing nuclear proliferation in terms of Pakistan's rapidly expanding nuclear capabilities, both in terms of fissile materials and delivery means. Situation is further exacerbated by attempts at miniaturisation to field TNWs which will result in lowering the thresholds and increasing instability. China on the other hand is not only modernising its nuclear forces but remains ambiguous about its 'no first use' doctrine. The aggravating Pakistan-Afghanistan scenario looms large on India's security landscape and would need to be addressed in a proactive and comprehensive manner to hedge India not only against the spill-over of violence but also safeguard other strategic interests in the region.

Imponderables

The US policy on Af-Pak has been ambiguous. Pakistan has been the recipient of US largesse all along but the Chinaisation of Pakistan should logically not be taken kindly, especially when it has strategic ramifications for the Straits of Hormuz with the Chinese bases at Gwadar and Jiwani. The US-China strategic brinkmanship will dominate the course and complexion of transformational world order, besides, given the US-China economic embrace, it is unlikely that they would risk a military confrontation or adopt a confrontationist strategic stance that harms their mutual interests. However, it is unlikely that the West will permit China free run to the Indian Ocean through Pakistan, hybrid wars being the flavour to contain the influence of opposing powers in the Great Game—as is happening in Afghanistan. US President Donald Trump has proposed a $54 billion increase in Defence spending, one of the largest increases in American history. The main reason obviously is China, even as US focus remains on retaining naval superiority in the South China Sea. HJ Mackinder in his article 'The Geographical Pivot of History' in the *Geographical Journal* wrote, 'Chinese might constitute the yellow peril to the world's freedom, just because they would add an oceanic frontage to the resources of the great continent, an advantage as yet denied to the Russian tenant of the pivot region'.[1] More recently, Robert D Kaplan in his book *The Revenge of Geography* has said, 'Pressure on land can help the United States thwart China at Sea'.[2] This is where hybrid war becomes relevant. The Taliban was created by the US to oust the Soviets from Afghanistan, simultaneous to Al Qaeda in Afghanistan through the US-Saudi-ISI nexus for similar reason. There is much more to the US policy than what meets the eye. Very significantly, a leaked 2004 classified US document titled 'Mapping the Global Future' exposes the 'Caliph Project 2020', that was enacted through Baghdadi, even as Baghdadi is being hunted today by the US[3].

An article in 2014 exposed secret decisions taken at a NATO summit in Newport to prevent not only Russia and China but, also India from continuing their development and that NATO could count on terrorism from the Islamic Emirate (read ISIS) which it pretends to condemn and fight.[4] But that was in 2014 and the US-India equation has undergone major change since then, in the backdrop of China's spectre threatening the Indo-Pacific, with new focus on the IOR particularly, the Arabian Sea. Pakistan, backed by China, seeking strategic depth in Afghanistan is increasing instability in Afghanistan; as per the Special Inspector General for Afghanistan Reconstruction (SIGAR), by end 2016, Afghan government was controlling only 57.2 per cent of Afghan territory, with a 6 per cent decrease from the previous year albeit Afghan government has rubbished the said report.[5] The refocusing of Al Qaeda and ISIS to Af-Pak region, therefore, should be viewed in context of moves by the West to contain the influence of China, Russia and Iran, with trapped Pakistan walking the fine line. This provides a window where Indian interests coalesce with those of the West, notwithstanding the fact that Pakistan's ISI is linked with the ISIS and organisations like the Lashkar-e-Jhangvi (LeJ), who are apparently operating in synch.

But in the event of any conflict between India and China, the US is unlikely to come to direct aid of India even as US seeks stronger strategic alliance with India to balance China. But this does not imply that the common aim of negating the China threat stands diluted and cannot be leveraged. India should leverage this unique opportunity to broaden and deepen its strategic partnership with the US in trade for high-end defence and dual-use technology. We should, however, be upfront with the US that India would cooperate with the US in consonance with its national interests and spirit of strategic autonomy.

Reports about Iranian support to Taliban need to be taken with a pinch of salt since Iran had always been in support of the erstwhile Northern Alliance in Afghanistan, particularly the Hazaras who are Shias. If it is engaging Taliban, it is perhaps only to keep them talking and oust the US-NATO from Afghanistan, which Iran too would want. At the same time hostility between Iran and Pakistan, because of Pakistan's proxies and targeting Shias, is very much alive. As recent as March 2017, Iranian border security forces reportedly fired rocket and mortar shells into Pakistan, for which there must have been a good reason.[6] Iran is also wary of Taliban, Haqqanis, Al Qaeda and ISIS in Af-Pak region, all of them being Sunni radical organisations, which have no compunctions in killing Shias. Similarly, Russian leaning towards Pakistan and Taliban need to be viewed in context of (1) partial capture of Kunduz was perhaps CIA engineered which alarmed Russia forcing it to double its military deployment in Tajikistan; (2) increasing economic sanctions against Afghanistan and lack of US-Russia rapprochement despite the Trump administration forced Russia sell weapon platforms to Pakistan; (3) engagement with Taliban is perhaps to assist them get control of more Afghan territory but spare Central Asia; (4) China has obviously coaxed Russia to join hands in evicting US-NATO from Afghanistan; (5) Russia is conscious of Al Qaeda and ISIS being refocused to Af-Pak and the reasons thereof, and is already wary of the Islamic Movement of Uzbekistan (IMU) aligned with ISIS and (6) Russia has always been wary of Pakistani support to Islamic radicals in Chechnya, and perhaps is engaging Pakistan akin to 'pest control'. But all this does not imply that the Indo-Russian relationship is no more strategically important and given the right impetus cannot grow.

Aim of Grand Strategy

The grand strategy option for India in developing multiple deep coalitions while retaining autonomy has been discussed in the previous chapter. The aim of this grand strategy should include the following:

- ✓ Unhindered economic growth.
- ✓ Maintain territorial integrity.
- ✓ Avoid conventional conflict, as possible.
- ✓ Create deterrence against and weaken China-Pak nexus.
- ✓ Protect Indian interests abroad including in Afghanistan.
- ✓ Open land access to Afghanistan-CAR.
- ✓ Protect SLOCs and freedom of Global Commons.
- ✓ Cripple China's aggressive moves by forcing it to look inwards in conjunction strategic partners.
- ✓ Generate effective global response to nuclear terrorism.
- ✓ Emerge as a global economic and militarily strong nation.

Focus Areas for Strategic Response

The focus areas for India's strategic response to the China-Pakistan hybrid war have been summarised in Chapter 8 as given below:

- ✓ Define a comprehensive National Security Strategy (NSS).
- ✓ Undertake Comprehensive Defence Review (CDR).
- ✓ Enunciate clear policy to deal with the China-Pakistan nexus.
- ✓ Revamping national security architecture and higher defence organisations.
- ✓ Initiate all-inclusive military jointness.
- ✓ Streamline national security planning process.
- ✓ Effective mitigation of internal security challenges.
- ✓ Build requisite cyber warfare capability.
- ✓ Effective border control.
- ✓ Develop credible deterrence for collusive hybrid threats.
- ✓ Maximise influence in strategic neighbourhood.

As soon as the fear approaches near, attack and destroy it.

—Chanakya

This quote by Chanakya aptly describes the China-Pakistan threat that is looming large and the need for a proactive response by India, shedding strategic restraint. Globally, the Indo-Pacific is witnessing a power shift with ensuing strategic brinkmanship between the US and China. India has an opportunity to leverage its status as a strategic swing state and enhance its own image and status. In this strategic milieu, it therefore becomes incumbent for policy maker to develop a comprehensive strategy to ensure that India successfully develops Comprehensive National Power (CNP), through sustained development, astute diplomacy, and effective deterrence. Strategic configuration of CNP will enable India to consolidate its pre-eminence in the region and extend its sphere of influence in the extended strategic neighbourhood. To have a favourable strategic balance in the region, India needs internal consolidation, be the anchor of regional economic integration, and provider of net security and international capability by strong deterrence. To achieve these goals, salient aspects required in achieving CND, diplomacy, and deterrence are elucidated in the succeeding paragraphs.

Comprehensive National Development

Concurrent to addressing comprehensive national security (including military security, political security, economic security, food security, health security, personal security, community security, energy security, and environmental security), India needs to go from the current 7 per cent economic growth to the sustained 10 per cent growth, in order to catch up with China's CND. This will require big bang economic and governance reforms, in which India continues to lag. Despite the push by the Prime Minister, we still have not progressed much in facilitating 'ease of business'. Innovation and Ingenuity must be optimised to fuel growth through projects like 'Make in India', 'Digital India', 'Skill India', and 'Start Ups'. For internal stability, de-radicalisation and political consolidation in Kashmir must be given top priority. For resolving the Maoists issue, reclaiming of the Dandakaranya Forest in the Tribal Corridor is also a must. Similarly, the security and development of our Northeast region must be aligned with India's Act East Policy. India must concentrate on integration and synergy of all instruments of national power.

National Security Architecture

Higher Defence Organisation (HDO). Our defence organisations are not well integrated, be it the inclusion of Service Chiefs in the Cabinet Committee on Security (CCS), representation of high-calibre service officers in the National Security Council Secretariat (NSCS), functioning of National Security Advisory Board (NSAB), Strategic Planning Group (SPG), Nuclear Command Authority (NCA), Ministry of Defence (MoD), and the three Services. Ironically, none of the operational commands of the three Services are co-located. There is an intra- and inter-politico-bureaucratic-military disconnect which does not augur well for security and development of the country. A detailed review and restructuring of our Higher

Defence Organisation is overdue. Allocation of Business (AOB) and Transaction of Business (TOB) Rules 1961 of Government of India must be amended. Participation of the Service Chiefs in the CCS and selected military officers in NSCS, NSAB, SPG, and MoD must be effected as indicated in the following Revamped National Security Architecture (see Figure 9.1).

Figure 9.1: Revamp National Security Architecture
(Review Allocation of Business & Transaction of Business Rules Act 1962)
(Service Chiefs must be part of CCS)

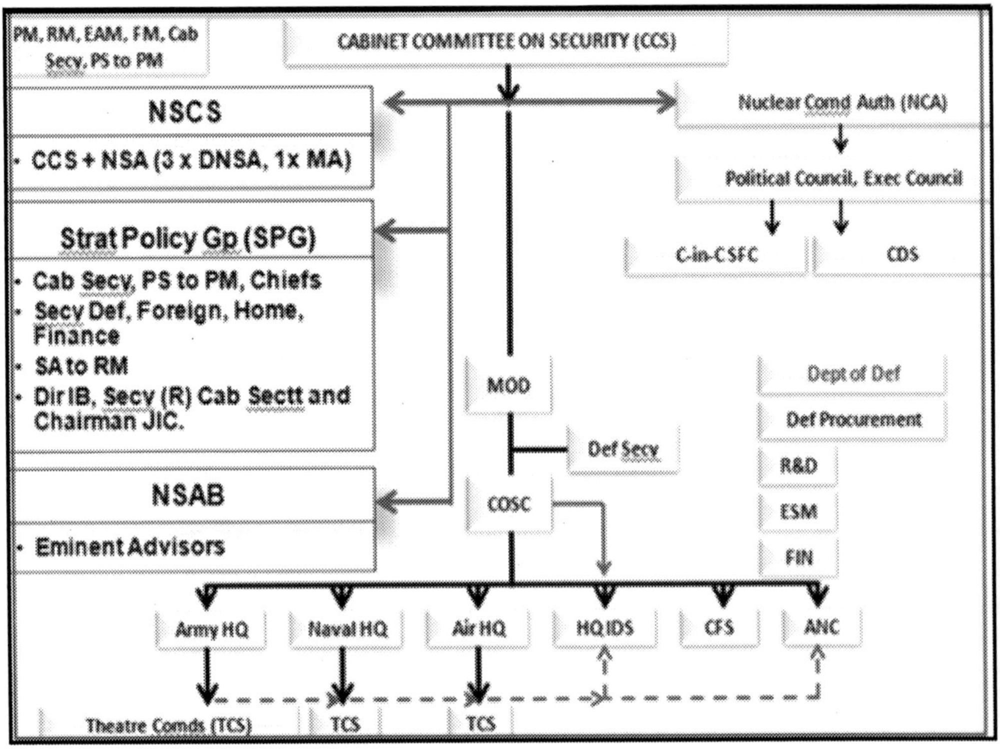

Streamlining National Security Planning Process

HQ Integral Defence Staff (IDS) has enunciated a six-step strategy for developing a long-term Tri-service force structure and capabilities as follows, which needs to be implemented:

- ✓ **Stage 1: Articulation of a National Security Strategy**. The starting point of the process is the articulation of the NSS. This broad-based document would draw inspiration from national core values and interests and provide the guidelines to various ministries to formulate policies and strategies.

- ✓ **Stage 2: Formulation of Defence Planning Guidelines**. The NSS will set the stage for the formulation of the Defence Planning Guidelines (DPG) which would address the National Aim, National Security Interests, National Security Objectives and other impellers of Defence Policy. The document leads to the specifics of National Defence Strategy as well as the National Military Strategy.
- ✓ **Stage 3: Formulation of a Defence Capability Strategy**. Formulation of Defence Capability Strategy will identify the capabilities required for the assigned roles of the armed forces. It would also suggest as to how, the forces intend to provide a flexible suite of capabilities within the planned financial outlay and governmental priorities.
- ✓ **Stage 4: Preparation of a Defence Capability Plan**. Defence Capability Plan would be the road map for the development of future capabilities of armed forces over a fifteen-year horizon.
- ✓ **Stage 5: Preparation of LTIPP**. The end product of the whole process would be the Long Term Integrated Perspective Plans (LTIPP) spanning over three 5-year plans. These plans should be finalised at HQ IDS and not merely stitched together without any meaningful intervention. LTIPP should be approved by the CCS for assured budgetary allocation.
- ✓ **Step 6: Preparation of Joint Military Strategy**. The Armed Forces should earnestly shed off their Services biases and work towards formulations of comprehensive joint military strategy at the national and theatre level. Once a joint military strategy is in place, the infructuous debate of which resource should be under whom and how it should be utilized will get resolved.

National Security Strategy (NSS). In pursuance of the enunciated vision, as the first and foremost step, National Security Council (NSC) should formulate a comprehensive National Security Strategy (NSS) which should encapsulate inter alia India's core values and beliefs, vital national interests and objectives and, economic policy, governance, foreign policy, science and technology, and defence policy etc. The strategy should clearly integrate ends, means, and ways for promotion of national interests. Our strategic planning should graduate from linear thinking to 360 degree horizon scan based on the process of 'Net Assessment', 'Scenario Building' and systematic approach to formulation of strategy. The planning staff in the Services and various ministries should be imparted formal training in this field. With regard to perspective planning in the Services, a five-step approach should be adopted.

Jointmanship

Jointmanship should be the overarching concept that provides the glue for integrating strategic vision, intelligence, thinking, planning, training and execution at national level and within the Services. Not only is the Ministry of Defence without military professionals, it has a major void in not having institutionalized set up for strategic policy formulation, which should be overcome by merging HQ IDS with MoD. This in fact was the premise on which HQ IDS was raised. The Chief of Defence Staff (CDS) should be appointed at the earliest and the raising of Unified Commands (Cyber Command, Aerospace Command, Special Forces Command, Joint Logistics Command, Joint Training and Doctrine Command, etc.) should be reviewed and decisions taken. The seminal work in producing joint military doctrines, strategy and concepts must be undertaken under aegis of HQ IDS and implemented by the Services in letter and spirit. It is time that we produce a comprehensive Information Warfare and Asymmetric Warfare doctrine. Crisis and conflict management require better integration of various organs of the government, the military and the non-mainstream elements. Led by the NSC, the policy-making processes should integrate the military and non-military components of national power. NSC and HQ IDS should plan and conduct strategic exercises to rehearse higher decision makers in formulation of comprehensive strategic assessments, analyse decision dilemmas, formulate comprehensive strategic responses, and exercise escalation domination control in crisis/conflict situation.

Proactive Diplomacy in Regional Integration

India is a pre-eminent power in South Asia and the IOR. This must be further optimised through the following:

- ✓ Speedily develop ports as part of Sagarmala Project.
- ✓ Lead in developing Blue Economy; establish Free Trade Agreements (FTAs) in the IOR; revive historical trade routes like Mausam, Spice Route, and Cotton Route.
- ✓ Integrate Delhi-Mumbai-Bengaluru-Chennai with Regional Corridors such as BBIN and BIMSTEC.
- ✓ Access to Eurasia, Chabahar-Afghanistan-Central Asia Axis, and INSTC.
- ✓ Make 'Act East' policy a success; operationalise Kaladan project, India-Myanmar-Laos-Thailand Transit Corridor with rest of South East Asia.
- ✓ Be a net security provider in South Asia/IOR.
- ✓ Soft power hub.
- ✓ Optimise military diplomacy.

FORCE DEVELOPMENT

Spotlight Pakistan

Focus of force development for dealing with Pakistan should include calibrated engagement; perpetuating two-front dilemma; non-contact asymmetric capability and punitive lethal deterrence. In addition, India must call Pakistan's nuclear bluff.

Spotlight China

Focus of force development for dealing with China should include perpetuating two-front dilemma in accordance to Sun Tzu's 'acme of skill'; credible deterrence through establishing A2-AD in Tibet and IOR (using ANC as strategic springboard); status quo at the border with full spectrum Quid Pro Quo (QPQ) capability up the escalatory ladder at Theatre level; rebalancing from the Western border to Northern borders and creation and posturing of tailor-made offensive accretion forces in Ladakh.

Firepower Asymmetry

The Army and the Air Force must pivot to the mountains as that is where the territorial disputes are and the probability of conflict highest. As large-scale manoeuvre is not possible in mountains and large-scale offensive operations in plains can likely threaten nuclear red line, the army and air force must upgrade their capabilities to engage targets and destroy them. Massive dose of accurate strikes by guns, rockets, missiles using terminally homing PGMs from ground, air and sea-based platforms (when in range) can tilt the balance in India's favour.[7]

Anti-Access and Anti Denial

Our ISR (Intelligence, Surveillance and Reconnaissance) and long-range targeting capabilities vis-à-vis China demand major up-gradation. Redundancy in communication and surveillance satellites, sub-meter resolution, and daily revisit with Direct Downloading Facility (DDS) at the Corps level must be accorded top priority. We need to develop viable Signal Intelligence (SIGINT) and Human Intelligence (HUMINT) capabilities to obtain reliable intelligence on both China and Pakistan. The strategic ISR capability should be complemented by deploying state-of-the-art reconnaissance aircraft and UAV with a live streaming facility at the surveillance centres at the national, theatre, and sector level. Long-range precision guidance weapon systems for key point/in-depth strikes, multi-barrel rocket launchers, BrahMos with high-altitude capability, air superiority fighters supported by AWACS and air-to-air refuelers should be inducted on top priority in adequate numbers. Fail-safe multiple means of communication are vital for sensor-shooter interface. With these capabilities in place, India can impede and degrade Chinese build-up in the Tibetan Plateau and the Indian Ocean.

Intelligence

While coordination and synergy between the nine major intelligence agencies needs to be built, a major shortcoming since past several years has been the lack of strategic intelligence and human intelligence, even of India's immediate neighbourhood. Special Forces have major role to play in providing continuous strategic intelligence, which is covered later in this chapter. HQ IDS is authorised to operate trans-border HUMINT sources since its establishment, which unfortunately has not been permitted till date. This needs to change since HUMINT is of prime importance in hybrid warfare. In fact, deployment of trans-border HUMINT resources must be done by HQ IDS in consultation of Services/Unified Commands. The National Information Grid (NATGRID) is running way behind schedule. This needs to be hastened. NATGRID also needs to be linked with the National Counter Terrorism Centre (NCTC) and State Counter Terrorism Centres (SCTCs) and in turn linked to nominated agencies that can draw upon it on need to know basis.

Pocket of Excellence (PoE) Forces

Besides nuclear weapons, India should develop anti-satellite weapons, laser weapons, e-bombs (Electromagnetic pulse), microwave weapons, etc. All modern armies are developing weapons with disruptive technologies. A case in point is the secretive 'Assassins Mace Weapon Programme' of China. The US is known to have its own secret weapons programmes. India should invest in R&D and develop its own variants of Assassins Mace. Cyber warfare units should be raised. Higher priority should be given to develop space-based Command, Control, Communications, Computers, Intelligence, Information, Surveillance, and Reconnaissance (C^4I^2SR), and guidance and navigation systems, operating in optical, infrared, and microwave regions of spectrum. Electronic Warfare and Information Warfare capabilities should be enhanced to conduct network-centric operations.

Cyber Security

China is a cyber-super power adept in refined skills to undertake cyber espionage and sabotage, and Pakistan is a beneficiary of China's hybrid warfare capabilities. China will rely heavily on cyber offensive in non-contact and contact stages of its hybrid warfare campaign. India must show great urgency in developing credible cyber warfare capability. India should establish Centres for infrastructure protection, information sharing, information assurance, and IT Product Security Test. These should be created at the national level under one single advisory council. Significantly, the cyber warfare programmes in the US and China are led by respective militaries, whereas in India this is not the case. There has been talk of establishing Cyber Command past few years but no progress has taken place. The advances in cyberwarfare may be gauged from the fact that according to a recent WikiLeaks report, 85 per cent of global smart-phones have been weaponised by the CIA using the Android operating system (OS) for spying and that a surveillance technique called 'Weeping Angel' infiltrates smart TVs, transforming them into microphones.[8]

National Coordination Centre for Information Sharing and Analysis. This should be an independent unit that defines the Meta data and data standards for information sharing between the NCIP, the intelligence agencies, and the public and private sector industry. This may be a part of NSC/NTRO.

National IT Product Security Test Centre (NIPSTC). This should operate and maintain a National Evaluation and Certification Scheme for IT Security.

Information Warfare

Information war, including psychological operations, is of special significance in hybrid warfare, which besides other means can be waged exploiting all types of media. The same goes also for countering digital jihad, enemy psychological operations as also as part of de-radicalisation programmes. Pakistan has been successfully waging psychological operations in J&K to radicalise and incite the population. The J&K police recently found at least two WhatsApp groups with Pakistani numbers as administrators, which were allegedly involved in rumour-mongering and crowd mobilization during anti-militancy operations in South Kashmir, aimed at disrupting security forces operations through stone-pelting and providing human screens to enable terrorists escape.[9] Many times, people did not even know that they were part of such a group which had Pakistan-based administrators. The police have launched a massive crackdown on such underground and fake news WhatsApp groups in Pulwama district. These groups have been mobilizing crowds to help the militants escape from search-and-cordon operations. India needs to do similarly to negate Pakistani psychological operations of this type, as well as for targeting Pakistani fault lines. This can also be done through select NGOs in addition to government agencies.

The IT Cell of the Bhartiya Janta Party (BJP) played a major role in the unprecedented enormous win of the BJP during the last elections in the State of Uttar Pradesh (UP), waging a smart-phone war for moulding perceptions of voters.[10]

Since 1980, no party has been able to clinch three-fourth majority in UP as BJP did this time; the BJP-led alliance won 325 seats, a significant amount of credit for this victory going to the IT Cell. In a span of just two years, from the urban landscape of Lucknow to a remote villages, BJP has successfully netted smart-phone users across UP and subjected them to an aggressive and meticulously planned new media strategy; aim was to capture the mind of the voter by messaging them night and day. The IT Cell aimed to enter minimum 5,000 WhatsApp groups, which they achieved comfortably six months prior to the election. By the time UP went for polls, the IT Cells had access to over 9,000 WhatsApp groups spread across the state, with an average 150 mobile users in each group. This meant that the seven to eight messages that were sent every day were read by at least 13.5 lakh people.

The above mechanics must be used for information war in Pakistan, which can even be waged through NGOs to help build suspicion against the Pakistani army and also the increasing presence of China. Given that most of the rural populace is of somewhat similar psycho-profile as UP. Could these same mechanics be implemented by China in India for disruption along our fault line? Or by China in Nepal against India, conversely in Nepal by India against increasing Chinese influence? While Pakistan is looking at increasing violence in J&K through such means, India can also use such means to isolate trouble makers, for example, induce distrust and hatred towards separatists. Clearly, it requires much deeper thought, dynamic strategy and continuity. Considering that the whole budget of the exercise would be a fraction of a cost of a war fighter, India needs to look at this aspect seriously especially with the ISI having a head start. India should establish a National Information Warfare Department for overall coordination and guidance in waging info war including psychological operations. Information and psychological warfare units comprising experts from different disciplines and ministries could be raised at national level as also within the military. Special efforts should be made to educate Indian media on security matters. Theme-based media campaigns should be undertaken to build political and public consensus on India's vital national interests, strategic objectives and policy options for dealing with intricate and vexed issues such as resolution of border issues. Publication and circulation of White Papers, Strategic Defence Reviews and literature on security issues is yet another way of shaping perceptions and portraying India's contemporary strategic culture. IW Cells should also be established in insurgency areas, and psychological operations launched by Services in required regions with well thought out themes. The proposed Special Forces Command too must have an integral IW Cell.

Special Operations

Despite India being subjected to decades of proxy war, our hierarchal understanding of trans-border employment of Special Forces ironically is limited to short-distanced physical or direct type of actions executed at unit or sub-unit level. Special Forces potential in asymmetric wars in furthering national security objectives and employment as extension of foreign policy is little understood. Special Forces should actually be central to our asymmetric response, which does not necessarily imply operating in units or sub-units. In most cases, such Special Forces response does not even automatically relate to physical attack, physical attack being only the extreme and potentially most dangerous expression of asymmetric warfare.[11] The key lies in achieving strategic objectives through application of modest resources with the essential psychological component. Our areas of strategic areas interests need to be kept under surveillance through HUMINT, to which Special Forces can be major contributors.

The Naresh Chandra Committee had recommended setting up a Special Forces Command. This should have been established forthwith directly under the Prime Minister with parallel links to the PMO and NSA.[12] However, during the Unified Commanders' Conference in July 2017, Defence Secretary announced Special Operations Division will 'soon' become reality. According to media, SOD will collate Special Forces of the Army, Navy and IAF, for supporting offensive and defensive operations. India needs a National Operations Division (NOD) under the Prime Minister.

The Prime Minister should have a Special Forces Cell under him manned by R&AW and Special Forces personnel, tasked with evolving policy and doctrine for strategic employment of Special Forces at strategic level; oversee their manning, equipping, training, tasking, intelligence, inter-agency synergy; coordinate and monitor their operational employment and coordinate joint training and operations with foreign Special Forces. The Special Forces Cell should have direct links to the DIA, R&AW, NTRO, and IB. It would be prudent to go for two-three Special Forces battalion strength ISFC taking the nucleus from military Special Forces. The NOD should have multiple Special Forces Teams assigned to specific countries/ regions. The other components of the NOD should comprise an Intelligence Cell, Insertion and Extraction Group, Support Elements, Logistic Elements, Cyber Cell, R&D Cell, and a Training Cell linked to the Special Forces Training School.

The balance Special Forces should be clubbed under the Chief of Defence Staff as a Special Operations Division (SOD) for supporting military operations; cross-border tactical tasks and within border tasks beyond capabilities of regular infantry.[13] Strategic sense dictates that SOD should also integrate relevant elements of NSG and SFF discarding turf wars. The case for raising a Marine Brigade gathering dust in MoD for last decade and a half should be activated and the Marine Brigade clubbed with SOD. Tasks of the NOD and SOD would complement each other in specific situations. Diplomacy and conventional war by themselves cannot contend with asymmetric wars of Pakistan and China. Conventional response to asymmetric threats does not work and merely fortressing one's house is no answer. We need a well thought out, coordinated proactive approach. Establishment of the NOD and SOD will be vital steps towards this.

Space

Space control, comprising Offensive Space Control (OSC) and Defensive Space Control (DSC), supports freedom of action in space for own forces, and when necessary, defeats adversary efforts that interfere with or attacks one's space systems, and negate adversary's space capabilities. Space situational awareness is dependent on integrating space surveillance; real-time collection and processing data; environmental monitoring; status of own and cooperative satellite systems; analysis of space domain and insights into adversary's space capabilities, and possible threats they pose. In addition to creating these capabilities, actions that India should take as part of techno-military orientation of its space programme[14] are as follows:

- ✓ Enhance space-based communications and surveillance in multiple domains and orbits.
- ✓ Evolve sharing of transponders and facilities within military and with civil sources for greater survivability and redundancy.
- ✓ Involve military in planning and execution of national satellite plans.
- ✓ Increase launch facilities with services earmarked by military and transportable launch stations on variety of platforms.
- ✓ Involve and train military in measures for passive protection of satellite systems.
- ✓ Missile defence, satellite communications, navigation, earth observation, ocean monitoring and surveillance, weather monitoring, and electronic intelligence systems should be operated jointly to start with and handed over to defence forces gradually.

Combining Intelligence, EW, Cyber and Space

Combining Intelligence, Technical Reconnaissance, Electronic Warfare, Cyber Warfare and Space Warfare under the newly constituted Strategic Support Force of the PLA has merit and is of tremendous operational advantage. This needs to be closely analyzed. It may be prudent for India to raise a Strategic Support Command on similar lines in addition to a Special Operations Command rather than going for three separate commands: Aerospace Command, Cyber Command and Special Operations Command. The army too should examine combining these functions. Presently, intelligence functions are under Military intelligence Directorate, electronic warfare with Military Operations Directorate, cyber with Signals Directorate and Space with Perspective Planning Directorate.

Border Defence Management

China's Western Theatre Command is responsible for China's border with Myanmar and thence running west to include Afghanistan. The Border Guard Divisions deployed to guard the entire length are directly under command the PLA. In contrast, we have different forces deployed on the border in contrast to the concept of 'One Border, One Force'. One example is the ITBP deployed in Depsang Plains and Chumar area in Eastern Ladakh, who report to their headquarters at New Delhi and consequently to the Ministry of Home Affairs (MHA). The Kargil Review Committee had recommended that Central Armed Police Forces (CAPF) can be deployed on the borders but these should be placed under Army command. This latter part has been ignored despite adverse ramifications to border security. One Border, One Force needs to be enforced with the CAPF deployed to defend international borders by placing them under command of the Army, or at best under MoD, not MHA.

The Prime Minister has publicly pointed out that the Kanpur train derailment was by enemy agents coming across our borders. Our concept of 'open borders' must comprise a series of mutually supporting integrated check posts with effective joint patrolling to cover the gaps along our international borders with Nepal, Bhutan, Nepal, Myanmar and Bangladesh. Movement across 'open borders' needs to be channelised to deter illegal immigration/infiltration, insurgents/terrorists/saboteurs, flow of weapons, narcotics, fake Indian currency and smuggling.

Army Chief, General Bipin Rawat stated on Army Day this year (15 January 2018) that of the 72 strategic roads, only 22 have been completed after so many years, and all of the 14 strategic rail-lines approved remain on paper only. This is a serious flaw which must be addressed through public-private partnership since resources of the Border Roads Organization are obviously short.

Technology

Technology will play an important role in any form of conflict in the coming decades. It is suggested that a Defence Technologies Commission be set up to oversee technology development for the Armed Forces, evolve a coherent policy on make/

buy decisions, and ensure that the vulnerability of the nation to technology denial regimes of various kinds is eliminated, or at the least reduced to the minimum. The Commission may work through various panels or task forces comprising a mix of experienced scientists, technologists, officers of the defence forces, and consultants from industry, R&D, academia, and the strategic community. Each service should be encouraged to set up its own technology advising mechanism in the form of a Technology and Systems Command to help its chief to provide well-considered inputs to the Defence Technology Commission. The Services should be encouraged to keep open their lines of communication with the scientific and industrial communities. Harnessing of scientific talent and allocation of more funds for R&D is necessary to reduce the country's dependence on technology imports. Speedy development of unmanned and robotic systems, additive manufacturing, directed energy weapons, nano-technologies, precision guided munitions (PGMs), data mining, quantum communications, and developing futuristic materials like high performance thermoplastic polymeric (GPAEK/PEI)-Carbon Fabric Composite with high thermal and mechanical properties, and the like must remain in our focus. Development of 'disruptive technologies' should focus on new technologies that can cause extensive damages within the natural and human domain:

- ✓ **The HAARP Theory**. The High Frequency Active Aurora Research Programme (HAARP) proposes tampering of ionosphere and geophysical domain for purposeful military and civilian application. Visible signs of its manifestation exist in terms of weather and geo-physical manipulations.
- ✓ **Mind Control Sciences**. This theory revolves around making a deliberate attempt to manage public's perception on a subject through sensitization. Although in its early stages of development, it is a potent threat for the future.
- ✓ **Extremely Low Frequency (ELF) and Directed Energy Weapons (DEWS)**. ELF uses radio waves as a weapon to create incapacity and disruption without resorting to destruction, whereas, 'Directed Energy' weapons are the newest in the range of destructive weapons but with tremendous potential and range of utility. Applications in this domain are presently experimental in nature but fast reaching operational status.
- ✓ **New Forms of Combat**. Space combat, cyber space combat, radiation combat; robotic combat, nano-technology combat will add to existing forms of combat, zombie war being the latest addition. We must be prepared to win such conflict situations. Leapfrogging technology requires special emphasis.

China is building a 1.2 billion yuan ($180m) Large High Altitude Air Shower

Observatory (LHAASO) to search for the origin of high energy cosmic rays, to study the evolution of the universe and high energy celestial bodies, as well as to push forward the frontier of new physics.[15] LHAASO will be mankind's first attempt to hunt for the highest-energy Gamma ray, which is the burst of radiation thought to be produced alongside cosmic rays in our Galaxy. It will without doubt have military applications. With Ramayana and Mahabharat replete with instances of use of cosmic power, India must initiate research in cosmic rays and cosmic power.

Defence Budget

The Parliamentary Standing Committee on Defence slammed the Government on 9 March 2017 through its report tabled in Parliament on Demands for Grants for 2017-18, for its adhocism, casual and lackadaisical approach saying it would adversely affect the country's defence preparedness as well as hit the morale of the armed forces. Getting back to the snubbing by the Parliamentary Standing Committee on Defence to the government, the highlights include the following: in terms of modernisation demands for FY 2017-2018, the Army, Navy, and Air Force have only received 60 per cent, 67 per cent, and 54 per cent, respectively; only Rs 86,488 crore has been earmarked for modernisation from the total defence outlay of Rs 2.74 lakh crore—what makes matters worse is bulk of this capital will be used to pay 'committed liabilities' of earlier arms contracts instead of new projects. The Committee had asked the government to allocate additional Rs 13,000 crores for defence in the current financial year. Unfortunately, the Defence Budget 2018-2019 too is 'negative' in actual terms. India's security challenges are unique. The country faces serious internal security threats, proxy war, and external security threats from two nuclear capable adversaries who are in a strategic alliance. India's defence spending has not been in tune with its strategic security needs. China's defence spending is approximately four times higher than that of India. The Armed forces need a defence budget which is a minimum of 2.5 per cent to 3 per cent of GDP with an assured annual increase of 14.5 per cent. If the higher defence allocations are not increased, the asymmetry in the defence capability vis-à-vis China will increase to an unacceptable level.

Ironically, most of our tanks and infantry combat vehicles are not fit to fight through a nuclear attack zone due to non-availability of particular type of air filters, as also perished rubber seals, that help create overpressure in the crew compartments. Procurement of new ICVs has just been cleared but the execution will need to be hastened. Also, the individual protection kits for soldiers under nuclear attack are either incomplete or grossly short in numbers. These are serious flaws that need to be addressed on priority.[16]

Nuclear Deterrence

India has already successfully test fired the PD Interceptor missile and the long range BrahMos (450 km range), following India's entry to Missile Technology Control Regime (MTCR). India must operationalise complete triad-based nuclear deterrence capability with assured second strike capability, fielding of Agni V, development of thermonuclear warheads, tactical warheads, Multiple Independent Re-entry Vehicle (MIRV) capability, Anti-Ship Ballistic Missiles (ASBMs) and Anti-Ship Cruise Missiles (ASCMs) nuclear submarines, making our nuclear deterrence credible. Concurrently, Ballistic Missile Defence (BMD) capability should be developed to protect major communication centres, strategic assets and NCA. Nuclear brinkmanship is a mind game targeted at the political leadership and people of target country. Our nuclear doctrine should reflect our resolve to use nuclear weapons, when our vital national interests or survival is at stake. To this end, India should review the tone and tenor of its nuclear doctrine and categorically indicate red lines, which if crossed, will warrant use of nuclear weapons. A more assertive nuclear doctrine will add sting to our nuclear deterrence.

Internal Security

Any future conventional/sub-conventional war in the Indian context will take place in a heightened insurgency/terrorism environment. It is imperative to ensure that the Armed Forces do not lose their combat edge by getting involved in fighting terrorism/insurgency. It is imperative to define a Comprehensive Internal Security Strategy and establish Central Armed Police Force (CAPF)-based national capability to effectively combat insurgencies and terrorism. Establishment of National Counter-Terrorism Centre (NCTC) and State Counter Terrorism Centres (SCTCs) is necessary to revamp intelligence agencies and Terrorism Evolution Monitoring Groups, with the view to coordinate and oversee all actions of different government departments. Networking of electronic and human intelligence, ability of hi-tech and dynamic Rapid Reaction Forces (RRF)/Special Forces (SF) to conduct precision operations against all forms of asymmetric threats including use of WMD from non-state actors should be the important thrust areas. India should set up a counter-terrorism grid in the whole country integrating all agencies and stakeholders to combat all forms of terrorism, including cyber terrorism. It must be ensured that the Armed Forces are not embroiled in fighting insurgencies but kept well equipped, trained and motivated to safeguard India's strategic frontiers, aerospace, and maritime space against all forms of aggression.

Virtual Terrorism. Virtual terrorism is a gigantic problem which requires huge amount of data mining and constant surveillance. In 2014, Mehdi Masroor Biswas, a Bengaluru-based executive, first discovered and reported by Channel 4 News of UK, confessed he was handling the pro-jihad tweeter '@ShamiWitness' for past several years. According to a former NSA, more than 100 individuals are involved in Mehdi-like activities. A National Investigation Agency (NIA) probe shows that Indian Mujahidin (IM) cadres are tech savvy and have been using proxy servers and complex code to chat, with exceptional knack for IT setting up email accounts that disappear if they not accessed in 24 hours, proxy servers to camouflage geographical location, encrypted files and complicated code language; use of US-based Yahoo Inc, Paltalk Inc, Sophidea Inc and Hurricane Electric, plus providers in Nepal, Canada and Ireland; IP address of Nimbuzz chat traced to Pakistan Telecom Company Ltd and others traced to France, Germany, Netherlands, Nepal and India. Asymmetry through non-war operation encompasses fields like finance, ecology, psychology, media, drug trafficking tech etc. Such asymmetric approaches will invariably be used in conjunction with others. In the US, a non-governmental initiative termed Counter Extremism Project (CEP) was launched in 2014 with Israeli assistance to confront the growing threat from 'extremist ideology'. CEP seeks to refute social media messaging, compile world's biggest database of extremist networks. The CEP would augment the US NSA already heavily committed albeit the NSA faced heavy criticism in recent times for snooping globally under the 'Prism' programme. Participation of the private sector is also essential because of the magnitude of the issues involved. CEP has been launched as a private sector organization that describes itself nonpartisan in its efforts to combat extremism. Its goals include compilation of the world's most exhaustive database on extremist groups and their networks, and places unmasking the funding sources for ISIS high on its list of immediate priorities. Though the CEP is a non-governmental organization, it works with governments exploiting the internet to, mobilize social media to counter extremist ideology by exposing the threat of extremists and mounting a global counter narrative. India needs similar public-private partnership to tackle this mammoth problem. Ironically, the radical Zakir Naik would have continued to preach hatred without Bangladesh pointing out to us Naik's radical activities that came to light post the terrorist attack on a Dhaka café.

CBRN Terrorism. Chemical, Biological, Radiological, Nuclear (CBRN) terrorism is a reality, some examples being the Sarin Gas attacks on Tokyo Subway in 1995, Anthrax attacks in the US in 2001 and Sarin gas use in Syria now. A study by the Center for Non-proliferation Studies reveals that during 2013 only, there were 153 cases spanning 30 countries where radiological and nuclear materials were lost, including 141 involving dangerously radioactive materials albeit not usable in nuclear weapons. On face value, India is inadequately prepared for CBRN attacks notwithstanding the hype created around the National Disaster Response Force (NDRF). A closer examination would lead to the same conclusion. India needs to look at this issue more seriously. An appreciation of likely targets, placement of advance warning, locating and response equipment, along with requisitely trained forces is the need of the hour. Merely responding to cross-border perpetrators should not be the only consideration with respect to CBRN terrorism.

Focus: China-Pakistan

All the issues discussed above are relevant to creating effective deterrence against the collusive hybrid threat by China-Pakistan. These include issues like force development, upgrading cyber warfare and information warfare capabilities, establishment of special operations organizations, establishing of deep coalitions and the like. China has developed massive infrastructure in Tibet with its military use in mind, in addition to the CPEC which is China's strategic highway to the Indian Ocean. India should speed up infrastructure development projects on the border with China. Inadequacies in critical infrastructure, construction of multiple axes of induction, airfields, ALGs, helipads, gun areas, defence works, habitat, communication and logistics nodes etc. should be built on war footing.

Establishing Deep Coalitions

To counter the China-Pakistan hybrid war, India needs to establish 'Deep Coalitions' at multiple levels without disturbing the various strategic partnerships, including the India-US Strategic Partnership. The concept of 'Deep Coalitions' has been discussed in Chapter 5 of this study; instead of a coalition being limited to few nations, the deep coalition besides select nations may also include few civil society organizations, even drug mafias, couple of private corporations with their own self-interest at stake, an individual speculator, and many other components. The deep coalition involves players at many levels of the system. It is multi-dimensional with all these groups operating all the time, in continuous flow—multiplying, fissioning then fusing into others, and so on. Such a system is based less on 'balance of power' relations among major nations than on the ability to configure the right combination of players at every level. More important than the balance of power is the 'power of balance'; the ability of a major state to keep its senses in the midst of this turbulence, and to match its economic and military capabilities with high-level knowledge resources.

This idea of 'deep coalition' is present in all but in name in Unrestricted Warfare, with its repeated references to the political role played by non-state actors ranging from credit rating agencies to narco-mafias, and its emphasis on the 'civilianisation of war' thesis: Precisely in the same way that modern technology is changing weapons and the battlefield, it is also at the same time blurring the concepts of who the war participants are; non-professional warriors and non-state organisations are posing a greater and greater threat to sovereign nations. Faced with warfare in the broad sense that will unfold on a borderless battlefield, it is no longer possible to rely on military forces and weapons alone to achieve national security in the larger strategic sense, nor is it possible to protect these stratified national interests. Obviously, warfare is in the process of transcending the domains of soldiers, military units, and military affairs, into the wholesome national domain involving politicians, diplomats, scientists, and even bankers.

Depending on the aim chosen for individual 'deep coalition', India will need to decide upon the nation or group of nations that need to be co-opted in the particular deep coalition. The broad aims of such deep coalitions should be to (1) isolate Pakistan as terror exporting country; (2) deter and weaken the China-Pak nexus; (3) open India's land access to Afghanistan-CAR; (4) stabilize Afghanistan and protect Indian interests abroad including in Afghanistan; (5) deter Chinese naval bases coming up in IOR; (6) protect SLOCs and freedom of Global Commons in Indo-Pacific; (7) cripple China's aggressive moves by forcing it to look inwards in conjunction strategic partners; (8) weaken China's gravitational pull to strategic neighbours; (9) generate declared global response to nuclear terrorism, and (10) enable progressing own CND.

Forcing China Inwards

The China-Pakistan-North Korea combination is perhaps the most dangerous on the global stage, China being the driving force with the other two rogue nuclear-cum-terrorist nations talons of the Chinese dragon. At the same time, China has infirmities in the restive non-Han Xinjiang and Tibet that can be exploited through deep coalitions. Also by 2030, some 400 million Chinese (population greater than of USA) is expected to transit from rural regions to urban regions, particularly the rich areas along China's eastern seaboard. China has already announced plans to relocate 9.81 million people living in 'impoverished and unsustainable conditions' in 22 provinces to geographically 'less disadvantaged' areas during 2016-2020 at a cost of $158 billion. This still leaves a great socio-economic divide and a massive chunk of 'have-nots' (which China does not want the world to see), whose strife can be exploited. A total of 54 per cent of China's defence budget is for internal threats, and in year 2015, Xinjiang was allotted a budget of $1.5 billion which was a 35 per cent increase from the previous year. If instability increases in China, it would be forced to look more inwards.

China is an economic giant; however, its external debt in March 2017 has been estimated at 272 per cent of its GDP by UBS Financial Services. Significantly, year 2015 saw a 30 per cent increase in protests by workers across China, as also 30 per cent unemployment in graduates. With slowdown of economy, considerable amount of money earned goes towards repaying interests on the external debts. It is for all these reasons that the success of the OBOR, CPEC and MST are vital to China, for sustaining the economy and creating jobs for Chinese population. A squeeze on OBOR, CPEC and MST would force China to curb its aggression.

Considerable scope also exists weakening, and possibly even reversing the China-Taliban and the China-United Wa State Army (UWSA) linkages through various 'deep coalitions'. Since UWSA are staunch Buddhists, their religious teachers (Buddhist monks) could be influenced by making them aware of China's Tibet invasion, China's continuing genocide in Tibet including sustained attempts to kill the Tibetan heritage and culture, and Chinese attitude towards the Dalai Lama. Similarly, the Taliban could be psychologically disillusioned towards China with bringing home China's treatment towards Muslims in general, and Uighurs and ETIM in particular. No doubt that both the Taliban and UWSA themselves are narcotics mafias, and money plays an essential part; however, it is a question of igniting spark(s) that would inflame itself as and when the killings get going.

India should also expand its cooperation with Taiwan. Knowledge of Taiwanese language implies one can automatically read and understand Chinese and Japanese languages. Interaction with Taiwanese government officials and military indicates they are more than willing to run Taiwanese language courses in India, knowledge of which would be invaluable in reading and understanding the Chinese, gathering intelligence, as well as for 'deep coalition' operations. Interestingly, hundreds of Taiwanese firms are operating in China which obviously will have elements of Taiwanese Special Forces.

Engaging Strategic Neighbourhood

India must re-invigorate its ties with the regional countries and reduce their dependence on China, including in the supply of military hardware. In order to contain China's influence, India should develop viable leverages to implement its 'Connect Central Asia Policy', 'Act East Policy' and 'IOR Rimland policy'. Engagement with Iran is pivotal for our Central Asia, Afghanistan and West Asia Policy as also for energy security. Full operationalization of Chabahar port, rail-road connectivity to Zaranj-Delaram (Afghanistan), and further to Central Asia should be accorded high priority together with the early operationalisation of the International North-South Transportation Corridor (INSTC). In our engagement with Iran, we must highlight the factor of sectarian violence against Shia population perpetuated in Pakistan and continued targeting of Shias in Afghanistan by Wahabi-Salafi inspired Pakistan-backed Taliban. For the fructification of 'Act East Policy', enunciated by the Prime Minister in the vision document 2012, engagement with Bangladesh and Myanmar is extremely crucial. Outstanding issues with Bangladesh must be diplomatically resolved in the interest of gaining access to North-eastern states thus mitigating Siliguri Corridor dilemma. Myanmar is India's strategic springboard to Southeast Asia and we have an excellent window of opportunity to make strategic investments in Myanmar. We should leverage our ties with the government in Myanmar to liquidate insurgent camps inside Myanmar territory through mutually agreed joint operations.

India should resolve the Teesta water sharing issue with Bangladesh to earn goodwill, encourage and assist Nepal to harness the potential of its rivers flowing into India to generate electricity and earn revenue by supplying it to India. The Nepal-China deal for China to explore gas in Nepal's Terai region during the erstwhile Nepalese government is a loss to India with security implications. Such instances need to be avoided by our foreign policy mandarins. The proposed three dams China is building over the Brahmaputra are likely to affect the flow of water into India and Bangladesh. India should build an opinion along with Bangladesh and other countries to urge China to sign the UN convention on water sharing and become a responsible stakeholder in sharing of global commons.

It is in China's interest to undermine the status of Nepal and Bhutan as strategic buffers and perpetuate our strategic security concerns about the Siliguri corridor. China is already pursuing this with occupying Northern Doklam, engaging Bhutan in talks of trade, and installing a China-favoured government in Nepal. Besides investing in Nepal's infrastructure, China is reportedly funding the Border Village Development Councils and modernising police stations on Nepal's border. Bhutan too is being wooed through slew of incentives, including package deal on the boundary issue, to open itself to diplomatic and trade relations with China. Our influence in Sri Lanka and Maldives is waning to China's advantage. This trend must be reversed. India can ill afford to allow these countries to fall in China's orbit.

China is beset with the issues of contested sovereignty in East China Sea with Japan and in the Western Pacific with Philippines and Vietnam. Taiwan issue is not yet resolved and it plays profoundly on the Chinese psyche. The 'US Asia Pivot Strategy', its security alliances with the regional countries and strong military posturing in the region are creating serious security concerns posing multi-front dilemma for China. The US, Japan, Vietnam, South Korea perceive India as a balancer/swing state and an important stakeholder in the region. India takes a principled stand on the right of access to global commons and freedom of navigation in the international waters. India also advocates collaborative security mechanisms for protection of SLOCS and critical infrastructure against all forms of threat. India should enhance its economic, cultural and military engagement with these regional countries. India should show the flag in the East China Sea/South China Sea and participate in bilateral and multi- lateral exercises at a scale and level that is demonstrative of its capability and resolve. Formation of the 'Quad' is a good beginning, whose involvement in regional security needs to be expanded.

From India's strategic security perspective, China should be kept embroiled in the Western Pacific. China's preoccupation in the East China Sea/South China Sea will provide India much desired window of opportunity to narrow the power asymmetry with that country. Special emphasis should be laid on developing strong and multi-layered defence ties with Japan and Vietnam. Xinjiang and Tibet are China's vulnerabilities and it stands isolated in the eyes of international community for oppressing the sub-national movements and violating human rights. India needs to develop subtle leverages with Uighur Diaspora and re-energise its linkages with Tibetan resistance as a quid pro quid, should China resort to coercion and abetment of anti-national elements.

From a long-term perspective, Sino-Russia relations will remain competitive. We should not allow a situation to develop that Russia completely distances itself from India and supplies high-end military hardware to China and Pakistan. In our policy reset on Russia, we should bring in the growing Chinese influence in Central Asia and dangers of Pakistan-China nexus in Afghanistan with consequences for Central Asia. Continued partnership with India is also helpful to Russia for balancing China in Greater Central Asia. India should support Russia's endeavours in strengthening of Custom Union/Eurasian Economic Community and Collective Security Treaty Organisation (CSTO). Given the undercurrents of mistrust between Russia and China, the former would welcome a closer alignment with India provided Russia's strategic concerns vis-à-vis Indo-US proximity are allayed.

Diplomacy

Wars are deterred/won/lost in the minds of a country's national leadership which gets influenced by the domestic and international public perceptions. Steps must be taken to shed off India's image as a pacifist and soft power state. Sound psychological and information operations themes propagated through diplomacy, diaspora, media and cyber space coupled with credible demonstration of soft and hard power should project India's political will to respond resolutely and effectively for safeguarding national interests. Proactive defence diplomacy in the form of joint military exercises, exchange of delegations, conduct of symposiums, demonstrations of military capabilities, export of weapons, etc. have the most direct and visible effect in shaping perceptions.

Due to lack of substantial trust and goodwill, Indian neighbours have employed military diplomacy with China. China's involvement in military affairs of South Asia is a worrying sign for India. There are two ways for India to tackle this: one is India should enhance its military diplomacy with Chinese neighbours like Vietnam, Japan, South Korea, and Philippines. This would be a 'Quid Pro Quo' policy to heighten China's insecurity in its backyard; second, India needs to intensify its military diplomacy in South Asia as well. A South Asian Defence University could be set up in India to take it further. Military conferences, joint maritime patrolling, disaster management exercises, anti-terrorism exercises and military sports events are some of the areas that should be explored by India with its South Asian neighbours. Conduct of joint training exercises with Nepal, Maldives, Sri Lanka, Bangladesh and Afghanistan needs to be upscaled. India also needs to export military hardware to these countries to reduce their dependence on China. Cyber, space and emerging weapon technology are some other areas where India can boost its cooperation with its South Asian neighbours.

Dealing with China

China is becoming stronger and assertive by the day. Confrontation with China is not in India's interest but India cannot allow coercion or intimidation by China. Therefore, multi-dimensional engagement at one level and developing credible deterrence capability at another is the best policy.

Economic Cooperation. The India-China economic cooperation has potential to reach the $120 billion mark. China seeks bigger investments in Indian markets and infrastructure sector. However, the imbalance in trade is two-thirds in China's favour. India will have to find measures to address the unfavourable trade balance and create a mutually favourable economic cooperation framework. China's strong economic relation with Japan and US is a restraining factor in their vexed relations India's strong and vibrant economic trade with China will make that country a stakeholder in India's security. China has evinced interest in boosting trade with India along Nathu La-Kalimpong-Siliguri-Kolkata Corridor. Other potential trade corridors between the two countries could be Myanmar-Northeast and India and even along the Sutlej (Himachal) and Demchok (Ladakh) corridor to Xinjiang and Central Asia or via Chabhar-Afghanistan-Central Asia-Xinjiang or along the North-South Corridor, which intersects with the East-West Eurasian Corridor. We must keep diplomatic options open to discuss these issues with China at a Track 2 level to gauge China's response.

Convergence Areas. The two countries cooperate on WTO, climate change and reformation of international institutions which are biased towards the US-led western world. BRICS, SCO, and India-China-Russia Triangular Dialogue are the other fora to engage with China. However, on the issue of India's candidature to UNSC and on Nuclear Supplier Group (NSG), China has been obstructive. Nonetheless, with India already full member of SCO, China should be nudged for cooperation on global commons and demonstrate sincerity in relations by supporting India's entry in the UNSC. Commonality of interest in managing energy prices is yet another area of cooperation. In addition are the civilization ties, institutionalisation of dialogue of which can pave the way for exchange of scholars, cross-fertilization of ideas and in developing mutual understanding, bridging trust deficit.

Border Issue. The border resolution is unlikely to be resolved in the near future. At the same time, India should not fall into the trap of China's indirect hints to part with the Tawang Plateau since Chinese claims continue to change periodically. Our border talks with China should include cession of Shaksgam valley by China, which was illegally ceded by Pakistan in 1963. India's concerns over Chinese presence in Northern areas, which legally belong to India, should be emphatically flagged at the diplomatic level talks.

China-Pak Economic Corridor (CPEC). Both China and Pakistan have been calling for India to join the CPEC. India should never join the CPEC because it does not give land access to India to Afghanistan and Central Asia through Pakistan, which India has always wanted; second, it may increase India-China trade but with the existing bilateral imbalance heavily in favour of China (according to information provided in Parliament, it stood at close to $45 billion in 2015-16 with India's exports amounting to only around $8 billion. The India-China trade touched US$80 billion first time in 2017 but although Indian exports to China have increased, the trade deficit in favour of China also crossed US$ 52 billion. China wants India to join CPEC to make it economically viable; however, it would result in increased imbalance manifold with increased Chinese belligerence, having conned India into such arrangement; it would legitimize PLA lodgment and projects in Gilgit-Baltistan (Indian Territory) undertaken without any reference to India; it would also indicate India's intransigence to Pakistan's genocide in Baluchistan, fully backed by China and most importantly it will fit into Chinese plans to keep India boxed within South Asia. Arrogant China doesn't understand why should India join the CPEC when it has trampled on India's sovereignty in Pakistan-Occupied Kashmir, which is India Territory.

Dealing with Pakistan

Pakistan's civil-military establishment has been soft on India-centric Jihadi outfits even when Pakistan itself is being devoured by the Frankenstein monster. Historical experience strongly suggests that in the event of India-China conflict, Pakistan is likely to play a role of China's proxy and perpetuate India's 'Two-Front Dilemma'. It would do its best to pin down Indian military on the Western front and help Chinese in creating an asymmetric ascendency over India. We must guard against this strategy. In the event of 'Two-Front' conflict scenario, the study group suggests the following measures in tackling Pakistan:

- ✓ Remain firm with the Pakistan Government in clearly enunciating India's concerns on terrorism and expectations from them to curb anti-India Jihadi activities bring perpetrators of terrorism living in Pakistan to speedy justice.
- ✓ In 1960, in the naïve hope that water largesse would yield peace, India entered into a treaty that gave away the Indus system's largest rivers as gifts to Pakistan[17]: 80 per cent of water, which is far in excess to the global norms of water sharing based on size of the river basin. Despite this, Pakistan is continuing with its proxy war on India while drawing the full benefits from the treaty and is now using the Indus Water Treaty (IWT) itself as a stick to beat India with, including by contriving water disputes and internationalizing them. The answer to India's serious under-utilisation of its share, which has resulted in Pakistan getting more than 10 billion cubic metres (BCM) yearly in bonus waters on top of its staggering 167.2 BCM allocation, is not a bureaucratic rigmarole but political direction to speedily build storage and other structures. Meanwhile, India can always restrict the outflow during the crop-sowing season in Pakistan if there is no let up on cross-border terrorism.
- ✓ Develop a multi-spectrum non-contact, clandestine, and lethal punitive deterrence capability against Pakistan.
- ✓ Broaden and deepen engagement in Afghanistan. Afghanistan should be our strategic outpost to perpetuate Pakistan's 'Two Front Dilemma' by covertly aiding pro Khyber-Pashtunistan (KP) movement. Covert support to resistance movement in Baluchistan is desirable to tie down Pakistan in its internal strife and thwart the CPEC. Fomenting anti-Pakistan unrest in the Northern Areas will also serve India's strategic security objective and weaken Pakistan-China nexus. The Islamic Movement of Uzbekistan (IMU) has struck Karachi Naval Base twice in the past. Terrorist strike(s) at Gwadar would be in India's interest.

Concluding Observations

It is ironic that India having fought five wars, hemmed in by nuclear-armed states, and contending with China-Pakistan collusive hybrid war does not have a formally declared national security strategy. Therefore, our defence policy remains ad hoc and the nation inadequately prepared to realize its global ambitions. Without due corrective actions, we are likely to face much higher levels of Chinese assertiveness and Pakistan's unrelenting proxy war in coming times, especially with China allowing President Xi Jinping to serve indefinitely—for life. India must move beyond conventional operations in nuclear backdrop and relying on diplomacy. We must adopt the strategy of 'deep coalitions' to deter hybrid threats preferably through non-contact operations employing non-kinetic means. Simultaneously, we must build and be prepared to employ kinetic means when warranted. A combination of hard and soft power needs to be progressively advanced.

It would be worthwhile to undertake a joint services study to identify optimum combat resources needed to deter the China-Pakistan hybrid warfare collusivity taking into account the unpredictable nature of future threats. The requirement is of light, lethal and wired 'Third Wave' forces with precision strike and stand-off kinetic capabilities and C^4I^2SR relevant to both the contact and non-contact battles, capable of conducting joint effect-based operations in a network-centric battlefield environment. State-of-the-art technology must be integrated with weapon platforms to gain the decisive edge.[18]

As discussed above, combining Intelligence, Technical Reconnaissance, Electronic Warfare, Cyber Warfare, and Space Warfare under the newly constituted Strategic Support Force of the PLA has merit and of tremendous operational advantage. This needs to be closely analysed. It may be prudent for India raise a Strategic Support Command on similar lines in addition to a National Operations Division (for strategic employment of Special Forces on politico-military missions) under the Prime Minister, and a Special Operations Division under the CDS, rather than going for three separate commands: Aerospace Command, Cyber Command, and Special Operations Command. Within the army also, combining these functions must be examined seriously, akin to China's Strategic Support Force.

Key Issues

- ✓ *India needs to define comprehensive national security strategy, streamline national planning process.*
- ✓ *The national security architecture and higher defence set up should be reorganised.*
- ✓ *Comprehensive defence review and military restructuring including appointing a CDS to ensure inclusive jointness.*

- ✓ *Multiple 'deep coalitions' need to be established to weaken the China-Pak nexus, open land access to and stabilize Afghanistan, deter Pakistan's proxy war, deter PLAN bases in IOR, deter China's all-round aggression and establish declared global response to nuclear terrorism.*
- ✓ *Establish credible deterrence to collusive China-Pakistan proxy war.*
- ✓ *Develop own set of 'Assassin Mace' weapons, akin to and including China's.*
- ✓ *Establish effective border control and border management, improve border infrastructure, and mitigate internal security challenges.*
- ✓ *Develop credible cyberspace, space and information warfare capabilities.*
- ✓ *India should establish National Information Warfare Department, and Information and psychological warfare units both in civil and in military.*
- ✓ *Light, lethal and wired forces required with precision strike and stand-off kinetic capabilities and C^4I^2SR relevant to both the contact and non-contact battles.*
- ✓ *Examine establishing Strategic 'Support Command' in addition to a Special Operations Command instead of three separate Commands for Aerospace, Cyber and Special Operations.*
- ✓ *Establish pocket of excellence and establish nuclear deterrence.*
- ✓ *Maximise influence in strategic neighbourhood.*
- ✓ *India's concerns over Chinese presence in Northern Areas, which legally belong to India, should be conveyed to China forcefully.*
- ✓ *Establish nodes of excellence for China and regions of strategic interest.*
- ✓ *Increase defence allocations and gear up indigenous industry for developing futuristic technologies and weapon systems.*

NOTES

1 Mackinder, HJ, 'The Geographical Pivot of History', *The Geographical Journal*, London, 1904, http://onlinelibrary.wiley.com/doi/10.1111/j.0016-7398.2004.00132.x/abstract

2 Kaplan, Robert D, '*The Revenge of Geography*': *What the Map Tells Us About Coming Conflicts and the Battle Against Fate*, New York: Random House, 2012.

3 'Mapping the Global Future', Report of the National Intelligence Council's 2020 Project, Washington, DC, USA, December 2004, http://www.futurebrief.com/project2020.pdf.

4 Meyssan, Thierry, 'NATO Intends to Prohibit Russia's and China's Development', *Investment Watch*, 14 September 2014, http://investmentwatchblog.com/nato-intends-to-prohibit-russias-and-chinas-development/.

5 Faizy, Mansoor, 'Afghanistan Rejects SIGAR Report', *Afghanistan Times*, 1 February 2017, http://afghanistantimes.af/afghanistan-rejects-sigar-report/.

6 'Rockets, Mortars Fired from Across Iran Border', *Dawn*, March 12, 2017, https://www.dawn.com/news/1319951/rockets-mortars-fired-from-across-iran-border

7 *The New Arthshastra*, NOIDA, India: Harper Collins, 2016, p. 379.

8 #Vault7: 85% of World's Smart Phones 'Weaponized' by CIA, RT Question More, rt.com, 7

March 2017, https://www.rt.com/news/379775-cia-weaponized-85pc-worlds-smartphones/.

9 Hassan, Ishfaq Ul, 'WhatsApp Groups with Pak Admins behind Crowd Mobilisation in J&K', DNA, 19 March 2017, http://www.dnaindia.com/india/report-whatsapp-group-with-pak-admins-behind-crowd-mobilisation-in-jk-2358531.

10 Bhardwaj, Amit, 'How BJP's IT Cell Waged War and Won in UP', Newslaundry, 17 March 2017, https://www.newslaundry.com/2017/03/17/how-bjps-it-cell-waged-war-and-won-in-up.

11 Katoch, PC and Datta, Saikat, 'India's Special Forces – History and Future of Indian Special Forces', New Delhi: Vij Books India, 2013.

12 Ibid.

13 Ibid.

14 *The New Arthshastra*, op. cit., pp. 264-265.

15 'China Starts Building Huge Cosmic-ray Observatory to Study the Evolution of the Universe', News Room, 16 March 16, http://english.cas.cn/newsroom/news/201703/t20170316_174968.shtml.

16 Chabbewal, Amarjeet S, 'India's Military Might: The Real Truth', *Indian Defence Review*, 18 March 2017, http://www.indiandefencereview.com/news/indias-military-might-the-real-truth/

17 Chellaney, Brahma, 'Shed the Indus Albatross: Indus Waters Treaty Offers One-sided Benefits to Pakistan, World Bank Too is Partisan', *Times of India*, 20 March 2017, http://blogs.timesofindia.indiatimes.com/toi-edit-page/shed-the-indus-albatross-indus-waters-treaty-offers-one-sided-benefits-to-pakistan-world-bank-too-is-partisan/.

18 *The New Arthshastra*, op. cit.

APPENDICES

APPENDIX 'A'

(Refers to Chapter 3)

PAKISTAN ARMY

(Extracts from Military Balance, 2017: International Institute of Strategic Studies, London)

Strategic Forces

1. Operational control rests with the NCA. The Strategic Plans Directorate (SPD) manages and commands all of Pakistan's military nuclear capability. The SPD also commands a reportedly 25,000-strong military security force responsible for guarding military nuclear infrastructure.

2. **Army Strategic Forces Command**. Command of all land-based strategic nuclear forces.

Equipment by Type

Surface-to-Surface Missile Launchers 60+

MRBM • Nuclear 30 Ghauri/Ghauri II (Hatf-5)/ Shaheen-2 (Hatf-6 – in test); Shaheen-3 (in test)

SRBM • Nuclear 30+: 30 Ghaznavi (Hatf-3 – PRC M-11)/Shaheen-1 (Hatf-4); some Abdali (Hatf-2); some Nasr (Hatf-9) GLCM • Nuclear Babur (Hatf-7); Ra'ad (Hatf-8 – in test)

Air Force 1–2 sqn of F-16A/B or Mirage 5 may be assigned a nuclear-strike role

Army – 560,000

Forces by Role

Command

9 corps HQ
1 (area) comd

Special Forces

2 SF gp (total: 4 SF billion)

Manoeuvre

Armoured

2 armd div
7 indep armd bde

Mechanised

2 mech inf div
1 indep mech bde

Light

18 inf div

5 indep inf bde

Other 1 sy div (1 more div forming)

<u>Combat Support</u>

1 arty div

14 arty bde

7 engr bde

<u>Aviation</u>

1 VIP avn sqn

4 avn sqn HELICOPTER

3 atk hel sqn

2 ISR hel sqn

2 SAR hel sqn

2 tpt hel sqn

1 spec ops hel sqn

<u>Air Defence</u>

1 AD comd (3 AD gp (total: 8 AD billion))

Equipment by Type

<u>Armoured Fighting Vehicles</u>

MBT2,561+: 415 Al-Khalid (MBT 2000); 320 T-80UD; 51 T-54/T-55; 1,100 Type-59/Al-Zarrar; 400 Type-69; 275+ Type-85; (270 M48A5 in store)

<u>APC 1,422</u> APC (T) 1,260: 1,160 M113/Talha; ε100 Type-63 APC (W) 120 BTR-70/BTR-80 PPV 42 Maxxpro AUV 10 Dingo 2

<u>Engineering & Maintenance Vehicles</u>

<u>ARV 117+</u>: 65 Type-653; Al-Hadeed; 52 M88A1; T-54/T-55 VLB M47M; M48/60 MW Aardvark Mk II

<u>Anti-Tank / Anti-Infrastructure</u>

MSL

SP M901 TOW MANPATS HJ-8; TOW

RCL 75mm Type-52; 106mm M40A1

RL 89mm M20

GUNS 85mm 200 Type-56 (D-44)

<u>Artillery 4,472+</u>

SP 375: 155mm 315: 200 M109A2; ε115 M109A5 203mm 60 M110/M110A2

TOWED 1,659: 105mm 329: 216 M101; 113 M-56; 122mm 570: 80 D-30 (PRC); 490 Type-54 (M-1938); 130mm 410 Type-59-I; 155mm 322: 144 M114; 148 M198; ε30 Panter; 203mm 28 M115

MRL 88+: 107mm Type-81; 122mm 52+: 52 Azar (Type83); some KRL-122; 300mm 36 A100

MOR 2,350+: 81mm; 120mm AM-50

Surface-to-Surface Missile Launchers

MRBM • Nuclear ε30 Ghauri/Ghauri II (Hatf-5); some Shaheen-2 (Hatf-6 – in test); Shaheen-3 (in test)

SRBM 135+: Nuclear 30+: ε30 Ghaznavi (Hatf-3 – PRC M-11)/ Shaheen-1 (Hatf-4); some Abdali (Hatf-2); some Nasr (Hatf-9); Conventional 105 Hatf-1 GLCM • Nuclear some Babur (Hatf-7)

RADAR • LAND AN/TPQ-36 Firefinder (arty, mor); RASIT (veh, arty); SLC-2

Aircraft

TPT • Light 14: 1 Beech 200 King Air; 1 Beech 350 King Air; 3 Cessna 208B; 1 Cessna 421; 1 Cessna 550 Citation; 1 Cessna 560 Citation; 2 Turbo Commander 690; 4 Y-12(II) TRG 87 MFI-17B Mushshak

Helicopters

ATK 38 AH-1F/S Cobra with TOW (1 Mi-24 Hind in store) MRH 115+: 10 H125M Fennec; 6 AW139; 26 Bell 412EP Twin Huey; 38+ Mi-17 Hip H; 2 Mi-171E Hip; 12 SA315B Lama; 20 SA319 Alouette III

TPT 76: Medium 36: 31 SA330 Puma; 4 Mi-171; 1 Mi172; Light 40: 17 H125 Ecureuil (SAR); 5 Bell 205 (UH1H Iroquois); 5 Bell 205A-1 (AB-205A-1); 13 Bell 206B Jet Ranger II

TRG 10 Hughes 300C

Unmanned Aerial Vehicles

ISR • Light Bravo; Jasoos; Vector

Air Defence

SAM • Point-defence some M113 with RBS-70; Anza Mk1/Mk2; FIM-92 Stinger; HN-5A; Mistral; RBS-70

GUNS • TOWED 1,933: 14.5mm 981; 35mm 248 GDF002/GDF-005 (with 134 Skyguard radar units); 37mm 310 Type-55 (M-1939)/ Type-65; 40mm 50 L/60; 57mm 144 Type-59 (S-60); 85mm 200 Type-72 (M-1939) KS-12

APPENDIX 'B'

(Refers to Chapter 3)

PAKISTAN NAVY

(Extracts from Military Balance, 2017: International Institute of Strategic Studies, London)

General

1. The non-naval elements of Pakistan's maritime capabilities remain rudimentary. The focus of this section, therefore, will be on its naval capability, and how this is likely to develop in the coming decades.

Submarine Holdings

2. Pakistan currently operates the following submarines:

- **Hashmat Class Submarines**. Two submarines of the French Agosta class, Hashmat and Hurmat, were commissioned in 1979 and 1980. Their primary weapon fit comprises SM-39 Exocet anti-ship missiles (range upto 180 Km) and 4 bow torpedo tubes; they can carry a mix of 18 torpedoes and missiles. The boats are over 37 years old and can be considered approaching the end of their useful life.
- **Khalid Class Submarines**. Three French Agosta 90B submarines, Khalid, Saad and Hamza, were commissioned between 1999 and 2006. The first was built in France, the second partially at KSEW and the last completely at KSEW. The weapon fit of the Khalid class is as for the Hashmat class. They have more modern sensors, AIP, a lower acoustic signature, improved battery performance and greater automation, leading to a smaller crew. A Turkish firm, STM, has been contracted to upgrade the submarines, probably at Jinnah Naval Base in Ormara. Details of the upgrade are not known, but speculation is that it relates to modernisation of the combat control system. These boats can be expected to continue in service till 2030 and perhaps a little beyond.
- **Midget Submarines**. Three MG 110 midget submarines built by KSEW are operated by the PN. Their role is mine laying, commando attacks and special force operations. They can carry two torpedoes.

Blue Water Ships

3. The second rung of the PN's maritime capability comprises its surface fleet capable of blue water operations. The current force level is as follows:

- **Zulfiquar Class Frigates**. The PN fleet currently operates four frigates of this class, named Zulfiquar, Shamsheer, Saif and Aslat. The first three were built in Shanghai and delivered 2009-2010. The last, built by KSEW at Karachi, joined the fleet in 2013. Their armament comprises 2x4 cell C-802 launchers (C 802 is the export version of the Chinese YJ-8 sea-skimming anti-ship missile with a range of 120 Km), an 8-cell short range (15 Km max) FM90N SAM launcher, 2x3 cell torpedo launchers, 2x6 cell anti-submarine rocket launchers, one 76.2 mm AK-176 gun, 2xType 730B CIWS and one Harbin Z-9EC ASW helicopter.
- **Tariq Class Destroyers**. Six ex-Royal Navy Type 21 frigates, built 1969-1975, were acquired by the PN from UK in 1993-94. One (Badr) was decommissioned in 2014, the others (Babur, Shah Jahan, Tariq, Khaibar and Tippu Sultan) remain in service. There armament comprises a quadruple Harpoon sea-skimming anti-ship missile launcher (range about 124 Km); the LY-60 short range SAM (max slant range 18 Km); a 4.5" gun; 2 triple ASW torpedo tubes; a Vulcan Phalanx CIWS; 2x20mm Oerlikon cannon and one ASW helicopter (Lynx). The ships are more than 40 years old and of limited utility.
- **PNS Alamgir**. An Oliver Hazard Perry class frigate first commissioned in 1979 and transferred to the PN in 2010 after undergoing a $ 65 million refit. The weapon fit comprises Harpoon anti-ship missiles, 2xtriple torpedo tubes, a Vulcan Phalanx CIWS; a 76 mm gun and anti-submarine helicopters. The ship is more than 37 years old.

Naval Platforms

4. These are as under:

- **Indigenous Capability**. KSEW has been able to turn out a Zulfiqar class ship (PNS Aslat), based on plans obtained from China. Indigenous design capability appears to have been restricted to small vessels. This cannot be expected to change over the next 15-20 years. During this period, the PN will have no option but to acquire plans from a foreign nation and build in Pakistan, or to acquire the platform itself from foreign suppliers.
- **Foreign Sources**. The traditional sources of supply have been USA and UK. These sources appear to have dried up for political and economic reasons. Both USA and UK are no longer likely to transfer warships at friendship prices, although UK may be willing to sell at market price. The PN, however, doesn't have the ability to buy at market prices. Essentially, the only reliable sources of supply appear to be China {PN vessels of Chinese

origin in service include Zulfiqar class frigates, Azmat Class FAC (M) and the fleet tanker PNS Nasr. Two 1500 ton OPVs for Pakistan's Coast Guard are under construction at KSEW}, Turkey (Turkish origin ships are the Zarrar Class FAC (M) and a 17000 ton fleet tanker launched by KSEW in August 2016, due for delivery in April 2017). Russia could emerge as a future source of supply.

Brown Water Platforms

5. Force levels of shorter range 'brown water' platforms in the PN are as follows:

- **Azmat Class FAC (M)**. Two ships (Azmat and Dehsat) are reported to be in service, the first build by China Shipbuilding and Offshore Company in 2012 and the second by KSEW in 2014. A third was launched on 17 Sep 2016 and a fourth is reported to be under construction. The ships are equipped with 2x4 cell C 802 SSM launchers, AK 630 CIWS and a 23 mm automatic gun. These are short range vessels, best suited defensive tasks and swarm attacks against more capable ships approaching the Pakistani coast, but they could be used for offensive measures on the West Coast of India, somewhat akin to the use of Osa class missile boats by India against Karachi.
- **Jalalat Class FAC (M)**. Two missile boats (Jalalat and Shujaat) were commissioned in 1997 and 1999 respectively. Built by KSEW, the boats are equipped with two twin C 802 SSM launchers and a twin radar controlled 37 mm gun.
- **Jurrat Class FAC (M)**. Two more missile boats (Jurrat and Quwwat), both built by KSEW based on a German design and in collaboration with a Thai company, were commissioned in 2002. Their weapon fit is similar to the Jalalat class.
- **Zarrar Class FAC (M)**. Two missile boats (Zarrar and Karrar) based on the Turkish Multi Role Tactical Platform 33 (MRTP 33) design have been commissioned in 2007 and 2008 respectively. Unconfirmed reports indicate these may be equipped with Harpoon SSMs and a short range SAM.
- **Landing Craft (Mechanised)**. Two LCMs built by KSEW have been inducted into the PN in April 2016. These will provide the PN the capability to land men and materials in areas on its coast. They may be seen as the beginnings of an amphibious capability, but are too small to enable amphibious landings on hostile shores.
- **Support Vessels**. Pakistan also operates a number of auxiliaries and support vessels suited for support or constabulary tasks, but with negligible warfighting capability. These include the fleet tanker PNS Nasr, an unnamed

tanker built in collaboration with Turkey, the Munsif (Tripartite) Class mine countermeasures vessels, 70 Ton MRTP 15 boats built in accordance with a design obtained from Turkey and maritime patrol vessels operated by the MSA (Pakistan's Coast Guard). These vessels have negligible offensive capability, hence they are not considered further in this paper.

Naval Aviation

6. Pakistan has three naval air bases: PNS Mehran at Karachi, PNS Makran at Pasni and PNS Siddique at Turbat. The naval aircraft inventory comprises the following:

- 7 Lockheed P3C Orion LRMP aircraft, of the total 10 received from USA from 1996 onwards. The aircraft are operated by 28 Sqn. One was lost in a crash in October 1999, while two were destroyed by terrorists in the attack on PNS Mehran in 2011. Two aircraft delivered in 2012 and 2013 are new, the rest are refurbished old USN aircraft. Their weapon package includes Harpoon ASMs, Mk 46 torpedoes, 127 mm rockets, depth charges, bombs and active and passive sonobuoys. Avionics include maritime surveillance radar and inverse synthetic aperture radar, an advanced electro-optical and infra-red imaging system, a sonobuoy receiver and acoustic processor, MAD and ESM. Designed as a long range maritime patrol and anti-submarine aircraft, these P-3Cs enable Pakistan to maintain good surveillance over the Northern Arabian Sea, up to a line linking the Red Sea and Mumbai.
- 3 ATR 72-212A transport and maritime patrol aircraft. Two were delivered in 2013 and one in August 2016. These are likely to be employed in a constabulary role.
- <u>Mirage 5PA/JF-17 Thunder Maritime Strike Aircraft</u>. The PAF acquired 41 second-hand aircraft from 1995 onwards. Some of them are dedicated to a maritime strike role and are reportedly flown by PN pilots for such missions. They have a combat radius sufficient to reach the approaches to Mumbai in a Hi-Lo-Hi profile. They are reportedly being replaced by JF-17 Thunder.
- Four Hawker 800 EW aircraft.
- Fokker F 27.
- Harbin Z-9 Helicopters.
- Westland Sea King Helicopters.
- Alouette III Helicopters.

UAVs

7. The PN has the following UAVs:

- 20 UQAB-II, inducted in 2011. These have a range of 100 Km and endurance in excess of six hours. They carry a 20 Kg payload comprising colour camera and a thermal imager with target tracking capability, transmitting real time information to the Ground Control Station.
- 8 LUNA UAVs, inducted in 2010.
- An unknown number of Scan Eagle UAVs, inducted in 2016.

Special Services Group Navy (SSGN)

8. The Special Services Group Navy is the PN's elite Special Operations Force, the counterpart of India's MARCOS. Their actual strength is estimated at between 700 and 1000 personnel, the actual strength being classified. Based on the US Navy SEALS and the British SBS, they are trained at USN facilities by the SEALS and tasked with unconventional warfare in coastal regions. Pakistan's midget submarines are operated by the SSGN. Their Headquarters are at PNS Iqbal, in Karachi. No information about the SSGN's expansion plans is available in the public domain.

APPENDIX 'C'

(Refers to Para 40 of Chapter 3)

PAKISTAN AIR FORCE

(Extracts from Military Balance, 2017: International Institute of Strategic Studies, London)

Strategic Forces

Operational control rests with the National Command Authority. The Strategic Plans Directorate (SPD) manages and commands all of Pakistan's military nuclear capability. The SPD also commands a reportedly 25,000-strong military security force responsible for guarding military nuclear infrastructure.

Army Strategic Forces Command.

- 12,000 to 15,000 personnel.
- All land-based strategic nuclear forces.

<u>Equipment by Type</u>

SURFACE-TO-SURFACE MISSILE LAUNCHERS 60+

MRBM • Nuclear ε30 Ghauri/Ghauri II (Hatf-5)/Shaheen-2 (Hatf-6 – in test); Shaheen-3 (in test).

SRBM • Nuclear 30+: ε30 Ghaznavi (Hatf-3 – PRC M-11)/Shaheen-1 (Hatf-4); some Abdali (Hatf-2); some Nasr (Hatf-9) GLCM • Nuclear Babur (Hatf-7); Ra'ad (Hatf-8 – in test).

Air Force 1–2 sqn of F-16A/B or Mirage 5 may be assigned a nuclear-strike role.

<u>Air Force</u> – **70,000**

3 regional comds: Northern (Peshawar), Central (Sargodha), Southern (Masroor). The Composite Air Tpt Wg, Combat Cadres School and PAF Academy are Direct Reporting Units.

<u>FORCES BY ROLE</u>

FIGHTER

1 sqn with F-7P/FT-7P Skybolt
3 sqn with F-7PG/FT-7PG Airguard
1 sqn with F-16A/B MLU Fighting Falcon
1 sqn with F-16A/B ADF Fighting Falcon
1 sqn with Mirage IIID/E (IIIOD/EP)

FIGHTER/GROUND ATTACK

2 sqn with JF-17 Thunder
1 sqn with JF-17 Thunder Block II
1 sqn with F-16C/D Block 52 Fighting Falcon
3 sqn with Mirage 5 (5PA)

ANTI-SURFACE WARFARE

1 sqn with Mirage 5PA2/5PA3 with AM-39 Exocet AShM

ELECTRONIC WARFARE/ELINT

1 sqn with Falcon 20F

AIRBORNE EARLY WARNING & CONTROL

1 sqn with Saab 2000; Saab 2000 Erieye
1 sqn with ZDK-03

SEARCH & RESCUE

1 sqn with Mi-171Sh (SAR/liaison)
6 sqn with SA316 Alouette III TANKER
1 sqn with Il-78 Midas TRANSPORT
1 sqn with C-130B/E Hercules; CN-235M-220; L-100-20
1 VIP sqn with B-707; Cessna 560XL Citation Excel; CN235M-220; F-27-200 Friendship; Falcon 20E; Gulfstream IVSP 1 (comms) sqn with EMB-500 Phenom 100; Y-12 (II)

TRAINING

1 OCU sqn with F-7P/FT-7P Skybolt
1 OCU sqn with Mirage III/Mirage 5
1 OCU sqn with F-16A/B MLU Fighting Falcon
2 sqn with K-8 Karakorum*
2 sqn with MFI-17
2 sqn with T-37C Tweet

AIR DEFENCE

1 bty with HQ-2 (SA-2 Guideline); 9K310 Igla-1 (SA-16 Gimlet)
6 bty with Crotale
10 bty with SPADA 2000

EQUIPMENT BY TYPE

AIRCRAFT 451 Combat Capable

FTR 195: 48 F-7PG Airguard; 60 F-7P Skybolt; 24 F-16A MLU Fighting Falcon; 21 F-16B MLU Fighting Falcon; 9 F-16A ADF Fighting Falcon; 4 F-16B ADF Fighting Falcon; 21 FT-7; 6 FT-7PG; 2 Mirage IIIB

FGA 208: 12 F-16C Block 52 Fighting Falcon; 6 F-16D Block 52 Fighting Falcon; 49 JF-17 Thunder (FC-1 Block 1); 20 JF-17 Thunder (FC-1 Block 2); 7 Mirage IIID (Mirage IIIOD); 63 Mirage IIIE (IIIEP); 39 Mirage 5 (5PA)/5PA2; 2 Mirage 5D (5DPA)/5DPA2; 10 Mirage 5PA3 (ASuW)

ISR 10 Mirage IIIR* (Mirage IIIRP)

ELINT 2 Falcon 20F

AEW&C 5: 1 Saab 2000 Erieye (2 more non-op); 4 ZDK-03

TKR 4 Il-78 Midas

TPT: 35: Medium 16: 5 C-130B Hercules; 10 C-130E Hercules; 1 L-100-20; Light 14: 2 Cessna 208B; 1 Cessna 560XL Citation Excel; 4 CN-235M-220; 4 EMB-500 Phenom 100; 1 F-27-200 Friendship; 2 Y-12 (II); PAX 5: 1 B-707; 1 Falcon 20E; 2 Gulfstream IVSP; 1 Saab 2000 TRG 142: 38 K-8 Karakorum*; 80 MFI-17B Mushshak; 24 T-37C Tweet

<u>**HELICOPTERS**</u>

MRH 15 SA316 Alouette III

TPT • Medium 4 Mi-171Sh

<u>**UNMANNED AERIAL VEHICLES**</u>

CSIR • Heavy CH-3 (Burraq)

<u>**AIR DEFENCE**</u>

SAM 190+ Medium-range 6 HQ-2 (SA-2 Guideline) Short-range 184: 144 Crotale; ε40 SPADA 2000 Point-defence 9K310 Igla-1 (SA-16 Gimlet)

<u>**RADAR**</u>

AD 6+: 6 AR-1 (AD radar low level); some Condor (AD radar high level); some FPS-89/100 (AD radar high level); MPDR 45/MPDR 60/MPDR 90 (AD radar low level); Type-514 (AD radar high level)

<u>**AIR-LAUNCHED MISSILES**</u>

AAM • IR AIM-9L/P Sidewinder; U-Darter; PL-5; SARH Super 530; ARH PL-12 (SD-10 – likely on order for the JF-17); AIM-120C AMRAAM

ASM AGM-65 Maverick; Raptor II

AShM AM-39 Exocet

ARM MAR-1

ALCM • Nuclear Ra'ad (in test)

<u>**BOMBS**</u> • Laser-guided Paveway II

APPENDIX 'D'

(Refers to Chapter 4)

CHINESE MILITARY

(Extracts from Military Balance, 2017: International Institute of Strategic Studies, London)

PLA Army Organization

- Part of the PLA's continuing reorganization includes the creation of a new national-level army headquarters in Beijing and a new theatre-command army headquarters in each of the five joint theatre commands that replaced the seven military regions (see above).
- Previously, four now-disbanded general departments served as the national-level army command, as well as performing joint functions for the other services. In bureaucratic terms, this configuration maintained army dominance among the forces. The new army headquarters in Beijing is organizationally equivalent to those of the navy, air force and rocket force. This has, in effect, lowered the prestige of the army and helped to better balance the four services. Eventually, the army is expected to bear the brunt of the personnel reduction (of 300,000 troops) that was announced in 2015.
- The former military regions commanded most of the operational army units, such as group armies, as well as the system of provincial military districts and their subordinate headquarters and units. Now that the military regions have been replaced, most operational army units come under the command of the five theatre-command army headquarters, while most military districts report to the Central Military Commission's National Defense Mobilisation Department. However, in an important exception, the central army headquarters directly oversees the Xinjiang and Tibet military districts, both of which command significant combat forces. The relationship between these military districts and the Western Theatre Command, where they are located, is unclear at the time of writing.
- The five theatre-command army headquarters are the principal link between the national-level army headquarters in Beijing and the joint theatre commands. They perform both 'construction' functions, such as personnel and organization, as directed by the national-level army headquarters, as well as 'operational' tasks, including war fighting and military operations other than war, as directed by the theatre commands. Accordingly, theatre-command army headquarters may serve as 'campaign headquarters' in time

of war or as 'emergency response headquarters' for non-traditional security missions.

- Furthermore, prior to the reorganization, army units wore the patches of the military region to which they were assigned. Now all army units wear generic army patches, which do not reflect the theatre command areas in which they are stationed.
- To date, all 18 group armies appear to be active and no divisions or brigades are known to have been eliminated as part of the reorganization. The only major change announced is the transfer of the 27th Group Army headquarters from Shijiazhuang to Taiyuan.
- There is also continued emphasis on developing 'new types of combat forces', which include army aviation, mechanized and light infantry units, special operations forces, and cyber-/electronic-warfare units. Despite the trend toward 'brigadisation' of the army, about 20 divisions remain spread among half of the group armies, with four assigned to the Xinjiang Military District.
- Group armies do not have a standard organizational structure. The number and type of mechanized, motorized and mountain/jungle infantry units within a group army ranges from two to five, along with a single armoured brigade/division. Army aviation and special-operations brigades or regiments are assigned to only about half the group armies. Smaller special-operations battalions or companies are being created in divisions and brigades, underscoring their primary focus on tactical and operational tasks rather than long-range strategic missions.
- Though the pace may be uneven and the force is reducing in size, the PLA Army is being equipped with weapons and technologies that allow its units to move more rapidly over difficult terrain (including water), to engage targets faster and at greater range, and – more than ever before – integrate their capabilities with those found in the other services. However, training personnel and units to operate and maintain their new equipment and execute more complex operations will be as great a challenge as is restructuring the force.

People's Liberation Army Air Force

- China's PLAAF continued to pursue broad modernization aims during 2016, progressing developments in combat, transport and special-mission aircraft, as well as in air-launched weapons. For tactical aircraft, Beijing is pursuing a twin-track approach of upgrading in-service types at the same time as developing at least two new multi-role combat aircraft.

- Following extended negotiations, early in 2016 the PLAAF signed a contract to purchase Russia's Su-35 Flanker E single-seat, multi-role combat aircraft, with the expectation that 24 aircraft would be purchased. The Su-35 is a development of the Su-27 Flanker design.
- Meanwhile, China's Shenyang Aircraft Corporation, which manufactures domestic versions of the Su-27 family, continued work on the J-11D. This is an improved variant of the J-11B, a variant of the Su-27 with domestic avionics and weapons. In all likelihood, the PLAAF will want to compare the 'D' model with the Su-35 before deciding which of the two types to acquire in order to replace early-model Su-27/J-11s as these come to the end of their service lives over the next decade.
- The PLAAF also continued its development of the Chengdu J-20 heavy fighter. Eight prototype aircraft have been built and are now being joined by production-standard aircraft. The type is likely to enter front-line service by the end of the decade. Work also continued on the Shenyang J-31 combat aircraft, though at a far slower pace than the Chengdu J-20, and as of the third quarter of 2016, no imagery of a second prototype had been released.
- At the same time, the PLAAF continued its attempts to address its relative weakness in heavy transport, airborne early warning (AEW), air-to-air refueling, and intelligence, surveillance and reconnaissance platforms. The first two Xian Y-20 transport aircraft were delivered to the air force in June 2016 and, assuming the aircraft's performance is acceptable, the type will likely replace the Russian Il-76 Candid as the core of the airlift fleet. It is possible that tanker and AEW versions of the Y-20 may also emerge.
- Reports also appeared in the Chinese media in 2016 that the PL-10 imaging infrared air-to-air missile was entering service with the air force. The PL-10 will likely replace the PL-8 and the R-73 (AA-11 Archer) as the PLAAF's primary short-range air-to-air missile; it is also likely that the PL-10 will be a credible offer in the export arena.

People's Liberation Army Navy

- Beijing continued to consolidate its presence in the South China Sea in 2016, notwithstanding the judgments against China by the UN Permanent Court of Arbitration in July. China's comprehensive naval modernization programme continued to make steady progress, encompassing not just further additions to the fleet of modern, more capable combatants, but also logistic-support capabilities and developments in training and doctrine. The Dalian Shipbuilding Industry Corporation is making rapid progress in building China's first domestically produced aircraft carrier, with the suggestion that the vessel could be ready for launch in 2017. The ship was only officially confirmed at the end of 2015, and it appears to be a close, although evolutionary, copy of the PLAN's first carrier, the Liaoning, which was built in Ukraine. The Liaoning's capability remains limited. However, it has been observed with up to eight Shenyang J-15 naval combat aircraft embarked, as the PLAN continues to develop its operational carrier experience and the military concepts required to use this new capability.

- There is now firm evidence that work is under way on the first of the anticipated Type-055 large destroyer/cruisers. Meanwhile, the PLAN's third and fourth Type-052D multi-mission destroyers were commissioned in December 2015 and June 2016. A fifth appeared close to completion, out of a total of at least 12 of these vessels now in service or under construction.
- In addition, more Type-054A frigates and Type-056A corvettes were added to the PLAN's inventory. Other significant additions during 2016 included the commissioning of a fourth Type-071 landing platform dock, which will be assigned to the East Sea Fleet, boosting the PLAN's amphibious capabilities. (The South Sea Fleet received the first three Type-071s.) Speculation persisted in 2016 about plans for an amphibious-aviation ship, which would be a logical next step for the PLAN's growing amphibious capabilities.
- Perhaps of equal significance was the commissioning of three more Type-903A large replenishment ships in 2016, as part of the modernization and strengthening of the PLAN's logistic support. Beijing also announced the decision to construct a naval facility in Djibouti. These developments reinforce the impression that the PLAN's blue-water capabilities are maturing.
- It remains more difficult to discern the Chinese submarine force's progress. It is still unclear whether the Jin-class Type-094 ballistic-missile submarines have begun regular patrols, and if not, why not, since the boats would seem to have been ready for some time. There is also uncertainty over the operational status of the latest, improved variant of the Shang class Type-093 nuclear-powered attack submarine, which features a vertical-launch system believed capable of accommodating the YJ-18 advanced anti-ship cruise missile.
- The China Coast Guard also continues to bolster its capabilities and appears to have adopted the basic design of the PLAN's Type-54A frigate (without weapons) for its latest ocean-going patrol vessel. It has also received modified

former PLAN Type 053H2G frigates, again with weapons removed, and completed a second 10,000-tonne patrol ship. Beijing continues to develop the different arms of its maritime capability in pursuit of broad policy goals, but these larger coastguard vessels will likely permit deployments of greater duration, at greater range and in larger sea states.

BIBLIOGRAPHY

Books

Bajwa, JS, *China: Threat or Challenge*? New Delhi: Lancer Publications, 2017.

Buzan, Barry, *Security: A New Framework for Analysis*, Lynne Rienner Publishers, 1998.

Chawala, Shalini, *Nuclear Pakistan*, KW Publishers, New Delhi.

Dhar, Maloy Krishna, *Open Secrets: India's Intelligence Unveiled*, New Delhi: Manas Publications, 2005.

Guangqian, Peng and Yao Youzhi, *The Science of Military Strategy*, Beijing, People's Republic of China: Military Science Publishing House, 2005.

Horybho, Andrew, *Hybrid Wars: The Indirect Approach to Regime Change*, Project of the Institute of Strategic Studies, Peoples' Friendship University of Russia, 2015.

Ispahani, Mahnaz Z, *Roads and Rivals: The Political Uses of Access in the Borderlands of Asia*, Ithaca, NY: Cornell University Press, 1989.

Kanwal, Gurmeet, *The New Arthshastra*, NOIDA, India: Harper Collins, 2016.

Kaplan, Robert D, *The Revenge of Geography': What the Map Tells us About Coming Conflicts and the Battle Against Fate*, New York: Random House, 2012.

Katoch, PC and Datta, Saikat, *India's Special Forces: History and Future of Indian Special Forces*, New Delhi: Vij Books India, 2013.

Lin, Chongn, *China's Nuclear Weapon Strategy: Tradition within Evolution*, MA: Lexington Books, 1988.

Michael, Howard, Michael and Parte, Peter, Carl von Clausewitz: '*On War', Princeton* University Press), 1976/1984.

Narang, Vipin, *Nuclear Strategy in the Modern Era: Regional Powers and International Conflict*, Princeton University Press, 2014.

Small, Andrew, *The China-Pakistan Axis: Asia's New Geopolitics*, London: Hurst & Co Publishers Ltd, 2015.

Zhang, Baouhi, *China's Assertive Nuclear Posture*, Oxford: Routledge, Taylor & Francis Group, 2015.

Periodicals, Reports, Articles, Web References

"#Vault7: 85% of World's Smart Phones 'Weaponized' by CIA", RT Question

More, rt.com, March 7, 2017, https://www.rt.com/news/379775-cia-weaponized-85pc-worlds-smartphones/

Agus Harimurti Yudhoyono Quotes, https://www.goodreads.com/author/quotes/7224099.Agus_Harimurti_Yudhoyono

Annual Report to Congress, 'Military and Security Developments Involving the People's Republic of China', 2016.

Ansari, Usman, 'Pakistan Seeks to Energize Naval Modernisation', *Defense News*, June 17, 2015, http://www.defensenews.com/story/defense/naval/ships/2015/06/17/pakistan-revive-naval-modernization-shipbuilding-china-frigates-dockyard-ksew/71074464/

Ansari, Usman, 'Pakistan, China Finalise 8-Sub Construction Plan', *Defense News*, October 11, 2015, https://www.defensenews.com/naval/2015/10/11/pakistan-china-finalize-8-sub-construction-plan/

Arora, Kamna, 'Two-Front War against India Possible', *Zee News*, October 23, 2011, http://zeenews.india.com/exclusive/-two-front-war-against-india-possible_3375.html

Asian Development Bank, 'Poverty in India', https://www.adb.org/countries/india/poverty

Bannon, Steve, 'We're Going to War in the South China Sea ... No Doubt', *The Guardian*, February 2, 2017, https://www.theguardian.com/us-news/2017/feb/02/steve-bannon-donald-trump-war-south-china-sea-no-doubt

Bernard D Cole, 'Reflections on China's Maritime Strategy: Island Chains and the Classics', US Naval War College, see https://www.usnwc.edu/Academics/Faculty/Derek-Reveron/Workshops/Maritime-Security,-Seapower,—Trade/Maritime-Working-Papers/cole-island-chains.aspx

Bhardwaj, Amit, 'How BJP's IT Cell Waged War and Won in UP', *Newslaundry*, March 17, 2017, https://www.newslaundry.com/2017/03/17/how-bjps-it-cell-waged-war-and-won-in-up

Blank, Stephen, 'The Chinese Concept of "Unrestricted Warfare"', *Global Competitors Up The Ante*, Second Line of Defense, April 11, 2014, http://www.sldinfo.com/the-chinese-concept-of-unrestricted-warfare-global-competitors-up-the-ante/

Boh Ze Ka, 'Narco Diplomacy: Foreign Policy of the United Wa State Army', *Mantraya Special Report*, January 27, 2016, http://mantraya.org/narco-diplomacy-foreign-policy-of-the-united-wa-state-army/

Burgers, Tobias J and Romaniuk, Scott N, 'Hybrid Warfare in the South China Sea: The United States' Little Grey (Un) Men', *The Diplomat*, December 31, 2016, http://thediplomat.com/2016/12/hybrid-warfare-in-the-south-china-sea-the-united-states-little-grey-unmen/

Byman, Daniel, 'Recommendations for the Commission on the Prevention of Weapons of Mass Destruction Proliferation and Terrorism', June 13, 2008, https://www.brookings.edu/wp-content/uploads/2016/06/0613_terrorism_byman-1.pdf

Calvo, Alex, 'Pakistan's Navy: A Quick Look', CIMSEC, March 23, 2016, http://cimsec.org/pakistans-navy-quick-look/23227

Campose, Phillip, 'India's National Security Strategy: Imperative of Integrating Defence Policy', *CLAWS Journal*, Winter 2016.

'Capabilities for Computer Network Operations and Cyber Espionage', Northrop Grumman Corporation, March 2012.

Chabbewal, Amarjeet S, 'India's Military Might: The Real Truth', *Indian Defence Review*, March 18, 2017, http://www.indiandefencereview.com/news/indias-military-might-the-real-truth/

Chellaney, Brahma, 'Shed the Indus Albatross: Indus Waters Treaty Offers One-sided Benefits to Pakistan, World Bank Too Is Partisan', *Times of India*, March 20, 2017, http://blogs.timesofindia.indiatimes.com/toi-edit-page/shed-the-indus-albatross-indus-waters-treaty-offers-one-sided-benefits-to-pakistan-world-bank-too-is-partisan/

'China Confirms Sale of 8 Attack Submarines to Pak, First Delivery by 2023', *Hindustan Times*, October 21, 2016,http://www.hindustantimes.com/world-news/china-confirms-sale-of-8-attack-submarines-to-pakistan-first-delivery-by-2023/story-kqSiZxhkB6r60QvhF2G7CK.html

'China GDP Annual Growth Rate Forecast 2016-2020', *Trading Economics*, http://www.tradingeconomics.com/china/gdp-growth-annual/forecast

'China has deployed more troops near Indian border: Pentagon', *The Indian Express*, May 14, 2016, http://indianexpress.com/article/india/india-news-india/china-has-deployed-more-troops-near-indian-border-pentagon-2799965/

'China Military Spending Quickens as Xi Seeks "World Class" Military', *Bloomberg News*, March 5, 2018, https://www.bloomberg.com/news/articles/2018-03-05/china-military-spending-quickens-as-xi-seeks-world-class-force

'China Rushing to Beat US in the Race to Space', *Pakistan Defence*, February 19, 2016, https://defence.pk/pdf/threads/china-rushing-to-beat-us-in-the-race-to-space.422675/

'China Starts Building Huge Cosmic-ray Observatory to Study the Evolution of the Universe', *News Room*, March 16, 2017, http://english.cas.cn/newsroom/news/201703/t20170316_174968.shtml

'China Tests Missile That Can Carry 10 Nuclear Warheads: Report', *The Tribune*, February 3, 2017, http://www.tribuneindia.com/news/world/china-tests-missile-that-can-carry-10-nuclear-warheads-report/358517.html

'China's Military Strategy', *China Daily*, May 26, 2015, http://www.chinadaily.com.cn/china/2015-05/26/content_20820628_2.htm

'China's Road & Belt Initiative: Indian Perspective', http://www.vifindia.org/article/2016/may/19/chinas-road-and-belt-initiative-indian-perspective

'China's Space and Counterspace Programs', Report to Congress, US-China Economic and Security Review Commission, November 2015. http://origin.www.uscc.gov/sites/default/files/annual_reports/2015%20Annual%20 Report %20to%20Congress.PDF

'China's Straight Deck Amphibious Assault Ship', Official Information, December 7, 2015, http://www.china-arms.com/2015/12/chinas-straight-deck-amphibious-assault-ship-confirmed-by-official-information/

'China's Xi Allowed to Remain 'President for Life' as Term Limits Removed', *BBC News*, March 11, 2018, http://www.bbc.com/news/world-asia-china-43361276

'Chinese Airfields Encircle Ladakh', *Defense News*, March 11, 2018, http://www.defence.pk/forums/indian-defence/138148-chinese-airfields-encircle-ladakh.html#ixzz2JGx2Ph7p

'Chinese Army Spotted along Line of Control in Pakistan-Occupied Kashmir, say sources', *Times of India*, March 13, 2016, http://timesofindia.indiatimes.com/india/Chinese-army-spotted-along-Line-of-Control-in-Pakistan-occupied-Kashmir-say-sources/articleshow/51380359.cms.

'Chinese Engineer and Driver Injured in Karachi Separatist Bombing', *The Guardian*, May 30, 2016, https://www.theguardian.com/world/2016/may/30/chinese-worker-driver-injured-karachi-bombing-claimed-separatists

'Chinese Military Modernisation and Force Development', July 2012, Burke Chair Study, csis.org.

'Chinese, Pakistani Businesses Build Ties as Beijing Splurges on "Silk Road"', *Dawn*, February 3, 2017, http://www.dawn.com/news/1312472

Clark, Wesley, 'We're going to take out 7 countries in 5 years: Iraq, Syria, Lebanon, Libya, Sudan and Iran', *Global Research*, 12 July 2014, http://www.globalresearch.ca/we-re-going-to-take-out-7-countries-in-5-years-iraq-syria-lebanon-libya-somalia-sudan-iran/5166

'CNS Global Incidents and Trafficking Database - 2015 Annual Report', March 2016, http://www.nti.org/media/documents/global_incidents_trafficking_report.pdf

Congressional Research Service, 'Pakistan: US Foreign Assistance', July 1, 2013. www.crs.org.

'Crime Index for Country 2017', https://www.numbeo.com/crime/rankings_ by_country.jsp

Dalton, Toby and George Perkovitch, 'Alliance is Unstable, not Pakistan's Nukes', Carnegie Endowment, May 16, 2011, http://carnegieendowment.org/2011/05/16/alliance-is-unstable-not-pakistan-s-nukes/2oi

Das, Pushpa, 'India: Internal Security Budget 2017-2018 – Analysis', *Eurasia View*, February 22, 2017, http://www.eurasiareview.com/22022017-india-internal-security-budget-2017-2018-analysis/

Dasgupta, Sunil and Cohen, P Stephen, 'How Not to Deal with Defence Corruption', *Indian Express*, April 2, 2013. http://indianexpress.com/article/opinion/columns/how-not-to-deal-with-defence-corruption/

Deep, Alex (2015-03-02), 'Hybrid War: Old Concept, New Techniques', *Small Wars Journal*, Small War Foundation, retrieved 2015-08-05.

Donnan, Shawn, 'World Bank Eyes Biggest Global Poverty Line Increase in Decades', *The Financial Times*, May 9, 2014.

Durrani, MA, 'Pakistan's Strategic Thinking and the Role Of Nuclear Weapons', Cooperative Monitoring Center Occasional Paper 37, Sandia National Laboratories, Sand Report July 2004, http://www.cmc.sandia.gov/cmc-papers/sand2004-3375p.pdf

El Mawy, Reda (2014-09-30), 'Islamic State Adapting to US-led Air Strikes', *BBC New*, BBC, archived from the original on 2015-08-05, retrieved 2015-08-05.

Fair, Christene, 'Denying Pakistan the Dividends of Terror', *Open Magazine*, September 23, 2016, http://www.openthemagazine.com/article/cover-story/denying-pakistan-the-dividends-of-terror

Faizy, Mansoor, 'Afghanistan Rejects SIGAR Report', *Afghanistan Times*, February 1, 2017, http://afghanistantimes.af/afghanistan-rejects-sigar-report/

Feldman, Dan, 'Successes and Challenges in Afghanistan and Pakistan', *United States Institute of Peace*, August 5, 2015,http://www.state.gov/p/sca/rls/rmks/2015/245767.htm

Fleming, Brian P (2011-05-19), 'Hybrid Threat Concept: Contemporary War, Military Planning and the Advent of Unrestricted Operational Art', United States Army Command and General Staff College, archived pdf from the original on 2015-08-05, retrieved 2015-08-05.

Forest, Kaya and Sierra Rayne, 'China and Russia Combined Now at Military Spending Parity with US', April 13, 2016, http://www.americanthinker.com/blog/2016/04/china_and_russia_combined_now_at_military _spending_parity_with_us.html

'Former British Army Officials Now Training ISIS Militants in Iraq: MI6, CIA', *News*, webindi123, 31 August 2014, http://news.webindia123.com/news/articles/India/20140831/2450603.html

Gard, Robert and Terryn, Greg, 'American Nuclear Strategy: The Case for a Minimal-Deterrence Policy', December 1, 2014, http://nationalinterest.org/feature/american-nuclear-strategy-the-case-minimal-deterrence-policy-11755

Ghosh, Partha S, 'Socio-Political Trends in Southern Asia Security Implications for India', http://www.satp.org/satporgtp/publication/faultlines/volume17/Article2.htm

'Global Strategic Trends – Out to 2040', Development, Concepts and Doctrine Centre (DCDC), Ministry of Defence, Government of UK, https://www.gov.uk/government/uploads/system/uploads/attachment_data/file/33717/GST4_v9_Feb10.pdf

Goldstein, Lyle J, 'China's YJ-18 Supersonic Antiship Cruise Missile: America's Nightmare', *National Interest*, June 1, 2015, http://nationalinterest.org/feature/chinas-yj-18-supersonic-anti-ship-cruise-missile-americas-13010

Grant, Greg (2008-05-01), 'Hybrid Wars', Government Executive, *National Journal Group*, archived from the original on 2015-08-05, retrieved 2015-08-05.

Green, Marcel A, 'China's Growing Cyberwar Capabilities', *The Diplomat*, April 13, 2015, http://thediplomat.com/2015/04/chinas-growing-cyberwar-capabilities/

Haider, Irfan, 'Details of Agreements Signed During Xi's Visit to Pakistan', *Dawn*, April 20, 2015, http://www.dawn.com/news/1177129/details-of-agreements-signed-during-xis-visit-to-pakistan

Hao, Zhan, 'Why Is the China-Pakistan Relation Unique in the World?', *Beyondnewsnet*, Apri; 22, 2015, http://beyondnewsnet.com /20150422/16557/

Hassan, Ishfaq Ul, 'WhatsApp groups with Pak Admins Behind Crowd Mobilisation in J&K', DNA, March 19, 2017, http://www.dnaindia.com/india/report-whatsapp-group-with-pak-admins-behind-crowd-mobilisation-in-jk-2358531

Hoffman G Frank, 'Hybrid Warfare and Challenges', NDU Press, JFQ/issue 52, 1st quarter 2009.

Hoffman, Frank, 'Conflict in the 21st Century: The Rise of Hybrid War', Potomac Institute for Policy Studies, Arlington, http://www.potomacinstitute.org/images/stories/publications/potomac_hybridwar_0108.pdf

Holmes, James, 'Will China Become an Aircraft Carrier Superpower', Foreign Policy, January 21, 2016, http://foreignpolicy.com/2016/01/21/will-china-become-an-aircraft-carrier-superpower/

Hoodbhoy, Pervez, 'Pakistan's Westward Drift', Islamic Research Foundation International Inc, September 8, 2008, http://www.irfi.org/articles2/articles_3251_3300/pakistan's%20westward%20drifthtml.htm

'How Does China's First Aircraft Carrier Stack Up', CSIS, http://chinapower.csis.org/aircraft-carrier/

'Hydropower in India: Key Enablers for a Better Tomorrow', FICCI, http://www.pwc.in/assets/pdfs/publications/2014/hydropower-in-india-key-enablers-for-better-tomorrow.pdf

iCasualties: 'Operation Iraqi Freedom and Operation Enduing Freedom/Afghanistan', icasualties.org, http://icasualties.org/

IISS Military Balance 2017.

'In India, a Military Strategy Guided by Precision', *STRATFOR*, October 6, 2016, https://www.stratfor.com/sample/analysis/india-military-strategy-guided-precision

'India Ranks 131 on Human Development Index, Norway No. 1', *Live Mint*, March 22, 2017, http://www.livemint.com/Politics/NcyY1Zr768TEl02yaRSh4M/India-ranks-131-on-global-Human-Development-Index-Norway-No.html

'India vs China Military Power Comparison | Indian Army vs Chinese Army | Full Documentary', *World Military Channel*, August 18, 2016, https://www.youtube.com/watch?v=yyRROSl5SSM

'Inter Services Public Relations', Press Release, No. PR130/2012-ISPR, May 29, 2012, http://www.ispr.gov.pk/front/main.asp?o=t-press_release&id=2074

Jain, Dipti, 'Was the Indian Economy "Healthy" Before Demonetisation?', *Live Mint*, February 17, 2017, http://www.livemint.com/Politics/P87C89as66H11KefFnba9J/Was-the-Indian-economy-healthy-before-demonetisation.html

'Jamaat-ud-Dawa Chief Hafiz Saeed placed on Pak's Exit Control List', *The Indian Express*, February 1, 2017, http://indianexpress.com/article/world/jamaat-ud-dawa-chief-hafiz-saeed-placed-on-paks-exit-control-list-4502943/

Jasper, Scott, Moreland, Scott, 'The Islamic State is a Hybrid Threat: Why Does That Matter?', *Small Wars Journal*, December 1, 2014, http://smallwarsjournal.com/printpdf/18345

Javeed, Nusrat, 'Indians Aiming at Strikes on Pakistan's Nukes', http://www.rense.com/general18/indiansaimingatstrikes.htm

'Joint Patrol along China-Pakistan Border', *People's Daily*, July 21, 2016, http://en.people.cn/n3/2016/0721/c98649-9089345.html

Jones, Sam, 'Ukraine: Russia's New Art of War', *Financial Times*, August 28, 2014, http://www.mediapool.bg/files/224/Ukraine_%20Russia%E2%80%99s%20new%20art%20of%20war%20-%20FT.pdf

Kalha, Ranjit Singh, 'The Dynamics of Preventive Diplomacy', New Delhi: KW Publishers, 2014.

Kanwal, Gurmeet, 'Why India Needs a National Security Strategy', *rediff.com*, June 17, 2016, http://www.rediff.com/news/column/why-india-needs-a-national-security-strategy/20160617.htm

Kapila, Subhash, 'India's Foreign Policy Challenges 2017 Analysed', South Asia Analysis Group, Paper No. 6205, December 16, 2016, http://www.southasiaanalysis.org/node/2100

Katoch, PC, 'The Currency of Terror', USI of India, 2013, http://usiofindia.org/Article/?pub=Strategic%20Perspective&pubilliono=37&ano=1883

Katoch, PC, 'Why India Should Never Join CPEC', SP's MAI, January 10, 2017, http://www.spsmai.com/experts-speak/?id=311&q=Why-India-should-never-join-CPEC

Katoch, Prakash, 'Demonitization: India Can't Win Its Black Money War by Going Soft on Political Parties', *First Post*, December 17, 2016, http://www.firstpost.com/india/demonetisation-india-cant-win-its-black-money-war-by-going-soft-on-political-parties-3161200.html

Katoch, Prakash, 'Make in India Found Floundering – But What Beyond?', *Indian Defence Review*, March 6, 2018, http://www.indiandefencereview.com/news/make-in-india-found-floundering-but-what-beyond/

Kenny, Stuart, 'China and India: A "New Great Game" Founded on Historic Mistrust and Current Competition', Indo-Pacific Strategic Papers, September 2015, http://www.defence.gov.au/ADC/Publications/IndoPac/Kenny_IPS_Paper.pdf

Kevin Pollpeter, 'China Dream, Space Dream: China's Progress in Space Technologies and Implications for the United States', US-China Economic and Security Review Commission, March 2, 2015.

Khan, Bilal, 'Is it Finally the Pakistan Navy's Turn', *Quwa*, October 3, 2015, http://quwa.org/2015/10/03/is-it-finally-the-pakistan-navys-turn/

Khan, Mubarak Zeb, 'Pakistan Rises to 122nd in Global Competitiveness Rankings', *Dawn*, September 28, 2016, https://www.dawn.com/news/1286493

Kingsbury, Alex, 'Why China Helped Countries Like Pakistan, North Korea Build Nuclear Bombs', *US News*, January 2, 2009, http://www.usnews.com/news/world/articles/2009/01/02/why-china-helped-countries-like-pakistan-north-korea-build-nuclear-bombs

Krepon, Michael, 'Nuclear Postures', Arms Control Wonk, 25 February, 2015, http://www.armscontrolwonk.com/archive/404492/nuclear-postures/

Kristensen, Hans M and Robert S Norris, 'Chinese Nuclear Forces, 2011', Taylor Francis, November 27, 2015, http://www.tandfonline.com/doi/abs/10.1177/0096340211426630

Kugelman, Michael, 'India's Environmental Security Challenge: Water, Coal, Natural Gas, and Climate Change Fuel Friction', New Security Beat, November 23, 2012, https://www.newsecuritybeat.org/2012/11/indias-environmental-security-challenge/

Lai, David, 'Learning by Doing: The PLA Trains at Home and Abroad', Carlisle, PA: Strategic Studies Institute, US Army War College, November 2012, http://ssi.armywarcollege.edu/pdffiles/pub1135.pdf

Lasica, T Daniel, 'Strategic Implications of Hybrid War: A Theory of Victory', United States Army Command and Staff College, AY 2009.

Laskar, Rezaul H, 'Nine Militant Groups of NE Form United Front with Chinese Blessings', *Hindustan Times*, April 24, 2015, http://www.hindustantimes.com/india/nine-miltant-groups-of-ne-form-united-front-with-chinese-blessings/story-6SuTFuFRymf27fSueYyoaP.html

Latif, Amir, 'A Comparative Study of Nuclear Doctrines of India and Pakistan', *Journal of Global Peace and Conflict*, June 2014, Vol. 2, No. 1.

Laxman, Beharam K, '"Make in India" for Defence: A Roadmap', Institute of Defence Studies and Analyses, February 5, 2015, http://www.idsa.in/policybrief/MakeinIndiaforDefence_lbehera_050215

Lei, Zhao, "New Rules Mean Ships Can Be Used by Military', *China Daily*, June 18, 2015, http://www.chinadaily.com.cn/china/2015-06/18/content_21036944.htm

Liang, Qiao and Xiangsui, Wang, 'Unrestricted Warfare: China's Master Plan to Destroy America', Pan American Publishing Company, Panama, 2002.

Listner, Michael J, 'Pakistan to Have a Functioning Global Navigation Satellite System by June 2013', *Space Safety Magazine*, November 7, 2012.

'Lodi, FS, Pakistan's Nuclear Doctrine', *Pakistan Defence Journal*, 1999, http://www.defencejournal.com/apr99/pak-nuclear-doctrine.htm

Lucian Kim, 'Russia Having Success in Hybrid War Against Germany', http://blogs.reuters.com/great debate/2016/02/07russia-having-success-in-hybrid-war-against-germany/

Macias, Amanda, 'Putin Once Casually Said Over Dinner That He Could Destroy America in a Half-Hour (or Less)', *Business Insider*, January 4, 2016, http://www.businessinsider.in/Putin-once-casually-said-over-dinner-that-he-could-destroy-America-in-a-half-hour-or-less/articleshow/50443170.cms

Mackinder, HJ, 'The Geographical Pivot of History', *The Geographical Journal*, London, 1904, http://onlinelibrary.wiley.com/doi/10.1111/j.0016-7398.2004.00132.x/abstract

Malik, Mohan, 'China Unveils "The Kashmir Card"', China Brief, Vol. 10, Issue 19, September 24, 2010, https://jamestown.org/program/china-unveils-the-kashmir-card/

'Mapping the Global Future', Report of the National Intelligence Council's 2020 Project, Washington, DC, USA, December 2004, http://www.futurebrief.com/project2020.pdf

Mary Ellen Connell and Ryan Evans, 'Russia's "Ambiguous Warfare" and Implications for the U.S. Marine Corps', CAN Occasional Paper, May 2015, https://www.cna.org/cna_files/pdf/dop-2015-u-010447-final.pdf

Mathur, Dhiraj, 'Unlocking defence R&D in India – Do We Have the Skill?', *First Post*, April 8, 2016, http://www.firstpost.com/business/unlocking-defence-rd-in-india-do-we-have-the-skill-2715650.html

McCuen, John J. 'Hybrid Wars', *Military Review*, 88 (2), p. 107.

McDermott, Roger N, 'Russia's Conventional Military Weakness and Substrategic Nuclear Policy', The Foreign Military Studies Office, Fort Leavenworth 2011, http://fmso.leavenworth.army.mil.

McDevitt, Michael, 'Does China Have an Effective Sea Based Deterrent', CSIS, http://chinapower.csis.org/ssbillion/

Medeiros, Evan S, 'Rightsizing the PLA: Exploring the Contours of China's Military', Strategic Studies Institute, US Army War College, Carlisle, Sep 2007.

Meyssan, Thierry, 'NATO Intends to Prohibit Russia's and China's Development', *Investment Watch*, 14 September, 2014, http://investmentwatchblog.com/nato-intends-to-prohibit-russias-and-chinas-development/

'Military Balance, 2017', International Institute of Strategic Studies, London.

Mirza, Nazir Abbas, 'A Monstrous Experiment', *Daily Times*, May 11, 2009, https://therearenosunglasses.wordpress.com/2009/05/12/a-monstrous-experiment/

Mizokami, Kyle, '5 Super Weapons China Would Use to Crush India in a War', The National Interests, February 6, 2017, http://nationalinterest.org/blog/the-buzz/5-super-weapons-china-would-use-crush-india-war-19332

Mizokami, Kyle, 'Five Chinese Weapons of War India Should Fear', The National Interest, June 28, 2014, http://nationalinterest.org/feature/five-chinese-weapons-war-india-should-fear-10774

Mizokami, Kyle, 'Five Indian Weapons of War China Should Fear', The National Interest, June 21, 2014, http://nationalinterest.org/feature/five-indian-weapons-war-china-should-fear-10714

Moss, Trefor, 'Bangladesh Eyes China Arms', *The Diplomat*, June 30, 2011, http://thediplomat.com/2011/06/bangladesh-eyes-china-arms/

Myres, Joseph C, 'The Quranic Concept of War', http://insct.syr.edu/wp-content/uploads/2013/03/MyersJoseph.Quranic-Concept-of-War.pdf

Nair, Vijai K, 'China's Evolving Strategic Capabilities: Doctrine, Concept, Force-Structure', South Asia Strategic Forum, May 25, 2013.

Naravane, Manoj, 'War Zone Campaign Doctrine a Revisit', http://www.claws.in/images/journals_doc/SW%20i-10.10.2012.71-79.pdf

NATO Review Magazine, 'Hybrid war – Does it even exist?', http://www.nato.int/

docu/review/2015/also-in-2015/hybrid-modern-future-warfare-russia-ukraine/EN/index.htm

O'Rourke, Ronald, 'China Naval Modernisation: Implications for US Navy Capabilities: Issues for Congress', CRS December 23, 2014,

'Operation Arachonophobia: Caught in the Spider's Web', http://paper.seebug.org/papers/APT/APT_CyberCriminal_Campagin/2014/ThreatConnect_Operation_Arachnophobia_Report.pdf

Osborn, Chris, 'China is Diminishing the US's Air Power Superiority', *Business Insider*, December 8, 2014, http://www.businessinsider.com/china-is-diminishing-the-uss-air-power-superiority-2014-12?IR=T

'Pakistan Could Put Nukes on New Submarines Sold by China', *Trib Live*, April 17, 2015, http://triblive.com/usworld/world/8194853-74/pakistan-nuclear-india

'Pakistan Economic Outlook', *Focus Economics*, January 24, 2017, http://www.focus-economics.com/countries/pakistan

'Pakistan Ranked 147th on HDI', *The News*, January 26, 2016, https://www.thenews.com.pk/print/93753-Pakistan-ranked-147th-on-HDI

'Pakistan Unemployment Rate Forecast 2016-2020', *Trading Economics*, http://www.tradingeconomics.com/pakistan/unemployment-rate/forecast

'Pakistan', SIPRI, https://www.sipri.org/research/armaments-and-disarmament/nuclear-weapons/world-nuclear-forces/pakistan

'Pakistani Army Chief Assures Full Security for CPEC', *Xinhuanet*, April 13, 2016, http://news.xinhuanet.com/english/2016-04/13/c_135274538.htm

Panda, Ankit, 'A First: China and Pakistan Conclude Naval Exercise in East China Sea', *The Diplomat*, January 4, 2016, http://thediplomat.com/2016/01/a-first-china-and-pakistan-conclude-naval-exercise-in-east-china-sea/

Panda, Ankit, 'Pakistan Army Seeks Greater Authority over China-Pakistan Economic Corridor Administration', *The Diplomat*, August 18, 2016, http://thediplomat.com/2016/04/pakistans-army-seeks-greater-authority-over-china-pakistan-economic-corridor-administration/

Pandit, Rajat, 'India Remains World's Largest Arms Importer, with 14% of Total Share', *Times of India*, February 22, 2016, http://timesofindia.indiatimes.com/india/India-remains-worlds-largest-arms-importer-with-14-of-total-share/articleshow/51095168.cms

Paul, TV, 'Chinese-Pakistani Nuclear/Missile Ties and the Balance of Power', *The Non-proliferation Review*, Summer 2003.

Pedesen, Chris, 'Flipping the Switch: A Look at India's Future Energy Demands', Energy, October 20, 2014, http://breakingenergy.com/2014/10/20/flipping-the-switch-a-look-at-indias-future-energy-demands/

'Pentagon Report and Chinese Nuclear Forces', Federation of American Scientists, May 18, 2016, https://fas.org/blogs/security/2016/05/chinareport2016/

Peri, Dinakar, 'Yaogan Satellites and Chinese ASBM Capability', http://www.claws.in/images/journals_doc/653652095_DinakerPeri.pdf

Petri Huovinen, Petri, 'Hybrid Warfare: Just a Twist of Compound Warfare?', National Defence University, Washington DC, April 2011.

Pilger, John, 'In Ukraine the US is Dragging us Towards War with Russia', *The News*, May 14, 2014, http://www.theguardian.com/commentisfree/2014/may/13/ukraine-us-war-russia-john-pilger

Pindják, Peter (2014-11-18), 'Deterring Hybrid Warfare: A Chance for NATO and EU to Work Together?', *NATO Review*, archived from the original on 2015-08-05, retrieved 2015-08-05.

Ping, Su and Kao Yi, 'Intensive Talks between Chinese and Pakistani Business Communities', *BBC China*, 2015-04 19, http://www.bbc.com/zhongwen/trad/world/2015/04/150419_china_pakistan_deals

'PLA Signs Preliminary Deal for 24 Russian Su-35 Jet Fighters', *South China Morning Post*, December 7, 2012, http://www.scmp.com/news/china/article/1099368/pla-signs-preliminary-deal-24-russian-su-35-jet-fighters accessed on January 3, 2013

'PN Fleet Tanker', *Naval Technology*, http://www.naval-technology.com/projects/pn-fleet-tanker/

'Poverty & Equality Data Portal, The World Bank', povertydata.worldbank.org

'Press Release of ISPR' on April 21, 2015, https://www.ispr.gov.pk/front/main.asp?o=t-press_release&date=2015/4/21

'Press Release of ISPR' on February 19, 2016, https://www.ispr.gov.pk/front/main.asp?o=t-press_release&date=2016/2/19

'Quran Allows Elimination of Troublemakers: M J Akbar', *The Times of India*, February 10, 2017, http://timesofindia.indiatimes.com/india/quran-allows-elimination-of-troublemakers-m-j-akbar/articleshow/57071594.cms

Rehman, Iskander, 'Murky Waters: Naval Nuclear Dynamics in the Indian Ocean', Carnegie Endowment, March 9, 2015, http://carnegieendowment.org/2015/03/09/murky-waters-naval-nuclear-dynamics-in-indian-ocean-pub-59279

Renz, Bettina and Smith Hanna, 'Russia and Hybrid Warfare: Going Beyond the Label', Aleksanteri Papers 1/2016, http://www.helsinki.fi/aleksanteri/english/publications/presentations/papers/ap_1_2016.pdf

Reza, Akash, 'China and India in the Perspective of Sun Tzu and Kautilya's Thought', July 29, 2008, https://ishakhan.wordpress.com/2008/07/29/china-and-india-in-the-perspective-of-sun-tzu-and-kautilya%E2%80%99s-thought/

Rickard, James, 'Sun Tzu, Nuclear Weapons and China's Grand Strategy', Centre for Contemporary Conflict, http://www.au.af.mil/au/awc/awcgate/nps/rickard_chin_grand_strat_jul08.pdf

Rinehart, Ian A, 'The Chinese Military: Overview and Issues for the Congress', CRS Report R44196, March 24, 2016, https://www.fas.org/sgp/crs/row/R44196.pdf

'Rockets, Mortars Fired from Across Iran Border', *Dawn*, March 12, 2017, https://www.dawn.com/news/1319951/rockets-mortars-fired-from-across-iran-border

'Russia to Deliver S-400 Air Defence Missile Systems to China Before 2020', defenseaerospace.com, November 10, 2016, http://www.defense-aerospace.com/articles-view/release/3/178669/russia-to-complete-s_400-deliveries-to-china-by-2020.html

'Russia's Use of Military Force as a Foreign Policy Tool: Is There a Logic?', http://www.ponarseurasia.org/node/8728

'Sardar Vallabhbhai Patel's letter to Jawaharlal Nehru on 7 November 1950' not only deploring Indian Ambassador KM Panikkar's action but also 'Warning Dangers from China', http://www.friendsoftibet.org/main/sardar.html

Sayers, Eric, 'China's Asymmetrical Strategy', *The Weekly Standard*, December 26, 2007, http://www.weeklystandard.com/chinas-asymmetrical-strategy/article/15628

Shahi, Agha, Zulfiqar Ali Khan and Abdul Sattar, 'Securing Nuclear peace', *The News*, October 5, 1990.

Sibal, Kanwal, 'Adrift Without a Strategic Culture', *India Today*, March 12, 2013, http://indiatoday.intoday.in/story/national-security-nuclear-age-armed-forces-british-rule-security-threat-china-military/1/257472.html

Siddiqui, Salman, 'Lagging Behind: 2040 – Pakistan's space Odyssey', https://tribune.com.pk/story/415738/lagging-behind-2040-pakistans-space-oddyssey/

'Six Principles of Sun Tzu & the Art of Business', http://www.suntzustrategies.com/resources/six-principles-of-sun-tzu-the-art-of-business

Sonwalker, Prasun, 'Pakistan "Very Concerned" at India's Military Modernisation', *Hindustan Times*, February 9, 2016, http://www.hindustantimes.com/world/pakistan-very-concerned-at-india-s-military-modernisation/story-JOrnmwTnk8B6CJ3vfrGhnJ.html

Subrahmanyam, K, 'Academic Contribution to National Security Policy Formulation in India', *The Institute for Defence Studies and Analyses Journal*, January 1969, Vol.1, No.2.

Tadjbakhsh, S, 'Human Security in International Organizations: Blessings or Scourge?', *The Human Security Journal*, Vol. 4, Summer 2007.

Tellis, Ashley J, 'India as a Leading Power', Carnegie Endowment for International Peace, April 2016.

Tellis, Ashley, 'The Menace That is Lashkar-e-Taiba', Carnegie Endowment for International Peace, March 13, 2012.

'The PLA Navy: A Modern Navy with Chinese Characteristics', http://fas.org/irp/agency/oni/pla-navy.pdf

'The PLA Navy: New Capabilities and Missions for the 21st Century', US Office of Naval Intelligence, 2015.

Thompson, Mark, 'The True Cost of the Afghanistan War May Surprise You', *Times*, January 1, 2015, http://time.com/3651697/afghanistan-war-cost/

Tiezzi, Shannon, 'The New Military Force in Charge of China's Nuclear Weapons, Goodbye Second Artillery Force; Hello PLA Rocket Force', January 5, 2016, http://thediplomat.com/2016/01/the-new-military-force-in-charge-of-chinas-nuclear-weapons/

'Trade between Pakistan and China Continues to Grow at Steady Pace', *Balochistan Times*, April 27, 2016.

Trofimov, Yaroslav, 'America's Fading Footprint in the Middle East', *The Wall Street Journal*, October 9, 2015, http://www.wsj.com/articles/americas-fading-footprint-in-the-middle-east-1444411954

'United States Political Warfare Policy', January 2015, http://orchestratingpower.org/lib/LIC/PW/2015%20draft%20PWP.pdf

'US and Allied Killed, Cost of War', Watson Institute, Brown University, http://watson.brown.edu/costsofwar/costs/human/military/killed

US DoD Annual Report to Congress on 'Military and Security Developments Involving the People's Republic of China 2016', https://www.defense.gov/Portals/1/Documents/pubs/2016%20China%20Military%20Power%20Report.pdf

US Joint Forces Command, 'The Joint Operating Environment: Challenges and Implications for the Future Joint Force', Norfolk, VA: U.S. Joint Forces Command, November 2008.

'US Senate Passes $800m Pakistan Fund', *Dawn*, June 16, 2016, http://www.dawn.com/news/1265197

Weidong, Sun, 'Interview: The Progress of the China-Pakistan Economic Corridor Goes Well', *Xinhua News*, June 26, 2016, http://news.xinhuanet.com/world/2016-06/24/c_1119108622.htm

Yaxin, Shen, 'China-Pakistan Relations in Xin Jinping's Eye', *People's Daily Online*, April 17, 2015, http://politics.people.com.cn/n/2015/0417/c1024-26862088.html

Yost, David S., 'Russia's Non-strategic Nuclear Forces', *International Affairs* 2001, Vol. 77, No. 3.

Zafar, Muhammad Saleh, 'Chinese Premier Vows to Support Pakistan at Every Forum', *The News*, September 21, 2016, https://www.thenews.com.pk/print/151751-Chinese-premier-vows-to-support-Pakistan-at-every-forum

CONTRIBUTORS

Lieutenant General PK Singh, PVSM, AVSM (Retd), Director, United Services Institution of India, was commissioned as a 2/Lt in the Indian Army in 1967. He retired as an Army Commander (C-in-C) in 2008. He is a graduate of Higher Command Course and the National Defence College. His academic qualifications include MSc, MPhil and Post-graduate Diploma in Business Management. He took over as Director of the United Service Institution of India in January 2009. He is a member of the Governing Council of the Indian Council of World Affairs, New Delhi, and also a member of the International Advisory Board of the RUSI International, London.

Major General BK Sharma, AVSM, SM and Bar (Retd) is Deputy Director Research and Head of Center for Strategic Studies and Simulation at United Service Institution of India, New Delhi. He specializes in Strategic Net Assessments, Scenario Building and Gaming. He is the editor of four books, a digital magazine, *Strategic Perspectives*, and also the *USI Strategic Yearbook* besides authoring monographs and articles. He also participates in TV debates and international conferences regularly.

Major General RPS Bhaduria, VSM (Retd) retired from NDC as SDS after 36 years of service. He was the first Chief of Staff of the Mountain Strike Corps. His command assignments include command of a newly raised Division in Arunachal Pradesh and a brigade and battalion in Sikkim. He has served extensively on India's Northern Borders in various other capacities. He was also a member of Army's VI Pay Commission Cell and served in DRDO on a project to develop computer war games for Army. He attended the NDC course in 2010 and a course on Politics and Strategy in Brazil.

Major General Rajiv Narayanan, AVSM, VSM (Retd), was commissioned in Dec 1978 in the Armoured Corps and retired after over 37 years of distinguished service on 29 Feb 2016. An Alumni of DSSC Wellington and DSCSC Mirpur, Dhaka, he is an expert in mechanized and mountain warfare and has seen service along India's both Western and Northern Borders. He has had the opportunity to serve as the Defence Attaché in the Embassy of India Dushanbe, Tajikistan, during the turbulent period post 9/11 from Oct 2003 to Mar 2007. His areas of interest areas include China, South and Central Asia, Indo-Pacific Region, and Future World Order and Regional Multilateralism. He has a large number of articles and papers published in Indian journals and magazines (including web editions).

Commodore Lalit Kapur (Retd) has served on many Western and Russian origin ships, served as the Defence Attaché at Muscat (1999–2002) and held a wide variety of seagoing assignments. He has served in the Defence Intelligence Agency as Defence Protocol and Foreign Liaison (DACIDS) in HQ IDS, the Strategic Forces Command responsible for strategic communications and the sea vector, and at Headquarters Offshore Defence Advisory Group, Mumbai. A prolific reader, his interests include international relations, human resource development and military history. He also writes professionally and has numerous published articles to his credit.

Dr (Mrs) Roshan Khanijo is a Senior Research Fellow and Research Co-coordinator at the Centre for Strategic Studies and Simulation (CS3), New Delhi. She is a strategic analyst. Her areas of focus are Security, Nuclear Issues, Indo-Pacific Region, Niche Technologies-BMD, HGV, etc. She has authored, edited books, monographs and occasional papers. Some of them are *Complexities and Challenges of Nuclear India, Indo-Pacific Region Security Dynamics and Challenges, Nuclear Security Summit – The Challenge Continues, China's Military Modernisation*, etc. She has been a panellist in a number of national and international Workshops/Seminars, and presented papers in China Institute for International Strategic Studies (CIISS); Beijing, Research Institute for National Security Affairs (RINSA), South Korea, etc.

Group Captain Sharad Tewari, VM (Retd), is a Senior Research Fellow at the Centre for Strategic Studies and Simulation (CS3) at the USI. He is an alumnus of Flying Instructors' School, Defence Services Staff College and College of Defence Management. He attended UN Peacekeeping Course at Narobi, Kenya. He specialises in Net Assessment and Scenario Building and has been a former Director (Net Assessment) at HQ Integrated Defence Staff. He has conducted a number of seminars and workshops related to Net Assessment and scenario building. He has been part of the research team for two National Security Studies and has undertaken a number of Net Assessment projects. He has been a guest speaker at a number of universities.

Lieutenant General PC Katoch, PVSM, UYSM, AVSM, SC (Retd), is veteran Special Forces officer. He is a prolific writer on international affairs, geopolitics, military, security, and technical and topical issues, having over 1,400 articles published, and has authored *India's Special Forces* and *Indian Military and Network-Centric Warfare*. He holds the Flying Officer Amandeep Singh Gill Chair of Excellence at the USI for the current year. He has been an active participant in national and international seminars and has presented papers in USA (Hawaii and Washington, DC), China, Taiwan, Japan, South Korea, Afghanistan and Maldives.

INDEX